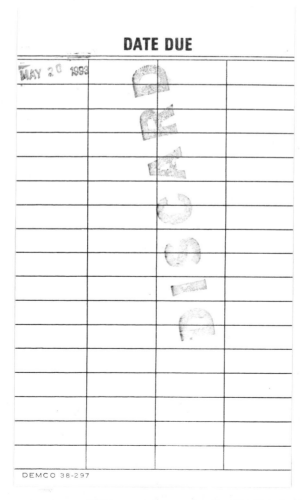

DATE DUE

MAY 20 1993			

DEMCO 38-297

THE TRUST MOVEMENT IN BRITISH INDUSTRY

THE TRUST MOVEMENT

IN

BRITISH INDUSTRY

A STUDY OF

BUSINESS ORGANISATION

BY

HENRY W. MACROSTY, B.A.,

LECTURER, LONDON SCHOOL OF ECONOMICS, AND EXAMINER IN COMMERCE, UNIVERSITY OF
BIRMINGHAM; AUTHOR OF "TRUSTS AND THE STATE," ETC.

AGATHON PRESS, INC.
NEW YORK, N. Y.
1968

Reprinted, 1968, by

AGATHON PRESS, INC.
150 Fifth Avenue
New York, N. Y. 10011

Library of Congress Catalog Card Number: 68-16355

Printed in the United States of America

THE TRUST MOVEMENT IN BRITISH
INDUSTRY

THE TRUST MOVEMENT

IN

BRITISH INDUSTRY

A STUDY OF

BUSINESS ORGANISATION

BY

HENRY W. MACROSTY, B.A.,

LECTURER, LONDON SCHOOL OF ECONOMICS, AND EXAMINER IN COMMERCE, UNIVERSITY OF
BIRMINGHAM; AUTHOR OF "TRUSTS AND THE STATE," ETC.

LONGMANS, GREEN, AND CO.

39 PATERNOSTER ROW, LONDON

NEW YORK, BOMBAY, AND CALCUTTA

1907

PREFACE.

In popular usage the term Trust is generally applied to industrial and trading combinations with an implication of tyranny on the part of the organisations so described; but in the following pages it is used solely in its secondary, not its original, meaning of combination, and is not intended to convey any sense of condemnation. The word is now thoroughly established, and it has the advantage of being free from any reference to the labour movement such as, for historical reasons, still clings to the phrase, "the combination movement". To award praise or blame in the moral sense for the operations of trade in no way falls within the scope of this book, whose only object is to detail, with as little bias as possible, as many facts as could be ascertained in relation to the modern organisation of industry. Description rather than criticism has been the aim mainly kept in view, and, therefore, every opportunity has been taken to let business men state their opinions in their own words.

The survey of the industries of the United Kingdom, which forms the greater part of the book, has been compiled from a variety of sources, and in a task so new and surrounded by so many difficulties many gaps have necessarily been left, and, doubtless, some mistakes have been made. The daily Press, the financial papers, and especially the trade papers, have been the main sources of information. All cannot be enumerated, but the Author's indebtedness to some must be specially acknowledged. The *Economist, Statist, Times* (*Financial Supplement*), and *Financial Times* have been the chief, though not the only, financial organs consulted, while the *Stock Exchange Year Book* and the *Official Intelligence* were, of course, indispensable. Wherever possible official sources have been used for financial results, and at other times the excellent summaries of company reports in the *Financial Times*; the *Draper* gives in full the annual reports of the great textile companies.

A great many newspapers have been at one time or another consulted, and the *Manchester Guardian* and *Yorkshire Post* have been found particularly useful for textile combinations, the *Birmingham Daily Post* for the iron trade, the *Liverpool Post* for shipping items, and the *Glasgow Herald* for general commerce. The annual reviews of trade published by the *Manchester Guardian, Yorkshire Post*, and *Glasgow Herald* are of the greatest value. Among trade papers the following have been freely utilised : *Iron and Coal Trades Review, Iron and Steel Trades Journal, Times* (*Engineering Supplement*), *Colliery Guardian, Textile Mercury, Fairplay, Ironmonger, Hardware Trades Journal, Grocer, British Baker, Miller, Draper, Tobacco*.

Wherever access could be had to prospectuses and reports these were carefully studied, and the leading points were extracted, so that the reader might be able to compare the views of the organisers of an amalgamation with its subsequent results. An amalgamation, indeed, may be studied with comparative ease, especially if it has not been very successful, for then the financial Press and the newspapers locally interested in the industry give plenty of space to reports of meetings, at which accusation and apology reveal many interesting details.   With terminable associations the case is very different.   Here market reports must be scrutinised with care for traces, and, perhaps, after all the illuminating fact is found tucked away in an obscure corner, or, frankly, is discovered by pure chance in a paper which does not generally pay much attention to industrial affairs.   Indeed, hunting down an association is quite an exhilarating sport; there is no cover so unlikely in which the game may not be started.

The chapter on "Grain-milling" has been reproduced, with some alterations, from two articles in the *Economic Journal* with the permission of the Editors.   The valuable assistance of Mr. C. M. Knowles, LL.B., Barrister-at-Law, who went through the proof sheets, must also be gratefully acknowledged.

HENRY W. MACROSTY.

CONTENTS.

CHAPTER III.

THE IRON AND STEEL INDUSTRIES—ASSOCIATIONS.

CHAPTER IV.

THE EXTRACTIVE INDUSTRIES.

CHAPTER V.

THE TEXTILE INDUSTRIES.

CONTENTS

CHAPTER XI.

THE RETAIL TRADES (*continued*).

CHAPTER XII.

THE TRANSPORT INDUSTRIES.

CHAPTER XIII.

MISCELLANEOUS INDUSTRIES.

CHAPTER XIV.

SURVEY AND CONCLUSIONS.

CHAPTER I.

A TRUST was originally a combination of a number of companies through a board of trustees to whom the shareholders assigned their shares in exchange for trust certificates. This special form of industrial organisation, which is now illegal in the United States, except in Massachusetts, has given the popular name to the general movement of industrial combination which includes a great variety of structures. The prominence of the Standard Oil, Sugar, and Whisky Trusts made the name familiar, and it passed over to the companies which were formed to replace the "trusts" declared illegal in 1892. From that to the whole problem of industrial organisation was an easy step, and every one speaks of the trust movement, the trust problem, the trust danger, including forms as various as the Beef Trust, the Westphalian Coal Kartell, or Messrs. J. & P. Coats. The one common point about all forms is the combination of several capitalists who formerly operated singly ; beyond that the structure may vary infinitely, it may be in intention permanent or temporary, it may be for all purposes or for some only, it may include manufacturers only, or wholesalers only, or retail vendors only, or any two or all three of those classes. The object of all forms is the same, so to regulate industry that it may become more profitable to those in whose interests it is regulated. In the words of Mr. S. C. T. Dodd, Attorney to the Standard Oil Co., a trust "embraces every act, agreement, or combination of persons or capital believed to be done, made, or formed with the intent, effect, power, or tendency to monopolise business, restrain, or

I

interfere with competitive trade, or to fix, influence, or increase the price of commodities" (*Harvard Law Review*, October, 1893).

The words "competitive trade" in Mr. Dodd's definition give a limit to the scope of this essay. It is not proposed to deal with those industries or services which obtain through grant from the legislature a position of monopoly. The supply of gas, water, and electric light, or tramway or railway services, need not necessarily be monopolised, but the permission of competitive services would be so wasteful that it is not granted, and other means of control are adopted. A patent, again, during its currency confers a monopoly, subject only to the competition of substitutes or to possible supersession by a newer discovery. The effects of patents and patent laws have been powerful and important but they will not be dealt with here. Our more limited theme is the discussion of those industries in which, up to a recent period, prices and output have been left to the free competition of manufacturers and retailers.

With every improvement in transport the market becomes wider and competition becomes keener through the advent of new producers, while at the same time it becomes more difficult to make rational forecasts of the course of trade. Even within tariff walls competition always rages as soon as it is discovered that there are certain industries to which the law has assigned the possibility of greater profits than the average. Alike in protected and unprotected markets free competition becomes cut-throat, prices fall, and over-production ensues in the wild effort of producers to reduce costs by a larger output. If the word normal were not entirely out of place in dealing with phenomena of which we do not know all the factors and cannot evaluate all those we know, one might say that the normal course of modern trade was that prices should always tend towards the cost of production, that this tendency developed itself with increasing speed, and from time to time ended in production at a loss. Now whatever one may say about a "social contract" or the working out of the welfare of society through the clashing self-interest of individuals, the fact remains that the first object with which a man enters business is to make

money, and his second to make as much as he can.   Similarly
a workman wants to get a subsistence wage and next as high
a wage as he can.   And if any social institutions or trade
methods stand in the way there will be a revolt.   Such a revolt
in a multitude of forms we are now witnessing, starting from
the simple combined refusal to trade at a loss and leading up
to a position of dominance of an industry scarcely distinguish-
able from a monopoly.

"Among the causes which have led to the formation of
industrial combinations, most of the witnesses were of opinion
that competition, so vigorous that profits of nearly all competing
establishments were destroyed, is to be given first place"
(*American Industrial Commission—Preliminary Report on
Trusts*).   The effect of the tariff is first that it creates the
industry, and then the rush and scramble for the high profits
brings the manufacturers to the bankruptcy court, from which
they are barely saved by the aid of the trust promoter.   Once
combination has been formed the tariff very usefully bars out
foreign competition, and if new domestic competition can be
prevented or suppressed the trust is in a very strong position
indeed.   More effective assistance has been given to trusts
through secret alliance with the railways, as in the case of the
Standard Oil Company, but that is not a generally co-operating
cause.   We have not to reckon with it either in Germany or
in the United Kingdom.

The phrase " free competition " has been used, but entirely
free competition has never existed in any trade, except within
very narrow limits.   Local physical advantages and difficulties
of transport profoundly affect markets, and sometimes even
create quasi-monopolies, which in turn are modified as facilities
become more abundant.   On what may be called the psycho-
logic side, again, common knowledge of each other's action in
open market leads to manufacturers and dealers arriving at
customary prices for a wide range of commodities.   Still more
important is the ever-spreading knowledge and recognition of
common interests within a trade leading to common action
locally and nationally for the improvement of trade processes,
the furtherance of general commercial purposes, and the defence

I *

of all against intervention by Parliament, aggression by work-people, and exploitation by railways. In this way trades and industries have built up a complex system of organisation—for scientific purposes, as in the Iron and Steel Institute; for Parliamentary action, as in the Federation of Master Cotton Spinners; for general commercial objects, as in Chambers of Commerce; for negotiating with trade unions, as in Employers' Associations everywhere. Competition and individual action have had to yield in all these directions to co-operation. While the nature and quantity of the goods produced by any one and the price at which he sells them have generally been left to his own judgment, even there inroads have been made on the sphere of personal decision. Market rules have been drawn up prescribing the conditions under which goods are to be sold, standardising regulations have been adopted detailing the permissible variations, and so it may be broadly said that only the volume of output and the actual sale price have been left to the manufacturer and distributor. To-day we are viewing the bringing of these last tracts of trade policy under regulation. Sometimes this development is described as artificial or as contrary to the normal course of trade, but these phrases are meaningless, for freedom includes liberty to combine as well as to compete, and if profits cannot be obtained in one way they will be sought in the other.

Combinations may be classified according as they deal with purchase or sale of commodities. The former class is not of special importance. The clearest cases are the agricultural associations of farmers for the joint purchase of seeds, manures, and implements, and occasionally associations of chemists and grocers buy part of their supplies in common. They seek to realise the economies, the lower prices and extra discounts which usually attend on large orders, they prevent waste and increase the economic strength of the members, but they do nothing for the regulation of the market or for the suppression of competition. On the contrary, they leave their members free and able to compete amongst each other more strenuously in the sale of their goods. Of course a large merger of many previously independent concerns is a combination for purchase as well as for sale, but the importance of the former function is sunk in the greater advantages of the latter. To some extent we find an approximation to a purchasing combination in joint stock companies for the opening up of fresh fields of supply, like the British Cotton-Growing Association or the Dunderland Iron Ore Company, but the new supplies so obtained are sold on the open market and not exclusively to the members of the company.

Combinations aiming at the sale of goods may be distinguished as either permanent or terminable, according to the intention of their organisers. In the former case the combining units lose their identity in a new company comprehending them all, or at best preserve only a formal independence. In the latter they combine only for an agreed period and for specific purposes apart from which they retain their independence and self-government. Terminable combinations come first in logical order, but before treating of them we must precisely exclude "corners" which are popularly spoken of along with trusts as if they were of the same nature. A combination is an organised effort for the regulation of the market; a corner is a speculative operation for the violent increase of prices by the artificial limitation or withholding of supply. A corner only resembles a combination when it is comprised of several temporary partners, but its engineers need not be and often are not connected with the industry in which they operate, and in all cases the object is a disturbance of the market. The cotton corner of 1903 and the corner in Cleveland warrants in 1905 each aimed at a control of the market, but only for the purposes of one particular speculation. Many of the participants had nothing to do with the cotton or iron industries and only sought a gambling profit. The object of combinations, on the other hand, need not be altruistic, but it is always the elimination of the aleatory element in trade.

Terminable combinations are based on contracts, written or verbal, for the attainment of specific purposes over an agreed period of time after which the members are free to revert to independence. So far as possible the term "association" will hereinafter be confined to this class of organisation, though unfortunately that will not be entirely possible since certain of the large textile amalgamations call themselves associations in their official titles.   The logical classification of associations will proceed from the weaker to the stronger according as the control over production and distribution is less or more, but it must not be supposed that every industry necessarily passes regularly from grade to grade.   Organisation may begin at any point in the sequence and may in its development omit several stages.   The lowest class of associations are what Dr. Grunzel, secretary of the Central Union of Austrian Manufacturers, in his book, *Über Kartelle* (Leipzig: Duncker und Humblot, 1902), calls " Konditionenkartelle," combinations for the settlement of the terms upon which business shall be done.   They deal with discounts, terms of credit, payment for packing and transport, and all the conditions attendant on the conclusion of a bargain. For example, the sale note adopted by the National Association of Millers prescribes the terms of delivery, the duration of the contract, the date of payment, and the adjudication of disputes.   The charter party or contract for hire of a vessel adopted for various trades by Chambers of Shipping contains stipulations as to loading, conduct of the voyage, and method of payment. The primary object of these agreements is the avoidance of disputes by the transaction of business according to settled forms, but they also ensure that competition shall take place in the open without secret rebates.   For the present purpose their chief importance is that they accustom traders to the regulation of the market.

Price Associations, the next highest grade, aim at the regulation of sale prices as well as of the conditions of bargaining, and exhibit a great variety of structure.   They are generally local, seldom national, though the locality may cover a wide area.   The simplest form is where the manufacturers or traders meet, either as individuals or as members of an association for general trade purposes, and determine on a rise in prices to meet some special circumstance, such as an increase in the price of raw materials.   The agreed rise may either be for an indefinite period so long as the conditions remain the same, or for a fixed period after which competition is once more free.

Thus we find the associations of coal masters raising the price of coal at the beginning of winter, and associations of grocers trying to make the retail price of sugar follow advances in the wholesale price. The next stage is where the members combine for a definite period, usually a year, for the specific purpose of fixing prices from time to time. Regulation may take place irregularly as trade demands, as is done by the Fife Coal Association, or normally at meetings weekly, monthly, or even quarterly, as in the case of the Midland Unmarked Bar Association. The government of the association may reside in the members themselves in their periodical meetings, as in the Cleveland Ironmasters' Association in 1881-82 ; or in a committee, subject to confirmation by a general meeting, as in the Midland Unmarked Bar Association ; or in a committee alone, as in the Millers' Associations. In the committee decisions as to alterations in price may be determined by the majority, which is the general rule, or by a minority in which case no change is made if a specified minority objects. This last form was adopted in some of the Millers' Associations, and is always a sign of weakness.

Generally speaking, the rules of a Price Association provide the ordinary machinery of a committee, president, secretary and treasurer, annual and other meetings. Sometimes a deposit of money, or securities, or a promissory note is required, out of which penalties for breach of the rules are levied. In other cases penalties are imposed, recoverable on demand, and in a third class no penalty at all is inflicted. Agreements which depend simply on the honour of the members for fulfilment are called " Gentlemen's Agreements " ; they are often characterised by complete want of formality, in which cases they are the hardest to detect but not the least formidable or the least strictly observed.

Price Associations are usually formed between persons in the same class of trade—manufacturers, or wholesalers, or retailers. Sometimes they embrace agreements between two or more of these classes, particularly in the retail trades where the manufacturers fix the retail prices below which goods must not be sold. In such cases the retail vendor is, as a rule, not

consulted as to the price paid by the public, his part being confined to making representations to the manufacturer that the
margin between the makers' price and the shopkeepers' price
must be large enough to afford the latter a living profit. A
further distinction may be made between associations as to the
means by which they seek to maintain their price lists against
outsiders. Beginning with persuasion they pass through retri-
butive competition, in which the association cuts prices below
the underseller, to the exercise of the boycott. The boycott
may be directed through third parties—customers, as where
Shipping Conferences refuse rebates to merchants who send
some of their shipments by independent steamers; or through
trade unions, as when the Birmingham Alliances arranged that
unionists should not work for non-associated firms; or, as in
the case of associations of manufacturers and retailers, by the
manufacturers refusing supplies to outside retailers.

The economic weakness of Price Associations is that while
fixing, that is, raising prices, they not only leave output unregulated but actually stimulate it by the better prices. If this
synchronises with an improvement in trade the extra supply is
carried off, but otherwise there is over-production and prices
must fall. Such difficulties are accentuated when the association contains members of different strengths, for the larger can
naturally both more easily exploit the increase in price and
maintain their production at a higher level of profit when prices
fall. Experience teaches that the next step is the regulation of
output. For this purpose the simplest form is a temporary
agreement to work short time until the glut is removed. Short
time and absolute closure are the last resort of a master, and a
common agreement will ensure the relief of the market before
matters have become absolutely desperate. Otherwise a manufacturer will keep his mill going so long as he can cover all or
the greater part of his standing charges. Such agreements have
been common in the tinplate industry and are usually concluded
with the consent of the men. The converse case to this limitation of supply in times of glut is the stopping of demand for
raw materials in times of actual or artificial scarcity—as in the
case of the cotton spinners on discovery of a corner. In both

cases the means adopted is the same, either the closure of the works or the adoption of short time for a definite period, and in both cases free competition is resumed when the necessity has passed away.

A more continuous control over production is exercised by pools, syndicates, or " Kontingentierungskartelle ". Dr. Grunzel distinguishes three classes: (1) The syndicating of production, where each member is assigned a quota of the total output of the associated firms; (2) a syndicating of sales, where each party is allowed to put on the home market an agreed quantum, but is left free to make for stock or export; and (3) a pooling of profits, which are paid into a common fund and shared out on an agreed scale. The essential feature of this grade of association is the attempt to determine what quantities ought to be put on the market. The output for the preceding three or five years is taken as the basis and, with perhaps an addition if the course of trade is favourable, is fixed as the amount to be produced during the currency of the agreement. The shares of the individual members normally bear the same relations to the agreed output as they did during the period covered by the statistics, but here all manner of difficulties arise. Some firms may have been declining in productive capacity throughout the period and others steadily increasing, so that while the former would welcome an arrangement which would stereotype their position the latter would object and would seek to obtain an additional share in consideration of their efficiency. Other firms may have had their works silent during part of the standard period owing to strikes, fires, or reconstructions, while others again may only have been in existence during a part of the time. All these questions are repeated at each renewal of the contract and are often complicated by the advent of new competitors who claim admittance and a share. This necessity for constant adjustment is the weak side of " pools ".

Usually a percentage of the total output is assigned to each member, and then if the committee considers that the course of trade demands a reduction or permits an increase it only requires to alter the total and the shares are modified mechanically. Prices may also be fixed, but that is. not a necessary feature since the limitation of production enables the producers to command the market. A pool or syndicate requires more machinery than a price association since it must collect statistics of current production and sales and keep a constant watch over the members to see that they adhere to the rules. Excess of production over the share-figure is generally visited with a fine, while a reduction of output below the allotted amount receives compensation. The most effective method of control is when profits are pooled, for as they generally have to be shared in the same proportions in which the output was allotted any member who exceeded his allotment would lose his share of the profit arising from the excess. For the ascertainment of profits a base price is fixed which is generally just enough to cover cost of production, and the difference between that and the sale price is paid into the common fund. This is the method adopted by the North of Ireland Corn Millers' Association. In some of the German kartells three prices are taken, the cost of production, the minimum sale price covering costs and interest, and the sale price actually obtained. The difference between the two former goes into the "pool," and the surplus obtained over the minimum selling price falls to the manufacturer concerned.

The manufacturer who takes part in a syndicate will be urged to reduce his costs as much as possible, since thereby he will secure for himself an additional profit which does not go into the pool. This he may do by improving his processes, but also by exceeding his output so as to reduce his standing charges; thus while losing the normal profit on his surplus he may gain more on his legitimate output. But this policy of exceeding allotments must, except in a rising market, tend to lower prices, and is a fertile source of weakness and quarrels. Individual interests are not entirely merged in the common interest even in a syndicate.

It is not easy to obtain information about associations of any higher grade than those confined to the regulation of prices. The Nitrate Combination regulates the output of nitrate from year to year, making adjustments for the introduction of new producers, alterations in demand, etc., but it does not appear to regulate prices. It is a pure production syndicate. The Gas

Strip Syndicate on the other hand regulated both production and prices. Sale-pools—Dr. Grunzel's class 2—do not appear to exist in Britain, but we find instances of the profit-pooling syndicates which at the same time regulate output and fix prices in the associations of omnibus proprietors and in the already mentioned Irish Corn Millers' Association.

The special temptation of the members of output associations to overstep their allotment is met in the next class, or Sales Associations, where the business of selling is taken entirely out of the hands of the individual members and given to a special department of the association. The normal output and the shares of the members are fixed at the establishment of the association, and for the agreed period form the most important part of the original pact. To the several firms is left only the technical management of their works. The sales department may be, though seldom, one of the member firms, or a trading firm outside the association; but most usually the association establishes a sales department of its own, sometimes in the form of a limited liability company. This form of organisation is what is known in Germany specifically as a kartell. The looser forms to which the name kartell is also generically applied are now usually spoken of under special titles—"price-conventions," "syndicates" to pool profits, and so on. The Sales Association is the highest form of terminable organisation, the form adopted by all the greatest kartells, and constituting the kartell *par excellence* gives rise to the "Kartell problem," the "Kartell danger," and the "Kartell movement".

The Rhenish-Westphalian Coal Syndicate may be taken as the type of the Sales Association. It is a joint stock company with a capital of 900,000 marks, all the shares being held by the coal-owners and only transferable with the consent of the general meeting. The government of the syndicate is divided between the general meeting, the committee (Beirat), the commission (Kommission) and the executive (Vorstand). The general meeting appoints the other bodies, decides questions of limitation of production, settles the compensation to be paid by or to mine-owners who have produced more or less than their allotment, and acts as a court of appeal against punishments for

breach of the rules.   The commission decides the total output
and the percentage shares of the members.   The committee
acts as a court of appeal from the executive and the commission,
and determines the base price (Richtpreis) of the different
qualities of coal which acts as the long-run regulator of or guide
to the syndicate's transactions.   The executive decides the price
at which the coal is to be sold to its customers (Verkaufspreis)
and the account price (Verrechnungspreis) at which it buys from
the mine-owners, and can propose fines for breach of the rules.
Each mine-owner has one vote in the general assembly for
every 10,000 tons of output allotted to him, and for every
1,000,000 tons he can nominate a member of the committee.

The mine-owners must sell all their production of coal, coke,
and briquettes to the syndicate at the account price, which is
based on and is generally higher than the base price.   The
actual selling price will vary according to the state of trade and
the competition to be met.   It can never fall below the base
price, but may easily fall below the account price, in which case
the difference is made good to the syndicate out of the regular
levies on its members for business expenses graduated according
to their allotment percentage.   The surplus of the sales price
over the account price falls to the member whose coal is sold.
Like all other German kartells of whatever class this syndicate
is clothed by the law with full legal personality, and can, through
the courts, enforce its regulations against its members.

Such closely knit organisations are not to be found in British
industry.   Where there are Sales Associations they are usually
to be found in those industries where the manufacturers do not
make for stock but on order.   In such cases the function of the
committee is to allocate the orders equitably among the members according to their capacity, and to fix the price at which
they are to be accepted.   We know that in the case of the
International Rail Syndicate of 1883-86 a percentage was
allotted to each participant country, which then divided the
orders among its members in rotation.   Each firm was allowed
to retain as far as possible its original clients, and if any firm
was, owing to conditions imposed by the buyer, given a contract
out of its turn, it had to compensate the firm which normally

should have had the order. It may be concluded that somewhat similar regulations are observed in the Ship Plate and Boiler Plate Associations. The Central Sales Agency, which formerly marketed the threads of the firms now composing Messrs. J. & P. Coats and still conducts the selling business of that company, the English Sewing Cotton Co., and Messrs. Lister, preserves a complete secrecy as to its methods. But the very fact that it transacts the business of the several companies on exactly the same terms enables it, through the information it sends to the factories, to control the production. An approximation to a Sales Association is to be found in the not infrequent instance of a "ring" of manufacturers who put in similar tenders for a public contract, the successful tenderer compensating the others, or arrange to modify their tenders so as to ensure a rotation of orders.

All these different forms of association may be regarded as so many governments each in its particular locality and according to its capacity passing laws for the regulation of its branch of industry, exercising a legislative function, so to speak. But while they maintain common action each in its own district, they frequently compete violently with one another or in neutral markets; thus the Scotch and English steel masters respectively regulated prices in Scotland and the North of England, but competed in each other's home district and in neutral markets such as Belfast. The same causes which lead to the cessation of competition between the firms situated in one centre of industry demonstrate the advisability of peace between the different districts, and so agreements, or, we might almost say, treaties, are signed demarcating their respective territories (Rayonierungskartelle). Most associations try to fix prices at such a level as will extract the maximum of profit from their own immediate district, observing such a measure that they are able to use the cost of transport from the nearest competing centre as a protective tariff. The output determined by this price will generally be below the capacity of the works, and so to enable the realisation of the economies arising from a larger output the members are allowed to "dump" their surplus outside the protected district. They are thus brought into conflict with both home and foreign producers, and to ensure peace with profit demarcating agreements are drawn up. The makers of shipbuilding steel in Scotland and the North of England, the Ship Plate and Angle Iron Associations, are at present agreed to respect each other's territory and to cease selling in Belfast at lower than the home rates. The International Rail Syndicate began by assigning to each nationality its home market. The tobacco war was ended by a treaty leaving Great Britain and India to the Imperial Tobacco Co. and the United States to the American Tobacco Trust. And numerous other examples could be given of similar arrangements between all classes of associations.

The Sales Association, as already said, is the highest form of terminable combination, in which the freedom of the individual is most completely subordinated to the common judgment of the associated members, but it contains the seeds of weakness in the liability to constant disputes arising out of claims for increased allotments of output. It is therefore natural that the next step should be taken of complete submergence of the individual in the community by the fusion of the associated firms into a new company. It has been frequently denied that this is the natural development. For instance, Dr. Grunzel says : " Kartell and Trust are very different, not in degree but in their nature. I know of no case in the thirty years of active kartell movement in Europe in which the one form has passed over into the other" (*Über Kartelle*, p. 14). In England, however, we have the evolution of Messrs. J. & P. Coats out of the Central Thread Agency, and of the English Sewing Cotton Company, the Bleachers' Association, the Bradford Dyers' Association, Wright, Bindley, & Gell, etc., out of actually existing associations, while countless other amalgamations have been built up on the ruins of associations which had proved unable to cope with the difficulties of the trade.

Old and well-established firms never welcome the complete loss of their identity that is implied in amalgamation, and even smaller firms seize that excuse for demanding a high purchase price. It was partly for these reasons, though no doubt also to avoid publicity, that the trust form was invented by Mr. Rockefeller and his colleagues. The owners of a majority of the shares in a number of oil-refining concerns deposited these in the hands of trustees, receiving in lieu trust certificates of an equivalent amount and retiring from the duties and responsibilities of ownership. The trustees thereafter managed the businesses, took the profits, and distributed them in dividends on the trust certificates. When this device was declared illegal the only alternatives were to revert to individual ownership, as the Standard Oil Trust did for a time, or to sell out to a new company, and the latter was taken in most cases. Amalgamation must take the form of purchase of the plant and assets if only private firms are being merged, but while it may also take that form in the fusion of companies it is not absolutely necessary. One company may acquire a controlling interest in other companies by buying up all or a majority of their stock which carries the right of management. Thus Dorman, Long, & Co. bought up the ordinary shares of Bell Brothers and the North-Eastern Steel Company, making an additional issue of its own stock for the purpose; its ordinary shareholders, who had the right to appoint the directors, thus obtained the power through those directors to appoint the directors of the other two companies. This method is cheaper than buying up the plant and assets, for the debenture holders and preference shareholders who rank as creditors of the company do not require to be bought out.

Sometimes, to effect the merger of a number of companies a new company is created, called a "holding company," which exchanges its shares for the shares of the separate companies and so acquires the right of appointing their directors and controlling their management. Sometimes the purchase money may be partly in cash, partly in shares, and the shares may be in different classes. The United States Steel Corporation purchased all the classes of stock of the separate companies. The Nobel Dynamite Trust Co., again, was formed to acquire by exchange of shares holdings in various explosive companies, and, for example, holds all the stock, etc., of the Nobel Explosives Co. It is common enough in the United Kingdom to acquire all the stock of several companies, take over the plant, and dissolve the original companies, but the "form in which the central corporation owns the stock instead of the properties of the separate companies has a flexibility and convenience in organisation and in retaining local brands, goodwill, etc., not found in corporations owning the plants" (*Final Report of American Industrial Commission*, p. 608). It also has the advantages of enabling the original owners to continue as directors of the subordinate companies, a consideration which much facilitates fusion, and of leaving greater opportunities to individual initiative and zeal. For these reasons the English Sewing Cotton Company organised its separate properties under companies in which it owned all the shares and of which it appointed the directors. At the same time, unless the subordinate directors are very closely under the control of the central board by, for example, receiving small fees in their quasi-independent capacity as directors and much larger salaries in an easily terminable capacity as managers, the holding company system affords opportunities for friction, misunderstandings, quarrels, and even rebellion. Although the disturbers of the peace can be removed at the next board election they may meanwhile have wrought much mischief.

The advantages which the amalgamation possesses over the association or kartell arise out of its permanency and the more complete control over production. Superfluous or badly equipped plants can be closed, mills can be specialised, concentration of establishments will enable greater economies of large-scale production to be made, and, above all, the best brains of the trade in any department are put at the disposal of all the branches of the combination. Such measures are impossible in a union which will come to an end in at most a few years. On the other hand, even in the strongest form of association, the Sales Kartell, a greater initiative is left to the individual member, or greater profit accrues to him if his goods command a higher price than those of his colleagues, and he is subject to a strong inducement to improve his processes since he can retain for himself the saving, at least for a time. To secure these advantages also has always been the aim of the promoters of amalgamations, and one very common device has been to represent all the combining firms on the board of directors and to retain some of their members in the management of the works they formerly owned. A manager, however, is primarily interested in the aggrandisement of his branch, while a director should be concerned only with the welfare of the company as a whole. When an amalgamation is formed virtually on the federal principle these interests inevitably clash and dire confusion results as in several of the textile trusts. In the most highly organised form of amalgamation all functions are carefully defined and graded so that proper subordination is observed, and the whole edifice culminates in a small board of directors who form, so to speak, the cabinet of the industry.

The ruling principle of the associations and amalgamations considered so far has been the union of firms in the same line of business—"horizontal combinations"—and this has necessarily been so since the motive for their creation has been the suppression of competition; to this principle the only exception is the combination of manufacturers and retailers where, however, the difference is only formal, since such a combination can be considered as, and in fact generally is, an alliance between two separate associations, one of manufacturers and one of retailers. Discussion of this class of combination forms the greater part of any treatment of the trust problem, since the elements of trade control and market dominance are thrust into the foreground at the very inception of an association or trust. Nevertheless, we must place by its side another class of combination, whose history is older, which is perhaps more closely involved in the evolution of industry, which is sometimes hostile to, sometimes ancillary to, the "horizontal" form. Employing the same metaphor we may call it the "vertical" form, where all processes of production, direct and lateral, from the extraction of the raw material to the sale of the finished product are concentrated or "integrated" under the same control. Full particulars of this development are given under the iron and steel industries where it is the typical form. Here emphasis must be laid on the fact that the object is to strengthen the main unit by the absorption of all intermediate and collateral profits. To this extent it may afford an outstanding firm a strong defence against a combin-

2

ation; on the other hand, if in the course of events the bulk of an industry has got into the hands of a very few large self-sufficient firms, the obvious costliness of internecine warfare will suggest the advantages of a common arrangement.

Whether integration of industry is antagonistic or favourable to combination will depend not on principle but on the circumstances of the individual case, often on purely personal considerations. Both are efforts to rise above competition, the former by direct increase of competitive strength, the latter by elimination of rivalry. Both seek to obtain a dominance over the market, in both there is ultimately a tendency towards monopoly. In every large horizontal combination, as soon as the amalgamation is complete, attention is directed towards efficiency, towards securing control of raw materials on the one side, and towards obtaining possession of the markets on the other. In almost every large integration there will be found some degree of removal of competition, and when the direct process of integration has been completed policy turns towards the absorption of rivals and also of firms making other finished goods from the same raw materials. The long run shows that both methods lead to substantially the same result, and both are therefore equally considered here.

The economic strength of industrial combinations is profoundly affected by their legal position. No one disputes the legality of an amalgamation, any man is free to sell his business to whomsoever he pleases, and twenty men can do the same; nor when the amalgamation is formed is there any law to prevent it from obtaining the highest price it can for its commodities. But the terminable associations of traders or manufacturers established for the regulation of their trade or industry are said to be " unlawful " since they are in restraint of trade; monopolies have always been repugnant to English law and contracts to restrict competition have always been viewed with the same hostility. Fortunately, in the *Mogul Steamship Co.* v. *McGregor and others*, decided in the House of Lords, December, 1891 (1892, A. C. 25), the law has been clearly laid down. The defendants were a " conference " or combination of shipping companies which had tried to exclude the plaintiffs from the Hankow tea trade by offering a special rebate to shippers who confined their shipments exclusively to the conference lines. Damages were sought for a conspiracy to injure the plaintiffs, and it was pleaded that the conference was unlawful, being in restraint of trade. Judgment was given unanimously against the plaintiffs, the Mogul Co.

Lord Chancellor Halsbury said: "There are two senses in which the word 'unlawful' is not uncommonly, though, I think, somewhat inaccurately used. There are some contracts to which the law will not give effect; and, therefore, although the parties may enter into what, but for the element which the law condemns, would be perfect contracts, the law would not allow them to operate as contracts, notwithstanding that, in point of form, the parties have agreed. Some such contracts may be void on the ground of immorality; some on the ground that they are contrary to public policy; as, for example, in restraint of trade, and contracts so tainted the law will not lend its aid to enforce. It treats them as if they had not been made at all. But the more accurate use of the word 'unlawful,' which would bring the contract within the qualification which I have quoted from the judgment of the Exchequer Chamber, namely, as *contrary to law*, is not applicable to such contracts. It has never been held that a contract in restraint of trade is contrary to law in the sense that I have indicated. A judge in very early times expressed great indignation at such a contract ; and Mr. Justice Crompton undoubtedly did say (in a case where such an observation was wholly unnecessary to the decision, and, therefore, manifestly *obiter*) that the parties to a contract in restraint of trade would be indictable. I am unable to assent to that dictum. It is opposed to the whole current of authority; it was dissented from by Lord Campbell and Chief Justice Erle, and found no support when the case in which it was said came to the Exchequer Chamber, and it seems to me contrary to principle." Lord Watson carried the definition of the legal status of terminable combinations a stage further in expounding the case, *Hilton* v. *Eckersley* (6 E. & B. 47), referred to by the Lord Chancellor: "The decision in that case," he said, "which was the result of judicial opinions not altogether reconcilable, appears to me to carry the rule no further than this—that an agreement by traders to combine for a lawful purpose, and for a specified time, is not binding upon any of the parties to it if he chooses to withdraw, and consequently cannot be enforced *in invitum*." In that case, which was tried in 1855, a body of cotton spinners had mutually bound themselves in effect to carry on their works in conformity with the resolutions of the majority of the body passed in general meeting. It follows that any penalty imposed for breach of the rules cannot be recovered, and it was so held in *Urmston* v. *Whitelegg Brothers* (63 L. T. 455), a case in 1890 in which an association of mineral water manufacturers bound themselves for a definite period not to sell mineral waters at any less price than 9d. per dozen or such greater price as the committee might from time to time direct. It also follows that a member of an association who has made a deposit as a guarantee of his observance of the rules could not, on expulsion from the association, recover at law his deposit. To establish his case he would require the aid of the illegal transaction, and as the illegal purpose of the association had been in part carried out by the mere forming of the association, he would be *in pari delicto* with the others.

Attempts, common in the retail trades, to bind the retailer not to resell below prices fixed by the maker have also failed. This was decided in a case in 1904, *Taddy* v. *Stevious* (1 Ch. 354), in which manufacturers of tobacco, who sold their packets with printed conditions on the wrappers, trade catalogues, and invoices to the effect that tobacconists were not to resell them at prices below those quoted, sought to restrain retailers from selling except upon such terms. Mr. Justice Swinfen Eady dismissed the action, though the sub-purchaser had notice of the terms, mainly on the ground that conditions of this kind do not "run with the goods" and so could not be imposed on chattels so as to bind successive purchasers. Mr. Justice Kekewich, however, in 1901, in *Elliman, Sons, & Co.* v. *Carrington & Son* (2 Ch. 275), an application for an injunction to restrain the defendants from selling the plaintiffs' embrocations below the prices fixed by them, held that, first, as Messrs. Elliman were free to manufacture or not as they pleased and could sell to the wholesaler at whatever price, high or low, that they pleased, so also they were at liberty to bargain with him as to the retail price, and that the contract was no more in restraint of trade than if they had imposed a high wholesale price at the beginning. " I do not think," he said, " that it is touched by the authorities at all. It is merely a question whether a man is entitled, when he is selling his own goods, to make a bargain as to the use to be made of them by the purchaser." The case is said to be of doubtful authority, and the decision is not, to a layman, easily reconcilable with the other cases. Twenty shillings damages were allowed, but an injunction was refused on the ground that Messrs. Elliman had the remedy in their own hands of refusing to supply their goods except on their own terms. This weapon of the boycott is the really effective way in which a manufacturer can enforce compliance with his rules. By abundant advertisement he can create a public demand for his goods so that a retailer will suffer in public estimation if he does not supply them, and, that demand once created, the shopkeeper cannot afford to be cut off from supplies.

The judges have repeatedly referred to the injustice of not allowing an association of traders to do those things which could be done by an amalgamation of the same persons. In all matters of competition an association has the same rights as an individual trader, who, to adopt the words of Baron Alderson, quoted by Lord Halsbury, in all matters " not contrary to law, may regulate his own mode of carrying on his trade according to his own discretion and choice ". Fraud, intimidation, molestation, obstruction, and the procuring of people to break their contracts are forbidden, but the right to trade freely is recognised by the law. Lord Justice Bowen said : " To say that a man is to trade freely, but that he is to stop short at any act which is calculated to harm other tradesmen, and which is designed to attract business to his own shop, would be a strange and impossible counsel of perfection ". A shipping conference can attract trade by offering rebates for exclusive patronage, though this involves boycotting of competitors. A manufacturer can refuse to supply an undercutting retailer, since by so doing he will attract other retailers to deal with him in faith that the minimum selling price will be observed. An eminent K.C. has passed an agreement allowing a miller to terminate a contract for the delivery of flour when the purchasing baker sells below the prices fixed by the local bakers' association. Prices can be fixed as high or as low as the maker pleases. Competition, however violent, is not "contrary to public policy," even if the stronger party carries on business at a loss for a time in order to drive the weaker out of business. "The object of every trader," said Lord Justice Hannen, "is to procure for himself as large a share of the trade he is engaged in as he can." Lord Justice Bowen said of the defendants in the Mogul case: "They have done nothing more against the plaintiffs than pursue to the bitter end a war of competition waged in the interest of their trade". And finally, to quote Lord Justice Fry: "To draw a line between fair and unfair competition, between what is reasonable and unreasonable, passes the power of the Courts". Those five quoted opinions, delivered by eminent judges in the course of the Mogul case, make clear the legal position of competitive traders.

The non-recognition of associations by the law has impressed on them a character of great fragility. Whatever may have been the period for which an association was originally formed, no member need belong to it or observe its rules a day longer than he likes. Nothing can keep him to his contract except a sense of honourable obligation, and that does not always resist the temptation of an advantageous order. This fragility is increased by the almost invariable incompleteness of an association, which very rarely includes all the competitors in a district. Some are always left outside to profit by cutting prices a shade below the association rates, or it becomes profitable for another district to invade the territory of the combined traders. Disintegrating forces are always at work, and when trade is bad and there is a mad rush for orders at any price so as to reduce costs by a large output they work with double violence until at length a point comes when by common consent the association is allowed to lapse until the frenzy has ended in exhaustion. The history of price associations, pools, and similar bodies will show how they "rose, and stoop'd, and rose again, wild and disorderly".

It was said at the beginning of this chapter that the whole combination movement originated in competition ; it must now be added that it does not begin until by mutual slaughter the competitors have been reduced to a manageable number. What that number may be will depend entirely on the circumstances of the trade and the locality. If entrance to a trade is easy it will be difficult for the members in existence at any time to combine, since their action in raising prices will at once attract fresh competitors. Obviously, too, it is easier for ten men to agree to a course of action than a hundred. The survivors, also, must be of about the same grade of strength ; where there are a few strong and many weak, as in the tinplate trade, the strong will incline to kill out the weak rather than to protect them by alliance.

Restriction has always been a trade policy, and attempts at regulation can be traced throughout the whole history of our industry. The limitation of the vend of coal at Newcastle and the combination disclosed in *Hilton* v. *Eckersley* are only two examples. Still it is significant that it is in the eighties, after the great depression which followed the boom of 1870-75, when the effects of international competition first began to be fully felt, that we first discover something like a general movement to control competition. After numerous experiments with all kinds of terminable associations, manufacturers, sick of warfare, turned to amalgamation of their interests, and followed in the same course as their brethren in the United States, only a little later. The first stimulus was given by the success of Messrs. J. & P. Coats in 1896, and the great development of 1899-1900 was distinctly imitative of the parallel development in America, just as the subsequent disfavour was to some extent due to the temporary financial failure of some of the great transatlantic trusts.

CHAPTER II.

THE IRON AND STEEL INDUSTRIES.

I.—AMALGAMATIONS.

No industry has been so much syndicated and combined in all the great industrial countries as that of iron. In a degree not shared by any other commodity but coal it is the servant of all other industries, its prosperity depends on their welfare, and its trade-cycle is modified by the curves of every other manufacture to which it supplies the tools, plant, and machinery. The factors on which iron and steel prices depend are therefore peculiarly insusceptible of control, and it is not surprising that development has gone mainly in the direction of the evolution of large units, businesses big enough to command the respect of competitors, strong enough to stand the stress of prolonged bad times, and so self-contained as to control a definite portion of the market. In the whole of the United Kingdom there are, after allowing for associated companies, some 101 blast furnace companies with an output exceeding 9,000,000 tons of pig-iron, and thirty of these in Scotland and on the North-East Coast are responsible for half the total output. There are about ninety-five steel-making concerns, of which some twenty-eight also possess blast furnaces. The several districts have a certain amount of specialisation; Scotland and Middlesbrough serving the shipbuilding industries; Yorkshire making heavy steel castings and forgings, armour-plate, rails, cutlery, and machinery; the West Coast, rails and machinery; South Wales, rails and tinplate; the Midlands, sheets, etc. In many of the finished branches of the industry the limitation of numbers has gone far; some half-dozen firms make projectiles, and the rollers of rails do not exceed a dozen. On the other hand, the number of firms making armour-plate has grown from two to five as the result of Government orders, but the number is still a manageable one. As the units become fewer they grow larger, and we have individual companies, like W. Baird & Co., the largest makers of pig-iron in Scotland, the Carron Co., which combines iron-smelting with the largest ironfounding works in the kingdom, and Messrs. Bolckow, Vaughan, & Co., of Cleveland, whose share and loan capital amounts to £3,939,000.

The tendency to embrace a whole line of manufacture from the raw material to the finished product—which is sometimes known as the "integration of industry"—was stamped on the iron trade from the beginning, and has always been its most noteworthy characteristic from the standpoint of economic philosophy. The ironmasters of Scotland and Cleveland owned their own iron-ore fields and coal-mines from the inception of the industry. When the black-band ores were exhausted the Scotch ironmasters bought mines in Cumberland and in Spain. In some instances several British companies have combined to own and work Spanish mines for their joint benefit. Most noteworthy is the Dunderland Iron Co. (capital in 1906, £2,250,000, of which £1,250,000 has been issued to the public), which was established in 1902 to exploit through Mr. Edison's patents ore fields in Norway. Twenty-four British companies are concerned in this enterprise besides private shareholders. With a little pedantry this undertaking might be likened to what some German economists classify as a kartell for the purchase of raw materials. To the British business man it is only one joint-stock company among some thousands, without any special significance. Beside it we may set the Talbot Continuous Steel Process (Limited), a company formed in 1902 to exploit a new method of making steel. Its capital was £250,000, and eight British steel and engineering companies were represented on the directorate. When the supplies of raw material have been secured operations are frequently extended to include several branches of manufacture in order to mitigate the effects of sectional depression. The further step, the absorption of competitors, brings the movement into closer line with what we ordinarily understand as trust development.

The history of the firm of Bell Bros. and the companies now associated with it is a typical example of the development characteristic of the British iron trade. The firm was established in 1844 and on the discovery of the Cleveland ore deposits threw itself into the new enterprise. Important royalties were secured on the Normanby estate and the Clarence works were established on the Durham side of the Tees mouth. Three furnaces were blown in in 1854, and the make for the year was 12,536 tons of pig-iron, a figure nearly doubled two years later. Further important iron-mines at Skelton and collieries at Pagebank, Browney, etc., were acquired, the necessary railway connections were made, the depression of 1857-62 was lived through, and great improvements were made in the technique of the pig-iron manufacture as the result of investigations with which the name of Sir Lowthian Bell will always be associated. The development of the firm followed closely the development of the district, with a remarkable rise during the Franco-Prussian war and a slower growth afterwards : —

	Cleveland Pig-iron. Tons.	Bell Bros. Pig-iron. Tons.
1868	1,233,418	88,470
1871	1,884,439	136,997
1897	2,138,378	195,598

The firm was converted into a private limited company in 1873 which was reconstructed in 1895, the whole of the property passing into the hands of the Bell family. In January, 1899, it became a public company, the complete purchase price being £900,000, and the paid-up capital £1,270,000, of which £500,000 was in debentures. According to the prospectus, Bell Bros., Ltd. "produced during the last three years an annual average of pig-iron, 320,000 tons; coal, 715,000 tons; coke, 305,000 tons; ironstone, 1,165,000 tons; and limestone, 206,000 tons". The minerals remaining unexhausted were certified at : coal, 37,500,000 tons ; ironstone, 40,000,000 tons ; and limestone, 25,000,000 tons, or altogether a forty years' supply. After providing for maintenance, but not for interest or reinstatement of capital, the profits for the ten years ended 30th September, 1898, averaged £78,180 per annum; for 1895-96 they were £84,712; for 1896-97, £101,372; and for 1897-98, £112,176.

So far we see that we are dealing with a firm which had grown to be a large unit in the single business of producing pig-iron, with full command over its supplies of raw material, and manufacturing nearly all the coke it required. It was, in fact, a self-contained firm. But now there was a fresh development. During 1898 the firm, with the assistance of the neighbouring steel-making firm of Dorman, Long, & Co., had been experimenting with the manufacture of steel from Cleveland ores by the open-hearth process, for the increasing scarcity of hematite ores was driving men to consider the utilisation of more phosphoric ironstone. The experiments were satisfactory, and £300,000 out of the new issue of stock were to be devoted to the building of steel works at Port Clarence for the manufacture of finished steel for shipbuilding and other purposes. Dorman, Long, & Co. subscribed one-half of the ordinary shares issued and the Bell family the other half—total £300,000—and the directors represented these two interests. It is to be observed that while the aid of the public was called in to assist in the extension of the business, control lay solely with the vendors and Dorman, Long, & Co. so long as debenture interest and preference dividend were maintained. This is quite a common feature of British flotations, and it demands from the cautious investor a careful scrutiny of the purchase conditions. In this case the purchase money was eleven and a half years' purchase of the profits reckoned on a ten years' basis, or nine times the average of the last three years—over-capitalisation was thus excluded.

Dorman, Long, & Co. were incorporated as a limited liability company in 1889. They began business in 1876 at the West Marsh Works in Middlesbrough, where they had puddling furnaces and made bars and angles for shipbuilding purposes. In 1879 they acquired the Britannia Works, and in 1886 began the substitution, now complete, of open-hearth steel for malleable iron. Their speciality in manufactures is girders which they first rolled in 1883; the trade was then entirely in the hands of the Belgians and Germans, but Messrs. Dorman, Long, &

Co.'s competition was so successful that they beat their foreign rivals and are now the largest makers of girders in Britain. In 1899 the sheetworks of Messrs. Jones Bros. and the wire works of the Bedson Wire Co.—both of which undertakings had for some time been carried on by members of the Dorman family—were incorporated with the firm.   Here again we have a case of typical development of a steel firm—gradual increase in size and at the same time extension to include the manufacture of new products.   All kinds of large and small sections are rolled, and in 1900 nearly 30,000 tons of structural steel were turned out at the Britannia Works where 600 men are employed in the building up of girders.   With the growing use of steel for structural purposes it is natural that an important part of the work carried on by the company should be the construction of large engineering shops.   At the wire works all classes of wire are made, from telegraph and fencing wire to high carbon wire for steel ropes.   At the sheet works galvanised corrugated iron and steel sheets for roofing purposes are made.   About 3,000 men are employed at all the works of the company, and the output in 1900 was about 3,500 tons of finished material weekly.

The beginning of steel making at Port Clarence and the starting of a rolling mill opened up possibilities of competition, and in September, 1902, a circular was issued to the shareholders of Dorman, Long, & Co., in which the chairman said: "To avoid the risk in the future of any conflict of interests in dealing with the finished product of the mill it is desirable, and even necessary, that there should be a more complete union of the interests of the two firms.   This has been fully recognised by all parties concerned."   The share capital of the company was raised from £525,000 to £1,000,000 (the debenture issue of £400,000 remaining unchanged).   The remaining half of the ordinary shares of Bell Bros. was acquired in exchange for £225,000 shares in Dorman, Long, & Co., four directors of Bell Bros. joining the latter.   £250,000 of the new capital was raised for another purpose.   This was the period when German and American competition was being most keenly felt after the boom.   "When I addressed you in December last," the chairman continued in the circular just quoted, "I intimated that no large capital expenditure was then in contemplation. Your Board have since had under consideration the reports made to them by one of the managing directors after a visit to America, and have found it expedient to remodel and enlarge your furnaces and mills, which has in part been already accomplished." The position of Dorman, Long, & Co. was further strengthened by being now based upon the large supplies of raw material—coal, ironstone, and coke—owned by Bell Bros. Hitherto Dorman, Long, & Co. went no farther back than the manufacture of steel ingots, so that they were liable to suffer during times of high prices of pig-iron. The new issue of £250,000 stock, it should be noted, was offered to the existing shareholders of Dorman, Long, & Co., Mr. Hugh Bell and Mr. A. J. Dorman agreeing to accept any shares not so taken up (not exceeding £125,000), so that the control was not affected. Bell Bros. still retained its separate existence and separate accounts, but its steel business was to be under the management of Dorman, Long, & Co.

Still a third step was taken in May, 1903, when Dorman, Long, & Co. acquired the ordinary shares of the North-Eastern Steel Co. (capital £800,000), a steel-making company with a basic Bessemer plant and rolling mills for tramway and other rails. Its fortunes had not of late been remarkably good, especially for 1901, when a loss was shown. "The unfavourable results," according to the prospectus of a debenture issue in 1903, "shown for 1900 and 1901 are exceptional, both these years, especially the latter, having been affected by the low prices obtainable for the company's products at that time, compared with the abnormal advances in wages and prices of materials, particularly fuel. These unusual conditions in trade have passed away, and may not be experienced again for a considerable period of years." The main features of the situation were set forth in the circular to the North-Eastern shareholders. "The works of Dorman, Long, & Co. are freehold, and contiguous with those of your company; the railway and shipping facilities are identical; the class of material manufactured at each works has much in common, but your company have no mineral resources, while Bell Bros., Ltd., and through them, Dorman, Long, & Co., Ltd., are in this respect in a very advantageous position. . . . The Boards of the two companies have long felt that their manufactured products could be more economically handled by a union of interests, and after negotiations commenced more than two years ago have come to the above arrangement which they are convinced will bring important advantages to the proprietors, without disadvantage to the public." The total capital involved in all these transactions now amounted to £3,059,594, namely, Dorman, Long, & Co., £1,259,594 ordinary shares (including the ordinary shares of Bell Bros. and the North-Eastern Steel Co.), and £400,000 in 4 per cent. debentures; Bell Bros., £500,000 in 6 per cent. preference shares and £500,000 in 4 per cent. debentures; North-Eastern Steel Co., £250,000 in 4½ per cent. debentures and £150,000 in 6 per cent. second debentures. A further issue of £250,000 6 per cent. debentures was made by Dorman, Long, & Co. in 1904 to provide for alterations and developments both at Britannia and Clarence Works which had been " more extensive and costly than was at first intended ".

This story of development and concentration includes all the chief factors which will be found recurring again and again in the last ten years: control over raw materials, extension of products manufactured, absorption of competitors, reconstruction of works in order to meet American competition. When we turn to the results there is little evidence that a market notoriously so fluctuating as that of iron has been brought under any effective control. But we do find an increase in efficiency. The new steel works at Clarence, the reconstruction of the Britannia Works, and the remodelling of the North-Eastern Steel Co.'s Works not only cost much money, but by causing a complete closure of the Britannia Works in 1902-3 seriously interfered with the earning of dividends. But after all this reconstruction "you may take my assurance that we were never in a better position than we are to-day of meeting competition of the severest kind, or of taking advantage of any improvement in trade". Among the three concerns "we produce," said the chairman of Dorman, Long, & Co., in December, 1905, "annually 1,150,000 tons of ironstone, 750,000 tons of coal, 500,000 tons of coke, and 550,000 tons of pig-iron. We manufacture upwards of 400,000 tons of finished steel and 30,000 to 40,000 tons of constructional or bridge work. These are large figures." It should be added that the ore and coal resources of Bell Bros. had by subsequent purchases been maintained at about the same level as in 1899. Their production of iron rose to 352,749 tons in 1905, and they employed in all 5,500 men, paying "roughly 1,000 guineas in wages every day". The Port Clarence Steel Works, at once the original cause and the fruit of the combination, cost over £300,000, but solved the problem of producing steel from Cleveland ore by the use of hot metal direct from the blast furnaces. The advantage of having not only a firm basis on possession of raw materials but also a large number of different products, so that the market may be entered at many points and not all the eggs may be in one basket, was excellently shown in Dorman, Long, & Co.'s report for 1904-5, for while owing to reconstruction and strikes no profit was obtainable from steel, profits were earned on pig-iron, wire, sheets, and the constructional work at the London yard. The financial results of the three companies before and after combination are shown by the following table of profits :—

Bell Bros.		Dorman, Long, & Co.		North-Eastern Steel Co.	
Year to		Year to		Year to	
30/9/96	£84,712	30/9/96	£33,513	31/12/96	£41,113
30/9/97	101,372	30/9/97	51,256	31/12/97	57,940
30/9/98	112,176	30/9/98	72,622	31/12/98	48,091
31/12/99	213,334	30/9/99	99,105	31/12/99	46,033
31/12/00	360,466	30/9/00	159,167	31/12/00	4,284
31/12/01	83,004	30/9/01	115,534	31/12/01	14,727 (loss)
31/12/02	129,730	30/9/02	43,959	31/12/02	25,925
31/12/03	101,175	30/9/03	54,476	31/12/03	3,664
31/12/04	68,579	30/9/04	23,566	31/12/04	122 (loss)
31/12/05	87,469	30/9/05	9,923	31/12/05	42.934
				(Nine months)	
31/12/06		30/9/06	176,232	30/9/06	27,049

In the case of Bell Bros. and Dorman, Long, & Co. the profits are shown before deduction of depreciation or debenture interest, but in the case of the North-Eastern Steel Co. debenture interest, renewals, maintenance, etc., have been deducted, but not expenditure at blast furnaces, and in 1906 a new reserve account was started with £7,500.

This minute analysis of the normal course of development

will make it unnecessary to go into similar details in other cases. Pursuing the investigation of amalgamations based on the manufacture of pig-iron and the possession of ore fields and coal-mines, we come to a group associated with the name of Sir Christopher Furness. The Weardale Steel, Coal, and Coke Company was incorporated in October, 1899, to take over the business of the Weardale Iron and Coal Company, whose average annual production for the preceding three years exceeded : coal, 1,350,000 tons; coke, 380,000 tons; steel ingots, 68,200 tons; and finished steel and iron, 47,300 tons. It possessed nine collieries, exceeding 15,000 acres, in Durham, with a valuable connection for the sale of coal for iron and steel making, gas manufacture, steam raising, and export purposes, besides supplying the demands of its own iron and steel works. In addition, it possessed 17,000 acres of royalties for ironstone, limestone, ganister, and fluorspar, all of which except the spar were almost entirely used in the company's works. Further, there were blast furnaces, steel-melting plant, and rolling mills at Spennymoor at which steel boiler plates and steel and iron bars, etc., were made. The manufacture of ship plates was to be added. Sir Christopher Furness, the vendor, sold at a profit, the purchase price and issued capital being £1,025,000, of which £350,000 represented the available capital in cash, stock in hand, and book debts.

The prospectus stated that £150,000 had been spent on the steel works in recent years, and that " the collieries, works, and mines are in first-class order, equipped with modern and efficient appliances, and in full and profitable operation". But at that time the cloud of imports had not risen to the magnitude to which it was soon to attain. The following table of imports is very instructive :—

| | Unwrought Steel. | | Girders, Beams, and Pillars. | Iron and Steel Unenumerated. |
	From United States. Tons.	From All Countries. Tons.	From All Countries. Tons.	From All Countries. Tons.
1897	26,000	40,000	76,000	173,000
1898	29,000	40,000	103,000	219,000
1899	59,000	77,000	95,000	227,000
1900	158,000	179,000	93,000	266,000
1901	51,000	183,000	123,000	321,000
1902	4,000	281,000	127,000	323,000
1903	1,000	274,000	145,000	561,000

Sir Christopher Furness at the annual meeting in September, 1901, announced that "at Tudhoe they had been unable to produce steel during the past year at a price which left them any profit. In other words, they were not producing so cheaply as other makers." Strenuous measures were at once taken. Quoting again from Sir C. Furness: "The Weardale Steel, Coal, and Coke Company, finding that their works at Tudhoe were geographically in a position which made competition with their principal competitors difficult, bought the entire share capital of the Cargo Fleet Company. The amount of that capital stood at £120,000, and the works were absolutely antiquated, but the purchase secured what the Weardale directors mostly desired, a large quantity of freehold land, an unrivalled situation on the sea-board, a magnificent frontage to the river Tees, low cost of carriage by sea and land, and the ironstone mines within a few miles of the works—what one may term the natural advantages of the property were very great indeed" (Annual Meeting of Cargo Fleet Company, 30th November, 1905). The purchase was made in 1900, and the Cargo Fleet Iron Company was incorporated in 1904. Modern blast furnaces with an annual capacity of 127,000 tons of pig-iron, a by-product coke plant with a capacity of 130,000 tons per annum, and a Talbot steel plant and rolling mills capable of producing 125,000 tons of finished steel a year were erected. In addition, there were ironstone mines with an estimated annual output of 360,000 tons.

This excellent equipment of the Cargo Fleet plant with its many advantages threatened, however, to bring it into conflict with another of Sir C. Furness's companies. This was the South Durham Steel Company, whose prospectus, issued in March, 1900, stated that "the company was incorporated on 29th December, 1898, to acquire the following properties at the price of £850,000: The Moor Steel and Iron Works, Stockton-on-Tees; the Stockton Malleable Iron Works, Stockton-on-Tees; and the West Hartlepool Steel and Iron Works, West Hartlepool. . . . The amalgamation of these three works was originally arranged with the view of avoiding undue competition in the purchase of raw material, and in the sale of finished steel, and this object has been entirely attained." The output of finished iron and steel in 1899 was 284,568 tons, of which 207,438 tons consisted of steel plates. At first successful, the years 1902-4 were disastrous, and it was plain that competition must result, again to quote Sir C. Furness, "in serious loss to both, a serious loss to the share-holders of each company, and the ultimate ruin of one of them". A union of interests was effected in 1905 "by the Cargo Fleet Company relinquishing its scheme for the manufacture of steel plates, leaving that field to the South Durham Company, and by giving the Cargo Fleet Company an opening with the South Durham Company for the delivery of raw material, further arranging that the Weardale's supplies of fuel should be available for the South Durham as well as for Cargo Fleet". The financial side of the transaction was the acquisition by the Cargo Feet Co. of £324,440 in preferred and ordinary shares of the South Durham Co., thereby acquiring full control. The issued share and debenture capital of the South Durham Co. is now £950,000, of the Cargo Fleet Co., £1,370,000, and of the Weardale Co., £1,125,000, the total amount involved in this community of interests being £3,143,000. The output of the South Durham Co. for the year to 30th September, 1906, was the largest on record, being 353,000 tons of finished material, but this, according to the report, was "only practicable through our association with the Cargo Fleet Iron Co. Ltd."; £100,000 in ordinary shares had been issued in the year to complete the new Talbot plant. The Weardale Co. acquired in 1906 a con-trolling interest in the Talbot Continuous Steel Process Co.; the Cargo Fleet Co. is now entering on the manufacture of rails.

The firm of Bolckow, Vaughan, & Co. is intimately connected with the development of the Cleveland district. It was the first to utilise the native ore, and with large ironstone properties in close proximity to their blast furnaces at Middlesbrough the original firm, founded in 1850, grew so rapidly that when it was incorporated as a company in 1865 its issued and paid-up capital was £699,510. In 1875 the share, debenture, and loan capital amounted to £2,528,000, in 1885 to £3,730,000, and in 1905 to £3,939,000. In 1899 the business of the Clay Lane Iron Co. was acquired out of profits for £215,000. Apart from this instance the development of the company has been one of steady growth in the production of iron and steel, and in the extension of its raw material resources both in Cleveland and by the purchase of hematite mines in Spain. It now has six separate works in or near Middlesbrough with twenty-six blast furnaces, and at the Eston Works there is a modern steel plant with mills for rolling rails, etc. It is the evolution of a large unit by its own power and not by the accretion of other units. One point to be noted is that while the mass of profit increased the rate has decreased. From 1865 to 1874 the ordinary dividend varied from 10 to $21\frac{2}{3}$ per cent., from 1875 to 1883 between 5 and $8\frac{3}{4}$, and in the bad years 1884 to 1886 it was only $2\frac{1}{2}$. Not even millions of capital are proof against bad trade. Coming to the latest cycle we find dividends as follows :—

Year to 31st December, 1895	3 per cent.
„ „ 1896	5 „
„ „ 1897	5 „
„ „ 1898	5 „
„ „ 1899	8 „
Eighteen months to 30th June, 1901	13 „
Year to 30th June, 1902	5 „
„ „ 1903	5 „
„ „ 1904	5 „
„ „ 1905	5 „
„ „ 1906	6 „

We trace the effects of the general fall of the rate of profit and also of the increased international competition in iron and steel.

In the year ending 30th June, 1906, the output of this great company consisted of 2,604,152 tons of coal, 1,935,000 tons of Cleveland ironstone, 700,233 tons of coke, 779,241 tons of pig-iron, and 226,214 tons of steel. Nearly all its Cleveland ore was used in its own furnaces, and out of the total of 1,733,677 tons of pig-iron produced from native ironstone in the Cleveland district it contributed 534,987, or very close on one-third. Its total sales were £3,393,958, of which only £23 were bad debts.

Pease & Partners, Limited, was formed in 1898 "to take over and continue the businesses carried on since 1882 by the private company of Pease & Partners, Limited, of Darlington, and before that year by their predecessors, Joseph Pease & Partners and J. W. Pease & Co., in connection with their extensive collieries and limestone quarries in the county of Durham, and their ironstone mines in the North Riding of York". The directors were six members of the Pease family and Sir David Dale. The capital was £1,400,000, of which the vendors took all the deferred ordinary shares (£300,000 not transferable for ten years), and one-third of the £700,000 8 per cent. preferred ordinary; the average trading profit before deducting directors' fees and depreciation for the three years to 30th June, 1898, was £121,208. The output from the mines, quarries, and coke ovens was: coal, 1,300,000 tons; coke, 715,000 tons; ironstone, 1,196,000 tons; limestone, 260,000 tons. This is a case of a company engaged in the extraction of raw materials and seeking to secure a market for its output partly through the business relationships of its directors—the Pease family being intimately involved in the business development of the North of England—and by investments in iron and other companies. At the time of its public flotation it owned a large interest in the Skinningrove Iron Co., a blast-furnace concern in the neighbourhood of Middlesbrough, which it supplied with ore from its Loftus mine free of railway dues. In 1903-4 a two-thirds' share was purchased in another Middlesbrough iron-making company, Messrs. Wilson, Pease, & Co., which, with a previously acquired interest, made the purchasing company almost the sole owners. The Normanby Iron Co., another subsidiary company whose capital is mainly held by the Pease family, has had a variegated career. The coal resources have been augumented by the purchase of the Eldon and Horden Collieries. For 1905-6 the output of coal was 1,895,339 tons, of coke 727,222 tons, of ironstone 1,210,221 tons, and of limestone 406,005 tons. The company is obviously dependent upon the open market for the sale of most of its produce, especially coal, and therefore finds itself in an unfortunate position when prices fall. In 1899-1900 gross profits amounted to £375,402, and 20 per cent. was paid on both ordinary and deferred shares; things grew steadily worse till in 1903-4 profits fell to £61,891 (the failure of the firm's bankers being a contributory cause of disorganisation), and only 3 per cent. was paid on ordinary shares and nothing on deferred. Since then matters have improved with improving trade, Wilson, Pease, & Co. being a good investment, and in

1905-6 profits amounted to £169,177, the highest since 1901, and 8 per cent. was paid on both classes of shares. It would be difficult to give a plainer example of the way in which a raw material company is exposed to violent fluctuations, a weakness which the directors have recognised by their efforts to strengthen their position by suitable investments and alliances. The capital of the company is now £1,525,000.

The Pearson & Knowles Coal and Iron Co. of Warrington, founded in 1874, whose present capital is £860,000, affords us another example of a manufacturing concern trying to secure its market. Besides raising coal and making iron it has an engineering department and manufactures railway wheels and axles and iron rods. "Some little time ago," said the chairman at the annual meeting in September, 1905, "we found that in our wire rod trade we had alternate busy and idle periods in consequence of foreign competition coming in at times to offer goods at low rates and stop the continuous supply which we had with our customers. This was particularly so with one of the large customers, with whom we were in close alliance, and an opportunity occurred, and we took it, of purchasing a considerable interest in shares in that company. The result has been most satisfactory to the continuous working of our wire rod mill, as foreign competition does not come in and stop the continuity. There is no doubt continuity means cheapness as well as other advantages in our work."

Passing to South Wales, the company of Guest, Keen, & Nettlefolds is not only the largest iron concern in the principality but one of our largest and most successful amalgamations. The company of Guest, Keen, & Co. was formed in July, 1900, to combine the businesses of the Dowlais Iron Co., Guest & Co., and the Patent Nut and Bolt Co. The two former, the Dowlais properties, had been operated for a century and a half; they consisted of collieries with an output approaching 1,500,000 tons a year, a large interest in the important Orcanera Iron Ore Co. in the north of Spain, and steel and iron works at Dowlais and Cardiff, including blast furnaces, open hearth and Bessemer steel plants, and rolling mills for the production of rails, sleepers, plates, billets, bars, etc. Their purchase money was £1,530,000. The

Patent Nut and Bolt Co. dated from 1853, and owned works for the production of bolts and nuts at Birmingham, plant for the manufacture of railway fastenings at West Bromwich, blast furnaces and plant for making bolts, nuts, railway fastenings, chairs, and other railway material at Cwm Bran, near Newport (Mon.); also a colliery with an annual output of 250,000 tons. Its capital was £400,000, but as the profits had never been fully divided, having been used for improvements, the purchase money was fixed at £1,000,000. The issued share and loan capital was £2,530,000, of which only £380,000 in preferred shares and debentures was issued to the public, the rest going to Lord Wimborne and the shareholders of the Patent Nut and Bolt Co. Nothing was paid for goodwill. Mr. Arthur Keen, in putting the question of amalgamation before the members of the Patent Nut and Bolt Co., said that the policy was "to give the company a position of complete independence, and to enable it to hold its own in competition with the whole world". This he had endeavoured to do in the past by accumulating undisclosed profits for extensions, and now by purchase of the Dowlais properties they obtained full control over their coal supply besides producing for sale; they acquired a large supply of ore which, though insufficient for their needs, enabled them to purchase the rest when markets were favourable, and "they would make for sale and for use a large quantity of pig-iron and steel, which, to a very large extent, would make them independent of market fluctuations".

Early in 1902 the company was enlarged to Guest, Keen, & Nettlefolds by the absorption of the famous Birmingham firm of Messrs. Nettlefolds, screwmakers. On the part of the latter the motive was to establish their business more securely, in view of the strong competition to which they were subjected, by obtaining control over their supplies of raw material and absorbing all intermediate profits. On the part of Guest, Keen, & Co. the motive was the extinction of competition. Mr. Keen said: "Messrs. Nettlefolds were not only screwmakers but manufacturers of goods so similar to their own in many cases that the line of demarcation between the two was so obscure that it could hardly be explained. In addition to that they were steelmakers on no small scale, and, in many instances, produced the same classes of steel which Guest, Keen, & Co. manufactured, and they had been regularly selling in competition with each other." A little later Messrs. Crawshay Brothers' steelworks and collieries at Merthyr were acquired, a firm which mainly made steel rails in competition with the Dowlais and Cardiff works. "They bought and sold," said Mr. A. Keen, "in very much the same markets as Guest, Keen, & Nettlefolds did, and it was for reasons of economy that the directors decided to make the purchase." The issued capital was then raised to £4,535,000. On the report for 1905-6 the chairman said that "in the departments that produced the smaller manufactured goods they had had to meet very severe competition from home and abroad, but they had held their own and maintained their markets. During none of the previous years had their amalgamation been of so much service to them in resisting the attacks of their opponents in these departments as it had during this year". Since the union with Nettlefolds profits have been remarkably uniform, the average for the five years being £419,224, and the extreme range of variation from lowest to highest only £43,000. The reserve fund is now £750,000. A proposal was made in 1905 to amalgamate with the Ebbw Vale Steel, Iron, and Coal Co. (capital £1,197,000), but it came to nothing.

By the side of such giants the absorption of the Calderbank Steel Co. (steel smelting and boiler plates) in 1898 by Messrs. Dunlop (blast furnaces, chemical works, and collieries), and their flotation in 1900 as James Dunlop & Co. with a capital of £500,000, appears trifling, but the same tendency is exhibited though on a smaller scale.

The amalgamations so far considered do not proceed beyond the production of rolling-mill products; the next series takes several steps farther in the finishing trades, and is of a more complex nature. Starting in some cases with the manufacture of pig-iron and in others only from the production of steel, it includes such branches as shipbuilding, engineering, tubes, and galvanised sheets. Here, too, we find the end of the evolution achieved in two separate ways—by growth of the large unit and by absorption. Palmer's Shipbuilding and Iron Co., on which the prosperity of Jarrow so largely depends, is probably a unique example of the former class.   By the progressive development of its own force without alliances it has covered the whole field of production from pig-iron to battleships.   Its capital is relatively moderate, £778,262; for 1899-1900 and 1900-1 it paid 8 per cent. on its ordinary shares and since then 5 per cent.   In 1906 it established a connection with an Italian shipbuilding company, La Società Cantiera of Genoa.

In many respects the most noteworthy of this class of amalgamations is Sir W. G. Armstrong, Whitworth, & Co., Limited.   The original firm of Sir W. G. Armstrong & Co. early attained a great reputation as makers of ordnance as well as for their steel and engineering works.   In 1882 the firm of Messrs. C. Mitchell & Co., shipbuilders, was added, and in 1897 the engineering business of Sir Joseph Whitworth & Co. of Manchester.   At one time the company possessed blast furnaces, but they have been abandoned for many years and the business now begins with the manufacture of acid and basic steel at Newcastle.   Over 12,000 men are employed at the Elswick Works, Newcastle-on-Tyne, and the average output of shipping tonnage, mainly battleships, for 1903-5 was 49,000 tons.   The Whitworth Works do a general engineering business, and in 1900 large armour-plate works were erected at Manchester.   In 1899 the sum of £30,000 was invested in ordinary stock of Robert Stephenson & Co., locomotive and marine engineers and shipbuilders at Newcastle-on-Tyne, and a ten years' agreement was made for the docking of all Messrs. Armstrong's war vessels in the graving dock belonging to the other company.   Although George Stephenson was the founder of the original firm, Robert Stephenson & Co. have not had a successful career.   Besides the investment by Messrs. Armstrong, Whitworth, & Co., Sir J. W. Pease, Sir C. Furness, and Sir Raylton Dixon guaranteed the subscription of 150,000 ordinary shares out of the capital of £750,000, and thus, in a way, through their common personal interests, linked together to some extent the interests of their companies.   Foreign Governments necessarily desire to exercise a close control over their supplies of war material, and insist on works being established inside their own territory. To strengthen their position with the Italian Government Messrs. Armstrong, Whitworth, & Co., in addition to their own works at Pozzuoli, secured, in 1904, an interest in the firm of Messrs. Ansaldo, of Genoa. Still a further alliance has been made, this time by an investment in the private company of Whitehead & Co., torpedo manufacturers. "Our firm," said the chairman, "has been carrying out important experiments on the effect of torpedoes, the mode of launching them, and of the improvement of their range and power. They are in possession of important patents bearing on their efficiency; and their connection with so important a firm as that of Messrs. Whitehead & Co. cannot but be advantageous to us" (Annual Meeting, 28th September, 1906). Thus another link in the supply of warlike material has been tightened up. The capital of the company is now £5,710,000. The assets on 30th June, 1899, were £5,295,115, and on 30th June, 1905, £7,236,412. A prospectus of July, 1900, gives the profits for 1896-97 as £446,872; for 1897-98 as £499,159; and for 1898-99 as £658,074. The average profits for the five years 1900-1 to 1904-5, after paying debenture interest, depreciation, and all other charges, was £568,948; and for 1905-6, £523,153. The improvement is intensified by the extinction of the good-will account in 1903-4.

Vickers, Sons, & Maxim are an example of a development characteristic of the heavy steel trade of Sheffield. Under the style of Naylor, Vickers, & Co. they were melters of crucible steel at Sheffield, making bar and sheet steel for tools. They had a large export trade to the United States, and about 1860 began to develop the heavy steel trade, such as marine shaftings, and in 1870 the very heavy trade. The firm in 1867 became the company of Vickers, Sons, & Co. with a capital of £150,000, and gradually developed the manufacture of railway material, heavy steel castings and forgings, and more lately guns and armour-plates. In 1897, so that it might be able to "build, equip, and arm the largest battleships that may be required," it purchased the Naval Construction and Armaments Co., of Barrow, as from 30th June, 1896, for £425,000, and the Maxim-Nordenfelt Guns and Ammunition Co., as from 1st October,

1896, for £1,353,334 in cash and shares. It then assumed its present title with an authorised capital of £3,750,000. An era of prosperity began; up to 1902 £1,350,000 of new shares were created out of reserve and to represent extensions made out of revenue; £250,000 new £1 shares were issued at £2 and £700,000 at £2 10s., and large expenditure was made on new works and machinery at Sheffield, Barrow, and Erith. In 1902 a half-share was acquired in the business of W. Beardmore & Co., steelmasters and shipbuilders, of Glasgow, 389,500 £1 shares in Vickers' being exchanged for 750,000 £1 shares in Beardmore's. The reason for this investment was apparent when, shortly afterwards, it was announced that Beardmore's had made highly successful experiments with a new armour-plate. The combined firms set about the erection of new ordnance works at Glasgow, and a new shipbuilding yard was also equipped. At Vickers' Barrow yard 41,500 tons of shipping, almost entirely warships, besides submarines, were turned out in 1905, and marine engineering of 64,900 I.H.P. W. Beardmore & Co. built in 1903 10,700 tons, in 1904 2,350 tons, and in 1905 4,196 tons, both merchant and warships, and in 1906 21,000 tons of shipping and 4,000 I.H.P. of marine engines. Messrs. W. Beardmore & Co. were themselves a combine, the shipbuilding business of R. Napier & Sons having been acquired in 1900; at the Parkhead Forge, established 1842, armour-plates, guns, heavy steel forgings and castings, railway material, etc., are manufactured. The issued capital is now £3,000,000, and the ordinary shares are all held by Mr. William and Mr. Joseph Beardmore and Vickers, Sons, & Maxim. At the end of 1905, Beardmore's bought the Mossend Steel Works to secure their supply of ship and bridge plates.

The share and debenture capital of Vickers, Sons, & Maxim is now £7,347,000, and the ordinary capital alone grew from £1,000,000 in 1898 to £3,689,500 in 1902, at which figure it now stands; preferred shares are £1,510,500 and debentures £2,147,000. Goodwill and patents stood at £1,452,767 in 1904 and £500,000 in 1905, and the record of dividends also tells a tale flattering to the management. Net profits have grown as follows :—

1898	.	.	.	.	.	.	£269,852
1899	.	.	.	.	.	.	404,046
1900	.	.	.	.	.	.	526,937
1901	.	.	.	.	.	.	701,691
1902	.	.	.	.	.	.	602,344
1903	.	.	.	.	.	.	526,883
1904	.	.	.	.	.	.	723,594
1905	.	.	.	.	.	.	787,778

The report for 1905 shows in the following passage how close the company follows on Armstrong's footsteps: "Encouraged by substantial orders for guns and mountings from Italian shipbuilders, your directors have entered into a combination with three of the largest manufacturing firms in Italy, the Terni Steel Works, the shipbuilding yards of Orlando, of Leghorn, and Odero, in Genoa, to erect gun works at Spezia in that country". Already in 1901 the company had widened its activity by purchasing the Wolseley Tool and Motor-Car Co. (the investment reaching in 1903 £160,000), and the Electric and Ordnance Accessories Co. (£110,000) for the manufacture of fuzes and small projectiles at Birmingham. The degree to which integration of industry proceeds in a large firm is shown by this extract from the chairman's address at the annual meeting on 18th March, 1903: "Two other items of about £62,000 and £120,000 respectively are holdings in a colliery from which we draw a large proportion of our coal supplies and in a powder company with which we have similar relations. The results of these two investments have been very satisfactory. Another item of £150,000 is an investment in a company which controls one of the works where our guns are manufactured abroad. The company's small works in Spain stand at £85,000, and the investment in the Swedish Works at £55,000. We sold last year a half-share of the latter to secure local influence."

With John Brown & Co., of Sheffield, we come to an organisation proceeding deeper even than Armstrong's or Vickers'. The firm began with the acquisition of the Atlas Works in 1854 and ten years later was converted into a limited liability company. The Bessemer patent was early acquired, and the firm rapidly became the largest makers of steel rails in the country, until about 1874 when the works established on the sea-coast gained a great advantage through their savings in transport. Armour-plates were also a speciality. On Mr. John Ellis becoming chairman in 1870 coal-mines with an output now exceeding 1,000,000 tons annually were bought, and ore fields secured in Spain and Lincolnshire. Blast furnaces were erected and their output is now about 45,000 tons annually. Open-hearth furnaces were afterwards built, and gradually in this way the company acquired full control over all operations, from the extraction of coal and ironstone, through the making of pig-iron and steel ingots, to the manufacture of armour-plates, shipbuilding material, rails, tires, boiler-plates, castings and forgings of all kinds. The output of the Atlas Works consists of armour-plates, 10,000 tons ; railway material, 20,000 tons ; forgings, 5,000 tons ; castings and other finished material, 14,500 tons. From armour-plate and shipbuilding material it was only a step to shipbuilding. In 1899 the Clydebank Engineering and Shipbuilding Co. (started 1846) was acquired for £923,255. Here from 20,000 to 55,000 tons are launched annually, including battleships, turbine liners, etc., and the marine engines turned out in 1906 were of 108,900 I.H.P. Seven-eighths of the ordinary shares of Thos. Firth & Sons, another Sheffield steel firm, were purchased in 1902, thereby greatly increasing the facilities for the manufacture of steel products as well as reducing competition. Their share capital is now £2,200,000. Net profits in the bumper year 1900-1 were £440,393, but fell to £185,750 in 1902-3, rising to the normal level of £223,881 in 1905-6. The firm employs about 16,000 men.

The career of " Cammell's " of Sheffield is similar to that of " Brown's ". Incorporated as a company in 1864, they have long been noted for the production of rails, railway material, armour-plates, and all kinds of heavy steel forgings and castings. They control their ore supply through their holding in the Sierra Company, which owns mines in the north of Spain, and they also possess mines in Cumberland. About 1883 they moved their rail works to Workington in order to realise the economies of cheap transport and a situation on the sea-board. There they have seven blast furnaces, including the property of the Solway Bay Iron Co., acquired in 1895. After having absorbed some years before the cognate firm of Wilson, Cammell,

& Co., of Sheffield, they purchased in 1903 the Mulliner-Wrigley Co., of Coventry and Birmingham ; the Birmingham business was separated as Mulliner's Ltd., the capital of which was held by Cammell's, and at Coventry ordnance works were erected which were transferred in 1905 to the Coventry Ordnance Co., a concern employing 3,000 men, and owned then in equal shares by John Brown & Co. and Cammell's. Later, in 1903, the engineering and shipbuilding business of Laird Brothers, of Birkenhead, was amalgamated, and the company became Cammell, Laird, & Co. The history of Laird Brothers is intimately connected with the history of British shipbuilding, although with the great growth of the Clyde and North-East Coast districts the Mersey has declined in importance. In 1902, in order to carry out extensions and reclaim the foreshore, Laird's promoted the Tranmere Bay Development Co. and bought the shipbuilding firm of Messrs. John Jones & Sons. The firm lives largely on Government orders, which are naturally fluctuating. Its output in tonnage and marine engines for the last four years has been :—

	Tons.	I.H.P.
1903	5,638	38,900
1904	9,800	56,800
1905	600	7,500
1906	8,541	16,800

The circular to the shareholders of Laird Brothers held forward as an inducement to the union that the intermediate profits on the material used in engineering and shipbuilding would be retained in the business. This prospect appears to have been realised, for in November, 1905, Cammell, Laird, & Co. increased their capital to £3,372,895 and purchased half the ordinary shares of the Fairfield Shipbuilding and Engineering Co., of Glasgow, and the latter company purchased an interest in the Coventry Ordnance Works for £187,500. The Fairfield Co., originally the famous old firm of John Elder & Co., was incorporated as a public company in 1885; capital now £1,050,000. Its output in 1905 was 37,835 tons, including a cruiser, and marine engines of 56,500 I.H.P. To facilitate the transport of their goods at Workington, Cammell, Laird, & Co. promoted an Act to incorporate a body of trustees with authority to acquire

Workington Harbour and Lonsdale Dock and to construct an extension pier, the funds of the undertaking being £100,000. Lastly, Cammell's issued £750,000 in debentures in June, 1906, to provide for other developments, making their gross capital £4,122,895. Their profits, less depreciation and debenture interest, averaged £209,595 in the five years 1896-1900 and £181,667 in the five years 1901-5. Reaching their maximum, £260,015 in 1900, they fell to £144,670 in 1903, and recovered to £231,806 in 1905, exactly mirroring the course of the general iron market. The combined capital of the "community of interests" represented by John Brown & Co., Cammell, Laird & Co., and the Fairfield Shipbuilding and Engineering Co., is, after allowing for duplications, £7,103,000—a worthy rival to Vickers, Sons, & Maxim. In May, 1906, preparations were being made to erect new ordnance works at Scotstown, on the Clyde, with a dock for battleships, to belong to this triple amalgamation. The company proposes to build extensive works in South Wales, near Swansea, where a colliery has been bought. The Russian Cammell File Co., established at Odessa in 1902, has been abandoned owing to the disturbed state of the country.

The tube trade has been for years ravaged by fierce competition, both in the home and foreign trade. Many attempts at regulation by means of price associations have met with no success, but out of the turmoil has arisen one large combination, which, though it does not completely dominate the trade, is certainly the most conspicuous unit in it. Three Coatbridge firms combined in 1890 as A. & J. Stewart & Clydesdale, becoming A. & J. Stewart & Menzies and the largest tube company in Scotland on the inclusion of a fourth in 1894. The capital was £1,050,000 and the company had its own steel works for the rolling of tube strip. Late in 1902 an amalgamation was achieved with Lloyd & Lloyd, of Birmingham, the largest tube makers in England. The express reason was the extinction of competition. " In the past," said the chairman of Lloyd & Lloyd, " they had continually crossed each other's paths in most corners of the globe. The fight had been severe, and victory had sometimes been secured by one side and sometimes by the other, but there had been one uniform result from all this fighting to the shareholders of both companies, that whether victorious or not it had diminished their profits. This competition would for the future cease to exist, and this concentration of practical experience should enable home and foreign competition to be more easily dealt with." One might say that here was the embryo of an " efficiency " trust which contemplated the extirpation of its rivals, and certainly it has surpassed them in dividend returns. The amalgamated company was called Stewarts & Lloyds, and its capital was raised to £1,750,000, only £150,000 of new debentures being offered to the public. Later in the same year a financial alliance was made with the Wilson's & Union Tube Co., of Coatbridge (a union of three firms in 1898, with a capital ultimately raised to £190,000), but it was dissolved after about twelve months owing to a dispute about the allocation of profits. To write off losses the capital of the Wilson Co. was reduced in 1903, and the amount subscribed is now £174,400.

Turning to the sheet industry, we find a combination achieved in 1902, which established the galvanised sheet businesses of Alfred Baldwin & Co., of Panteg and Pontypool, E. P. & W. Baldwin, of Stourport, etc., and the Blackwall Galvanised Iron Co., of London, on a sure foundation composed of the Bryn Navigation Colliery Co., of Glamorganshire, and the blast furnaces, steel works, ore-mines, and collieries of Wright, Butler, & Co., of Swansea, etc. The new company was called Baldwins', Limited, and its capital was £1,050,000—£165,186 of which, or rather less than two years' purchase of profits, represented goodwill—and all the ordinary stock was taken by the vendors and directors. For the next two years the holders of the ordinary shares applied the profit, which might otherwise have fallen to them, in extensions. Large as it is, however, Baldwins' does not dominate the industry for there is also the large company of John Lysaght, Ltd., which has a capital of £1,000,000. At the annual meeting in October, 1906, it was announced that the company had entered into an agreement with the Gloucester Railway Carriage and Wagon Co., to purchase the Port Talbot

Steel Co.'s Works. In this way the field for utilisation of the
company's products will be considerably widened.

We now pass to unions which although partly aiming at
increased efficiency were mainly brought about in order to extinguish competition. The most extensive is perhaps the Rivet,
Nut, and Bolt Co., a union of the fifteen leading Scotch firms in
1900, whose capital is now £550,000. Though it suffered from
the depression in the shipbuilding industry it justified its existence, while a co-operative concern, started by Clyde shipbuilders
to free themselves from its monopoly, failed. It has since started
branches at Gateshead and West Hartlepool. Each branch of
the textile machinery trade contains but a few names. Eight
large firms in Lancashire manufacture cotton machinery and, in
addition to monopolising the home trade, export to the value of
about £4,500,000 annually. Repeated suggestions have been
made for an amalgamation of their interests but they have
always broken down. Mechanical industries lend themselves
to inventions which when patented produce a monopoly for
a term of years, and while it lasts a patent is an argument
against combination. Unwillingness to sink a world-famous
name, especially when it has been gained by the exercise of
individual enterprise and ingenuity, in an impersonal amalgamation must also be reckoned as a powerful deterrent. Still
there is to be counted the Textile Machinery Association, a
fusion in 1899 of seven firms engaged in making wool-combing
machinery, etc., and doing 90 per cent. of the trade. Its capital
is £290,000, and the vendors hold all the ordinary shares,
£90,000, and altogether £167,000 of the total capital. Goodwill was £38,000, paid in shares. It has not been able to make
great headway against the difficult times through which the wool
industries have been passing, and the debit balance in 1905 was
£21,502. Fairbairn, Lawson, Combe, Barbour, capital £1,100,000,
was an amalgamation in 1900 of the three largest manufacturers
of machinery for preparing and spinning flax, hemp, and jute.
All the firms were well established, two in Leeds dating from
1820 and 1828 respectively, and one in Belfast from 1845. The
capital included £381,309 for patents and goodwill, or 4·63 years'
purchase of the average profits for the previous five years, and

only one-third of the ordinary shares was taken by the vendors. Depression abroad producing a lack of foreign orders was a circumstance beyond the power of the combined firms to modify, as the dividend results for 1902 and 1903 show, and in fact the company has to follow the fortunes of the textile industries to which it is ancillary.

The marine engineering and shipbuilding industries give several examples of combinations mainly intended to reduce competition but also to promote efficiency. The Thames Iron Works Co., favourably known for its introduction of the "eight hours' day" and the "good fellowship" or profit-sharing system, and also remarkable as the last large shipbuilding concern on the Thames, strengthened its position in 1899 by the purchase of John Penn & Sons' old-established engineering business. Its capital is £871,200, and it is largely dependent on Admiralty contracts for shipbuilding business, a fluctuating source of revenue as its dividend returns show. The following year saw the formation of Richardsons, Westgarth, & Co. with a capital of £1,050,000. The constituent members were Thomas Richardson & Sons, of Hartlepool, Sir Christopher Furness, Westgarth, & Co., of Middlesbrough, and William Allan & Co., of Sunderland, and the prospectus significantly added that "the union of these companies will result in a more close alliance with the shipbuilding industry carried on at Hartlepool by Messrs. Furness, Withy, & Co. (Limited), and Irvine's Shipbuilding and Dry Docks Company (Limited), and the company will in consequence secure important orders from these firms, to mutual advantage". £100,000 was to be spent in improvements. The amalgamated concern was asserted to be the greatest marine engineering concern in the world, and a few months after its formation the chairman stated that already good results had followed from the concentration of management and the closer alliance with the shipyards. The marine engineering output for the three years 1903-5 averaged 61,840 I.H.P., while that of the North-Eastern Marine Engineering Co. was 98,677 I.H.P., and in 1903 Harland & Wolff and John Brown & Co., and in 1904 Hawthorn, Leslie, & Co., and Cammell, Laird, & Co. had a larger output. Still it is well in the top half-dozen marine engineering companies of Britain. The prospectus contemplated that the ordinary dividend would reach 8 per cent., but that has not been quite realised.

Furness, Withy, & Co. was itself a combination, but one of a somewhat different nature from those so far described in that it went quite outside the steel industries. It was a union in 1891 of the businesses of Christopher Furness, proprietor of the Furness Line of steamers, and Edward Withy & Co., shipbuilders and repairers and graving dock proprietors, and it held a controlling interest in the Irvine's Shipbuilding and Dry Docks Co. Its shipbuilding output (including Irvine's Co.) in 1906 was 69,899 tons, or 23 per cent. of the total output of the Tees and Hartlepool district. All the ordinary shares, £700,000, were taken by the directors and their friends, and no public issue was made till 1898, when £300,000 in preference shares were issued to cover extensions of business. By 1902 the reserve fund was £1,000,000, and "in addition to the steamships, freeholds, dry dock, shipbuilding yard, and investments in steamships and shipping companies, the company has the large sum of £1,340,096 invested in industrial and other companies". Its capital is now £2,000,000. For the ten years, 1887-96, the profits averaged £113,840, and for the following ten years £234,511. Sir C. Furness, at the annual meeting in July, 1906, said: "The interests of the company were diversified. They did not rely wholly on ships and engine building, ships repairing, or on the proprietorship of lines of steamers trading with different parts of the world. They also derived income as coal-owners and distributors, from their connection with the iron and steel trades, and from their operations as general forwarders and insurance and freight brokers. The number of proprietors at present was 4,481, and the turnover for the past year was £4,708,508 as against £4,450,213 for the previous year." Here we have a picture of a great complex of interests resting upon investments, and carrying therewith a share in the control of numerous other businesses. Furness, Withy, & Co. do not stand alone in this respect; we shall find the same feature repeated in the case of J. & P. Coats, and in fact most large companies can show something of the same sort. Beneath all competition there runs a golden lode of common interests.

In 1903 three Tyne firms, C. S. Swan & Hunter, Whigham Richardson & Co., and the Tyne Pontoons and Dry Dock Co., were united into Swan, Hunter, & Whigham Richardson, with a capital of £1,413,000, which includes a holding in the Wallsend Slipway and Engineering Co. Their capacity is 120,000 tons of shipping and 50,000 horse-power in marine engines annually, and the reputation of the company stands high in the ship-building world. In 1904 J. I. Thornycroft & Co., the famous torpedo boat builders, found that their position at Chiswick, on the narrow reaches of the Thames, was a hindrance to their taking orders from the Admiralty which was always demanding larger boats, and so they purchased the firm of Mordey, Carney, & Co., of Southampton. They thus increased their efficiency by becoming able to build boats of any size. At the same time the Thornycroft Steam Wagon Co. was brought into the fold and the capital was raised to £466,500. Further increases of £40,000 debentures in 1904 and £100,000 in June, 1906, were made to provide for machinery for building turbines. Lastly, in June, 1906, a provisional agreement was made for the acquisition of Stirling, Limited, by Babcock & Wilcox, Limited. Both had been for some years keen competitors in the manufacture of water-tube boilers. The capital of Babcock & Wilcox is £900,000, and its dividends have steadily risen from 12½ per cent. in 1900 to 20 per cent. in 1904 and 1905.

The British railway companies build and repair most of their own rolling-stock, and consequently the private makers of locomotives and wagons are dependent mainly on the export trade, on the smaller railway companies, and on private owners such as dock, ironworks, and colliery companies, receiving only occasional orders from the large railway companies. There were eleven private engine-building firms in 1902, employing 14,853 men, and therefore the combination of the three Glasgow firms of Neilson, Reid, & Co., Dubs & Co. and Sharp, Stewart, & Co., with a total staff of 7,570 men, marked an important change in the trade. The North British Locomotive Co. thus formed had a capital of £1,750,000, while its largest competitor, Beyer, Peacock, & Co., is capitalised at £800,000, and in 1902 had a

4 *

staff of 2,165 men ; two other firms employ over 1,000 men each. In 1900-2 the average number of men employed by all the private firms averaged 14,304, of whom 7,319 worked for the three firms in question ; for the three following years the numbers were 14,594 and 7,601 respectively, showing that practically all the increase went to the combination. The vendors took all the ordinary shares, £1,000,000, and £200,000 out of £750,000 preferred shares.

A few months earlier, April, 1902, had seen the flotation of the Metropolitan Amalgamated Railway Carriage and Wagon Co. Five of the leading companies making railway rolling-stock for collieries, iron works, etc., and, mainly, for export, which had regularly paid dividends from 7½ to 15 per cent., combined, because, to quote one of the circulars, "the keen competition to which the trade is subjected has convinced your directors that a union of interests is necessary, and that the greater resources of an amalgamated company can secure advantages which are not possible in the case of smaller undertakings with separate administrations and duplications of special plant"—a clear and succinct statement of the case for combination. Unfortunately, several of the oldest and largest of the rolling-stock companies were left outside, but towards the end of 1902 the position was strengthened by the inclusion of the Patent Shaft and Axletree Co., a blast-furnace and steel-smelting concern at Wednesbury. In this way the company secured control of its supply of channels and became able to make its own axles and tires. Its paid-up capital is £1,184,100.

The following table shows the dividends paid on their ordinary stock by most of the companies just discussed, the dividends prior to the date of amalgamation being also given in some cases. A few which less strongly exemplify the combination principle have been omitted :—

Date.	Name of Company.	Present Capital.	Ordinary Dividends for: Year Ending	1898.	1899.	1900.	1901.	1902.	1903.	1904.	1905.	1906.
		£										
1891	Furness, Withy, & Co.	2,000,000	30th April	5	5	10	10	20	10	10	10	15
1897	Sir W. Armstrong, Whitworth, & Co.	5,710,000	30th June	15	20	20	$12\frac{1}{2}$	15	15	15	15	15
	Vickers, Sons, & Maxim	7,347,000	31st Dec.	15	20	20	15	$12\frac{1}{2}$	10	$12\frac{1}{2}$	15	—
1898	{A. & J. Stewart & Menzies	1,050,000	,,	10	10	10	10	10	—	—	—	—
	{Stewarts & Lloyds (1902)	1,750,000	,,	—	—	—	—	—	10	10	10	—
	Wilson's & Union Tube	174,400	,,	—	10	10	*nil.*	*nil.*	*nil.*	*nil.*	*nil.*	—
1899	Textile Machinery Association	290,000	30th Sept.	—	—	*nil.*	*nil.*	*nil.*	*nil.*	*nil.*	*nil.*	—
	Thames Ironworks	871,200	31st Dec.	—	—	5	*nil.*	*nil.*	*nil.*	5	5	—
	John Brown & Co. (with Firth's 1902)	2,200,000	31st Mar.	$6\frac{2}{3}$	10	15	20	15	10	$8\frac{1}{3}$	$8\frac{1}{3}$	10
1900	Rivet, Bolt, and Nut Co.	550,000	31st Dec.	—	—	—	6	8	7	5	5	—
	S. Durham Steel & Iron Co. (1898) } United 1905.	950,000	30th Sept.	—	—	10	10	*nil.*	*nil.*	*nil.*	10	$12\frac{1}{2}$
	Weardale Steel, Coal, & Coke Co. (1899) } United 1905.	1,125,000	,,	—	—	$14\frac{8}{9}$	6	6	6	6	6	6
	Cargo Fleet Iron Co. (1900) } United 1905.	1,370,000	,,	—	—	—	—	—	—	—	5	5
	Guest, Keen, & Co.	2,530,000	30th June	—	—	—	10	—	—	—	—	—
	Guest, Keen, & Nettlefolds (1902)	4,535,000	,,	—	—	—	—	10	10	10	10	10
	Richardsons, Westgarth, & Co.	1,050,000	25th Aug.	—	—	—	—	6	6	6	6	6
	J. Dunlop & Co.	500,000	31st Dec.	—	—	10	5	6	4	4	7	10
	Fairbairn, Lawson, Combe, Barbour	1,100,000	,,	—	—	$7\frac{1}{2}$	$7\frac{1}{2}$	4	1	$7\frac{1}{2}$	$8\frac{1}{2}$	—
1902	Baldwins', Limited	1,050,000	30th June	—	—	—	—	—	*nil.*	*nil.*	$1\frac{1}{4}$	$2\frac{1}{2}$
	Metropolitan Amalgamated Railway Carriage and Wagon Co.	1,184,100	31st Mar.	—	—	—	—	—	10	10	10	10
	Dorman, Long, & Co. } 1902. } 1903	1,909,594	30th Sept.	8	11	15	$8\frac{1}{2}$	6	4	*nil.*	*nil.*	5
	Bell Brothers } 1902. } 1903	1,270,000	31st Dec.	—	$33\frac{1}{3}$	$44\frac{4}{9}$	$3\frac{1}{3}$	$9\frac{4}{9}$	$7\frac{7}{9}$	$5\frac{5}{9}$	$8\frac{1}{3}$	—
	North-Eastern Steel Co. } 1903	800,000	30th Sept.	$6\frac{1}{4}$	$6\frac{1}{2}$	*nil.*	*nil.*	*nil.*	*nil.*	*nil.*	*nil.*	5
1903	North British Locomotive Co.	1,750,000	31st Dec.	—	—	—	—	—	10	8	10	12
	Swan, Hunter, & Whigham Richardson	1,413,000	,,	—	—	—	—	—	5	$2\frac{1}{2}$	5	$6\frac{1}{4}$
	Cammell, Laird, & Co.	4,122,895	,,	15	$17\frac{1}{2}$	$17\frac{1}{2}$	15	10	$7\frac{1}{2}$	$7\frac{1}{2}$	10	—
1904	John I. Thornycroft & Co.	606,500	,,	—	—	—	5	5	$7\frac{1}{2}$	3	*nil.*	—

The preceding figures must only be used with caution, for many other factors must be taken into account in determining the position of a company. For example, the heavy costs of reconstruction must be borne in mind in the case of Dorman, Long, & Co., and in the case of Baldwins' the directors who held all the ordinary stock devoted their share of the profits to extensions and renewals of plant. In many cases the ordinary stock is held largely or solely by the original vendors in order that they may retain control, in which case the amount of the ordinary dividend is of less consequence to the public. One of the most satisfactory features of most of the large iron combines is that goodwill plays a very small part. Nothing was charged for goodwill in Guest, Keen, & Co. or the North British Locomotive Co., for example; one year's profits in the Metropolitan Railway Carriage Co., two years' in Baldwins', and four and a half in Fairbairn, Lawson, Combe, Barbour. In most cases it has been largely written down since the flotation. The danger of over-capitalisation may therefore be taken as non-existent.

The twenty combines or groups listed above represent a capital exceeding £45,000,000. The list could have been swelled by the inclusion of smaller concerns—such as the United Horse Shoe and Nail Co., which has the special interest of having been formed in 1883 out of two companies which had previously worked together on an agreement; its career has been unfortunate, for its share capital of £326,300 was reduced to £131,400, foreign competition being probably largely responsible. Another example from a trade severely cut up by foreign imports is the United Wire Works, an Edinburgh concern dating from 1897, when several wire-cloth businesses were united with a capital of £126,000. Its dividends have ranged from $2\frac{1}{2}$ to 4 per cent. A more favourable example is the John Wright and Eagle Range Co., which in 1900 combined two gas engineering and stove businesses formed in 1890 and 1894; its capital is now £292,000, and it has paid 20 per cent. annually since 1899. Such instances serve to remind us that amalgamation is no novel or extraordinary device but an ordinary part of business statesmanship.

Speaking broadly, the iron combinations have followed the

course of trade but not controlled it. Those making a variety of goods have been able to enter the market at whatever point —raw material, half-stuff, or finished goods—most profit offered, and have in addition saved all intermediate profits. What this means may be illustrated by the case of the Steel Company of Scotland which out of a turnover exceeding a million sterling was only able to divide about £11,000, or a dividend of 2½ per cent., for 1901-2, and the chairman said "they had done quite as well as any of their competitors who were similarly situated as themselves, that is to say, those who had no adjuncts to their steelmaking, and had to buy their raw material and did not possess blast furnaces or mines or coal-pits". In all the recent amalgamations the main desire has been to increase the power of resisting American competition, and the opportunity has been taken of raising fresh capital from the public for the purpose of extending works and modernising plant. It is still too early to expect the full beneficial results from these technical changes, but it is a matter of universal agreement that never were our ironmasters so well equipped as now to meet foreign competition. Their financial strength has enabled them to utilise favourable turns in the market and to resist disadvantageous circumstances in a way impossible to small firms. At the last annual meeting of Guest, Keen, & Nettlefolds Mr. Arthur Keen publicly testified to the advantages his company had derived from combination. The belief in the big unit is universal, and if one considers the strength of Bolckow, Vaughan, & Co., with sales amounting to £3,394,000 in 1905-6, or Guest, Keen, & Nettlefolds, with a reserve fund of £750,000, the most casual observer is bound to acquiesce. Just as the fundamental branches of the iron and steel industries fluctuate with the course of general trade, so do the makers of textile machinery follow the course of the textile industries and shipbuilders and marine engineers the course of shipping—movements all reflected in the dividend list. Wherever trade is cyclical, where it does not rest on an absolute monopoly or is not buttressed by a popular patent, a large capital is advantageous, and if it is held by a limited liability company the shock of loss is reduced by being spread over many owners.

While we are compelled to deny to the large amalgamations any direct power of controlling the market, it is to be observed that in proportion as the number of firms or companies is reduced so is it possible for them to agree, at least temporarily, for the exploitation of favourable market conditions. This tendency is strengthened by the fact that many of the large companies are connected through their boards of directors, thus creating a community of interest antagonistic to violent competition. The slightest glance at the lists of directors will show how widespread these ramifications are, both through companies which one might expect to be competitors and through companies which may be customers of one another. So notorious is this fact that it is used in prospectuses as an argument favourable to investment—for example in the case of Richardsons, Westgarth, & Co. already quoted. The prospectus of Pease & Partners affords another illustration: "Several of the directors of the Vendor Company are also directors of, or shareholders or partners in, other important companies or firms in the East and West Coasts, in which they hold a considerable, and in some cases a preponderating interest; and trade contracts have been for many years entered into, and are now subsisting, with such other companies or firms, to the mutual advantage of the parties to such contracts". There is thus no great risk in hazarding the conclusion that during the last five-and-twenty years—partly as the result of increased foreign competition, partly owing to reduction in the number of competitors, and partly owing to the spread of common interests —conditions have become more favourable to the prosecution of attempts to control the production of iron and iron goods in the interests of the producers. This movement we shall now proceed to study, premising that it follows from what has so far been said that we shall expect the movement to be vigorous where the producers are few and large, and weak where they are many and small.

CHAPTER III.

II.—ASSOCIATIONS.

COMMENCING with the production of pig-iron, we note that in each district the number of independent and associated blast-furnace concerns is small—eighteen on the North-East Coast, fourteen on the West Coast, twelve in South Staffordshire, twelve in Scotland, five in South Wales, and so on—and that they are organised into associations for the purposes of collecting statistics, negotiating with trade unions, railways, etc., and defending their general trade interests. The ironmasters or their representatives also meet regularly in the daily or weekly pig-iron markets, held at the local Metal Exchanges, and at the quarterly trade meetings at Birmingham, where they have opportunities of discussing the condition of trade and exchanging views. In this way they informally thresh out a common price, for in a restricted market each man's business is easily known. When any attempt is made to regulate production it is usually done through the local pig-iron trade associations, and not by the formation of any special kartell; this flexibility of constitution is peculiarly English. In September, 1881, the price of Cleveland No. 3 G.M.B. pig-iron fell to 36s. 9d. and Scotch Warrants to 46s., while stocks had increased heavily. After some unsuccessful negotiations the Scotch and Cleveland ironmasters agreed on a 12½ per cent. reduction of their ordinary iron from 1st October for six months. Within a few weeks prices rose from six to seven shillings, though they subsequently receded a little. At this time there was a brisk demand for steel, which was now effectively ousting wrought-iron from many markets, and both in Scotland and Cleveland the reduction in ordinary pig-iron was brought about by changing the furnaces to hematite. By combined action there was thus brought about a needed and profitable change in production, which individual action had not attempted. The agreement was renewed for other six months, and, as there was a heavy reduction in stock, Cleveland iron was kept at 43s. 6d. and later at 45s. The Cleveland masters met regularly before the weekly Tuesday market and fixed their price, and by their strong combination were able to defeat the desperate efforts of the merchants to bear the market. When the agreement terminated at the end of September, 1882, it could not be renewed because Messrs. Baird & Co., who then were reported to be producing about one-fourth of the Scotch output, withdrew as they had good orders in hand and could sell more than they were making. This is the essential weakness of a voluntary association to regulate trade. It is necessarily an alliance of the weak and the strong, and sooner or later a time comes when a strong firm, whose products are always in good demand among the public, or which has special markets, finds a restriction of output to be burdensome. Regulation of trade always benefits weak firms who are thereby secured their share. It would probably be healthier if they could be forced out of existence, but experience in the iron trade shows that if an iron-making business goes into the hands of a receiver he cuts prices in order to make a good show of a large trade in order to dispose of the business on good terms, and in this way the market is more disorganised than ever.

The Cleveland ironmasters, after the defection of the Scotch Association, maintained their policy of restricting output, renewing their agreement every three months. For some time prices were maintained, but the dependence of Middlesbrough on the Scotch market made prices fall in sympathy with speculation. Merchants and non-associated masters cut prices, the boom in shipbuilding came to an end, bad trade spread on the Continent. The fixing of prices gave way to a " tacit understanding that quotations should not go below certain figures," and by the autumn of 1883 masters were left to get the best price possible. This policy was inevitable, for any attempt to hold up prices would have concentrated demand upon the most favourite brands, and the makers of other brands would, by their inability to keep on stocking their iron, have been forced either to secede from the association or to close their works. Early in 1884 the Cleveland makers in the Middlesbrough port district agreed to shut down eighteen furnaces on terms of compensation to their owners, for now a change to hematite was no good. This equalisation of supply to demand enabled them to reduce their stocks and maintain prices in the neighbourhood of 37s. most of the year. Although the association could not control the market, yet it was able to offer a more tenacious resistance to the disorganising effects of the depression. On 1st September, 1881, Cleveland iron was quoted by makers at 36s. 9d. ; on 25th December, 1884, it was quoted at 36s. 6d., and had not fallen below 36s. 3d. Scotch Warrants, on the other hand, being unregulated, fell from 46s. 6d. to 42s. 6d., and had been as low as 41s. Reduction of output was what the circumstances called for, but for any individual ironmaster to blow out a furnace meant increasing the proportion of his standing charges and thereby diminishing his power to compete. The Cleveland Association, even if it could not keep up prices, was at least able to bring about a necessary change in trade by spreading the cost over its members.

These details show the strength and weakness of a local association. As over-production increased and prices dropped, reaching the unprecedented depth of 30s. 6d. for Cleveland No. 3 in the spring of 1886, it is not wonderful that the longing for more effective means of control grew. First the Scotch ironmasters suggested a national combination to restrict output, and a little later the British Iron Trade Association proposed a 25 per cent. reduction on the output of every maker. All particulars were to be verified by sworn accountants, and the whole of the operations were to be supervised by "arbitrators" —Mr. Goschen, Mr. Shaw Lefevre, and Sir Louis Malet being suggested as qualified persons. The milder suggestion that all makers should give an undertaking not to increase their output for three months was actually carried by a large trade meeting. But all these proposals broke down because they were unfair to the strong ironmasters and to those districts which had not accumulated or had but slightly increased their stocks. The insoluble problem was solved by the revival in trade, and, except in the shallower depression of 1893, has never been raised in a very insistent form.   Since then, however, costs have risen as well as prices, and the margin for profit has probably become narrower.   The Cleveland Association was only partly successful, because it did not include all the ironmasters in its district and could not bring the other districts into line.   To-day the number of competitors is reduced, the several businesses are larger, and the principle of community of interests is more widespread.   Since 1895 ten of the members of the association appear either to have gone out of business or to have amalgamated with others.   The history of the policy of 1881-84 has been given in detail because the important point is that it was so far successful in a time of deep depression.   To-day a similar attempt would have better chances, and the next depression may bring about a more successful repetition.   As it is, the Lincolnshire ironmasters fix the price of their iron at their fortnightly meetings and Derbyshire prices follow automatically.   Occasional consultation as to prices, if not actual regulation, seems to be the rule in Scotland, if one may judge by such market advices as " Pig-iron makers have raised their quotations by about 1s. per ton all round for special brands" (*The Times, Financial Supplement*, 21st August, 1905). Scotch pig-iron is very largely sold in special brands, and a study of the market quotations will show that they move closely together.

Coming to the malleable iron trade, regulation of prices is so much a matter of course that Prof. Sexton, in discussing the grades of malleable iron in his *Outline of the Metallurgy of Iron and Steel*, says: " As the makers in each district are more or less associated and sell at the same price, the iron of the various firms must be similar in quality".   The most successful and oldest is the informal ring, or combine, of the " Marked Bar Houses"—some half-dozen old-established firms in the Midlands who have long had a reputation for the quality of their " marked" bar iron.   Being few and making a speciality they have been able to maintain prices for long periods, *e.g.*, from

May, 1901, till early in 1904 they kept the price at £8 10s. per ton.   Yet this special iron is liable to competition from ordinary or merchant iron, and in January, 1895, the price of marked bars was reduced from £7 10s., at which it had been kept for two years, in order to meet the competition of second quality iron. Most of the marked bar houses also made ordinary bars, and to prevent complete disorganisation, the Unmarked Bar Association was formed in the spring of 1895.   It included the makers in the counties of Stafford, Worcester, Derby, Nottingham, South Yorkshire, Lancashire, and Salop.   Members were to be admitted by the committee, and if excluded for non-payment of subscriptions could only be re-elected at the general meeting of the association.   Four ordinary meetings were to be held each year.   The principal rule ran as follows : " The association shall issue quarterly in every year on the Thursday preceding the date of the ironmasters' quarterly meeting in Birmingham, a list to be compiled by the committee and confirmed by a general meeting of the association to be held on the said Thursday preceding the said quarter-day, announcing the selling prices of second-class iron of the makers mentioned in Clause 2, which is not recognised in the trade as 'marked list iron'; and such list prices respectively shall be at sellers' works, but the seller may, if desirable, deliver the iron to the buyer or his nominee upon being paid by the buyer, in addition to the list price, delivery charges at the following rates, *viz.* : For all distances within five miles from seller's works at the rate of 5s. per ton ; for longer distances there shall be added to list prices the recognised railway rate per ton ; and such official list shall be signed by the chairman and secretary for the time being of the association, and posted on the Birmingham Exchange on the Thursday before such quarterly meeting.   And the respective prices charged on such list shall be the minimum prices at which their respective kinds of iron shall be sold during the quarter of a year following the posting of such list, unless the association shall in general meeting otherwise decide ; and such list prices shall be subject to the following discounts on the different modes of payment below, *viz.*, 3 per cent. for prompt payment within seven days after delivery, 2½ per cent. for cash monthly on the 10th of the month following delivery, or four months' acceptance net, bearing date the 10th of the month following delivery. All iron which is sold and exported and consumed out of the United Kingdom, and delivered f.o.b. in English, Scotch, or Irish ports shall not be in any way affected by the terms of this deed." This last clause permitted exportation at reduced prices, the policy which in more recent years has aroused so much resentment when practised by American trusts and German kartells. The minimum price was fixed at £5 5s. per ton, and was raised to £6 10s. by the end of the year. The Lancashire trade was separately organised in 1898. When the great boom came there was no difficulty about prices, for the average net selling price of bars, etc., as ascertained by the Midlands Wages Board, rose till it was £9 8s. 6d. in 1900, and the margin above the price of South Staffordshire pig-iron rose from £3 7s. 3d. to £5 10s. 1d. In the hope of retaining some of this gain in bad times the National Consultative Council of the Iron Trade of Great Britain was formed in 1900 to bring about joint action between the different bar iron associations. One meeting was held, but when the slump came this high-sounding association did nothing and prices fell to an unremunerative level. The second meeting of the Council was held in July, 1902, when representatives were present from North Staffordshire, South Staffordshire, Lancashire, Yorkshire, and Shropshire, and the common price of £6 15s. was fixed, a rise of 7s. 6d. in the quarter, partly due to improved demand, partly to the higher price of iron. This, once again, was following the market, but the attempt was unsuccessful. Some time later the Unmarked Bar Association fell into abeyance, but was revived on the improvement of trade in the spring of 1904, and it and other bar iron associations—such as the South Yorkshire and North of England—are from time to time reported as being active.

Combination in the Scotch malleable iron trade is at least twenty years old, and as there are only about two dozen iron rolling mill firms, and Scotch malleable iron owing to its world-wide reputation has maintained its competition with steel and declined but little in output, circumstances have been more favourable to the movement.   An extract from the *Iron and Coal Trades Review* of 15th October, 1886, commenting on a general rise of 2s. 6d. to 7s. 6d. per ton in Scotch malleable iron, is interesting as showing the local movement in its inception : " There is no combination of a hard and fast character amongst the makers, but almost as if by common consent they have fallen in with the suggestions of those of their number who took the initiative in the matter.   Even the largest concerns such as the Glasgow Iron Co. and Messrs. David Colville & Sons have identified themselves with this upward movement."   Scotland and the North-East of England have always been competitors not only in shipbuilding but also in the manufacture of shipbuilding materials—steel and malleable iron.   It therefore marked a distinct step in the organisation of the industry when in 1902 the malleable iron makers of the two districts to the number of forty entered into an agreement not to encroach on each other's territory.   The Scotch makers were so satisfied with the results of their combination that a good part of 1902-3 was occupied with negotiations for an amalgamation of all the works with a capitalisation reported as £1,000,000 sterling. The parties, however, were not able to agree as to whether the businesses were to be purchased with cash or paper and the scheme broke down.   Another " arrangement " between English and Scotch bar-makers was reported to be under discussion early in 1907.

The rail trade was for long the backbone of the steel industry, and it had developed at the same rate as steel itself which had nearly doubled in production in the United Kingdom and rather more than doubled in Germany and the United States between 1876-80 and 1881-85.   The extension of capacity kept down prices and the American market was largely closed by the tariff.   Consequently in 1883 was formed the International Rail Syndicate which was for long the most famous of industrial combinations.   The members were Great Britain, where all of the seventeen or eighteen firms in the industry except one joined, Germany, where all joined but two, and Belgium.   On the basis of the previous three years' trade, Britain was allotted 66 per cent. of the business, afterwards reduced to 63½ per cent.

in consequence of disputes; Germany 27, afterwards 29 per
cent. ; and Belgium 7, afterwards 7½ per cent.—and orders were
allotted to the three countries in those proportions, each retaining its domestic trade so far as it went.   In each country the
individual works were assessed according to their capacity, and
orders were divided according to the ratio of the individual to
the total capacity, adhesion to the rules being secured by a
penalty.   Prices were at once raised from £4 to £4 13s. per
ton, but any maker who could get ten shillings a ton for his
product above the standard price was left free to treat with
his customer.   According to a witness before the Royal Commission on the Depression of Trade and Industry, " The price
was fixed at very much what we considered the cost price
would be at the least favoured works, and any amount of profit
upon the prices we fixed is due to the better position and better
plant of the various works ".   The smaller works, which were in
the minority, were thus virtually offered painless extinction.
From January, 1884, to the spring of 1886, prices were kept at
£4 15s. to £5 5s. despite the bad trade on the Continent.   But
for some time there had been grumbling, and in April it was
officially announced that the " pool " was dissolved and that in
lieu the English and German makers had agreed to respect each
other's territory.   Prices at once fell to £4 3s. and the German
works, keeping their home prices just below the British price
plus duty and freight, were able to make a profit of 35s. a ton
on the two-thirds of their output consumed at home, while the
other one-third was squandered on foreign contracts at 73s.
The price maintained by the " pool " was no doubt excessive,
for a few months later we hear of the North of England rail-
mills being full of work at 20s. below the old price.

Rail prices fell to a yearly average of £3 18s. 3d. in 1888,
and rose to a yearly average of £5 9s. 1d. in 1890, sinking
once more to a minimum of £3 10s. in 1895.   Once more we
hear of a rail pool which, with the help of better demands from
India, China, and Japan, raised prices to £4 15s. by the end of
the year.   This time the combination was British only.   " Practically what we know," said the *Ironmonger* (22nd February,
1896), " is that about ten of the rail-manufacturing concerns have

associated themselves together for the 'maintenance' of prices, whilst the other five or six concerns, which also produce rails regularly or occasionally, are understood to give a benevolent support to the combination.   All the principal British makers are in the ring, so that it will not be easy for the smaller mills to run against it with good results to themselves." *Post hoc* at least prices went up in the general iron boom, and in 1898 the trade papers reported that the syndicate still controlled the trade, but some time later it was allowed to lapse—when high prices can be got there seems to be no need for regulation.   Late in 1902, however, a sensational report was circulated that the eight great rail-making concerns—Barrow Hematite, Bolckow's, Guest, Keen, & Co., Crawshay's, Moss Bay, Cammell, North-Eastern, and Rhymney—were to be combined with a share capital of £12,000,000.   This brought to light the fact that the old Steel Rail Manufacturers' Association had been resuscitated about two years earlier, since which time it had been regulating prices and output in the old fashion.   In the depression which followed the boom its utility became once more apparent.   But the depression of 1901-3 was universal, and Germany was dumping rails at 30s. a ton below her home price.   Throughout 1904 negotiations had been proceeding between British and German steel-makers for the avoidance of unprofitable competition, and in November an agreement was signed between the railmakers of Britain, Germany, Belgium, and France.   To each country its own territory was assigned, and the export trade was syndicated for three years on the basis of 1,300,000 tons annually, at a minimum price of 10·625 francs per 100 kilogrammes—say £4 7s. a ton.   The British works were to be allotted 53·50 per cent. of the export trade, with priority to the trade of British possessions, German works 28·83, and Belgium 17·67, the French being allotted 4·8, 5·8, and 6·4 per cent. for the three years respectively, in addition to the shares of the other countries. British prices were then about £4 per ton.   The leading British firms involved were said to be Cammell's, Guest, Keen, & Nettlefolds, Barrow Hematite, Bolckow's, Moss Bay, Ebbw Vale, North-Eastern, Walter Scott, and Steel, Peech, & Tozer (*Daily Chronicle*, 17th December, 1904).   In January, 1905,

5

prices rose to £4 10s. a ton and pretty soon reached £5 5s. In July the agreement was extended to the United States, to which probably the American continent was assigned as a market, and by the end of the year the price was £5 17s. 6d. per ton, and at the end of 1906, £6 12s. 6d. We consequently have now an international syndicate comprising several national trusts, pools, and kartells, with the net result that British rail-makers are "protected" from foreign competition. Not all the rail-making firms, however, are in the syndicate, and it is reported that the Glengarnock Iron and Steel Co. and the independent foreign firms have profited by the high level at which prices have been kept. Lancashire makers complain of want of orders and of the reduction of profits by the high price of steel.

The decade 1878-87 marked the transition from iron to steel in shipbuilding. The new material was taken up most actively on the Clyde, to the great advantage of the open-hearth steelmakers of the south of Scotland whose product was peculiarly adapted for ship-plates. The years 1880-83 were very brisk in shipbuilding, and not till 1896 did the Clyde surpass its output of 1883; with 1884 the tide turned, and not till 1887 was there another upward movement. The growing use of steel to some extent counterbalanced the decreased output of ships, for in 1885 about 45 per cent. of the Clyde output was steel ships. The Scotch steelmakers had quite a monopoly in supplying the local demand for boiler-plates, and their position was almost unquestioned in ship-plates, bridge-plates, and angles. To secure themselves against possible competition from the North of England, the four leading Scotch steelmakers formed a combination to control the local market early in 1885. In the course of the year they raised prices 10s. a ton, but in the winter the English makers, notably the Consett Iron Co., set up a sharp competition and in January, 1886, forced a reduction of 7s. 6d. This was the beginning of a warfare frequently to be repeated in later years. In May, 1886, the Scotch Steelmakers' Association was dissolved, prices being then lower than before its formation, but the "dissolution" was only temporary, for in January, 1887, we hear of a conference of Scottish steelmakers which advanced prices in consequence of a rise in hematite.

Coming to more recent years we find the *Iron and Coal Trades Review* (16th December, 1898) stating that : " We have now in operation agreements or understandings as to prices in the rail, ship-plate, boiler-plate, bar iron, and other branches of the iron and steel trades of this country by means of which prices are fairly well maintained, and cutting is largely prevented ". There were separate Plate Associations in Scotland and the North of England, and in Scotland there were separate Associations for Boiler-plates and Ship-plates. In Lancashire a Boiler-plate Association was organised in the spring of 1898. It lapsed in 1900, but was re-established in 1901 on a wider basis, and put up prices 10s. per ton. Both prices and output appear to have been regulated. Throughout 1902 the Ship-plate Associations had to struggle against the high price of pig-iron, due to American demand, and the depression in shipbuilding, but ultimately they reduced prices in concert, thereby calling forth fresh orders. There does not appear, however, to have been any demarcation of territory. The Scotch Boiler-plate Association was in a much stronger position and adopted very high-handed methods. There is no reason to suppose that they were more wicked than manufacturers in general, and therefore we can only take their action as significant of what may be expected from any combination which fancies itself strong enough. Messrs. Denny & Co., the shipbuilders, wrote to the newspapers, under date 11th November, 1902 : " A short time ago we bought a quantity of steel boiler-plates from a firm of Glasgow iron merchants, stipulating the usual Scotch brands, as in previous similar contracts. Against this purchase we recently placed with these merchants a specification, in which were four plates somewhat above ordinary size. The specification was placed by the merchants with a firm of steelmakers outside the combination or association of Scotch steelmakers. This firm found these four plates above referred to somewhat beyond their power to roll. Unknown to us they ordered these plates from a German firm. . . . On learning this we refused to take German when we had contracted for Scotch plates. . . . We then

5 *

approached a firm of Scotch steelmakers, who are in the combination, and with whom we had a large business directly, and explained to them the situation.   Their reply was a refusal to supply the four plates in question unless we gave them the order for the entire specification, but, as the balance of the plates had already been made, this proposal meant the scrapping of approximately 110 tons, and this we hardly saw our way to agree to.   We explained to these makers that no price in reason, or even beyond reason, would stand in the way, but we were told that at no price whatever would the plates be supplied. . . . We are accordingly, by the action of our home makers, forced to accept these German plates, and having once done so, we shall naturally have less hesitation in following the same course again.   From the same firm we further learned that no one of the combination of steelmakers would undertake our order, and that outside of the combination no one could turn out plates of the size required.   We understand that their extraordinary attitude on this occasion is due to the determination of those in the combination to coerce all those outside of it to join them.   And still employers complain of the tyranny of trade unions.   As a further example of the methods of this combination, we may state, of our own knowledge, that its members are prepared to supply boiler-plates for shipment abroad at about £1 less per ton than the rate charged by them to boilermakers in this country.   American methods are not regarded with entire approval on this side, but, after all, it would appear that the tyranny of combinations is not quite unknown here."

Besides the boycott and low export prices the Boilermakers' Association adopted another " American " device.   While keeping up the price of boiler-plates they undersold the makers of ship-plates, but in the spring of 1903 they were hoist with their own petard, for a Scotch maker of ship-plates converted his rolls to make boiler-plates, and severely undercutting the association price obtained plenty of business.   The persistent competition of outsiders defeated the efforts of the association to maintain prices at £7 10s. a ton, the combination collapsed, and prices fell to £6.

The steel trade had suffered heavily in 1902 and 1903 from

the "dumping" of German steel, and the autumn of 1903 was occupied with the negotiations leading to the formation of the German Steel Union, destined to place the German steel industry on a sounder footing. These facts, coupled with the dulness in shipbuilding, led to a meeting of all the steel producers in Scotland in December, 1903, "probably," said the *Glasgow Herald*, "the first meeting of the kind in the history of the trade at which all makers were represented". Prices had fallen to—ship-plates, £5 7s. 6d., angles, £4 15s., and bars, £5 15s. in small lots; so minima were fixed which were expected to prevent loss—boiler-plates, £6 per ton, ship-plates, £5 10s., and angles, £5, all less 5 per cent., and bars, £6. These prices were still unprofitable, and in February a combination was formed and an advance made of 2s. 6d. per ton in ship-plates, bars, and angles, and 5s. on marine boiler-plates. The association was to hold fortnightly meetings. The members each made a deposit of £1,000 and agreed to forfeit £1 for every ton sold below the association price—the money to be divided among the loyalists. The agreement only related to Scotland and the North of Ireland; in England the members had a free hand. The first result of this reconstitution of the Scotch Steelmakers' Association was that the rise in prices called forth fresh orders, merchants being at last obliged to cover their requirements. In the autumn an agreement was made with the platemakers of the North of England not to sell in each other's territory, and with the cessation of needless competition important savings were made in railway charges. After several fluctuations prices at the end of 1904 were ship-plates, £5 15s., angles, £5 5s., bars and marine boiler-plates, £6 5s.

Complaints were not slow to follow this enhancement of prices. A correspondent writing to the *Times* (*Financial and Commercial Supplement*, 5th December, 1904) asserted that such combinations led to increased importation from foreign countries. "The first consequence of this arrangement," he said, "was the shipment of a cargo of ship-plates from New York to the Clyde, and it was followed by offers of ship-plates from Germany." He added: "For some time there was a combination among British producers of crude steel to maintain the prices of bars and billets. They did so, and German, Belgian, and American bars and billets streamed into our markets. They may not be so good as our own make, but they were so much cheaper that our manufacturers bought them freely, and out of imported raw material they make finished products of which they in turn regulate the home prices by combinations, to the advantage of their foreign competitors." And his moral was that "profits should be sought in economy and efficiency in production and management, not in artificial restraint of business". The other side of the case was put forward by another correspondent in the *Times* (*Financial and Commercial Supplement*, 19th December, 1904), who pointed out that it took 22 cwt. of pig-iron to make a ton of finished steel, and that pig-iron had risen 4s. a ton since the inception of the combine. "Your correspondent," he said, "refers to the fact that steel ship-plates are about £1 higher now than they were sold at in the previous period of depression before the great revival of trade in 1897-98. The lowest price ship-plates were sold at then was £5 per ton, and angles, £4 7s. 6d. To-day prices are, as he states in his article, £5 15s. for ship-plates, and £5 5s. for angles, both less 5 per cent. This makes a difference in the one case of 15s. and in the other of 17s. 6d.; but pig-iron is to-day 14s. per ton higher than it was in the period referred to. Ore was 3s. 3d. per ton less, coal 2s. 6d. per ton less than it is to-day, and wages were 5 per cent. less than they are to-day, and during the depression referred to, few in the steel trade were able to make ends meet, as could be seen from the reports. . . . But for the improvements that have been made in the methods of manufacture and the greater care and economy exercised in all the works, material could not be made at to-day's prices without loss. Even with prices as they are controlled by the combination, with perhaps two exceptions, Scotch makers are not making sufficient money to give their shareholders a return in the way of dividend, and I think the same remark applies to the most recent creation of up-to-date works in the North of England." On this reply it is only necessary to comment that it is very doubtful if all the economies of improved methods were presented to the consumers, and that steelmakers who have their own blast furnaces are able to appropriate the profit arising from the rise in the price of pig-iron. It is, however, only fair to quote from the *Glasgow Herald Shipbuilding and Engineering Annual* for 1904, which one would expect to be biassed in favour of the shipbuilders, the following opinion : " In the case of the Scotch steelmakers it cannot be said that the agreement amongst producers has been at all hurtful to consumers, while it has certainly been very beneficial to manufacturers and their employees. . . . It may, indeed, be said that by the moderation in their terms makers have not excited hostility on the part of consumers, it being the desire of the combine at all times to meet their wishes as far as possible."

With the boom in shipbuilding which occupied 1905, the steel trade was in a happier position. Prices were advanced in January, in September, and in December, plates and angles being then £7 2s. 6d. and £6 15s. respectively, or rises of 27s. 6d. and 25s., but the price of Scotch hematite had risen from 59s. in January to 75s. in October, and in December was between 72s. and 73s. In January, 1906, ship-plates were at £7 2s. 6d. and rose to £7 7s. 6d. in February, at which price they continued till December, when they were raised to £7 12s. 6d. During the same period Scotch hematite fell from 74s. 6d. in January to 67s. 6d. in July and then rose sharply to 83s. 6d. in December. The margin between the prices of plates and hematite rose from £2 15s. 6d. in 1902 to £3 15s. 8d. in 1906. The steelmakers had a firm hold on the market, and were able both to follow the upward course of hematite and to retain the profit arising from its frequent downward fluctuations by steadying the prices of plates for considerable periods. German competition was absent, the makers there being fully occupied with their home trade. An incident narrated by the *Times* (*Financial Supplement*, 4th June, 1906), shows at once the advantage drawn from combination by a weak or temporarily embarrassed firm, and at the same time the sacrifices which must occasionally be made by those more fortunately placed : " One of the Scotch firms, which also runs a large shipbuilding concern and whose steel plant produces about 5,000 tons of plates per month, has become so scarce of orders that the association has had to be approached with the object of getting relief. To cut prices would mean a break-up of the association, and in order to avoid this it is understood that other parties to the combine have agreed to give a portion of their orders to the firm in question to tide them over their shortness of work." Such an arrangement is undoubtedly advantageous to the firm in question which at least avoids the loss of idle plant, to its employees who escape being thrown out of work, and to the other firms who avoid competition and lower prices, but the purchasers of steel plates have to resign the opportunity, formerly in their power, of profiting by the necessities of one of their suppliers. The proceeding, however, is comically like the disbursement of unemployed benefit by a trade union, but no doubt the imitation is quite unconscious. Only ship and boiler-plates were included in the agreement of 1905, but severe competition still went on in angles which were "dumped" at Belfast at 10s. a ton below Clyde prices, giving a marked advantage to the Belfast shipbuilders over their Clyde rivals. English angles were also sold on the Clyde at £6 5s. a ton, less 2½ per cent., whereas the Scotch price was £7, less 5 per cent. The Scotch makers similarly cut rates in England. In July, 1906, angles were included in the agreement, export prices were raised from 5s. to 10s., and Belfast was placed on the same level as the Clyde. The immediate result was to call forth a large amount of orders from Belfast which were placed at prices 15s. to 16s. above those previously current.

South Wales is an important steel-making district, turning out rails, billets, and tinplate bars, but except in rails it has never gone in much for combined action. In billets it has been much exposed to American and German competition, and for a long time its tinplate bar trade suffered from the unsatisfactory condition of the tinplate trade. The retirement of the Germans from the market in 1904 eased the situation a good deal, but in the spring of 1905 the bar trade suffered from the high price of pigs and the competition of West Coast steelmakers. An association was formed to maintain prices, but it only lasted a month when one firm withdrew and prices at once relapsed to their former level. In September, 1906, a new association was announced, the South Wales Siemens Steelmakers' Association, for the purpose of regulating output, allotting orders, and determining prices. All the makers but one were included.

Up till 1891 when the Americans resolved to establish the tinplate industry in the United States and imposed a duty on tinplate of $2\frac{1}{5}$ cents a pound, the tinplate trade was one of our most flourishing and prosperous trades, in which we had practically a monopoly. Yet it was not free from the blows of ill-fortune; for example, in July, 1885, the manufacturers arranged a stop week to get rid of the glut arising from over-production. When the American tariff was imposed a futile policy was adopted. The men in 1893 started the plan of restricting each man's output and did not give it up till late in 1900. The masters, no wiser, set up the Tinplate Manufacturing Board of Control in 1895 to reduce the output by one-third and so keep up prices, although the high prices of 1890 had supplied the Americans with one of their chief arguments for the creation of a domestic industry. "The effort," said the *Iron and Steel Trades Journal* (6th April, 1895), "to force up prices by a combination to restrict the make and cause a scarcity, seems to us to be playing into the hands of the American works. By all means let those makers who cannot produce at present prices stop their mills, but to tie the hands of those who are content with a small percentage of profit on a big turnover is neither wise nor fair." The Board of Control was dissolved the following year, and at the same time a proposal to raise capital to form a company for sending agents to the Colonies to create new markets for tinplate collapsed, being only supported by half the manufacturers.

Since those disastrous days the trade has expanded its home sales very largely and found new foreign markets which have replaced the lost American one. The chief makers manufacture their own tinplate bars, thus saving from 10s. to 20s. per ton. Much attention has been given to improvement of processes, and much profit has been made from "dumped" foreign bars. Yet the general profits have not been commensurate with the expansion of trade. By the side of large, new, well-equipped

works there are a large number of old works with obsolete
machinery which manufacture under most disadvantageous circumstances, and only exist because their capital value has long
since been written off. The result is a frantic and hopeless
competition like the handloom weavers against the power loom,
bringing jealousy, envy, and discord in its train, and therewith
complete disorganisation in the trade. The *Iron and Coal
Trades Review* (22nd March, 1901) wrote: "At the present
time the South Wales manufacturers are more or less at sixes
and sevens, and are carrying on a competition against each
other at a rate that is certainly uneconomical, if it is not ruinous. The effects of that competition are extremely prejudicial
to the trade, preventing it from controlling labour, from taking
up a firm and effective attitude as to the cost of everything
they buy (including transport), increasing standing charges, and
otherwise weakening the competitive hold over both the home
and the foreign markets. Assuming that these works were,
like the union of tinplate works in the United States, amalgamated into one concern, with one management, one staff, and
one central office, it would become possible to keep a certain
limited number of works always fully going, at a great saving of
standing charges, instead of nearly a hundred irregularly as at
present ; to keep certain works employed on certain sizes and
sections with little need for changing rolls ; to buy raw materials,
including tin and steel sheets or bars on much more advantageous terms; perhaps to acquire the control of tin-mines, tending
to make the works independent of market fluctuations ; to
negotiate for transport on the basis of thousands of tons where
the quantities are now hundreds of tons only ; and to employ a
special staff of qualified men to open up new markets, where
that would be a serious cost in the cases of individual firms.
All these advantages appear to have fallen to the American
company, and there seems to be no reason why they should not
equally fall to South Wales." It is an admirable exposition of
the advantages of amalgamation, but for combination there
must be some equality between the units. To propose an
amalgamation of all the South Wales tinplate works would be
like asking a turbine steamer to combine with a dodo. So little

has been learnt that when the rise in the price of raw materials and the loss of business on account of disturbances in Russia caused a serious shrinkage in demand, the employers' association and the trade unions could devise nothing better than a stop-week in June, 1906. The number of manufacturers in the tinplate industry is still too great, their circumstances too diverse, and their interests too discrepant for effective combination to regulate their industry.

Lord Glantawe, formerly well known in the tinplate trade as Sir J. J. Jenkins, speaking at the annual meeting of the Swansea Metal Exchange, said, " that the new steel combine brought into existence a state of things which might well press out of the trade the tinplate maker who was not also the maker of his own steel, and might eventually place it in the hands of tinplate makers who also had steel works, and steelmakers who had controlling interests in tinplate works. His lordship had no hesitation in expressing the opinion that this in the long run would prosper neither the Welsh Siemens tin bar manufacturer nor the Welsh tinplate maker" (*Times*, 19th September, 1906). The " pure" tinplate makers would in that case have to confine themselves to imported steel, and would even then be liable to be undersold by those who profited by the economies of mixed works. This would facilitate the freeing of the trade from many small and inefficient works.

The galvanised sheet manufacture resembles the tinplate trade in that it has always been an industry in which Great Britain has occupied a dominant position and has had a flourishing export business. Being largely a Midland interest—though of late years there has been a migratory movement to South Wales for the purpose of saving transport expenses by getting close to tide water—the manufacturers have been more favourably inclined to combined action. We must also note the existence in the industry of large companies like John Lysaght & Co. and Baldwins', Limited. As early as October, 1883, we find a Galvanised Iron Trade Association fixing prices at £13 10s. per ton f.o.b. London, but six months later, in the general depression, it decided " in the present unsettled state of the iron market to fix no price for galvanised iron ". In

1895 we again find this association fixing prices for the Midlands, and, according to the Birmingham trade reports, it appears to have exercised some controlling influence over the trade. In April, 1905, a considerable advance was made by the constitution of a National Galvanised Sheet Association to which 95 per cent. of the manufacturers of the Midlands, Lancashire, North of England, London, Scotland, and Wales gave their adhesion. An immediate advance of 7s. 6d. per ton to £10 5s. called out a brisk demand, hitherto latent in expectation of lower prices. Thereafter, further increases were rapidly made, partly on account of the rapid rise in the prices of spelter and pig-iron, and by the end of the year the official price was £12 2s. 6d. Still, so brisk was the demand that at that time manufacturers were easily getting from £12 15s. to £13 a ton. Prices at the end of 1906 were £13 5s. officially and actually up to £14, but since the formation of the association pig-iron had risen 10s. and spelter £4 7s. 6d. a ton. It was stated that the object of the association was to regulate output as well as prices, but for this there is little need while trade is good.

The tube trade has always been a prey to fierce competition. There are two main centres of the industry, Coatbridge and Birmingham, and the chief products are bicycle tubes and boiler tubes. About 70 per cent. of the trade is for export, and as some firms make mainly for export and others mainly for the home market it is natural that the disposal of the surplus output in each branch has given rise to much bitterness. There are between fifty and sixty leading firms in the United Kingdom, and their aggregate output is about 300,000 tons a year. An association of English boiler-tube manufacturers was attempted in 1898. In 1901 there were Scotch and English associations working in alliance, but relations were broken off owing to the severe cutting of prices. The British Tube Association was revived in 1902 and made two advances in home prices, the competition of Germany and Belgium being too severe to permit export prices to be touched. The amalgamation of Stewarts & Lloyds did something to improve the industry by removing the competition between the two companies which had been particularly severe in foreign markets, and the payment of a

steady dividend of 10 per cent. has shown how fully the combination was justified. Disputes with regard to foreign trade
and export prices appear to have brought the association to an
end. Mr. Arthur Chamberlain, in presiding over the annual
meeting of Tubes Limited, in December, 1902, expounded the
situation in a way which not only cast a good deal of light on
the tube business but also on the conditions of successful combination. He said: "He had been approached by other tube
makers in regard to the formation of a ring for the raising of
prices to their customers. The difficulty was not that prices
were too low; they complained of price in proportion to their
output. There were two or three times too many of them in
the trade. A great number of people who had now gone out of
the competition still had the requisite machinery, and if there
was any chance of making any plunder, there was no doubt
they would speedily reappear as tube manufacturers. If they
had to make a profit, it could only be done by reducing the cost
of manufacture, or reducing in proportion their dead charges.
And the only way of reducing the dead charges was by bringing
them down proportionately by increasing the turnover, which
probably involved a still lower range of prices. Everything
depended upon the amount of business they could succeed in
doing. In previous years they tried to effect a narrow trade at
higher prices, and had lost more than they had gained by it.
Now they had determined to have their share of the orders."
This was a declaration of war, and two years later Mr. A.
Chamberlain was able to say that in cycle tubes "what they
sold eight years ago for £50 they now only got £7 10s. for.
They had not only to meet other makers of weldless tubes but
great companies, whose proper business was lap-welded tube, and
who devoted a portion of their profits on this to the underselling
of weldless tubes at an absolute loss on production." At the
general meeting in 1905 he pointed out that "the total amount
paid for cycle tubes in Great Britain last year was only £90,0c0,
and for that there were eleven cycle tube companies fighting.
With their four works they could have done it all. The cycle
tube trade was bad and the boiler tube trade was nearly as bad."
The end of Mr. A. Chamberlain's bold determination to compete

for "their share of the orders" was very sad. In November, 1906, the directors issued a report to the effect that they felt that "a liquidation of the company's affairs cannot be any longer delayed" (*Times*, 5th November, 1906). The German tube makers had unsuccessfully tried in 1903 to persuade the English makers to agree to a division of foreign markets. The Gas Tube Association of manufacturers in the Midlands, London, and the North of England failed to maintain a minimum price which only covered the cost of production and collapsed early in 1905. After that the pendulum seems to have swung again towards combination. In the spring of 1905 we hear of the Cased Tube Manufacturers' Association and, a year later, of the Wrought Iron Tube Association—both regulating prices with some success. And in September, 1906, the British Tube Association was re-established to control both home and export prices. All the makers but one, a Glasgow firm making boiler tubes, have joined the combination. Prices have been raised for all classes of tubes—5 per cent. on export prices and home discounts reduced 2½ per cent. except for boiler tubes, where there is still to be free competition till the erring maker is made to enter the fold. It is also added that the support of the American makers has been obtained.

Lastly, coming to a group of sundry trades making more or less finished iron goods and generally centred at Birmingham, we find the germ of combination in a general meeting of the finished iron manufacturers of South Staffordshire and East Worcestershire at Birmingham in February, 1887, to bring about a general rise of 10s. a ton. It failed, but in 1895 we find Associations of Axlemakers, Tinned Sheet Manufacturers, Hoopmakers, and Heavy Ironfounders regulating prices in quarterly meetings at Birmingham. In 1901 the Gas Strip Association was formed by eighteen out of the twenty Midland firms, and in the following year it had a sharp tussle with German competitors whom it beat out of the market by lowering prices 2s. 6d. per ton. When the competition was crushed the old standard price was of course restored. In January, 1903, the Small Iron Makers' Association was set up, including sixteen out of eighteen houses rolling small bars, rounds, etc.

Both the Gas Strip and the Small Iron Associations were " pools "; each firm had a definite output allotted to it, and any excess entailed a penalty, divided among those who did not manufacture their full quota. Observance of the rules was secured by each member making a deposit. The Small Iron Association fell into abeyance after about a year's existence, and in the summer of 1905 the Gas Strip Association was in trouble with a firm accused of underselling. Expulsion of the offender, sharp competition, and collapse of the association followed. Late in 1904 an association was formed of thirty firms in the cut nail trade in England, Scotland, and South Wales—practically all of the manufacturers. A revised price list was issued and underselling forbidden by severe penalties. The German screw manufacturers syndicated themselves in 1905, and the long rate-cutting war was ended by the formation of an international syndicate in September, 1905, by which the British and German manufacturers agreed to accept no further orders from each other's country. This result was partly due to the vigorous attack made on German markets by Messrs. Guest, Keen, & Nettlefolds. In September, 1906, a combination of all the hinge makers in the country was formed, with headquarters at Birmingham. To stop underselling a new price list has been issued to which all the members have assented. Other Midland associations which are mentioned in the current market reports of 1906 are, Ironfounders' Association, Tinned Sheet Association, Galvanised Hollow Ware Association, Galvanised Wire-Netting Association, the Master Brassfounders' Association. The following extract appears to show the working of combined even if not regular action in other cases : " Discounts have been revised in builders' ironmongery, gas fittings, plumbers' brassfoundry, fenders and fire-irons, enamelled hollow ware, tin and japanned goods, etc. In most cases the change means an advance in price of from $2\frac{1}{2}$ per cent. to 5 per cent." (*Times, Financial Supplement*, 22nd January, 1906).

No account of attempts to regulate competition would be complete without a reference to the once famous " Birmingham Alliances," now happily defunct, never, it is to be hoped, to reappear in British industry. They were started by Mr. E. J.

Smith in the metallic bedstead trade in 1891, and spread to the manufacture of spring mattresses, metal and cased tubes, spun brass mounts and ornaments, rope and twine, metal rolling, fenders, china door furniture, china electrical fittings, iron plateware, coffin furniture, pins, marl, bricks, and jet and rockingham ware—trades including 500 masters and 20,000 workpeople. Mr. Smith's first principle was that no article should be sold except at a profit, and when he was called in to "organise" a trade his first task was to work out the cost price of all the goods, a task in which he found that only about a third of the manufacturers could give him reliable help. He took the average cost of the trade, holding that if a man with large capital could make advantageous purchases of raw material, or if by exceptional skill or by specially improved processes he could make savings in production above the average, he ought to retain these advantages for himself and not distribute them to the consumers in lower prices. Having ascertained average costs, a percentage of profit was added and uniform price lists issued. In this way the public was to be deprived of their due share in the improvement of industry by a combination which was at bottom anti-social in its tendency. Observance of the price lists was ensured by an alliance with the trade unions, the masters binding themselves to employ only unionists, and the latter agreeing to work only for members of the masters' association and to call out the employees of any offending master, the strikers to be maintained from a fund raised by levies from the employers. Ten per cent. was at once added to wages, a sliding scale was drawn up, and a conciliation board instituted. This alliance also was anti-social, for it is one of the tacitly recognised safeguards against high prices that if they are too high the men will step in and demand their share. Thus for many months the Scotch Ship Plate Association refrained from raising prices, because to do so would entail under their sliding scale a rise in wages, and only raised prices when the market had improved to such a degree that they were able to make an advance which would more than compensate for the extra wages; meanwhile, their customers profited. But under the alliance system both sections of producers combined at the expense of the consumer. Foreign competitors who tried to cut British prices were to be met by " well-arranged, careful, judicious, and systematic underselling," or by offering rebates to customers, conditional on their buying only from members of the associations.

For some time this system had remarkable success, but in the bedstead industry the number of makers increased from 40 to 56 between 1891 and 1899, and this brought trouble. Prices were cut by giving double discounts, making cash commissions, drawing out incorrect invoices, and supplying goods of a higher quality than charged. The association also tried to impose high entrance fees on firms applying late for membership. A private detective force was employed to check underselling, and the workpeople of offending members were called out. In 1900 about a third of the makers were outside the alliance, and the maintenance of the workmen on strike was a severe tax on the funds. The bedstead alliance was dissolved, and gradually the same fate befel the other alliances. Since then competition has been rampant in the bedstead trade, and several attempts to set up some regulating body have been made. In 1905-6 a determined effort was made to get all the makers into a combination to maintain a uniform price list, but it too failed.

The constitution and proceedings of associations for the control of production are naturally kept very secret, and consequently the preceding account is full of gaps. Still we observe that in every branch of the crude and finished iron and steel industries there has been a persistent movement towards the regulation of competition. The form varies from a " Gentlemen's Agreement," depending solely on the honour of the members and seeking only the determination of prices, to a closely organised association which regulates prices, fixes the amount of output, and allots to each member his share of trade, while loyalty is ensured by penalties. The strength of the associations varies from the casual exploitation of a market to the determined utilisation of a monopoly. As with the amalgamations so with the associations, they do not control the market, but while following it they take more speedy and

6

thorough advantage of rising prices and offer a more tenacious resistance to a fall.   Whether prices are high or low they prevent undercutting by their members; even outsiders though selling at lower prices follow close on the association prices, and thus get a greater advantage for themselves than they could with free competition.   It is only when a depression comes that the outsiders break clear away from the association, and in their frantic rush for trade at any cost bring about the collapse of the combination.   So far as the associations make prices steadier they are on the whole a benefit to industry, for they remove competition from cheapness to quality.   On the whole they do not seem to have misused their power much, and where in overconfidence they have played the tyrant, as in the cases of the Scotch Boiler-Plate Association and the Birmingham Alliances, retribution has followed.

Summing up the situation in the iron and steel industries, the conclusion forced on us seems to be that the tendency is towards the evolution of a comparatively few large units in each branch, and then that these units should combine into a loose organisation for the regulation of their trade.   It may so happen that a manufacturer may belong to several associations according to the variety of his products.   At present there is no prospect of a British imitation of the United States Steel Corporation.   Syndicates or "pools," like the Rail Makers' Associations, which establish a standard price, assign to each member an agreed output, and allot orders according to that scale, appear to be the highest form of organisation of which the iron industry is at present capable.   From regulating home prices we see the associations stretching out to control export prices, as in the Steel and Tube Associations.   The next step, which has been taken in the rail and screw trades, is to enter into treaties with foreign trusts or kartells for the cessation of competition, and the demarcation of territory.   This is a dangerous development, for by removing the potential and actual competition which free trade has hitherto secured, it creates the possibility that prices in this country may rise to the level of the highest protected prices anywhere.   And it raises the further question, which may one day become serious, as to how far it is consistent with national freedom that national industries should be controlled by international associations of producers.

Apart from special associations for the regulation of a trade, we meet with more or less permanent groupings of manufacturers into syndicates or even limited companies for the purpose of undertaking contracts, and some of these are to be found in the iron and steel industries. For example, British engineering firms are usually content to carry on their foreign trade on a competitive basis, except in Egypt where the principle of co-operation is successfully applied. "There are at least two large and well-known organisations engaged in promoting British engineering interests in Egypt. One is the British Engineering Company of Egypt, which consists of an amalgamation, for this particular purpose only, of the following firms: Gwynne's (Limited), Babcock & Wilcox (Limited), Dick, Kerr, & Co. (Limited), Callender's Cable and Construction Co. (Limited), and J. Gibb & Co. (Limited). Another organisation of a similar nature, but apparently on a larger scale, is the Egyptian Engineering Company (Limited), established at Chareh Kasr-el-Nil, Cairo. This is an alliance of twenty-four British engineering firms 'who,' as it is put, 'between them cover all the ground of mechanical and structural engineering in Egypt and the Sudan.' It may be inferred from these two organisations alone that British engineering is likely adequately to be represented in the Egyptian and contiguous markets" (*Times, Engineering Supplement*, 22nd August, 1906).

Another example is the assignment in July, 1906, of the contract with the Australian and New Zealand Governments for the fortnightly mail service (now carried on by the Orient Company) from 1st February, 1908, to a syndicate consisting of William Beardmore & Sons, of Dalmuir; Vickers, Sons, & Maxim, of Barrow; Sir James Laing (Limited), of Sunderland; Lord Armstrong (representing Armstrong, Whitworth, & Co.); and Mr. J. W. Potter, of Messrs. Birt, Potter, & Hughes, shipowners, London. The first four members are interested in the building of the new mail steamers required to carry out the contract, two steamers being allotted to each, and here we find a reversion to the policy of Robert Napier, the first great Clyde shipbuilder, who helped to finance the shipping lines for which in the early days he built steamers.

These " contract combinations," as they might be called, grow naturally out of the trade custom where one firm takes a contract and sublets part of it to other firms. They are not usually considered as part of the modern combination movement, but as they manifest the same characteristics—suppression of competition and co-operation in technical knowledge— they are rightly considered here. The chief misconceptions that cling around combinations are due mainly to undue limitation of view and blindness to many of the forms in which they present themselves.

CHAPTER IV.

THE EXTRACTIVE INDUSTRIES.

THE coal industry of the United Kingdom is distributed through half a dozen large and a number of small districts. The total available resources were estimated by the Royal Commission on Coal Supplies at 100,914,668,167 tons in seams of at least a foot thick and not more than 4,000 feet in depth, in addition to 5,239,433,980 tons in proved coal-fields, but below 4,000 feet, and 39,483,000,000 tons in concealed and unproved coal-fields. These supplies can be effectively supplemented by the reduction of waste in working, by the use of coal-cutting machines, and by the utilisation of poor coal in coke and briquette-making. Any attempt to form a universal coal trust would therefore be at once subject to potential competition from new mines, and on the other hand its power over consumers would be seriously limited by the many economies which are possible in consumption. The use of turbines instead of reciprocating engines, the extended employment of electricity and of gas engines, the use of petroleum in steamships and in internal combustion engines—these are only some of the ways in which the tyranny of coal can be combated. The difficulties of local combination are also not small. Each district has an advantage in supplying its own domestic and manufacturing consumption, but a great part of its trade is subject to the competition of other districts. The North of England coal-field is liable to the competition of Fifeshire in its export trade, as well as to that of the Midland field when the price is high enough to counterbalance the cost of railway carriage to the Humber ports; its facilities for water carriage long gave it a dominance in the London market, but now it must reckon with the railway borne coal of the Midland field.   South Wales alone possesses something like a monopoly in its excellent steam coal, containing from 80 to 90 per cent. of carbon, invaluable for steamship and especially for navy use.   Its export trade is not like that of Newcastle, subject to the competition of the Westphalian coal syndicate, and the steam coal of the North of England only comes into serious competition when prices are high.   The small field of pure anthracite in the extreme west of South Wales is unique in Britain, but its uses in this country are restricted and about half the output is exported.   In all the other districts the local advantage of position is always liable to be upset by the abundant facilities for railway transport, which make competition easy as soon as prices become tempting.   Not only do localities compete, but also classes of coal.   Although coal may be roughly graded according to its use for household, manufacturing, gas, or steamship purposes, there are always a number of intermediate qualities which a rise in price or some new invention at once brings into effective competition.   Incandescent mantles and methods of gas enrichment have come to the aid of the gas companies as the best supplies of gas coal are getting exhausted, and the introduction of producer gas plants has enabled a great quantity of inferior coal to be utilised.

Despite its position as the fundamental industry without which all other industries are impossible, the coal industry of the United Kingdom does not seem to be one well suited for combination.   Yet we have to reckon at least one gigantic plan for converting the whole industry into a large trust, and it was put forward not by a fantastic visionary but by a man thoroughly well acquainted with the trade.   The late Sir George Elliot, in a remarkable article in the *Times* (20th September, 1893), put forward proposals to remedy the evils from which the coal-mining industry was then suffering, and which had led to the industrial war with the men then raging.   The artificial way in which coal properties were developed led to considerable waste in leaving subterranean boundary walls and in unscientific and expensive methods of drainage, ventilation, and haulage, all of which could be obviated by treating each district as a whole with due regard to its geological peculiarities.   At that

time it was usual to take out only the best paying kinds of coal
and to throw small coal and inferior kinds into the waste ; by
systematic extraction he reckoned that the whole of the coal,
good and bad, could be brought to the surface on paying terms.
Great savings would also accrue from the organisation of sale
since each group of collieries would supply its natural market,
according to the class of coal it produced, instead of indulging
in insane competition in distant markets where railway carriage
ate up the profit. Lastly, there was the necessity of paying
wages " on a liberal basis as compared with other classes of
labour," which was impossible so long as the price-depressing
competition of the mine-owners continued. He also proposed
the creation of an insurance fund for worn-out and disabled
workmen. From the output of 1892, nearly 182,000,000 tons,
he deducted 20 per cent. for the coal used in iron and steel
manufactures, a great deal of which was raised by the ironmasters themselves, thus leaving 145,000,000 tons to be dealt
with under his scheme. For this operation he reckoned on a
capital of £110,000,000, one-third in 5 per cent. debentures, and
taking the average selling price of coal at 7s. 3d. a ton and the
pit head cost at 6s., he estimated that, taking into account the
economies resulting from scientific working, it would be possible,
after meeting the debenture interest and providing a reserve
against exhaustion of supplies, to pay a minimum 10 per cent.
dividend on ordinary shares. No dividend above 15 per cent.
was to be paid except with the consent of the Board of Trade,
when the shareholders, the miners, and the consumers were to
participate equally in the excess. The trust was to be governed
by a central council elected by the different mining districts on
the basis of one member for each 5,000,000 tons of output,
which would deal with the " general management, supervision,
and control of the business of the company," while the working
of the collieries, wages, and general local business were to be
entrusted to about thirty district committees, representing both
the shareholders and the miners. About 2,000 circulars advo-
cating the plan were sent out, but the replies were unfavourable.
It was felt that the difficulties of valuation were insuperable
since the owners would wish their actual expenditure to be

taken into account, while that would very often be in excess of what was scientifically necessary, as well as above the basis of 15s. per ton which was to be taken as a guide to the capital value of the output.

The lessons taught by the coal war, and also the opportunity offered by the exhaustion of stocks at its close, turned the coal-owners' minds towards other forms of combination. The great troubles of the trade had been caused by the want of equivalence between supply and demand, and the project of maintaining prices, and therefore through sliding scales, wages, by means of regulation of the output for long haunted the minds of both masters and men. Such an idea, indeed, was traditional in the coal industry, for the "Limitation of the Vend," a plan whereby the total output of the Newcastle coal-field was regulated and divided among the different mine-owners, only broke down in 1844 through the impossibility of reconciling the conflicting claims to a share in the trade. Lancashire was the first theatre of the new movement. Early in 1893 a Coal Traders' Association was formed to take action against increased railway rates, with successful results. In November a meeting of the coal-owners of South-West Lancashire was held at Wigan to dis-cuss arrangements "which might form the basis for, at any rate, the next two or three months". Some of the representa-tives of the large collieries wanted a list based on the prices of the winter of 1890, which would have affected the best qualities of coal but little, while others desired to take a fuller advantage of the depletion of stocks and the increased demand. The want of unanimity "prevented any really fixed basis of prices being definitely accepted, but an understanding was come to with regard to a list of prices as a minimum at something like the following rates: Best Wigan Arley coal, 14s. to 15s.; Pemberton Fourfeet, 13s. to 13s. 6d.; seconds house coal, 11s. 6d. to 12s.; steam and forge coals, 10s. to 11s.; burgie, 8s. to 8s. 6d.; slack from 6s. to 7s. per ton and upwards, according to quality. . . . The arranged prices for house coals generally represent an advance of 1s. 6d. to 2s. per ton upon those ruling three years ago, whilst for engine fuel prices return to the level which was reached during the winter season in 1890" (*Colliery*

Guardian, 1st December, 1893). The Manchester coal-owners followed suit with a similar common agreement to raise prices. A few weeks later the Lancashire and Cheshire Coal Sales Association was formed, by which it was hoped that " some effective check may be put upon excessive competition for contracts, as it is proposed that before tenders are sent out all important contracts shall be submitted for consideration to this association, and it is probable that periodical meetings will be arranged for the general regulation of prices " (*Colliery Guardian*, 8th December, 1893). The control was not very close, for " it was distinctly intimated by the representatives of some of the leading collieries that there was no intention whatever that this association should attempt in any way to exercise coercion in the matter of prices; its object was to be merely to protect the coal-owners from unfair competition and to enable them mutually to compare notes with regard to the large contracts which come upon the market, with a view of securing greater uniformity of prices " (*Colliery Guardian*, 15th December, 1893).

The association appears to have sub-divided its area into districts, each with a committee, and to have held monthly meetings to consider the official list prices. At first prices were fairly well maintained, but with the general slackening of demand consequent on the incoming of spring weather, outside districts naturally tried to profit by the action of the Lancashire Association, and it became difficult to maintain the list against their competition as well as that of the non-associated proprietors. " Some of the collieries outside the association are undercutting, and there is a good deal of keen competition with coal coming in from outside districts. The result is that the Associated Coal-owners have in many cases to see no inconsiderable portion of their trade taken out of their hands, but notwithstanding the competition which has to be contended with, there is little doubt that the association is rendering good service in enabling a better stand to be made with regard to the prices at which tenders are now being sent in for gas contracts " (*Colliery Guardian*, 1st June, 1894). Gradually the official list lost control of the market, and at last on 3rd September, 1894, several of the large firms withdrew, alleging underselling by some of the other members, and thereupon the association was dissolved.

The origin of the Durham Coal Sales Association of 1894-95 is best described in the words of the official statement issued to correct the " unauthorised, inaccurate, and misleading " press statements. It was published in the *Colliery Guardian* of 23rd February, 1894, and the salient parts of it are as follows : " Colliery owners in the county of Durham, representing nearly 80 per cent. of the output of that county, together with those interested in similar classes of coal in the county of Northumberland, have from time to time during the past two months conferred for the purpose of ascertaining whether, as regards all descriptions of coal and coke, some judicious organisation cannot be adopted to diminish the evils which are commonly supposed to arise from unrestricted and unorganised competition of which, perhaps, the most important are the great variations in price to which the trade is now subject. They have come to the conclusion that the object is one worthy of a serious attempt, and they contemplate the formation of an association to endeavour to accomplish it. At the same time they are not unmindful of the fact that fluctuations in price, even of very large extent, depend upon circumstances which are extremely obscure, very difficult to foresee, and, perhaps, impossible to prevent. The association will seek to confine its operations within those strictly legitimate limits which govern any well-managed industrial enterprise, and it is hoped that the magnitude of the interests involved will permit it to form a better judgment as to the course of trade than can be done by any single member. . . . It is anticipated also that, without endeavouring to thwart the natural course of trade and of prices, a careful and continuous survey of the market, such as can be taken by a large combination of owners, may curtail, if not entirely prevent, those losses to which the trade has from time to time been compelled to submit. . . . The intended association will deal with all descriptions of coals and coke, and its constitution will be such as to secure, by means of sectional committees, adapted as far as possible to each class of trade, discussion and uniform action suited to the varying trade conditions. From what has been said it will be apparent that there is no intention to seek to raise prices to such an extent as to prejudice the maintenance and development both of the coal trade itself and of the industrial interests dependent on it. The rise and fall of prices are, it is believed, largely beyond the control of any organisation, even one as powerful as that now contemplated ; but the careful watching of the changes may permit the members of the association to minimise or guard against dangers which they cannot altogether prevent. An attitude of explanation and co-operation will be adopted towards gas companies, railway companies, iron-masters, and any other large body of consumers. The consignment of coals on speculation and the making of contracts of longer duration than twelve months, except on sliding scales varying with the price of manufactured products, will be discouraged. The colliery owners of Durham and the adjacent points of Northumberland are encouraged in their views by the belief that similar steps are in contemplation in other districts."

The minimum price of gas coal was fixed at 7s. 3d. to 7s. 9d. per ton, according to quality, with a penalty of 2s. a ton for underselling; discounts were limited to 2½ per cent. The great competition for the continental gas contracts showed that the list price was too high, and it was reduced in March, 1894, to 7s. to 7s. 3d. per ton, f.o.b. There was plenty of ordinary coal in the market at 6s. 9d. to 7s. a ton, and naturally association coal could not be sold to those who preferred cheapness to quality. The association, however, commanded the bulk of the supply, and, to quote a market report, "as a rule quality tells in the long run, and the dearer coal has as much of the trade as the other". The strength of the association was shown when the London spring contracts for gas coal were placed at the association prices, and when throughout the summer prices were kept at 7s. 3d. to 7s. 6d. The membership was confined to the Durham coal-owners, for the coal-owners and fitters (or agents) in the Northumberland trade could only agree on a minimum price for small coal. The coke makers appear to have been separately organised, or at least to have managed their affairs separately. Throughout 1894 and the early part of the following year the prices of coal and coke were well held, though in January, 1895, the output of coke had to be reduced. But 1895 was a bad coal year ; while the total output rose 1,400,000 tons above that of 1894, the average value at the pit head fell from 6s. 7·43d. in 1894 to 6s. 0·42d. in 1895, the lowest since 1888, and the export price fell from 10s. 5d. to 9s. 2½d. The approach of the usual summer slackness found the trade face to face with the increased competition which had been attracted by the good prices, not merely local competition but also competition from Yorkshire. When plenty of gas coal was to be had at 6s. 6d. a ton, the large gas companies with their big orders were in an excellent position for battering the list prices, and at last in July, 1895, the association collapsed with prices ranging from 6s. 3d. to 6s. 9d. Once more was it demonstrated that prices cannot be fixed irrespective of the state of trade even by an association representative of the bulk and of the best of the output, so long as it is possible for local outsiders to extend their production and for outside districts to cut into the market.

There was also in 1894 a Price Association in Fifeshire which fixed the relative prices of the several grades of coal, not the actual prices that is to say, but the standard differences between them. It does not seem to have been very cleverly managed, for trade was diverted towards the lower classes of coal on account of their relative cheapness. To-day most of the coal-owners are members of the association. They meet from time to time as occasion requires for the adjustment of prices, but do not allocate contracts or attempt to regulate output. Their coal is graded in three classes, the first class including best coal and also coal from a few mines which may be sold at 3d. per ton below the price of best, as it is slightly inferior in quality. Second class coal, of which there is very little, and third class coal vary in relation to first class according to the state of the market. In October, 1906, second class coal was from 6d. to 9d., and third class coal 2s. 3d. per ton below the price of first, but when first class coal was at its lowest level of 6s. 6d., third class coal fetched from 6s. to 5s. 9d. a ton, f.o.b. The association prices are minimum prices, every owner being free to get as much more as he can, and are for shipment only, not for home sales. As the Fife Coal Co. has about half the output of the whole field, it can practically dictate prices, but its power is limited by the competition of Newcastle coal. Prices appear to be maintained above the level possible under free competition, and certainly the large buyer is deprived of the benefit of his position and can no longer get a lower rate quoted in consideration of his larger demand.

The Welsh miners clung to the sliding scale long after it had been abandoned in other districts, and thus, reminded at every turn that their wages depended upon the market price of coal, they naturally acquired the belief that by limiting the output they could increase their wages. The miners in other districts for some time held the same view, for it was the natural deduction from the doctrine dinned into their ears by their employers that prices were determined by supply and demand and wages limited by what prices permitted. But that opinion was held most strongly in Wales where it even secured the adhesion of many of the masters, and it has lingered to the present time in the policy of "stop days". At the International Miners' Conference in London in 1897, the French and Belgian miners proposed a resolution in favour of the international regulation of the output of coal, insisting at the same time that the lead in this matter must be taken by England, the greatest coal-exporting country. Mr. William Brace, as the representative of Monmouthshire, said that "over-production and low wages were inseparable, and he was quite willing to support any proposal to limit production. Idle days, or idle weeks, or idle months would not solve the question. If the men were working four days a week, they endeavoured to fill as much in four days as they did in six. He wanted a practicable scheme for the limitation of the output. Wales was a great exporting country, and in that country they were endeavouring to arrange a scheme in this direction. The men had put forward a scheme, and he was glad to say that 90 per cent. of the employers had accepted it. An Output Committee had been appointed which would allot to each colliery its output according to the returns of the previous six months. The men went further, and said that the Output Committee should have the power to allot to each workman the amount of coal he should get per day or week. There was to be a conference in a week or two in which the scheme would take shape. He was arguing in South Wales that before this limitation of output scheme was adopted, the men should be guaranteed a minimum wage. But having seen so much of the evils of over-production, he was quite ready to consider any scheme for a remedy, and he saw no reason why an international scheme, on the lines of that which was now being put forward in South Wales, should not be brought into existence." The resolution was carried, Northumberland and Durham alone dissenting. Mr. Brace's views about the Welsh scheme proved to be too optimistic, for a few weeks later the Monmouthshire and South Wales Coalowners' Association announced the abandonment of the proposal owing to their inability to obtain the concurrence of a sufficient number of colliery proprietors to make it a success.

The output of coal has risen from 181,786,871 tons in 1892—the figures on which Sir George Elliot worked—and 202,129,931 tons in 1897, the year of the Welsh scheme, to 236,128,936 tons in 1905, and for the same years the export has been 29,048,056 tons, 35,354,296 tons, and 47,476,707 tons. The average export price was 11·04s. per ton in 1892, 8·98s. in 1897, and 10·56s. in 1905. The bogey of over-production has been laid, and the better times which began with 1899—the average export price of coal for 1899-1905 was 2·64s. per ton higher than during the previous seven years—brought better profits to the masters and better wages to the men. Even the Welsh miners have given up the sliding scale and with it the belief in the dependence of wages on prices. The dominant idea among the miners to-day is that a living wage should be a first charge on the industry. With some security, therefore, we may hope that the last has been heard of such a thoroughly unsocial idea as the limitation of the production of a national necessary for the profit of a single class.

Although there are quite a considerable number of colliery firms and companies with a production exceeding a million tons per annum, and in some districts even a fair amount of concentration—as in Fifeshire where the Fife Coal Company is responsible for half the output, or in South Staffordshire where half the coal is raised by about half a dozen iron firms, or South Wales where twenty firms produce 80 per cent. of the steam coal output—singularly little has been achieved in the way of amalgamation.   One noteworthy union, however, was the purchase of Lord Durham's collieries in 1896 by Sir James Joicey & Co.   The Durham properties included a fleet of nineteen steamers, and fourteen collieries producing over 2,000,000 tons per annum and giving employment to 8,000 persons.   Sir James Joicey & Co. thus gained control over an output of 4,500,000 tons of coal and over 12,000 men.   There has been a certain amount of fusion of adjacent collieries—as the Tunstall Coal and Iron Co. (1899), uniting two collieries, with an output, partly estimated, of 150,000 to 200,000 tons, issued capital, £75,000; or the Groesven and Caradog Collieries, Limited (1900), also uniting two collieries, issued capital, £60,000.   Somewhat larger was the Broomhill Collieries, Limited, incorporated in 1900 " for the purpose of purchasing as going concerns, amalgamating, and carrying on the businesses of the Broomhill Coal Company, Limited, the Radcliffe Coal Company, Limited, and the steamers of the Broomhill Shipping Company, Limited, and also for the purpose of purchasing the whole of the debentures of the Warkworth Harbour Commissioners, of the nominal value of £170,000," but acquired for £50,000.   The collieries were adjacent, with an average annual output during 1896-99 of 611,583 tons, and the directors were of opinion that " the amalgamation will be decidedly advantageous, both from the underground and surface point of view".   Warkworth Harbour was the natural outlet for the collieries, and the purchase of the debentures practically secured full control over it.   The issued capital was £675,000.   In 1900-1 6 per cent. was paid, and in 1901-2 5 per cent., but since then nothing on the ordinary shares.   The output in 1905-6, was 851,167 tons.

Then followed a period in which Mr. Pierpont Morgan acted as the bogey man coming to eat up the British coal industry. In the autumn of 1901 he was supposed to be concerned in a fusion of Welsh coal firms with a capital of £20,000,000; the report next took the form of an intended kartell on the Westphalian model, and finally dwindled away to nothing.   Next year he was credited with the desire to buy up the South Staffordshire mines, and the reported amalgamation of the Fifeshire collieries followed. At last in July, 1902, the prospectus of the United Collieries, Limited, was placed before the public, announcing the union of twenty-four Scotch businesses owning collieries, mostly situated in Lanarkshire, the exceptions being a property in Ayrshire, and two or three properties in Stirlingshire and Linlithgowshire. The total output, partly estimated, was 6,000,000 tons, or nearly one-fifth of the total output of Scotland and fully 28 per cent. of the output of the four counties of Lanark, Dumbarton, Linlithgow, and Stirling. Only 15 per cent. of the output of these counties was exported, the rest finding its market in the great manufacturing district of the Clyde, from which the other counties, according to the prospectus, were shut out on account of the cost of railway transport. It was estimated that five-sixths of the output of the company would be sold in the local markets. The quantity of proved accessible coal was estimated at thirty years' supply, and the total valuation of the properties was £2,650,762. The gross profits of sixteen of the companies for 1899-1901, with an output of 4,150,000 tons, averaged £224,751 ; the other eight properties were during that period in course of development. The United Collieries Co. had been established in 1898 to amalgamate eight firms with a capital of £200,000, increased in 1900 to £300,000, and now in order to purchase the twenty-three other companies its capital was raised to £3,000,000—in equal proportions of 5 per cent. debentures, 6 per cent. cumulative preference shares, and ordinary shares. The debentures were purchased by Messrs. J. S. Morgan & Co., and offered at par.

Lord Belhaven and Stenton, the chairman, in a letter embodied in the prospectus, said: " The extension of the business should thus ensure the following results: (1) The elimination of competition, amongst the concerns now purchased, in the markets. (2) The power of regulating to some extent the prices of fuel and the adjustment of wages. (3) Economies of management ; in certain cases, the mineral fields adjacent to our existing properties being acquired, a great saving will result in not having to sink pits as, in some cases, existing pits on newly acquired properties will serve undeveloped fields of our company. (4) The advantages of arranging central pumping stations to avoid unnecessary duplication of plant and labour. (5) The economies of being in a position to purchase large quantities of furnishings, pitwood, stores, etc. (6) The arrangement to supply customers from the work nearest their point of delivery and consequent saving of carriage. (7) The avoidance of competition for labour and many other advantages, including the absorption of many small collieries that for want of capital were frequently working hand-to-mouth, and underselling the market. In ascertaining what the above will represent in additional profit, I am of opinion that at a moderate estimate 6d. per ton should be easily obtained, but some well-known experts are of opinion that even more should be gained." The last sentence was given prominence in large capitals. Here were united the economies of combination, the advantages of scientific working, and an anticipated control over prices and wages as a guarantee for the expected large increase of profits.

Before the great extension dividends of a handsome character had been paid on the ordinary shares: 1898-99, 10 per cent.; 1899-1900, 20 per cent.; 1900-1, 25 per cent.; but after that period nothing was paid, and reports were issued with extreme irregularity. For the two years and nine months, ended 31st December, 1903, the gross profit was £232,300, a figure not bearing much resemblance to Lord Belhaven's estimate. Notwithstanding the large subscribed capital the directors proposed in 1904 a fresh issue of debentures in order to obtain working capital. Profits in the coal industry had certainly fallen off greatly since the " boom " years, on the strength of which the company had been capitalised and there had been much delay in taking over some of the properties, but there were abundant complaints of inefficient management and the existing debenture holders insisted on the appointment of a committee of investigation. The issue of the £200,000 new stock was agreed to on somewhat onerous terms. The preference shareholders then petitioned the Court of Session for a winding-up order, which was refused by the judge on account of the large loss that would be incurred by a forced sale. The Debenture Holders' Committee had reported in July, 1904, that "the company's business is, and for some months past has been, carried on at an actual loss," and it does not occasion surprise that after all this chaos the accounts for 1904 showed a debit balance on profit and loss account. Despite a considerable improvement in 1905-6, there is still a heavy accumulation of unpaid interest. This is a poor result for a share and debenture capital now amounting to £3,251,717.

The anthracite coal district would appear to be better suited for control by a trust than any other district in the United Kingdom, for it alone possesses a monopoly, its product need fear no competition, and it commands a special price. The output, also, is of manageable dimensions, about 2,250,000 tons annually, of which half is exported to the Continent for domestic purposes and the remainder consumed at home in hop and malt drying, distilling, etc. Some sixty-two collieries, employing about 9,500 miners, are at work in Breconshire, Carmarthenshire, Glamorganshire, and Pembrokeshire—the extreme western corner of the South Wales coal-field. Of these, thirty-three employed less than 100 men each in 1903, and only one over 1,000. The industry is thus very much split up, and it is alleged that the sale of anthracite is much hampered by lack of uniformity in the preparation of the coal for the market. In 1903-4 prolonged efforts were made to effect an amalgamation, the promoting syndicate proceeding on the American plan of obtaining options on the properties by the deposit of, in this case, 1 per cent. of the price asked. According to an announcement in the autumn of 1903, 90 per cent. of the owners had given options over properties with a reserve of proved coal amounting to 90,000,000 tons, of which an exhaustive examination and valuation was being made. Great hopes were expressed of a profitable increase of trade by thoroughly working out the area and systematically developing both the home and foreign markets. Various reports put the probable capitalisation at almost every figure up to £5,000,000, and as owners had made good profits during the years of the boom it was obvious that they would not be too modest in fixing their prices. In fact on this very rock the project shattered, for the syndicate wanted to pick only the best properties and could not come to terms with their owners. A period of depression followed, and then in the summer of 1905 a new syndicate took the matter in hand, hoping to find the coal-owners more amenable to reason, but while the small and less efficient firms were ready enough to negotiate, those who had weathered the depression still, naturally enough, insisted on their own terms. Some thirty firms were approached and the syndicate were ready to find £500,000 to carry through the amalgamation, but their experts were "unanimously of opinion that the aggregate of the price asked for the properties offered is excessive, and that an amalgamation carried out on the basis of these prices would be over-capitalised and its prospects of successful working severely handicapped". It is probable, however, that the realisation of the scheme is only postponed, for the Share Guarantee Trust, in communicating the just-quoted opinion to the South Wales Anthracite Amalgamation Syndicate, also wrote: " Our investigations have revealed the fact that there is undoubtedly a well-founded consensus of opinion that, without tending to become a monopoly, an amalgamation of the interests of the anthracite colliery owners in order to systematise and standardise the output could have but the result of benefiting the producer and the consumer, and of firmly establishing the trade upon the substantial and lasting basis befitting so important a British enterprise ".

There is an ineradicable belief among the public that retail prices of coal are fixed by rings of merchants and mine-owners. The strong local associations of colliery proprietors lend a fictitious appearance of reality to this view. Coal is an article of universal, and, as regards house coal, of seasonal demand, and it moves in price by customary increments or decrements of 6d. or 1s. per ton. In every large town there is a Coal Exchange where those interested in the sale of coal meet to exchange views and transact business, and thus, as in the case of pig-iron, there is every facility for arriving at a common opinion and simultaneous action in the matter of price fixing without any formal organisation for the purpose. The general rise in the price of coal which takes place every autumn is thus

7 *

no proof of the existence of a ring of coal merchants.   Indeed the readiness with which colliery proprietors advance into the retail trade is a permanent obstacle to effective organisation among the middlemen.   All the large contracts for the sale of coal to railways, gas companies, etc., fall directly into the hands of the coal-owners, and usually the large consumers show themselves to be in the stronger strategic position.   Instances of seasonal fixing of prices by coal-owners are given in the following quotations : " As already announced the coal-owners in the Sheffield district decided a week ago to advance prices for house coal by 1s. per ton as from the 1st inst." (*Iron and Steel Trades Journal*, 6th October, 1906); and : " Advance in the Price of Coal.—At a meeting of West Lancashire and Staffordshire coal-owners, held in Manchester yesterday, an advance of 1s. per ton in the price of all descriptions of coal was decided upon.   When the news became known on the Coal Exchange there was some excitement, and the opinion of merchants was dead against it with strong declarations that it was not justified" (*Times*, 24th October, 1906).

A few interesting amalgamations exist among coal merchants. Wm. Cory & Son was a union of eight large London firms doing business as "coal factors, coal and coke merchants, coal contractors, lightermen, owners and dischargers of steam colliers, sea-going lighters, and other vessels," and was incorporated in the autumn of 1896.   Only the home business was taken over, the several firms retaining their colliery and export departments. From the prospectus : "The firm of Wm. Cory & Son was founded nearly a hundred years ago, and has always held the leading position in the trade.   This firm was one of the first to bring coal by steamer to London, and the first to discharge the cargoes by mechanical appliances. . . . An extensive and valuable retail trade in house and other coal by trucks and vans is secured to the company by the inclusion in this amalgamation of G. J. Cockerell & Co., Limited, and D. Radford & Co.; further, W. Cory & Son bring with their other assets the business of the Sea Coal Co., and Lambert Bros.' assets comprise the old-established business of Davey & Son, of Blackfriars."   The tonnage of coal, coke, and patent fuel handled by the firms in their home

business averaged 5,108,717 tons annually for the three years
1893-95, or about one-third of the 16,000,000 tons of coal coming
to London every year.   About half of London's coal is sea-borne,
and the company was equipped for that branch of its business by
the entire or partial ownership of steamers with an aggregate capacity of 42,000 tons, besides eleven sea-going lighters, twenty-one
steam tugs, and about 1,200 barges with a carrying capacity varying from 50 to 200 tons each, and shares in steamship companies.
For its rail-borne trade it owned 2,560 railway wagons.   The
average profits for the seven years 1889-95, excluding charges
for interest and management, but after providing for depreciation,
amounted to £143,023.   The assets taken over were valued at
£1,565,965 and the total purchase price was £2,374,000, making
goodwill equal to about nine years' profits.   The capital issued
amounted to £2,500,000, £800,000 in 4 per cent. debentures
issued at 103, £850,000 in 5 per cent. cumulative preference
shares, and £850,000 in ordinary shares; the vendors took one-
third of the debentures and preference shares and all the ordinary shares.

Wm. Cory & Son was an amalgamation of wholesale and
retail firms.   In June, 1899, a fresh amalgamation and rearrange-
ment was brought about by the formation of Rickett, Cockerell,
& Co., "to acquire the whole of the wholesale and retail business
of Rickett, Smith, & Co., Limited, of King's Cross, London, and
elsewhere, and the retail business of Wm. Cory & Son, Limited,
inclusive of that acquired from G. J. Cockerell & Co. and other
firms in 1896, and their coal merchants' railway truck trade
within a defined area.   The consolidation of these businesses,"
continued the prospectus, "should enable economies to be
effected in working, while the new company for the purposes of
its supply secures a permanent connection with the exceptional
sea-borne resources of Wm. Cory & Son, Limited, in addition
to the old-established railway-borne trade of Rickett, Smith, &
Co., Limited."   The tonnage of coal, coke, etc., handled by the
constituent companies and transferred averaged 1,875,102 tons
per annum.   The aggregate profits of the businesses acquired for
the year to 31st March, 1899, were £73,675.   The aggregate
purchase price of the goodwill and assets (other than existing

book debts, cash balances, and stock) was fixed at £688,092, of which £238,092 represented assets, goodwill being equal to 6·1 years' profits. The capital issued was £900,000, half in 4½ cumulative preference shares and half in ordinary shares; after providing for purchase of stocks, etc., the issue left £150,000 for working capital. The ordinary shares were taken by the vendors, Rickett, Smith, & Co. and Wm. Cory & Son, and the latter company had the right to nominate four members of the Board of ten directors, thus retaining "a substantial and permanent interest in the trade". Included in the sale of Rickett, Smith, & Co.'s business were the subsidiary businesses owned by them or in which they held a preponderating interest.

The working arrangements between the two companies continued for about three years but were not altogether satisfactory. In the spring of 1902 three of the directors in Rickett, Cockerell, & Co., who had been members of Rickett, Smith, & Co. retired, transferring their interest to Wm. Cory & Son, who thus obtained an absolute control over both companies by ownership of the ordinary stock of both. The capital of Wm. Cory & Son now amounts to £2,715,000, and their progress is shown in the following table, profits being taken after provision for depreciation, etc. :—

	Net Profit.	Ordinary Dividend.
Year to 30/9/97	£124,619	7
6 months to 31/3/98	65,418	3½
Year to 31/3/99	175,447	7½
,, 1900	215,897	11
,, 1901	357,199	15
,, 1902	151,940	10
,, 1903	152,614	10
,, 1904	162,001	10
,, 1905	151,271	10
,, 1906	171,661	10

And the reserves amount to £340,000.

Rickett, Cockerell, & Co. paid 12 per cent. for the year to 31st March, 1900; 6 per cent. for 1900-1; 1901-2, nil; 1902-3, 5 per cent.; 1903-4, 5 per cent.; 1904-5, 2½ per cent.; 1905-6, 4½ per cent.

The average profit of Wm. Cory & Son is well above the £143,023 for the seven years before amalgamation. The effect of high prices in 1900 is evident, but on this point the chairman said (12th June, 1900): "In the past year, which was a good year, their profit divided over their tonnage amounted to just over 10d. a ton. Theirs was not a company of coal dealers, but a company of coal distributors, and a coal distributor was a very different person from a coal dealer. The coal dealer had his coal delivered to him and sold it at a margin of profit, but their company were large shipowners, ship dischargers, lightermen, barge and wagon builders, engineers, and they were concerned in many other trades. The 10d. a ton which he had mentioned represented the entire profit made by the company on the whole of their business. Eliminating the profit belonging to other trades—which in the ordinary way a coal dealer had no connection with—the profit was considerably less than 10d. a ton." A boom also leaves disadvantages behind it. As the chairman said in discussing the trade for 1902-3: "After a coal boom the times are very anxious for some considerable period, because prices are very unsettled, and it wants the greatest care and very hard work to take care that everything is done for the very best, because one small mistake in the purchase of coal, to the extent of a penny a ton, means several thousands of pounds."

From Sauerbeck's tables we can get the average prices of Wallsend Hetton coal in London and from the Board of Trade reports the price of Northumberland coal at the pit-head, namely :—

	London. £ s. d.	Pit Head. s. d.
1896	0 15 0	5 1
1897	0 15 9	5 3
1898	0 16 9	6 1
1899	0 18 6	7 1
1900	1 3 6	10 4
1901	1 0 0	8 9
1902	0 18 6	7 5
1903	0 16 6	7 0
1904	0 16 3	6 4
1905	0 15 6	6 2

These prices are not strictly comparable, since the Northumberland price is an average for several qualities, but they indicate roughly the relation between pithead and London wholesale prices. When taken into consideration with the table of profits and the detail about 10d. per ton profit on the trade of 1899-1900, they enable us to establish some relation between the production and distribution of coal. They further show that the trade of Messrs. Cory & Son must have largely grown, in the matter of tonnage handled. Two things stand out saliently, the advantageous position occupied and the security enjoyed by a company doing a very large business when the rate of profit is low, and the importance of the subsidiary trades connected with a large combination in effecting economies.

It is interesting to observe that representatives of Wm. Cory & Son are directors of large colliery companies like Pease & Partners, the Broomhill Collieries, etc. Much smaller in size than the London amalgamation, but of considerable local importance, is the Bradford Coal Merchants' and Consumers' Association, incorporated in the summer of 1899. It was formed "to acquire, carry on, and further develop" the businesses of eight firms of coal merchants, turning over "upwards of 90 per cent. of the steam coal trade done in the city of Bradford" and controlling "a large proportion of the household coal trade of the city". Their annual sales were at the rate of 700,000 tons per annum, and the profit, though not actually stated, was certified to be in excess of £13,200 after providing for depreciation, etc. The assets were valued at £80,000 and the issued capital was £199,790—£80,000 in 5½ per cent. cumulative preference shares, and £119,790 in ordinary shares. The ordinary shares, which were taken by the vendors, thus represented goodwill. Later in the year the capital was raised to £249,790, the Bradford Dyers' Association investing £50,000 with the right to appoint two directors. The Coal Merchants' Association then became sole coal suppliers to the Dyers' Association. The progress of the company may be measured by the dividends paid: Year to 31st March, 1900, 8 per cent.; 1900-1, 8 per cent.; 1901-2, 5 per cent.; 1902-3, nil; 1903-4, 4 per cent.; 1904-5, 4 per cent.; 1905-6, 4 per cent. The lack of a dividend in 1902-3 was due to heavy losses from bad debts. Their capital is now £350,000.

The shale oil industry of Scotland was started by James Young in 1850, and up to the advent of American competition was on the whole very profitable, many fortunes being made.

In the eighties all that changed and there are now only some nine works. It is not within the object of this chapter to tell the story of the struggle or how it was accentuated by the competition of Russian oil in the nineties. These matters belong to the general history of international trade. It is sufficient to say that the companies which survived did so only by their tenacity, by painful attention to economies, and by the development of the trade in by-products. Besides burning oil, lubricating oils, paraffin wax, and sulphate of ammonia are now manufactured. Only four companies are quoted on the Glasgow Exchange— Young's, Broxburn, Pumpherston, and Oakbank—and their results have been generally satisfactory. Being so few in number and their trade being generally done in yearly contracts, it is easy for them to regulate their prices within the limits which American and Russian competition permit; they can also avoid undue publicity. At the same time the system of annual contracts has several times prevented them from utilising favourable trade conjunctures which have developed after the contracts had been made. In 1899 the Scotch companies had an agreement with the Standard Oil Co. as to the price of wax, but in 1904 they were strong enough to fix their own prices. For sulphate of ammonia they have only to face the competition of the blast-furnace by-product plants. In 1903-4 the Russian syndicates came to an agreement with the Scotch producers as to the price of lubricating oils. In the summer of 1906 the Scotch papers announced the fixing of prices by the Scotch companies, showing that the unrest in the Caucasus had lessened the strain on them.

The exploitation of the Caucasian oil-fields has been largely brought about with British capital through such companies as the European Petroleum Co., the Russian Petroleum Co., the Baku Russian Petroleum Co., etc. Over-production followed on prosperity in the manner characteristic of oil-fields, and that placed the producers in the power of the refiners and exporters. In turn the producers themselves entered the distributing business, and since 1900 there have been a series of alliances and arrangements to place the price of petroleum on a sounder basis, while there has been alternate combination and competition with the Standard Oil Co. wherever they have come into rivalry. All this belongs to the history of the world's oil industry, and does not concern British industry, further than indirectly through its effects on the fortunes of investors. A little more germane to our subject is the Shell Transport and Trading Co. formed in 1897 to amalgamate the interests of eleven firms engaged in " the transport of illuminating oil, mainly by means of tank steamers, and its storage in bulk, sale, and distribution in India, China, Japan, and the Straits ". To secure its sources of supply it acquired large oil-producing territories in Dutch Borneo, and is thus producer, transporter, and distributor. After negotiations with the Standard Oil Co. broke down, the Shell Co. entered into an alliance with the Royal Dutch Petroleum Co. to combine their marketing business and place the Eastern trade of the company on an impregnable basis. Four other companies came in, and in July, 1903, the Asiatic Petroleum Co. was formed to do the distributing business with a capital of £600,000, subscribed by the Shell Co., the Royal Dutch Co., and Messrs. Rothschild. That ended a ten years' war of prices between Russian and Borneo oil. Finally in 1906 a closer alliance still was achieved by the formation of a " holding company " in which the Royal Dutch Co. was to take 60 per cent., and the Shell Co. 40 per cent., the Royal Dutch Co. also taking 25 per cent. of the ordinary shares of the Shell Co. This is a significant instance of the ever-growing internationalisation of capital. The capital of the Shell Co. was originally £1,800,000, and was increased in 1902 to £3,000,000; it paid in 1898, 6 per cent.; 1899, 8 per cent.; 1900, 10 per cent.; 1901, 10 per cent.; 1902, $2\frac{1}{2}$ per cent.; 1903, 5 per cent.; 1904, 5 per cent.; 1905, 5 per cent.

The extractive industries dealing with stone and similar products afford us several instances of combinations, mostly small.

The nature and history of these firms is indicated in the table. The Bath Stone Firms, Limited, was a union of the seven chief firms in the industry, three Portland firms being added later; the Leeds Fireclay Co. originally included six firms and afterwards bought four more; the Buxton Lime

		Present Capital.	Year Ending	Ordinary Dividends.											
		£		1895.	1896.	1897.	1898.	1899.	1900.	1901.	1902.	1903.	1904.	1905.	1906.
1887	Bath Stone Firms	315,090	31st Dec.	8	9¾	9¾	12	15	15	15	15	15	15	15	—
1890	Leeds Fireclay Co. . . .	1,280,000	30th June	5	6	6	6	6	7	5	5	4	5	15	—
	Fullers' Earth Union . .	101,467	31st March	1	1½	2	3	3	4	3	4	5	5	7	11
1891	Buxton Lime Firms Co. . .	532,800	30th June	5	5	5	5	5	5	5	5	5	5	3⅛	4½
1900	Rowley Regis Granite Quarries . .	100,000	31st Dec.	—	—	—	—	—	—	3	nil.	nil.	nil.	nil.	—
	Associated Portland Cement Manufacturers . . .	6,571,540	30th June	—	—	—	—	—	—	nil.	nil.	nil.	nil.	nil.	nil.

Firms twelve, and the Rowley Regis Granite Quarries eight. All these companies are of the nature of monopolies, though incomplete. In the case of the Rowley Regis Granite Quarries, which owned two-thirds of the quarries at Rowley Regis, near Dudley, it was claimed that there was " practically no competition within a radius of about twenty miles," and that a large business was done in road material with railways and municipal authorities.   Here, however, it was plainly open to substitutive competition in a way to which the Bath Stone Firms Co., for example, was not exposed.   The Leeds Fireclay Co. has investments in a number of subsidiary companies, and in 1902 amalgamated the gas engineering works of the company with a gas engineering firm, Jonas Drake & Son, of Halifax, under the title of Drakes, Limited, capital (£115,000).   The Fullers' Earth Union consolidated the fullers' earth works at Redhill, Surrey, and Bath, Somerset.

The Associated Portland Cement Manufacturers, Limited, was formed in July, 1900, to purchase the undertakings of twenty-seven firms and companies.   " With the exception of three, all the works are situated on the Thames and Medway, and possess such advantages in the quantity and quality of raw material that the neighbourhood of these two rivers, from being the cradle of the Portland cement industry, has now become the chief seat of the manufacture.   It is believed that upwards of 80 per cent. of the entire output of the Portland cement is produced on the Thames and Medway, where the supplies of chalk and clay are of the finest quality for the manufacture.   The total production of cement on these rivers in 1899 has been estimated at 1,700,000 tons, whereas the estimate of production in 1895 was only 1,350,000 tons.   This difference is due to the largely increasing demand for Portland cement " (Prospectus).   The production of the firms taken over averaged for the three years 1897-9, 1,321,359 tons, and in 1899 was 1,404,569 tons; in addition Messrs. John Bazley White & Brothers, the largest combining firm, were erecting new plant with a capacity of 160,000 tons for making cement on the rotary kiln system on royalty.   Working arrangements were also made with four other firms; altogether the undertakings acquired and those four firms possessed about 89 per cent. of the total capacity of the Thames and Medway districts. In addition to cement, several of the businesses manufactured lime, whiting, bricks, Keene's cement, Roman cement, etc., and several possessed engineering works, enabling the association to carry out a great part of its own renewals and repairs.   In one of the four firms with which arrangements were made, the Wouldham Cement Co., which was established by S. Pearson & Son, the large contractors, mainly to supply themselves with cement, the association had a holding of £50,000.

The firms in the cement industry had always " kept themselves to themselves " until a few years before the formation of the association, when some of them formed an alliance which chiefly dealt with the purchase of fuel.   The cement industry, being based on the possession of a local monopoly of raw materials, seemed well fitted for consolidation, but proposals for amalgamation though often made met with no favour until the present occasion, when the negotiations were undertaken by an outside company of promoters whose independent position commanded respect.   The sale price to the association was £6,325,000, out of which the promoters had to meet the expenses of formation, but not cost of conveyance, etc.   Against this sum there were land, works, buildings, plant, machinery, etc., valued at £4,522,000, and the difference £1,803,000—or 3·2 years' purchase of the last three years' average gross profits (£561,103) before charging interest, depreciation, directors' fees, and income tax—stood against goodwill, brands, and trade marks ; the gross profits for the last year of account were £658,356.   An additional sum of £1,050,000 was required for purchase of the new rotary plant, stock, raw materials, etc., and for working capital.   The total capital offered for issue was £7,375,000—£2,475,000 in 4¼ debentures, £2,450,000 in 5½ per cent. cumulative preference shares, and £2,450,000 in ordinary shares, the vendors taking one-third of each class.

Unluckily for the association flotation took place at a most unfortunate time when the money market was in a semi-panic owing to the disasters in Africa and bad news from Pekin. Although there was a large subscription, particularly from agents, distributors, and customers, the total was not taken up by the public, and consequently the vendors, feeling absolute confidence in the undertaking, substituted a considerable further amount of stock, especially ordinary shares, for the cash to which they were entitled. The directors alone held £1,400,000 of the capital, and with their connections their total holding amounted to half of the ordinary shares, one-third of the preference shares, and one-fourth of the debentures, or £2,660,000 in all. A further severe blow was caused by the sudden refusal of three firms to fulfil their contract of amalgamation; they represented a production of 140,000 tons on the Thames and Medway, and 50,000 tons on the Tyne. Prolonged negotiations followed by litigation ensued, and the difficulty was not settled for five years when the contracts were rescinded on the three firms paying the expenses incurred.

The state of trade proved the most serious obstacle to success. First of all the association drew its supplies of coke from the London gas companies, who, having a monopoly, exploited the coal boom of 1900 by forcing up the price of coke from the normal figure of 10s. to 22s. per ton. This item alone raised their expenditure £200,000 above the level of 1899. On the other hand the market for cement was bad. In Germany the trade had been most unsatisfactory owing to over-production, underselling, and the tariff policy of the other European countries; in 1895 and the years following there had been a great extension ·of production, chiefly in expectation of the construction of the Great Midland Canal, so that the capacity of the German works was 29,000,000 casks, or double the home consumption. German exports rose from 600,386 metric tons in 1900 to 742,381 in 1903, of which Britain's shares were 12,500 tons and 36,700 tons, respectively. Belgium also produced large quantities of cheap " natural " cement, which though not so good as Portland cement was good enough for the cheap builder. Our imports of cement from all sources have risen as follows :—

							Tons.
1900	.	.	.	.	.	.	104,771
1901	.	.	.	.	.	.	220,962
1902	.	.	.	.	.	.	240,893
1903	.	.	.	.	.	.	261,077
1904	.	.	.	.	.	.	272,945
1905	.	.	.	.	.	.	234,588

Lastly there has been some competition by slag cement, a by-product of the blast furnaces at Middlesbrough, good for subaqueous works.   And to make matters worse, there was progressive depression in the building trade at home and stagnation in the South African market.   These hard facts not only affected profits disagreeably but had an important influence on the price policy of the association.

The prospectus stated that "an agreement has been entered into with George E. Wragge, on behalf of the principal London cement merchants, which provides, *inter alia*, for all merchants joining them taking their whole requirements of cement from this association for the term of seven years".   These merchants, of course, had the power of diverting a considerable portion of the trade, and towards them the policy was conciliation.   "We are daily impressing upon our customers," said the chairman at the first statutory meeting of the company, "that the object of this company is not to injure the merchant, or to squeeze out the middleman.   We know the advantages of working hand in hand with the distributors, but in return for the hand we hold out to the distributors we ask for a 'tied trade'".   This agreement antagonised some of the merchants, and when the high price of coke compelled a revision of cement prices the ill-will was increased and some trade was lost.   The anticipations that this agreement would be profitable were not realised; "chiefly," said the chairman at the annual meeting,[1] 27th November, 1901, "on account of certain restrictive clauses, which, in the changed circumstances, worked against the parties to them, including this company, without conferring on any of us the contemplated advantages of the arrangement.   There seemed, then, nothing for it but for these agreements to become inoperative." A letter to the press from Mr. Wragge, of date 1st February, 1901, gives a less detached view of the occurrence: "The agreement was duly sealed and exchanged, and for six months has been acted upon by both the manufacturers and the merchants.   At the beginning of January the associated manufacturers gave the merchants notice that they were advised the agreement was not enforceable.   The merchants thereupon took the opinion of

[1] *Financial Times*, 28th November, 1901.

eminent counsel, and were advised that the agreement was enforceable, and were prepared to enforce it but for the fact that the action taken would take considerable time and accentuate the present critical and disorganised state of the cement trade in London. Under these circumstances the merchants under protest agreed to the agreement being cancelled, and have now arranged to supply their customers' requirements from elsewhere." Such disputes always favour foreign producers, but in this case the association owned all the best brands. "We are sufficiently powerful," said the chairman at the same meeting, "to make it clear that where we do not get our products actively handled and distributed by merchants, there we shall organise our own agencies, so as to secure what we have a right to claim—not a monopoly, but our fair proportion of the trade." The merchants, in fact, were strong enough to injure the manufacturers, but the latter could in the long run, though at a loss, do without the merchants. This fact explains the submission of the middlemen.

The rise in the price of cement attracted considerable foreign competition. At first, the directors confessed, they were tempted to drive the foreigner out of the market by quoting prices too low for him to undercut, but fear of their shareholders withheld them. The middle course was adopted of letting the foreigner have all the market where cheapness was preferred to quality. Prices were reduced below the level of 1899 indeed but a moderate profit was aimed at, even at the cost of a diminished output. Slackness of demand caused a further restriction of output by about 7 per cent. in 1901. The ordinary expedient of making for stock is only possible to a limited extent in the cement industry, because cement is a bulky article to store and requires a considerable superficial storage area to allow aeration. Not till the spring of 1906 were the directors able to put up prices, thanks to improvements in the building trade and to the San Francisco earthquake. On the accounts for 1905-6 the chairman said that "if the company had been getting the price which ruled six years ago they would have had in the year under review a profit of nearly £500,000 more to deal with, less any extra cost of materials that might have been due to the circumstances which had given them greater prosperity ". For all their millions the Associated Manufacturers could not maintain prices, and even in 1905 had to complain of serious depression. The only alternative open to them was to reduce costs. At the time of the amalgamation there were differences in the cost of production at the different works amounting to 25 per cent. In the first four years about £550,000 was spent in additions to plant, buildings, and machinery, besides what was spent on repairs and renewals. The new rotary kiln process proved a success and brought about an economy of coke, though it cost more than was anticipated ; an exclusive licence was therefore purchased, and the process was introduced into more of the association's works. Labour-saving machinery was introduced, causing a re-arrangement of staff and some reduction. The opportunity was taken to re-model works which were temporarily closed on account of the state of trade, and ultimately the business of those which manufactured under disadvantageous conditions was transferred to others better situated. The directors were disinclined to close works permanently on account of the dislocation of local labour and trade which followed on such a policy, but the compulsion of necessity was too severe for them ; it is to be reckoned to their credit that in 1904-5 they undertook a lot of special clearing of chalk quarries in order to find work for the unemployed, and owing to the less efficiency of the labour had to charge their accounts with £989, the sum expended beyond the normal cost. The subsidiary industries of lime, whiting, bricks, etc., proved profitable and added an element of stability to the business.

The results of the trading are shown by the following table, profits being taken after providing for repairs and renewals, but not for depreciation, directors' fees, and income tax :—

Average profits for three years before amalgamation	.	.	£561,303
Profits—Year to 30th June, 1901	.	.	.	.	.	248,216
,,	,,	1902	.	.	.	.	.	279,742
,,	,,	1903	.	.	.	.	.	313,329
,,	,,	1904	.	.	.	.	.	335,722
,,	,,	1905	.	.	.	.	.	333,194
,,	,,	1906	.	.	.	.	.	335,462

The prospectus forecast a 10 per cent. dividend on the ordinary shares; nothing has been paid.   The capital issued is now £6,571,504.

The management of the association is entrusted to nineteen directors in addition to fourteen managing directors who give their whole time to the business.   The managing committee meets weekly and reports in full to the monthly meetings of the whole Board.   Directorial and other official appointments under a combination always represent a compromise.   " In the negotiations "—to quote a reminiscent passage [1] from one of the chairman's annual addresses—" there were many individual interests that had to be considered.   It was most important to retain the services of all those who had been most instrumental in conducting the businesses.   On the other hand, there were many who had posts in them who stipulated for employment in the new company.   Nearly all these arrangements are favourable to this company's interests; where there are exceptions time will enable the requisite changes to be made, but definite agreements have to be adhered to while they last."   After five years it was found possible, as these contracts lapsed, to make rearrangements producing a saving of about £10,000 a year. The first task after amalgamation was the substitution of one central office for many scattered offices and the adoption of one system of accounts.   The latter was a lengthy and complicated undertaking—involving as one single item the transfer of 6,000 customers' accounts—but without it there could not be obtained that ready access to statistics and that facility of comparison which are necessary in the control of a large business with many branches.   Not less important is the organisation of sales.   " Our selling operations," said the chairman on 24th October, 1902,[2] " are managed by a sales committee.   The members of it are those who, before they joined us, sold the cement of their respective firms.   Their work is, however, only to a small extent carried on in committee.   They meet together to determine the larger matters of policy, but each takes charge of a definite department, and keeps touch, by personal interview as well as by correspondence, with the customers of his own section.   We realise how important the

---

[1] *Financial Times*, 25th October, 1902.   [2] *Ibid.*

personal element is. . . . But, in addition to what I may call the daily routine of the business of selling our large tonnage, there is cast upon the sales directors the responsibility for watchfulness concerning new channels and new methods; for initiating, in fact, a policy of distribution. The directors felt at an early stage that many of the firms whose businesses had been purchased had localised their trade, and had to some extent neglected the great markets of the world. Business had come to them in good times, and they had formed the habit of waiting for it to come. With such large quantities to sell this company could not follow that example. The sales directors felt the importance of seeking business wherever it is to be found, and have been prepared to face the fact that it may be necessary to go to the other side of the world to obtain personal acquaintance with facts, conditions, and, above all, persons." The essential features of modern business could hardly be put more clearly than in Mr. F. A. White's speech, and he gave it further weight by adding that special visits had been paid in the past year by directors to South Africa, Australia, British Columbia, and California.

The organisation of the manufacturing side of the business was described by the chairman in his 1903 address:[1] " I told you on a former occasion that the works were managed by a small executive committee of two of your managing directors, responsible to the works committee" (of managing directors), " and through them to the managing directors' committee and the Board. The works committee sits once a week in London, and it was found that time did not allow of all that deliberation in concert with the executive committee that is demanded by the importance of what has to be done, especially in the way of work that involves capital expenditure. The executive committee work early and late; their duties embrace the daily supervision of the works, with whose managers they are in constant contact; and although from this fact they are the persons most likely to be struck with the necessity of construction and reconstruction of all sorts, and are in a position to initiate improvements, the decision as to these ought not to rest with them nor to be re-

[1] *Financial Times*, 24th September, 1903.

commended to the Board without the fullest examination by them, jointly with some of their colleagues; and so it was found desirable to form a small sub-committee of the works committee, consisting of those most conversant with the different works. This sub-committee meets for a day's work at the company's office at Gravesend once a week. The result has been very satisfactory."

By way of comparison with the Associated Portland Cement Manufacturers we append the results of some independent cement manufacturers, bearing in mind that some of them by their geographical position may have entire command over a local trade. Thus the Sussex Portland Cement Co. was the only concern having works on the London, Brighton, and South Coast Railway until the opening of Hall & Co.'s works at Beddington in 1905.

	Capital.	Year Ending	Year Ending						
			1900.	1901.	1902.	1903.	1904.	1905.	1906.
Sussex Portland Cement Co. (Newhaven)	£ 149,666	30th Sept.	15	15	12	7½	7½	6	6
Martin, Earle, & Co. (Rochester) . .	457,015	30th June	10	10	10	10	*nil.*	5	2½ (int.)
Jos. Robinson & Co. (Carlisle) . . .	95,000	,,	6	5	5	5	5	4	2
Wouldham Cement Co. (Grays) . .	459,480	31st Dec.	*nil.*	*nil.*	*nil.*	*nil.*	*nil.*	*nil.*	

It must be added also that these firms have profited by the efforts of the Association to maintain prices; direct arrangements also exist between it and Martin, Earle, & Co. and the Wouldham Cement Co. The Association sold out its interest in the last-named company in 1903-4.

In May, 1905, a conference was held of English, French, Belgian, and German cement producers which arranged the conditions of export to the Dutch market until 1914. Further arrangements were contemplated but do not appear to have been concluded.

CHAPTER V.

THE TEXTILE INDUSTRIES.

THE structure of the textile industries is completely different from that of the iron and steel industries. Whereas in the latter the dominant tendency is the concentration of all processes from the extraction of the raw material to the sale of the finished product under one government and the establishment of businesses on the possession of the sources of raw material, the former is characterised by entire separation from the raw material and by a very thorough specialisation in all the branches of manufacture. In the cotton industry importing, spinning, weaving, dyeing, printing, bleaching, merchanting, all constitute separate trades carried on by separate groups of manufacturers, and only in a comparatively few instances are spinning and weaving carried on by the same firms. In the worsted industry the wool is bought or imported and sorted by a topmaker who, if he has not a combing establishment of his own, sends it out to a commission comber. The "top" is then sold to a spinner to be made into yarn, and he sells it to a manufacturer or weaver to be woven into cloth. In turn he sells it to a merchant who "finishes" it or gets it dyed by an outside dyer. The related branch of woollens shows less specialisation, for carding, spinning, and weaving are usually done by the same firm. Linen again shows the same separation between flax growing and preparing, spinning, and weaving. Carpets, curtains, lace, hosiery, sewing cotton are all separate industries. And lastly, there is considerable specialisation among the individual firms in cotton and wool. The three main textile fabrics—cotton, wool and linen—may in some respects be taken as forming one industry, since they serve in many branches the same purposes and compete severely with each other. Recent inventions have increased this competition, for cotton in the form of linenette imitates linen, in the form of flannelette woollen goods, and in mercerised fabrics silk. All the other textile fabrics, in fact, are dominated by cotton. Fashion, again, the most incalculable of all economic factors, plays a decisive part in settling what shall be worn and therefore made.

The special feature of the cotton industry is that while British manufacturers have a practical monopoly of the home market, the imports of foreign yarns and goods being negligible, 80 per cent. of the trade is done for export. The Continent of Europe and the United States have largely developed their cotton manufacture in the last thirty years, but they supply only their own markets and that only in the coarser fabrics. In neutral markets only the competition of India in the Far East and of the United States in China have been serious. The consumption of raw cotton in the United Kingdom rose from an average of 11·20 million cwt. in 1876-80 to 15·05 million cwt. in 1896-1900, and reached 15·7 million cwt. in 1899. For the last five years the consumption and price of cotton have been :—

	Million Cwt.	Price— Pence.		American Crop. Bales.
1901	14·32	$4\frac{3}{4}$	1900/1	10,425,000
1902	15·07	$4\frac{27}{32}$	1901/2	10,701,000
1903	13·90	6·03	1902/3	10,758,000
1904	13·99	6·60	1903/4	10,124,000
1905	16·25	5·09	1904/5	13,577,000

These figures have an important influence on the position of the companies afterwards to be criticised. As the world's consumption grows at the rate of some 500,000 bales annually, there was an actual scarcity of cotton in 1903 and 1904.

The various branches of the woollen industry have suffered severely from foreign competition since the early seventies, when the change of fashion from lustre to soft goods gave an enormous advantage to the weavers of Roubaix and Rheims. The position has been largely regained and, though the export trade has declined, a large home trade has been developed as well as a considerable export trade in combed wool. Messrs. Helmuth, Schwarze, & Co.'s reports show that British consumption of wool rose from 351,000,000 pounds in 1871-80 to 522,000,000 in 1896-1900. Competition between merino and cross-bred wools has been pronounced, but even more serious were the effects of the great Australian drought which immensely reduced the supplies of wool after 1899. Subsequently there was a reduction in the South American supplies. The effect on prices was catastrophic, for a panic as to short supplies seized the trade. One class of merinos which in 1898 had been 21d. per lb. rose in 1899 to 33½d. and fell to 19½d. in 1900 when the scare had put a stop to trade. The subsequent annual consumption and prices are shown below :—

	Wool, Mohair, and Alpaca. Million lb.	Merino, Port Phillip. Average Fleece. Pence per lb.
1901	541	13
1902	490	15
1903	448	16
1904	437	16
1905	468	17¼

Besides foreign competition our wool industries are exposed to the competition of goods made from shoddy and mungo, that is, second-hand wool extracted from rags. According to the Bradford Chamber of Commerce the consumption of shoddy, mungo, etc., rose from 130,000,000 lb. in 1900 to 180,000,000 lb. in 1904.

The growth of the cotton industry is not fully shown by the statistics of consumption of raw cotton. While the consumption of cotton was 14·8 million cwt. in 1890 and 13·99 in 1904, the number of spinning and doubling spindles rose from 44,504,819 to 50,964,874 and the number of power looms from 615,714 to 704,357. This is partly due to the change from spinning coarse to fine counts, but it is partly also a sign of increased competition. After every spell of good trade capital flows into the industry, and the building of new mills is not always accompanied by the destruction of old. One cause of this is the facility with which money can be raised by joint stock companies, and the consequent growth of unjustifiable competition was the subject of voluble complaints before the Royal Commission on the Depression of Trade in 1886. One of the witnesses before Mr. Chamberlain's Tariff Commission made a statement: "For the last twenty years the extension has been under the limited liability system, but what I call rather the illegitimate. It has been by a combination of machinist and engineer, who have wished to keep their works going in order to find orders for their workpeople ; the landowner who has probably got adjoining land on which he wishes to build cottages; the mill furnisher, architect, lawyer, commission agent, and cotton broker in Liverpool, all of whom will make their profit out of the erection of the mill, or in the working of it after it is started. Very often when trade was bad, I have known mills that were practically at times insolvent, and they could not pay up the loan capital if it was recalled. The lenders dared not call it in, and did not when times improved, because they thought it safe again. They lent their money on no security, but came in as ordinary creditors. The money was generally lent in small sums. A great many people who were in the mill invest their money in this way, though it is most risky, and if they were capitalists they would never do it. In weaving the extension is done through the speculator building weaving sheds, which he lets out to manufacturers on the rent and power system, with or without looms. The manufacturer gets either a fortnight or a month's credit for his yarn and gets cash for his calico, and probably an advance for his wages from the bank. He is made or marred very often by a lucky speculation in yarn " (*Report on the Cotton Industry*, par. 217).

Even allowing for some exaggeration in this account—though the statements are by no means new—it is of special importance as showing the ease with which fresh competition can spring up in the cotton spinning and weaving trades. Mr. William Tattersall in his cotton trade circular issued in September, 1906, gave a list of twenty-eight spinning mills with 2,400,000 spindles which had got to work during the previous twelve months, thirteen with 1,100,000 spindles which had partly started, and thirty-seven with 3,100,000 spindles which were in course of erection—altogether seventy-eight mills and 6,600,000 spindles—while three more mills were projected. These new mills would altogether cost about £8,000,000 and give employment to about 16,000 hands. From 90 to 100 limited liability spinning companies publish their reports every year. A trade which is in so many hands is not in a favourable position for combinations, either temporary or permanent, to be effected. "Our manufacturers are too jealous," said another witness before the Tariff Commission in explaining his failure to form a price association in the cotton trade. Where potential competition may easily become actual no combination or amalgamation to raise prices is possible, unless very special circumstances are present. In cotton spinning and weaving we only find two amalgamations—Horrockses, Crewdson, & Co., and The Fine Cotton Spinners' and Doublers' Association. Very much the same account may be given of the woollen industries; it is in the derivative and not in the primary industries that we find combination attempted.

Temporary associations in the textile industries have not existed in many cases, but where attempted they have generally blossomed into permanent amalgamations. Messrs. J. & P. Coats were preceded by a sales association—the Central Thread Agency; the English Sewing Cotton Company grew out of an association of English Sewing Cotton Makers for trade purposes; the Bleachers' Association was amalgamated to realise more fully the advantages which had been found in price associations; the Yorkshire Woolcombers' Association was built up on the ruins of an unsuccessful attempt to regulate prices, and the various amalgamations in the dyeing trade of Yorkshire had the way paved for them by the "alliance" for regulating wages and prices which was inaugurated in 1894. These associations will be dealt with in connection with the respective amalgamations. Almost more significant are the attempts which have been made of recent years to enable a trade apparently so unfitted for combination as that of cotton spinning to act as a unit in times of emergency. On several occasions—1897, 1900, 1903, 1904—the two great masters' associations, the Federation of Master Cotton Spinners and the Bolton Association, have combined with the trades unions to run short time in order to counteract the effects of a short supply of cotton and the manipulation of the cotton market by speculators. After a general stoppage in Whitweek, 1903, short time was run for four months, June to October, 75 per cent. of the whole trade coming into line. Throughout 1904 up to the middle of September, except for a few weeks in June and July, a short week of forty hours only was worked. High prices and comparative scarcity of cotton for three years led to the formation of the British Cotton Growing Association in July, 1902, to promote the cultivation of cotton in suitable parts of the British dominions. Although the movement is quite in its infancy it has had a considerable amount of success. Private firms and companies in the cotton and allied industries, trade unions, co-operative societies, individuals, have co-operated to find the capital for this effort to widen the source of supplies. It cannot be said that there is anything of the trust or combination about the scheme, but it shows that the cotton industry is beginning to recognise the solidarity of its parts, and to see that it has economic interests which it cannot afford to leave to the self-interest of its members but must deal with as an organised industry. It is out of this spirit that combination to regulate production grows. With this attempt to free the industry from dependence on the American cotton-fields may be compared the partly successful effort of the spinners to free themselves from the Liverpool cotton brokers. They established the Cotton Buying Company which consisted originally of some twenty cotton-spinning companies and now numbers ninety-two members with 6,450,000 spindles. In its twenty-five years of existence it has bought for its members 2,733,341 bales of cotton, valued at £26,306,830, making a total profit of £73,466, which has been distributed partly in bonuses partly in interest on capital. Not only England but all cotton-manufacturing countries are interested in the supply of cotton and the regulation of the cotton trade, and on the initiation of Lancashire the first International Conference met at Zurich in Whitweek, 1904. A meeting was held in July, 1905, to consider the high prices of cotton ; one resolution which was carried urged spinners " to refrain from buying American cotton during the next three months, except for immediate wants " ; another provided for the collection of information from the spinners as to stocks of cotton in hand at the end of the season. Possible expansions of this international co-operation may be seen in proposals discussed at the 1906 conference to establish a reserve of cotton, to guarantee a minimum price for cotton so as to foster its production, and to establish a buying company in which every spinner should take shares and from which he should undertake to purchase one-tenth of his requirements. The American representatives urged that European consumers should get into ·closer touch with American growers, " who were full of progressive spirit and willing to co-operate in many ways of which Europeans did not dream ". All these indications show that the cotton-spinning trade is finding that its old individualist spirit which carried it so far is insufficient to meet modern conditions.

The great amalgamations in the textile industry are quite different in form from those that exist in the iron industry. Instead of the " vertical " combination extending upwards from the raw materials we find " horizontal " combinations embracing a majority of the firms and companies engaged in one branch of trade. The object is not primarily the increased efficiency of the dominant unit but the extinction of competition. Once the combination is effected, however, the management is driven to the pursuit of efficiency, just as the large iron firms having achieved self-sufficiency are forced to take steps to reduce competition. The large textile combines have also displayed a certain amount of " vertical " organisation in seeking to get control over their second most important raw material—coal. Lastly, by means of mutual investments a kind of general community of interests has been set up which prevents the textile associations from trespassing on each other's territory.

A list of the textile amalgamations showing their financial results is subjoined :—

Est.	Company	Present Capital. (£)	Year Ending	1897.	1898.	1899.	1900.	1901.	1902.	1903.	1904.	1905.	1906.
1887	Horrockses, Crewdson, & Co.	757,100	30th June	20	*Reports*	*not*	*obtainable.*	20	20	20	20	20	25
1896	J. & P. Coats	10,917,420	31st March	—	30	40	50	20	20	20	16	8	8
1897	English Sewing Cotton Co.	2,957,694	31st March	—	*nil.*	8¾	7½	3¾	*nil.*	*nil.*	*nil.*	*nil.*	14
1898	American Thread Co.	3,018,095	30th Sept.	—	—	6	10	6	6	4	6	8	6
1898	The Linen Thread Co.	2,844,560	31st March	—	—	8	8	9	8	6	8	6	6
1898	Fine Cotton Spinners' and Doublers' Association	7,250,000		—	*Reports*	*not available.*							
1898	United Turkey Red Co.	1,500,000		—	—	8¾	8	7	7	7	7	7	7
1899	Bradford Dyers' Association	4,810,227	31st Dec.	—	—	8¾	9	7	7	7	7	7	7
1899	Yorkshire Indigo, Scarlet, and Colour Dyers	468,000	30th June	—	—	—	*nil.*	8	8	3½	*nil.*	*nil.*	*nil.*
1899	English Velvet and Cord Dyers' Association	711,444	31st Dec.	—	—	—	*nil.*	*nil.*	7	6	3	3	—
1899	Yorkshire Woolcombers' Association	1,965,800	30th June	—	—	—	*nil.*	*nil.*	*nil.*	*collapsed.*			
1900	Calico Printers' Association	8,226,840	31st March	—	—	—	—	*nil.*	*nil.*	2½	2½	2½	2½
1900	British Cotton and Wool Dyers' Association	1,891,684		—	—	—	—	3	3	*nil.*	*nil.*	*nil.*	2
1900	Bleachers' Association	6,820,096	31st Dec.	—	—	—	—	*Reports*	*not*	3	*nil.*	3	4
1900	United Velvet Cutters' Association	200,000	31st March	—	—	—	—	6	6	6	*not*	2	2½
1900	Extract Wool and Merino Co.	201,186	30th April	—	—	—	—	7	6	6	6	7½	4
1900	J. & J. Baldwin and Partners	751,895	30th Sept.	—	—	—	—	6	8	8	6	7½	7½
1900	Leeds and District Worsted Dyers	226,000		—	—	—	—	*Reports*	*not*	*obtainable.*			
1904	English Fustian Cutting, etc., Co.	500,000		—	—	—	—	*Reports*	*not available.*			5	5
1904	Mitchells, Ashworth, Stansfield, & Co.	674,646	"	—	—	—	—	*Reports*	*not available.*			7½	7½
1904	Woolcombers, Ltd.	585,000	31st Dec.	—	—	—	—	—	—	—	—	*nil.*	15

Like many another Lancashire business Horrockses, Crewdson, & Co. goes back to very small beginnings. The founder, John Horrocks (1768-1804), the son of a small quarry-owner, set up a spinning-frame in a corner of his father's workshop and worked there with the help of his sisters. He attained some reputation for the quality of his yarn and set up in business at Preston in 1791, where he did his own carding, giving out the cotton to be spun by spinners in their own homes and the yarn to be woven by handloom weavers. The business grew and when he died in 1804 he was worth £150,000. He was succeeded by his brother, and the firm continued under the style of Horrockses, Miller, & Co. till 1887—though for many years there was neither a Horrocks nor a Miller connected with it. In 1885 the adjoining Preston firm of Hollins Brothers and in 1887 the Bolton firm of Crewdson, Crosses, & Co. were absorbed, and the company took its present name. The firm possesses works at both Preston and Bolton, the centres respectively of the plain and fancy trade, and warehouses at Manchester, London, and Glasgow. It employs 5,300 workpeople, owns over 7,000 looms and nearly 250,000 spindles, and the output weekly is 29,000 pieces of cotton fabrics of thousands of varieties and makes, or 58,000,000 yards annually. The bulk of the trade is in the home market, but a large export business is also done. " Always the foremost manufacturers of long-cloth and calicoes in England, the home trade of the firm has undergone a tremendous development in recent years as the result both of its amalgamation with the firms of Hollins Brothers and Crewdson & Co. and its introduction of direct dealing with the retailer. Until twenty years ago the firm had supplied its goods through wholesale merchants only ; in addition to that channel of distribution the firm now sells direct to the draper. . . . During the last twenty years . . . the output of the firm has been more than doubled " (*Times*, 17th January, 1906, *Advertisement*).

Nothing gave so great an impetus to the combination movement in the textile industries as the success of the Coats group. James Coats built a small mill in Paisley in 1826 for the manufacture of sewing thread. From that tiny beginning the business grew till it literally spread through the entire world.   Three generations of able business men by strenuous effort and sheer ability built up a concern so huge that when it was put before the public in 1890 as the limited liability company of J. & P. Coats, the purchase price was £5,750,000.   In these modern days so much is talked about the greatness and wealth and strength of the large "trusts" that it is well to emphasise the fact that it was by individuals that the component firms have been actually built up.   Messrs. Coats took one-third of the debentures and shares issued, and actually received in cash the tremendous sum of £3,833,350. The average profits of the seven years ended 1889 were £426,048, and in 1889, £474,775.   Included in the sale were stock valued at £1,015,287 and cash £400,000, so that the balance of the purchase money represented about ten years' profits.   Besides the mills at Paisley J. & P. Coats owned the Conant Thread Co., with works at Pawtucket, Rhode Island, through which they were able to utilise the American tariff laws.

Even so gigantic and successful a firm was not free from competition and a new policy was adopted.   The firm of Kerr & Co., of Paisley, was bought up from 1st August, 1895, and in the following year a great amalgamation was brought about by purchase of their chief rivals—Clarke & Co., of Paisley, James Chadwick & Co., of Bolton (founded 1820) and Jonas Brook & Co., of Meltham, near Huddersfield (1810).   For some time previous the four great rivals had been allied through the Central Thread Agency, a sales association which marketed the products of all its members.   Such associations have not been very common in British industry, and it is interesting, as proving the natural evolution of the amalgamation from the terminable association, to observe that it was the experience of the advantageous working of this association which led to the permanent union.   The additional capital required for the pur-chase, about £4,000,000, was obtained by the issue of 50,000 preferred and 125,000 ordinary shares, each of £10, and the ordinary shares were issued at £50 per £10 share.   In a cir-cular to their shareholders the directors of J. & P. Coats stated that "the aggregate profits of the various businesses, according to their last statements of account, are equal to 4½ per cent. on the £2,000,000 of debenture stock, 6 per cent. on the £2,500,000 of preference share capital, and over 23 per cent. on the £3,000,000 of ordinary share capital"—or about £930,000 altogether. The Coats firm itself had paid 20 per cent. on its ordinary shares for 1895-96 besides providing £50,000 for depreciation and £50,000 for reserve, raising the latter to £750,000, so that it contributed nearly two-thirds of the total profit. The circular continued : " These aggregate profits will be largely increased by the benefits which must necessarily result from the amalgamation of the four concerns. It is not intended to sell at higher prices than those charged by the various companies when they were separate ; but a marked improvement in values will necessarily take place in markets where they have been unduly depressed by unhealthy and excessive competition. Quite apart, however, from such readjustment of selling prices, large savings will result, not only in the cost of manufacturing, but also in the cost of distributing." The property of the company then included sixteen factories—including mills in the United States, Canada, and Russia—sixty branch houses and 150 depôts. Their staff of workpeople numbered 5,000. Since then they have acquired a coal-mine and 200,000 ordinary shares in the Fine Cotton Spinners' and Doublers' Association, thus obtaining some control over their supplies of raw material—cotton yarn. In 1901 the assets of the company exceeded the liabilities by about £5,500,000, which consisted partly of undistributed profits and partly of the premiums on the issue of 1896 ; of this sum £4,500,000 was issued to the ordinary shareholders in £1 ordinary shares, which were to receive the surplus profit after paying 6 per cent. on the preference shares and 20 per cent. on the old ordinary shares, now to be called preferred ordinary. In this way the capital was increased to £12,000,000— £2,000,000 being in debentures. Of this £10,917,420 is now outstanding. During the six years 1891-96 the total profit income —trading profit, interest, rents, etc.—after allowing for depreciation, averaged £567,552. The financial history subsequent to the amalgamation is summarised in the following table :—

Year to 30th June.	Net Profit.	Reserve Fund.	Ordinary Dividend.
1897	£981,692	£950,000	20 per cent.
1898	1,396,746	1,150,000	30 ,,
1899	1,858,232	1,500,000	40 ,,
1900	2,479,300	1,850,000	50 ,,
1901	2,680,153	1,310,000	*20 ,,
1902	2,662,412	2,050,000	*20 ,,
1903	2,737,636	2,850,000	*20 ,,
1904	2,633,039	3,550,000	*20 ,,
1905	2,379,429	4,050,000	*20 ,,
1906	2,974,088	4,500,000	*25 ,,

In 1904-5 the unrest in Russia cost the company about £200,000 in profits, a serious matter, remembering that in 1899 Sir Archibald Coats said that "by far the larger part of the company's profits was now derived from shares in foreign manufacturing companies, and not from mills in the United Kingdom".

The charge has frequently been made that Messrs. Coats have forced up the price of sewing cotton. Hereon may be quoted an article on "The Trade in Sewing Cotton" in the *Times* (*Financial Supplement*, 31st December, 1906): "The average price of the standard length of 200 yards six-cord (the basis for the price of the other lengths) has actually been less than 2d. per gross of 144 spools higher than the average price ruling during the twenty-five years preceding the amalgamation; but with the larger discounts to the trade allowed since the amalgamation the price is actually less. Wages have risen considerably, as also has the fine cotton used, as well as coal. Spool-wood—an important item—is 25 to 30 per cent. dearer than formerly. In effect, then, thread costs more to make by the combination even with the economies attainable under the combination, yet the consumers (or at all events the retailers) are paying somewhat less for it than they did when it cost less to make. It is not the case that the Coats combination has forced out competitors by underselling them. . . . The combination has improved the character of the products, while it has immensely reduced the cost of distribution. . . . What the 'Combine' has done has been to destroy the business of the middlemen, who stood between the thread manufacturers and the drapers and large customers. All these smaller dealers

* On Deferred Ordinary.

and consumers can now buy direct from the Central Agency on the same terms as the wholesale dealer."

The Coats group was almost unique in the history of large combinations in that it was composed exclusively of the strongest units in the industry; there was no "lame duck" in the company. Outside were left twenty thread-making firms in the United Kingdom, some forty on the Continent, and two large and many small firms in the United States. These were the weaker brethren, but though they were overshadowed by their mighty competitor that did not prevent them from indulging in reckless price-cutting. As the table just given shows the lower prices did not hurt Coats, but it was otherwise with the outsiders. In 1888 an Association of English Sewing Cotton Makers was formed for trade purposes, but after a few years it was dissolved though it was subsequently revived. In 1897 an amalgamation was mooted among the members of the association, and at last in December, 1897, fourteen firms (including three subordinate companies, one of which was situated in France and one in Montreal) combined to form the English Sewing Cotton Co., with a capital of £2,250,000. Of the fourteen eleven were sewing thread manufacturers— amongst them the firm of Sir Richard Arkwright & Co.; a firm of linen thread manufacturers, a firm of sewing silk manufacturers, and a firm of silk throwsters were included in the amalgamation "for trade reasons, as the acquisition of their businesses will, in the opinion of the directors, be beneficial to the company". After the company had got to work 63 per cent. of its business was done in sewing cottons, and the rest in yarns for manufacturing purposes, small wares, silk, and linen. A strong light was thrown upon the condition of the trade by the statement in the prospectus that "the difficulty of arriving at reliable figures on a common basis is so great, and the fluctuations owing to the excessive price-cutting are so considerable, that the directors decline the responsibility of putting forward a detailed statement. They think it right, however, to state that the average profits of the past few years have been comparatively small, a result due almost entirely to the undercutting already named, and would therefore form no criterion of the earning power of the separate businesses under the new conditions; moreover, the advantages which will be derived from the amalgamation in cheapening production and reducing the costs of distribution will materially help to produce satisfactory results." Under such circumstances the valuation of "trade marks, patent rights, and goodwill" at £447,131 was distinctly optimistic. The vendors, therefore, wisely sought to strengthen their position by establishing friendly relations with J. & P. Coats, who took up £200,000 of the ordinary shares. The total purchase money was £1,728,651, of which the vendors took £554,550 in equal proportions of debentures, preferred, and ordinary shares; the issue further provided £180,000 for working capital and £341,348 for additional capital.

The amalgamation was to be so organised that the original businesses should retain their individuality, and for this purpose subsidiary limited companies were to be formed, bearing the original names, all the shares in these companies being held by the English Sewing Cotton Co. At least one partner or director of the old firms was to remain in responsible management of his branch, and the board of seventeen directors contained representatives of all but one of the separate firms. In this way it was hoped to combine the special interest of each man in what he might still continue to regard in some respects as his own concern with the utilisation of the aggregated individual experience of all for the common good.

The next step was the absorption of the Glasgow firm of R. F. & J. Alexander, an active competitor in the Central and South American markets; it had been formed into a company in 1892 with £475,000 capital, but had paid only two ordinary dividends of 12 and 2 per cent. in its first year. Monopoly of the British thread industry became almost complete with the purchase of L. Ardern, of Stockport, in 1899, and, meanwhile, the American industry had been "organised" by the formation of the American Thread Company in December, 1898. In that amalgamation, which was brought about by the "advice and co-operation" of the English Sewing Cotton Company, thirteen firms were included, capitalised at £3,720,000, of which trade marks, patents, and goodwill accounted for £718,715. The English Sewing

Cotton Company took a majority holding, or 720,000 out of 1,200,000 five-dollar shares in the ordinary stock, and Messrs. J. & P. Coats subscribed for £100,000 worth of preferred shares. The union was made closer in 1899 when the American Thread Company invested in 125,000 ordinary shares of the English Sewing Cotton Company at 35s., part of a new issue. As with the British trade so with the American: " The business of the above companies," said the prospectus, "has for a considerable time been injuriously affected by excessive competition among themselves ; and the cutting of rates having, during the past three years, resulted in a very large portion of the trade being done below cost of production, it was realised that a complete consolidation of the various interests was necessary to ensure renewed prosperity ". The three managing directors of the English Company had seats on the American board of directors. Thus through the investment alliance of the three great units, J. & P. Coats, Limited, the English Sewing Cotton Company, and the American Thread Company, complete domination over the world's trade in sewing thread seemed to be attained, and it was only natural to expect that harmony would reign and prosperity ensue. The English Sewing Cotton Company had now an issued capital of £3,000,000, and the number of share-holders of all classes was about 15,000. The English and American companies ran a million spindles, and employed be-tween 13,000 and 14,000 workpeople.

Trouble soon arose over the working arrangements between the Coats and English Sewing Cotton Companies. According to the *Economist* (2nd December, 1899), " the proportions of the trade in those markets in which both companies were in the habit of competing were restricted to the ratios existing at the date of the agreement. Neither company was to be at liberty to extend its business in any one of these markets at the expense of the other, and when a market itself increased in volume there were provisions for dividing the increase. In some markets—as in Spain—the English Company was debarred altogether from competing, and in other markets—as in Cuba —the Coats Company was debarred." Now the English Company had a mill at Barcelona which they acquired with the

Alexander Company, and from their Cuban trade they made large profits under the Spanish protective tariff; but after the Spanish-American war this market was lost and Cuba became a possible market for the Coats' American mills. The agents of the English Company then tried to market the products of the Barcelona mill in Spain and elsewhere, but Messrs. Coats objected to this breach of the engagement. About the same time they sold half their holding in the English Company and invested the proceeds in the Fine Cotton Spinners' and Doublers' Association, doubling their holding and increasing their control over their raw material. The hint, if hint it was, was taken ; the Spanish mill was converted to the spinning of cotton yarn for piece-goods, and the English Company agreed to bring their agents under proper control by transferring the foreign sales business of their numerous branches to the Central Thread Agency which still continued to act as the sales department of the Coats amalgamation.

The first two years of the English Sewing Cotton Company's existence appeared to be prosperous, but the trading profit for 1900-1 was £69,846, or 38 per cent., less than that of the preceding year, the interim dividend which had been paid was not justified, and £50,000 had to be transferred from reserve. This astounding *débâcle* in a year in which J. & P. Coats distributed 50 per cent. on their ordinary shares naturally caused great turmoil among the shareholders, and the next two years were spent in continuous recrimination and investigation, ending in administrative reconstruction. The net profits of the company for 1898-99 were £172,992 ; for 1899-1900, £97,335 ; for 1900-1, £43,382 ; and for 1901-2 a loss of £127,006 was shown ; the price of the ordinary shares fell from 47s. 6d. in 1899 to 9s. 6d. in 1902. The finance of the company had been deplorable, for £112,000 of adventitious profits arising from the flotation of the American Thread Company had been mixed up with the ordinary trading profits. Mr. Diamond, a director and a leader of the reform movement, showered pungent criticisms on the management. He said that " he found that the cost of selling their goods in Canada was 32 per cent. He had made an arrangement with the Central Agency, who were already conducting the company's foreign business, whereby they stated that they could sell in Canada at a cost of 9 to 10 per cent. In the home department they had no protection ; everything was done in a haphazard, hand-to-mouth fashion " (Meeting of London shareholders, 13th March, 1902).[1]   And in a circular he spoke of " the gross over-capitalisation, the questionable finance, the extravagant and inefficient management, the bad buying, bad manufacturing, and bad selling ".[2]

With regard to over-capitalisation, the land, buildings, and machinery were valued in the ordinary way by a firm of valuers at £744,497, but as, according to Mr. Waterhouse, the new chairman appointed in 1902, " for some time, if not from the beginning of the combine, the machinery had produced barely half the total possible output," it would appear that the company was burdened with a quantity of machinery and buildings for which it had no use, and whose value, however correctly reckoned out by the valuers, was for the purposes of the company nil.   The auditors presented with the accounts for 1902-3 a report [3] on the sums paid for goodwill to the several vendors. The average profits of the several concerns " during the few years immediately preceding the formation of the company— not to be regarded as absolutely correct, but sufficiently so for the purpose of comparison "—aggregated to £56,537, and the sum paid for goodwill, £447,131, was nearly eight years' purchase.   In one case the vendor received nothing for goodwill, in three others less than three years' purchase of their profits, one, who showed a loss of £602, received £1,158, and the others from five to twenty years' purchase.   These sums were arranged by the accountant in consultation with a committee of the vendors.

On the question of management, experience showed that the whole scheme of organisation was faulty. Mr. Lawton, the vice-chairman, admitted at the annual meeting in August, 1901, that " it was an awful mistake to put into control of the various businesses purchased by the company the men from whom the businesses were purchased, because these men had

---

[1] *Financial Times*, 14th March, 1902.   [2] *Ibid.*, 27th March, 1902.
[3] *Ibid.*, 4th August, 1903.

got into one groove and could not get out of it ".[1] Many of these managers were also members of the board of directors and could not be active in both capacities, with the result that the three managing directors were overburdened. The board was not only composed of men of—to put it gently—unequal ability, but it was also too large for effective working. An executive committee of five was appointed by the board, but it became a prey to dissensions. Little wonder that Mr. Lawton and other directors should openly, and almost ostentatiously, confess that " the administration of the company had been inefficient and extravagant "[2]—it could hardly be anything else. They did not even adopt Messrs. Coats' system of costing, by which " every halfpenny stamp could be traced," although it had been put at their disposal. " They did not do so," said Mr. Lawton, " because they were ineffective in their management." There were indeed many difficulties in the way of economy. The constituent businesses were widely scattered, making concentration difficult, and if any branches were closed—as three were up to 1903—their value still burdened the books of the company. On the other hand, if the mills were left open their capacity was in excess of the volume of trade, and standing charges went on while the machinery stood idle. And to crown all, 1900 was a year in which coal rose in price nearly 50 per cent., cotton doubled in value, and silk rose one-third with severe fluctuations.

The contrast with the Coats' Company is striking. We begin with a comparison of an amalgamation composed only of sound efficient firms with one in which the only object apparently was to sweep every one into the net, and we go on to the antithesis of ability admirably equipped at every point and " inefficiency and extravagance ". Nor is this the last occasion on which the lesson is driven home in the history of English combinations that the mere aggregation of numbers is by itself no guarantee of success. Moderate capitalisation, economy, and, above all, good management, are the indispensable requisites.

[1] *Financial Times*, 30th August, 1901.
[2] *Manchester Guardian*, 24th April, 1902.

The shareholders appointed a committee with Mr. Philippi, of Coats, at its head to prepare a scheme of re-organisation, and their recommendations were adopted in the autumn of 1902. The directors were reduced to seven at salaries of £500 a year each and £1,000 to the chairman. Not more than five of the directors might get, by vote of the board, an additional £500 each, per annum, on condition that they should give their whole time to the company; in any year in which the ordinary dividend exceeded 5 per cent. the board was to get an additional £2,000 for every 1 per cent. in excess, to be divided among their members—a premium upon efficiency. Messrs. J. & P. Coats, who had supported the "reform" movement throughout, agreed " to give the necessary financial assistance as also advice regarding suitable manufacturing and selling arrangements". The company was, in fact, put under the tutelage of the great Paisley concern, and it was significant that the new board only contained two representatives of the old vendors. Messrs. Coats, however, declined to nominate a representative. The old agreement between the two companies had been that "the parties to it shall preserve, maintain, and have protection for the trade they have done in the recent past, not interfering with each other's business". To ensure the satisfactory performance of this agreement, the Central Thread Agency, which marketed Lister's silks as well as the products of Messrs. Coats, took over in 1900 the foreign trade of the English Sewing Cotton Co. with unquestionable advantages to all parties, and some years afterwards the home selling business of the English Co. was similarly taken over. The old Spanish quarrel was finally disposed of in 1905 by concentrating all the leading thread mills in Spain under one management controlled by J. & P. Coats.

The difficulties were not entirely removed by the reconstruction. " Any business man knows," wrote J. & P. Coats to the English Co. in 1905, "that it is very much easier to maintain a business than to transform one working at a loss into a remunerative one, or to regain trade lost by carelessness and mismanagement, and how difficult it is to shake off the effects of failure and of the distrust and disorganisation resulting therefrom."[1]   Yet the new board met with considerable success, and reduced the expenses of administration and distribution.   The debit balance brought forward from 1901-2, £110,793, was increased to £224,635 by writing back to capital reserve account the profits of the flotation of the American Thread Co., but by 1904-5 the whole of the arrears of preference dividend were wiped off and £31,052 was carried forward.   The high cost of cotton in 1904 produced a great falling off in the profits derived from the American Thread Co. for 1904-5, the reduction in its dividend from 16 to 8 per cent. representing a loss of £69,500. In the autumn of 1904 power was taken to sell three of the businesses in whole or in part; these were Sir Richard Arkwright & Co., S. Manlove & Co., and John Dewhurst & Co., and had originally cost £713,000.   "Principally owing to re-arrangements," said the deputy-chairman, "consequent upon the concentration of the manufacturing processes, they were no longer required for the purposes of the company."   The price was not disclosed, but it was to be made by a cancellation of debentures.   Other vendors had also agreed to surrender debentures without receiving any consideration in exchange.   With the general improvement in trade came prosperity to the English Sewing Cotton Co. also.   For the year 1905-6 their net profit, after providing for depreciation and directors' remuneration, was £286,582, which enabled them to pay a welcome dividend of 8 per cent. and put £70,000 to reserves.

The Linen Thread Co. completes the organisation of the thread industry.   It was formed in 1898-99 by the union of six firms—Wm. Barbour & Sons, Limited, Lisburn; Barbour Bros. & Co., New York; Barbour Flax Spinning Co., Paris and New Jersey; Finlayson, Bousfield, & Co., Johnstone, N.B., and Grafton, U.S.A.; W. & J. Knox, Kilbirnie, N.B.; and the Marshall Thread Co., New York.   The nominal capital is £2,000,000 but there was no public flotation.   Although far behind the cotton thread group in size the two are alike in their international character and in being dominated by one large constituent.   Messrs. Barbour were reported to be the largest linen thread manufacturers in the world.   Messrs. Coats are connected with the undertaking, and are represented on the board by Sir T. G. Coats. In March, 1906, a fresh issue of £200,000 was made, and the Boston Thread and Twine Co. was to be acquired.

Few of the large textile combinations have fully met the expectations with which they were founded, but among the number the Fine Cotton Spinners' and Doublers' Association occupies a prominent position. It was formed in May, 1898, " for the purpose of amalgamating into one concern the under-mentioned companies and firms "—which numbered thirty-one —" engaged in spinning fine (Sea Island) cotton, or in doubling yarns made from this and other staples of cotton ". The prospectus claimed that the business was steady and non-speculative and possessed of a kind of monopoly-value. " The extreme difficulty of inducing consumers of fine yarns to accept the risk of using new or unknown marks in the manufacture of the expensive fabrics into which this class of yarns so largely enters renders an established connection indispensable. This fact adds to the value of those long existent concerns which have won a reputation and gained the confidence of buyers, and at the same time places an obstacle in the way of new competitors." This, besides, was a peculiarly British industry, safeguarded by well-known suitability of the climate of Lancashire for fine spinning. Additional profits were expected from the cessation of unnecessary competition, " the centralisation of office work and of buying, selling, and distribution," the specialisation of mills, the " application to each individual concern (as far as possible) of the combined practical experience of the whole of the board of directors, which is exclusively composed of experts in this branch of business ". These were the common-places of amalgamation finance. The capital issued was £4,000,000, equally divided into 4 per cent. debentures, 5 per cent. cumulative preference shares, and ordinary shares, and one-third of each class was taken by the vendors. " Goodwill " was moderate, being reckoned on a three years' basis. The prospectus held forth the probability that the ordinary dividend would be at the rate of 8½ per cent., " assuming the same profits as in the past ". The management was entrusted to a board of twenty-six directors, of whom seven formed the "executive board".

Sea Island cotton is narrowly limited in quantity, for it is only grown on the islands off the sea-board of the southern United States, and it is only approached in quality by the best Egyptian staples. There was thus a clear possibility of a monopoly before the Fine Spinners, and the process of consolidation of the industry went merrily on. During the first year five additional businesses were purchased, including a Lisle company, and shortly afterwards the Musgrave Spinning Co., of Bolton, with 377,000 spindles was added, raising the total spindleage to 2,873,000, besides 220,000 in France. Five more businesses were acquired in the next two years, and in addition a dominant interest was purchased in La Société Anonyme des Filatures Delebart Mallet Fils—an old-established firm with a capital of £400,000, the most important French competitor of the company. In the course of 1900 the Bradford Colliery Co. was purchased by the issue of £450,000 debentures, an acquisition which produced a very considerable mitigation of the effects of the high price of coal on the cost of production. By the end of the fourth year there were forty-two associated companies, besides subsidiary companies which included the Colliery Company, Delebart Mallet Fils, Carver Bros., and some smaller concerns, and the capital was raised to £6,350,000. Five further acquisitions were made up to 31st March, 1905, and the capital raised to £7,250,000.

The financial history is summarised in the following table :—

Year Ended 31st March.	Profits, less Depreciation, etc.	Placed to Depreciation, etc.	Placed to Reserve.	Dividend on Ordinary.
1899	£362,927	£70,038	£80,000	8 per cent.
1900	469,421	102,981	100,000	8 ,,
1901	493,935	130,836	100,000	9 ,,
1902	364,008	132,118	50,075	8 ,,
1903	416,749	140,000	50,000	8 ,,
1904	384,267	140,000	nil.	8 ,,
1905	241,447	140,000	*40,000	4 ,,
1906	402,441	140,000	†40,000	6 ,,

* Withdrawn.   † Making total reserve, £700,000.

The bad results of the two years 1903-4 and 1904-5 reflect the condition of the whole cotton industry in those years—the years of the cotton corner and short supplies. The advantageous position which a trust is supposed to occupy in relation to those from whom it purchases proved to be of little use in face of the universal upward movement in the price of cotton. In 1903 Middling American cotton rose from 4·66d. in January to 7·46d. in December, and from January to April, 1904, it ranged from 7·64d. to 8·96d., the prices of fine Sea Island varying similarly; the prices of "good fair Egyptian" rose from $7\frac{9}{16}$d. in January to $10\frac{15}{16}$d. in June, 1903, keeping afterwards above 8d. in the first four months of 1904, and reaching in that period a maximum of $10\frac{1}{2}$d. a lb. Throughout 1904 the price of Egyptian cotton was 60 per cent., and in 1905 75 per cent. above the normal. In fact the growers for once had the game in their own hands—a short crop and a demand which had increased all over the world were "bull" factors too strong for any combination to contend with, however strong its sectional position might be. Not only were the prices of raw cotton high, but the demand for fine cotton goods was slack, partly on account of the increased cost of the raw material, partly on account of the diminished power of consumption which had been evident in the country since the close of the South African war. Even when the cotton position improved and prices fell with the incoming of the new crop of 1904 matters did not improve for the Fine Cotton Spinners' Co., for the stock which they had accumulated in the first part of 1904-5 now seriously depreciated in value and their loss under that head during the year was £100,000. Something has already been said of the ease with which fresh competition may be started in the cotton-spinning industry, and on this point Sir W. Holland, M.P., said at the annual meeting in May, 1905: "There had been during the year an extraordinary mania for building new mills for the spinning of fine counts—a matter which of course the directors could not put a stop to. Obviously the result of the new spindles started was to increase the production, and to that they must add the diminished demand in accounting for the position. He did not regard the state of affairs with alarm, however. At present there was a big demand for the coarser counts, and a good many of those new spindles were being diverted for that purpose. When the present gap in the Far East was filled these spindles, it was not unreasonable to suppose, would return to fine counts, and the demand for their output would increase." In 1905 the demand improved with the return of prosperity at home, and the improvement is amply shown in the returns for 1905-6. But the experience of this time of stress makes it plain that the Fine Cotton Spinners, despite their monopoly of the spinning of Sea Island cotton, are not really a monopoly ; they cannot free themselves from the competition of the spinners of fine Egyptian yarns, they cannot free themselves from the cotton growers in time of scarcity, and they cannot control a demand which is mainly dependent on the general prosperity of the country.

The career of the Fine Cotton Spinners having been prosperous, its domestic affairs have come less under the notice of the public than has been the case with less fortunate companies. Three small branches have been closed and their machinery transferred to other branches. All the works spin the counts of yarn they were in the habit of doing before the association started, but there is a certain amount of specialisation in that some firms spin certain counts for which they are best suited. Details of organisation are largely a matter of inference. We may assume that since the directors are managers of branches, and in that capacity must take orders from the executive board, the balance of power probably lies with the latter. That is always a delicate situation, and depends for its possibility entirely on the personal qualities of the men concerned ; in some companies the powers of the managing directors have been cut down after experience, in others the powers of the managers have had to be reduced. The managing directors meet daily, the executive board weekly, and the general board monthly. Mr. Scott Lings, in an address to the Millers' Convention in 1901, spoke of the necessity of ensuring that the directors of the future should be at least equal to those who had been trained in the hard school of competition, and said : " In the case of the Fine Cotton Spinners the difficulty had been foreseen. . . . Young men of good family were put into the different works as apprentices. They were there for a year on trial first, and if they liked the work and were themselves liked, an arrangement was made with them, and they had always the inducements before them that they could rise to the head of the branch; they might afterwards go to the central office and become executive directors, and they might be chairmen of the institution at some future time."

The central office keeps all the branches in hand through the statistical department which enables a close comparison to be made of the concerns doing the same class of work. Buying and selling and machinery form other main departments in addition to the ordinary secretarial and accounts work. The central office passes all prices. The strength of the association lies in its power, through the suppression of competition, to undertake large contracts absorbing sometimes the total output of three or four mills. The recent revival in the cotton trade has been mainly in connection with large orders and 1906 has been called "a big man's year".

The Bleachers' Association dates from July, 1900, and is an amalgamation of fifty-three firms and companies engaged in the bleaching and finishing of cotton piece-goods of every description. Here for the first time something of the character of a natural monopoly is encountered, for the prospectus claimed that "the great and ever-increasing difficulty of obtaining an adequate supply of water renders the position of the old-established bleachworks a very strong one, while enforcement of the law against pollution of rivers tends still further to prevent the erection of new works". This is also one of the comparatively rare cases in which we can trace the evolution of an amalgamation from terminable associations. "For a great number of years past," said the prospectus, "there have existed in the Manchester bleaching trade voluntary associations for the regulation of prices in different branches of the business, and for other purposes, and these have worked in harmony with the merchants as well as to the advantage of the trade; but it has been realised that the full advantages of co-operation can be secured only by amalgamation, for the success of which the existence and organisation of these associations give exceptional facilities. The present amalgamation has secured the adhesion of many firms who were not previously members of any price association." All the firms were situated within easy distance of Manchester, except four Scotch and two Irish firms engaged in special branches. A few firms had dyeing businesses, one of which was to be sold to the Bradford Dyers' Association ; the trusts quickly see that it does not pay to fight each other. The board of directors consisted of forty-nine members, the general management being vested in two general managers who were to be paid by a commission of 2½ per cent. on the net profits after payment of debenture and preference interest. The branches were to remain in the hands of their previous owners who were to be remunerated in part by a commission on their individual profits. " Each firm will continue to deal personally with their own customers, and arrangements which have been made by individual firms with regard to special finishes for particular customers will be strictly adhered to."

The average profits for the five years 1895-99 were stated to be £372,465, and a 6 per cent. ordinary dividend was foretold. The purchase money was £6,480,813 ; as quick assets were valued at £3,456,911, and £269,187 cash was provided, goodwill, patents, etc., amounted to £2,754,715, or a little over seven years' profits—distinctly excessive even for a business described as " steady and prosperous . . . pre-eminently a safe trade ". The issued capital was £6,750,000, equally divided into 4½ per cent. debentures, 5½ per cent. cumulative preference shares, and ordinary shares. In part payment of purchase money £710,310 of each class was allotted to the vendors, but the market was already sick with the strain of the South African war, and all the ordinary shares had to be taken up by the vendors, an action which redounded greatly to their credit.

The capital at the end of 1906 stood at £6,820,096, issued and paid up. Three businesses were subsequently acquired in 1900-1, one in 1901-2, and in January, 1906, a fifth, the River Etherow Bleaching Co., was purchased for £475,000 in cash. At least one branch has been closed. It was soon found that the troubles of combination only began after formation of the " combine," and at the annual meeting in 1901 the chairman spoke of the " difficulties which were inseparable from the early days of a large combination like their own—the mastering of details, the working up of backward concerns, and the wheeling of the whole into line". After the known experiences of the Calico Printers it is hardly to be supposed that the work of re-organisation was particularly furthered at mass meetings of forty-nine directors, each specially and keenly interested in the welfare of the branch on the profits of which he was paid a commission as manager. At all events in June, 1904, the articles of association were altered so that the board might be able to delegate to a smaller body the multitudinous questions which came before them, and at the same time the unusually extensive powers of the general managers were restricted.

Like every other manufacturing concern the Bleachers' Association was enormously hampered by the very high price of coal. The average price of Newcastle steam coal for 1888-97 was 9s. 10½d. a ton ; in 1899 the price was 12s. ; in 1900, 17s. 6d. ; in 1901, 12s. 6d. ; in 1902, 11s. 3d. ; in 1903, 10s. 6d. ; in 1904, 9s. 6d. ; and in 1905, 9s. 3d. With other commodities it was the same ; the price of bleaching powder in the three years of the syndicate, 1899-1902, was 26 per cent. above 1898-99, which were years of uncontrolled competition. Like all the other cotton trades the bleaching industry was seriously affected by the stagnation in the home market, by the high prices and short supply of cotton and by fluctuations in the export trade due first to famine in India, then to disturbances in China, and latterly to the Russo-Japanese war. The exports of bleached piece-goods have been as follows :—

	Million Yards.
5 years' average, 1895-99	1,294
1899	1,355·6
1900	1,306·2
1901	1,533·3
1902	1,383·7
1903	1,326·5
1904	1,528·1
1905	1,709·8

In comparing these figures with the revenue figures which follow the overlapping of the periods must not be overlooked. The net profit shown is after deduction of depreciation.

	Net Profit. £	Depreciation and Maintenance. £	Reserves. £	Ordinary Dividend. Per Cent.
15 months to 30/6/01	334,138	174,789	nil.	nil.
9 ,, 31/3/02	300,776	115,590	80,000	3
Year to 31/3/03	395,176	159,600	80,000	3
,, 31/3/04	321,779	165,896	80,000	nil.
,, 31/3/05	364,658	170,665	80,000	2
,, 31/3/06	477,670	149,900	50,000	4

The average profit for 1895-99, when the export trade was much less, was £372,465, but of this, if a 6 per cent. dividend had been paid, only £12,000 would have been available for reserve. The policy of building up a strong reserve is unquestionably sound but it only brings into stronger light the over-capitalisation of goodwill. That two and three-quarter millions was equal to all the ordinary stock issued and nearly a quarter of the preference shares, and even if a handsome allowance be made for patents still patents run out and must be written down. It is true that the vendors took all the ordinary stock themselves, and that if they chose to capitalise in anticipation the advantages they hoped to gain from amalgamation that was their own look-out, while persons who have bought in the open market since have done so at prices (as low as 7s.), which took no regard for the water in the stock. That is all very true but the standing of a company is disadvantageously affected by such finance. The American habit of looking upon common stock as a gambling counter has never been popular in Britain where investors perversely expect dividends, and good dividends too, from ordinary shares.

The last stage in the production of cotton fabrics is the ornamenting of them either by turkey-red dyeing or calico printing. Both arts originated in Scotland in the eighteenth century, and were later introduced into Lancashire. The turkey-red trade is associated with the family of Orr Ewing and has been the source of great fortunes. To meet English competition the three leading Scotch firms united to form the United Turkey Red Co., and in 1898 a fourth firm was absorbed which turned out fancy dyes. It has a practical monopoly of the trade, and beyond that its capital is £1,500,000 particulars of its working are not forthcoming. The calico printing industry is mainly shared between F. Steiner & Co., Ltd., and the Calico Printers'

Association. The former company was incorporated in 1897, but originated in the beginning of the nineteenth century, and its capital is £1,375,000. The prospectus of the Calico Printers' Association, issued in December, 1899, announced the amalgamation of forty-six firms of printers, fourteen located near Glasgow and the rest in the neighbourhood of Manchester, five firms of Glasgow merchants, five Manchester merchants, and three merchant firms with branches in both towns—fifty-nine firms and companies in all. Three of these also did a spinning and weaving business. The plant included 830 printing machines, 277,264 cotton spindles, and 6,656 power looms. "The businesses acquired comprise about 85 per cent. of the calico printing industry in Great Britain. The strength of the association is shown by the fact that it includes nearly every leading house of the trade, and that these supply goods not only to all branches of the home trade, but practically to every open market of the world. The businesses also deal with all sections of the trade, and include the production of every description of printed cotton, dress goods, furnitures, cretonnes, linings, flannelettes, and also of delaines and mixed fabrics. . . . Though some of the firms included in this Association have been and are earning large profits, the results of the trading generally for the past few years have been of an unsatisfactory nature, attributable chiefly to internal competition and cutting of prices" (Prospectus).

The average profits of the preceding five years, after deducting salaries of management, but before charging income tax and interest on capital and loans, were certified to be £455,826, from which the valuers considered £100,000 should be provided for depreciation. The directors considered that the two years 1897 and 1898 were years of exceptional difficulty and depression, and desired "to emphasise their opinion that as the outcome of the amalgamation far different and more profitable results may be confidently expected in the near future than have been realised for many years past". The reasons for this opinion were that in the past much loss had arisen from undercutting and overlapping and "an immense waste in sampling, engraving, and pattern distribution," while "large economies" were to be effected by "the centralisation of buying and finance and concentration of production". "In regard to possible competition the directors point out the following elements of security for the business of the association : (*a*) That the magnitude of the operations will practically insure to them the first offer of all new inventions and discoveries relative to the trade, and also the best productions of the designer and engraver. (*b*) That calico printing is in itself a difficult and complicated business, and that the best quality of work is obtainable, not so much by the skill of any one individual as by the combination of skilled workers under highly organised and experienced management. (*c*) That owing to the very large savings which can be made in the expenses of production, all competition, whether in the home trade or in neutral foreign markets, will be met upon much more favourable terms than hitherto. Certain markets are at present closed to English prints owing to hostile tariffs. It will in the future be possible to carry on works in foreign countries under most favourable conditions as regards designs, engraved rollers, etc., and in a way which was not practicable when such action depended solely upon the initiative of individual firms. The association already owns a large works in France."

The purchase price of the amalgamated properties was £8,047,031, and the issued capital was £3,200,000 in 4 per cent. debentures, and £5,000,000 in ordinary shares, the vendors taking £1,066,666 debenture stock and £1,595,170 ordinary shares. As the certified profits, less depreciation, only showed a produce of £4 6s. 10d. per cent., it was plain that the vendors had capitalised their expectations and included them in their sale to the public. Of course, it may be said that had they not done so the realisation of the economies resulting from the amalgamation would simply have increased the market price of the shares, whereas the enchancement in value ought really to belong to those to whose efforts it was due. But expectations are always ticklish things to convert into cash, and the immediate effect was that the company started with a heavy burden of over-capitalisation. There were no intermediate profits in the purchase of the businesses, but Mr. Ernest Crewdson, who negotiated the amalgamation, received from the vendors 2 per cent. on their purchase price, out of which he had to discharge all the preliminary expenses except investigation of title and some other legal charges. But the company started under an almost worse handicap still—the board of directors consisted of eighty-four members, of whom eight were managing directors. The form of administration, in fact, resembled the crude democratic expedient of government by mass meeting. The Calico Printers' Association at the time of its formation was, measured by capitalisation, the largest in the kingdom, but it was a lumbering leviathan.

The first fifteen months' trading, ending 31st December, 1900, showed a net profit of £446,452, after deducting head office charges, and providing £219,334 for upkeep and depreciation. Debenture interest was met but no ordinary dividend was paid; owing to delay in completing the contracts of purchase, £202,550 was paid as interest to vendors, which may be taken as the equivalent of $3\frac{1}{4}$ per annum on the £5,000,000 ordinary shares. The speech of the chairman at the annual meeting [1] was even more ominous than the figures in the report. " The eighty directors," he said, " were but imperfectly acquainted with each other, or, what was of greater importance, with each other's views." As for the economies foreshadowed in the prospectus, " it must be apparent to them that all changes aiming at reduced expenditure could not but be unpopular with those who were affected thereby, and who were to get less in order that the shareholders might get more than the old order of things admitted of. They had, in consequence, met with much opposition and obstruction. . . . He would go further and admit that it took many months before they fully realised the magnitude of the task of organising so large a company on suitable lines, or efficiently controlling the numerous businesses for which they had become responsible, and of initiating the reforms and improvements from which increased profits were to be derived. In plain English, they were not equal to the task. The situation created by the amalgamation of concerns which had in the past

---

[1] *Financial Times*, 1st May, 1901.

keenly competed against each other, and which had been worked upon widely different lines, was so novel that, in attempting to deal with matters which undoubtedly required to be adjusted, serious mistakes were made which affected their business injuriously, alienated the sympathy of many of their customers at a most critical time, and gave their competitors the opportunity of securing a great amount of business at their expense." In this apology there was much that was just, but these arguments should have been taken into account in capitalising the economies, while they obviously were not.

The results for 1901 were even worse. After deducting £191,684 for upkeep and depreciation, the trading profit was £74,714, and after deducting administration expenses, law charges, interest and bank charges, depreciation of copper stock, and preliminary expenses, there remained £22,140. With the help of the balance from last year, £144,367, the debenture interest was met and £38,525 was carried forward. A good deal of this loss was due to bad foreign trade. For the five years, 1890-94, exports of cotton prints averaged 954,473,620 yards, and for 1895-99, 992,899,900 yards, while for 1900 they fell to 957,914,800 yards, and in 1901 to 909,998,500 yards. There had also been heavy losses in reducing the stocks carried forward from the previous year. Fifteen indifferently equipped works had been closed, laying up £528,000 capital, after allowing for transfers; this reduction had not, however, affected the output, for out of the 175 machines involved twenty-two were transferred to other works and 140 had not been running before the association was formed. A central authority, both for finance and buying, and a central warehouse had been set up since August, 1900, with good results. Apologies, however, were now useless, and the directors tore away the veil which had shrouded the dissension of the past. Mr. Lennox Lee, one of the managing directors, explained the existing scheme of management to the shareholders:[1] "First there was a general body of directors, a body consisting of seventy or eighty members, upon whom rested the direct responsibility to the shareholders, and which

---

[1] *Manchester Guardian*, 25th March, 1902.

had the absolute control of the business of the association. These seventy or eighty gentlemen were for the most part members of a large body of vendors, and were selected by a mechanical process based upon the number of machines which their respective branches possessed. Secondly, there was the large body of 128 vendors, each of whom had an agreement giving him the management of his own branch for five years, and was, under his agreement, largely independent of and free from control by the managing directors. Thirdly, there was a board of managing directors having certain specific powers in addition to most of the other powers of the directors, but with the limitation that their powers in many respects could at any time be cancelled or overridden by the general board. The position between the managing directors, the directors and the 128 vendors was, and had been, an unworkable one. . . . In fact the whole branches became unsettled, and the *esprit* which was essential to successful working was lost. Failure to carry out instructions, lack of continuity of policy, and unrest and discontent were bound to bring about unsatisfactory results in the conduct of the association's business as a whole, and, to his mind, these, more than anything else, were responsible for what had occurred." On the motion of the directors they were empowered to appoint a committee to draw up a new scheme of management. This committee consisted of six directors and six outsiders—Messrs. O. E. Philippi, of Messrs. J. & P. Coats ; Frank Hollins, of Horrockses, Crewdson, & Co. ; Sir William Mather, M.P., of Mather & Platt ; Edward Partington, of the Kellner Partington Paper Pulp Co.; John Stanning, Joint Managing Director of the Bleachers' Association ; and John Thomson, Chairman of the Manchester Chamber of Commerce, and China merchant. The assemblage of so many notable business men to draw up a business constitution was a unique event, and the result of their deliberations was worthy of the men who framed it. The instances are rare indeed in which the public are favoured with the views of business men about business policy, they are usually reserved for private consumption in their own businesses. The report of the Investigation Committee is the most important individual document at our disposal in the history of British combinations, and for that reason it is given in full in the Appendix.

The report confirmed to the fullest the disclosures which already had been made, and laid down the elementary principles that close central control and firm discipline were at the basis of good management.   The central feature of the Calico Printers' Association, as of all large combinations, was that it must be treated as "one concern, consisting of a number of component parts, controlled by a central authority," and not as a mere aggregation of disconnected businesses.   This harmony cannot be attained by "scattered individual effort," and the following scheme of administration was propounded: A, a Board of Directors of six to eight members; B, an Executive of two to four members; and C, Advisory Committees of three to eight members.   "The co-existence of three different bodies," said the Committee, "for the purpose of management is unusual, but a careful scrutiny of past and present difficulties leads to the belief that they are necessary separately to: (1) *Supervise* (Board); (2) *Administer* (Executive) ; and (3) *Advise* (Advisory Committee), whilst co-operating in the general control of the business and directing its policy."   The Executive and the Chairman of the Board were to form a Finance Committee, dealing, *inter alia*, with salaries and bonuses.   The members of the Executive were to attend the meetings of the Board with power to speak but not to vote.   "The Executive shall send to the Chairman of each Advisory Committee weekly, on fixed days, a list of the subjects requiring the attention of his Committee, and these agenda shall determine the frequency of the meetings of the Advisory Committees.   One or more members of the Executive shall be present at the meetings of the Advisory Committees.   It is essential that they follow the discussions and take part in them, so as to understand and appreciate the reasons for the recommendations of these Committees.   It is intended that the Advisory Committees shall primarily decide upon the measures necessary to increase the efficiency of the branches, and upon other matters allotted to them, and it will be the duty of the Executive to carry the recommendations of the Advisory Committees into effect.   It must, however, not be inferred therefrom that the members of the Executive merely occupy the position of managers, whose duty it is to carry out the instructions of Committees competent to enforce their decisions. They will have the right to decline to adopt any recommendation of the Advisory Committees if they think that it would be hurtful to the interests of the association to carry it into effect. Should such difference of opinion arise, it shall be submitted to the Board of Directors whose decision, must be final. If the Board of Directors is applied to with reference to a matter of this kind, it should give to the chairman or any other member of the Advisory Committee in question an opportunity of explaining its views." Detailed reports as to the proceedings of these Committees were to be laid before the Board at its monthly meetings. Seven Committees were recommended : Works Production ; Designs, Styles, etc. ; Concentration ; Prices ; Trading ; Cloth Buying ; Drugs, Stores, Coal, etc.

The Investigating Committee further insisted that " any useful or even intelligent control " was impossible without a statistical department " for the purpose of collecting information upon every matter concerning any one of the businesses belonging to the Association, and of furnishing such information at a moment's notice ". The reward of merit received prominence as one of the most difficult problems before the management. Commission on profits would operate unjustly owing to differences in the profitable character of the classes of work done at different branches, but " it is necessary to introduce in some form the system of payment by results, and a suitable method of doing so will have to be devised," so as to reward men who did good work in any direction. One method of encouragement would be appointment to an Advisory Committee, where men, after a good training in the best branches, would be placed in positions of influence and responsibility.

The salient points of the scheme are : First, the concentration of power into a few able hands instead of its dispersion among a discordant mob which only needed shillelaghs to make a Donnybrook Fair. Second, the creation of machinery for bringing the best brains to bear upon every department of the business instead of leaving that desirable object to chance.

Third, insistence on the need of efficiency, in fact, that it still requires business ability to run a combination, an elementary fact generally forgotten in the extinction of competition. "Too much reliance is placed upon the possibility of obtaining higher prices, whereas it is in the case of a public company of the greatest importance to supervise every item of expenditure, to closely compare the cost of production and of distribution with what it was formerly, and to reduce it wherever this can be done with safety." Sir William Mather added a separate report, urging the formation of a Central Research Department " equipped with necessary appliances for research and experimental work, conducted by the ablest and best-trained chemists, specially qualified to pursue investigations, in which chemical processes and mechanical and electrical appliances are involved. This department would form a ' Clearing House' for difficulties experienced in any branch works in carrying out complicated processes, and in the introduction of new colours and methods of production. It would conduct research work having a direct bearing on desirable improvements and changes in processes. It would inquire into, and test if necessary, all new inventions, and obtain information from other countries of new developments in calico printing. It would form the brain of the business, always active and alert to supply the managers of the branches with expert knowledge without interference with the responsibility of such managers in obtaining the best practical results." This proposal was adapted from the best German practice in chemical and other industries.

The report was placed before the shareholders in September, 1902, and adopted. All the directors retired, and a new board of six, including Messrs. Hollins, Stanning, and Thomson of the Investigation Committee, was appointed, as well as an executive of three and the seven committees as recommended.

It will be convenient to insert here in tabular form the financial history of the association, profits being taken less upkeep, depreciation, head office charges, legal expenses, and depreciation of copper stocks.

	Net Profit.	Placed to Reserves.	Ordinary Dividend.
Average for 5 years, 1893-98	£455,826	—	
Fifteen months to 31st Dec., 1900	446,452	—	*
Year to 31st Dec., 1901	39,325	—	nil.
Six months to 30th June, 1902	225,366	£75,000	nil.
Year to 30th June, 1903	452,708	125,000	2½ per cent.
,, 1904	273,433	50,000	2½ ,,
,, 1905	323,680	50,000	2½ ,,
,, 1906	486,223	150,000	4 ,,

* Vendor's interest, £202,550 paid.

The first fruits of the new régime in its first eighteen months of operation were the creation of capital and revenue reserve funds, which met the complaint of the auditors that an insufficient amount had been written off for depreciation, and the allocation of £25,000 as bonuses to employees to be distributed according to the principles laid down in the report of the Investigation Committee. On the 30th June, 1903, goodwill stood at £510,292, and had not been written down; closed works stood at £675,184, after taking account of sales and transfers. About twenty works altogether have now been closed, and their value was £763,000 on 30th June, 1905, but the utility of the whole capital has thereby been increased, the surplus productive power existent in 1899 has been reduced, and the closed works are withheld from employment as competing printworks. Five additional printworks, one merchant's business, and one finishing business have been purchased, the last-mentioned increasing a department which had always been insufficiently equipped. A colliery has also been acquired. During the last few years the mills belonging to the association have been more largely employed in making cloth suitable for the requirements of the company, especially for the home trade, thereby increasing the profitable character of their merchant business. Bearing on Sir William Mather's report is the statement of the chairman at the annual meeting in September, 1905 : "The special commercial education of young men in their warehouses and technical education of lads in their works was making progress. They wished it to be known that youths who desired to enter their employment in either sphere, and who took advantage of the opportunities offered them for advanced education at Victoria University and the technical schools would be preferred." The

Research Department, however, has not yet been established, and the bonus granted to employees in 1903 has been dropped.

The greater part of the more satisfactory results of the last few years must be mainly attributed to the improved organisation. The bad effects of the disastrous cotton years 1904 and 1905 are manifest. Exports were in 1902, 961,289,300 yards; in 1903, 1,028,013,000 yards; in 1904, 1,036,733,000 yards; and in 1905, 1,053,674,000 yards. What the calico industry requires is a plentiful supply of cotton at a moderate price, for only on these conditions can an abundant demand from all classes of the community be expected. It will be useful to compare the results achieved by F. Steiner & Co.

		Ordinary Dividend.
Year to 30th June, 1899	. . . . .	8 per cent.
,, 1900	. . . . .	8 ,,
,, 1901	. . . . .	3 ,,
,, 1902	. . . . .	*nil.*
,, 1903	. . . . .	*nil.*
,, 1904	. . . . .	*nil.*
,, 1905	. . . . .	4 per cent.
,, 1906	. . . . .	5 ,,

Here we observe the same fluctuation and it must not be concluded that the higher dividend is proof of an essentially stronger position. The works in the association which are actually employed are doubtless as strong as the rival firm, but they have to bear the burden of practically paying the closed works not to compete. That makes the whole industry more effective and Messrs. Steiner & Co. profit indirectly thereby.

CHAPTER VI.

THE TEXTILE INDUSTRIES (*continued*).

In October, 1904, an agreement was signed between the Amalgamated Society of Dyers, the Gasworkers' and General Labourers' Union, and the Master Dyers' Association for the regulation of prices and wages in the dyeing industry of the West Riding of Yorkshire. Members of these trade unions undertook to work for the associated masters only, and the latter undertook to employ unionists exclusively except in the case of foremen, women, and children under sixteen, or if the unions were unable to supply suitable members. The *Labour Gazette* for October, 1894, summarised the method of working as follows: "A Wages Board is to be formed, which will consist of an equal number of employers and workmen, and its functions will be to prepare a list of minimum prices based upon the present wages, and a list of minimum wages for the (1) Bradford district, (2) Leeds and Halifax district, and (3) country districts; to take steps for carrying out the decisions of the Board, to consider the conditions of labour, and decide where an alteration in the price lists shall be made. It will also decide any disputes between employers and the unions as to the employment or discharge of men. For every 10 per cent. increase or decrease in the minimum price list there will be an increase or decrease of 5 per cent. in the wages list, subject to the proviso that there shall be no reduction upon the present rate of wages during the existence of the agreement." Any firms paying less than the minimum wage a year after signature of the agreement were to be required to raise their wages, unless by doing so they would reduce their profits below 5 per cent. The agreement was for twelve months, and em-

braced 60 per cent. of the employers and 90 per cent. of the
workpeople.   Attempts to force the non-associated employers
to sign the agreement led to three strikes in December, 1894,
and the Bradford Chamber of Commerce censured the Dyers'
Association for its coercive measures.   During the dispute the
Secretary of the Master Piece-Dyers' Association published a
statement that no attempt to enforce a uniform price list was
being made, that differences of price would exist as before, but
that prices below cost were to be abolished.   In March, 1896,
the minimum price list and the sliding scale were dropped and
standard lists of time wages' were drawn up.

So ended the attempt to organise the dyeing industry on
the model of the Birmingham Alliances, but nevertheless it was
the beginning of a movement which has ended in the complete
consolidation of the dyeing industry, there being no fewer than
five different amalgamations in its separate independent sections.   The most prominent of these, and the one which has
attained the greatest success, is the Bradford Dyers' Association.   This company was placed before the public in December,
1898, and was an amalgamation of twenty-two firms.   "The
businesses to be acquired," said the prospectus, "comprise about
90 per cent. of the Bradford piece-dyeing trade; two of the
firms have also extensive warp-dyeing departments.   These
works are situated in the midst of the great textile industrial
district of which Bradford is the centre, and thus the goods
pass from the manufacturers to the dyers, and from them to
the merchants with the greatest convenience and despatch, and
with the least amount of carriage.   As the value of the goods
dyed annually by the associated firms amounts to some 12
to 15 millions sterling, this constitutes an important factor.
The industry is one of great importance and magnitude, the
number of persons (mostly men) employed by the association
being about 7,500, and the consumption of coal alone about a
quarter of a million tons per annum.   The goods treated are in
use in almost every household in the United Kingdom, besides
being shipped to all parts of the world, and are of a very varied
character, embracing the finest silk, mohair, and wool fabrics as
well as the lowest cottons.   The business of the association is

thus not dependent on any particular market or branch of trade. At the same time the commercial risks attached to the business are reduced to a minimum, as the dyers do not trade in the goods, the work being all done on commission and on cash terms ; there is thus no risk or loss by falling markets, and the bad debts are inappreciable. The trade marks of many of the firms and companies in the association, representing a very large percentage of the work done, are known all the world over, and goods dyed under such trade marks are demanded by the users and distributors." The ordinary economies of combination were then set forth, and on the question of organisation the prospectus said : " It is intended as far as possible that the control of each firm shall remain in the hands of those who have been responsible for its conduct in the past, and in order that such management may have an inducement to continue to give their best efforts to the business, the directors are empowered under the articles to pay commissions on the profits of each individual branch, thus safeguarding the principle of individual effort, to which so much of the success of the past has been due. It is felt that this policy will be as much in the interests of the general trade as that of the company, seeing that thereby healthy competition and rivalry between the associated firms for excellence and quality of work will be maintained and encouraged." Seventeen of the firms were represented on the board of thirty-seven directors, three of whom were managing directors. The issued capital was £3,000,000 in equal proportions of 4 per cent. debentures, 5 per cent. cumulative preference shares, and ordinary shares, one-third of each class being taken by the vendors. Goodwill was valued at £681,388, or three years' purchase of the average profits of the preceding three years—£225,656. The total purchase price was £2,870,640.

By the spring of 1903 thirteen additional firms had been included and the chairman could say : " Thus, in four years from the inception of the association, the whole of the Bradford piece-dyeing trade has come within its folds. True, outside competitors have arisen ; and without cavilling at these in the slightest degree, we owe it to you to express ourselves clearly on one point. We have indisputable evidence that, in at least one instance, the root idea of the venture was to trade for a time and then sell to the association at a profit.   We are not buyers" (*Financial Times*, 27th February, 1903).   In a prospectus issued in April, 1906, the association were able to say that they had thirty-seven branches in Yorkshire and Lancashire—not including of course mills that had been closed, of which there were at least three.   One interesting point is that in two cases, at least, the dyeing branches of firms included in the Calico Printers' Association and Bleachers' Association were acquired, while certain mercerising branches were sold to the British Cotton and Wool Dyers, thus rounding off the borders of all three and preventing competition.   With the same object a community of interest was established with the British Cotton and Wool Dyers in 1900, when each company bought a holding of £50,000 shares in the other's stock.   The mutual agreement to regulate prices came to an end in 1901 but friendly relations were maintained; in 1906 the block of British Cotton shares was sold as there was no longer any object in holding it.   In 1906 £500,000 was issued in preference shares for extensions of branches and the equipment of new works for the dyeing of lower class goods, work which had hitherto been done by outside concerns, it being the opinion of the directors "that the earnings of the association can be considerably increased and its general position strengthened by undertaking" this class of work. Control over fuel supplies was to some extent secured when the Dyers' Association in 1899 took £50,000 shares in the Bradford Coal Merchants' Association, with the right to appoint two directors, conceding to the latter the sole right of supplying coal to all the branches.   Year by year the directors have carried out the policy of concentrating and sectionalising the various classes of work, upon which the success of combinations so largely depends.   But it is a policy which can only be carried out gradually, for as it involves the transfer of machinery between the branches and the reorganisation of equipment, "not only," as the chairman reminded the shareholders in 1903, "is the divisible revenue lessened by the consequent abnormal expenditure on repairs and renewals, but it suffers further from the temporary dislocation of trade and the greater difficulty and expense of production at the branches whilst the work of transfer and re-organisation is in progress ".   A central buying department was early established and considerable economies accrued from the advantageous terms on which dye-wares could be obtained. Testing laboratories for this department were also instituted, and a department for the sale of job goods was set up.   Work-men's compensation, insurance, banking, and patents were also dealt with from the central office with much saving of time and energy.   Other important points of policy were the appointment in 1902 of a representative at Shanghai to attend to the interests of the company and develop its trade with the Far East, and the undertaking in 1903 of an extensive and methodical plan of advertisement in the United States.   These are specially interesting as the enterprising efforts of a subsidiary trade to improve its position indirectly by attempting to further the general development of the textile industry, or at least that section of it concerned with Bradford piece-goods.

Naturally this policy of absorption and enterprise could not be carried on without an increase of capital, which now stands at £4,810,227.   The net profits are shown as under, after pro-viding for repairs, renewals, and depreciation :—

				Profits.	Ordinary Dividend.
1900 .	.	.	.	£250,916	9 per cent.
1901 .	.	.	.	233,463	7 ,,
1902 .	.	.	.	262,260	7 ,,
1903 .	.	.	.	239,994	7 ,,
1904 .	.	.	.	266,748	7 ,,
1905 .	.	.	.	274,166	7 ,,
1906 .	.	.	.	366,087	7 ,,

The reserve fund amounts to £285,372, of which £130,000 is invested in trustee securities and the rest in the business.   These figures show that the association has progressed in strength despite the vicissitudes of a period characterised by unfavourable conditions in the wool market and diminished purchasing power among the general population.   The profits before amalgamation have in every year been exceeded, and the prospectus forecast of a 7 per cent. dividend has been fulfilled.

The price policy of the association contains many points of interest.   With the object of crushing out the competition of some new firms, which had been started in some cases by former employees of the association, an attempt was made to induce merchants to agree to deal exclusively with the association. The *Yorkshire Post*, of 30th January, 1902, published the following document:—

"Memorandum of Agreement between Messrs. and the Bradford Dyers' Association (Limited), dated 190 , and extending till   19 .

"The Bradford Dyers' Association (Limited) undertake for the above period:—

"(*a*) To keep you automatically on its lowest prices and most favourable terms and rebates.

"(*b*) To give preference in time, in case of pressure of work, to your orders, and preference in the offer of any new process which may be initiated by the Bradford Dyers' Association (Limited) over those firms who have not entered into an agreement similar to this.

"(*c*) To make you a rebate from this date on quantities to a shade, as per particulars herewith. (This rebate will be made by credit note from the branch on receipt of the dyeing order.)

"(*d*) To pay you a rebate of $2\frac{1}{2}$ per cent. on the amount of annual net cash payment in excess of £   (sum stated).

"(*e*) An additional rebate of $2\frac{1}{2}$ per cent. on any one line of goods done with one branch reaching £5,000 net in the course of a year. (These rebates (*d*) and (*e*) to cover the period from   to   and be payable   .)

"Signed (on behalf of the Association)."

"We undertake to the Bradford Dyers' Association (Limited) to send it all our dyeing work from the present date till   , with the exception of such as is now endorsed on the annexed sheet or may be added by mutual agreement from time to time.

"Signed (on behalf of the Merchant Firm)."

"Accompanying the agreement" (continued the *Yorkshire Post*), "is a table of 'exceptions from the guarantee of the whole business for the period ending . . .,' and in this the 'guarantor' (such is the euphemistic term for the 'tied-house' merchant) is asked to set out: (1) The class of goods for which he asks exception; (2) the outside dyer he prefers; (3) the approximate quantity of goods; and (4) the reasons for exemption. This latter document is an especially ingenious method of conducting an inquisition into the affairs of the outside dyers. This much is frankly admitted by the management of the Dyers' Association, but in addition they reserve the right of veto, *i.e.*, 'they agree or they do not agree to the exceptions proposed'. The manner in which they then work is this: If a certain number of merchants claim exemption from one class of goods in favour of a certain dyer, the Association, by the 'approximate quantity' clause, obtain an estimate of the amount of trade that dyer is doing in those goods. It is a simple thing by observation and in other ways to check quantities; it is equally simple to arrive at prices by inquiry among the 'guarantors'. Thereafter a circular is issued cutting prices in these particular lines too low to make competition possible."

That is a hostile view. The case as put forward by the Association in a circular was that: "Our intentions are: (1) To make you secure, against your competitors, of proper protection and all reasonable advantages, according to the proportion of your trade; (2) to resist cutting of prices below normal proportions where this cannot increase the total business, and where the only effect can be to give a temporary and undue advantage to one firm over another; (3) to devote any such cutting of prices to lines which will increase the total amount of business. . . . We shall not hesitate to give you immediate exemption for all goods which you are having at present more satisfactorily treated in your opinion, or at any time for any goods which we cannot deliver in reasonable time. . . . You will observe that we keep you automatically, and without any attention on your part, on the most favourable prices and terms that we may give from time to time, but with regard to chance quotations lower than those of our Association, we expect you to forego any small temporary advantage in return for the extra rebate we are giving. At the same time, as you and we are mutually interested in any loss of business, if we find that your competitors, either in this district or abroad, are able to take business from you, and so from us, by aid of lower dyeing rates, we shall be prepared to meet them in an active way."

The early signatories to the agreement had an undoubted advantage over their competitors, but when about half the merchants had signed the trade took alarm and appointed a committee of manufacturers and merchants to negotiate with the Association. At the same time they passed a resolution " that, in consideration of the Association's present great efforts to keep abreast of the requirements of the trade, and their promise to continue on the same lines in the future, regard is due to their interests by manufacturers and merchants ". The Dyers' Association gave satisfactory assurances, and the committee made the following recommendations which were adopted at a meeting of the Bradford Chamber of Commerce in March, 1902: "(1) That in substitution for the second part of the agreement, the customers shall subscribe to an assurance recognising the right of the Association to a first preference in respect of dyeing work, and will also from time to time afford all fair and reasonable information in their power to enable the Association to adapt itself in all respects to the varied requirements of the trade; (2) that a joint committee be formed, consisting of representatives of the Dyers' Association, and of each of the leading sections of their customers, the latter to be nominated by the Council of the Bradford Chamber of Commerce. In case of a vote the voting power of each side shall be equal, with power to appoint an independent umpire or chairman; (3) that any difference or matter of dispute arising between the Association and their customers shall, if not capable of settlement between the parties, be referred to this committee for their arbitration, and their decision shall be final. Among the matters so to be referred shall be the question whether or not any customer has duly carried out the spirit of the assurance given by him under clause 1, so as to entitle him to the special terms given in consideration of that assurance, it being understood that existing business shall not be diverted from the Association (except for reasons which the committee shall at the next meeting after such diversion approve as sufficient) until after conference with the committee; (4) that during the period of the arrangement no advance shall be made on the prices current immediately prior to 27th December, 1901, without the concurrence of the committee, which, however, shall not be withheld in the case of an abnormal addition to cost." [1]

In this way was formed the Bradford Piece-Dyeing Board of twenty-three members, three of whom represent the Dyers' Association. It is certainly remarkable that two trades should thus agree to settle by negotiation the relations between them, the price at which work should be done, and the proportion of work which should go to a particular company. A vista of great possibilities is opened up in the way of trade regulation, and as the chairman of the Dyers' Association said at the annual meeting on 27th February, 1903 : "The justification of a body of this kind is not to be measured solely by the frequency of appeal to its arbitrament. Rather would we suggest that mutual recognition of each other's rights sufficiently to have created a body of appeal commanding joint confidence tends to a more harmonious and expeditious settlement of differences without resort to it." But behind all this harmony lies the great fact that the association cannot raise its prices, nor a merchant withdraw his trade without the consent of the board, and thus the two main points of business policy are placed under communal control.

For the rest, the price policy of the association has admittedly been moderate, and the directors were able to point out in their prospectus of April, 1906, that " the concessions to customers now ruling, as contrasted with the terms obtaining at the inception of the association, exceed £100,000 per annum ".

In sharp contrast with the Bradford Dyers' Association stands the next largest dyeing combine, the British Cotton and Wool Dyers' Association, familiarly known as "the Slubbers," which was formed in the spring of 1900 to amalgamate forty-six companies. Quoting the prospectus: "The businesses specified include the leading firms and companies engaged in dyeing, bleaching, printing, and sizing cotton yarn in warps and hanks, and wool in the loose state, and slubbing, and all kinds of worsted yarns. The former are used principally by manufacturers of various plain and fancy cloths, and the latter by worsted spinners in the production of mixture and coloured

---

[1] *Yorkshire Post*, 6th and 8th March, 1902.

yarns, used in the manufacture of dress goods and high-class cloth for men's clothing.   The associated firms, with the two firms of the Bradford Dyers' Association engaged in warp and hank dyeing, represent about 85 per cent. of the volume of both branches of the trade.   The process of mercerising, which has become such an important industry, has been very largely developed by certain of the concerns now amalgamating. . . . According to the returns of the vendor firms and companies, the total aggregate turnover of the associated concerns for the last year amounts to upwards of 70,000,000 lb.   An agreement has been entered into with the Bradford Dyers' Association (Limited), under the seal of the respective Associations, whereby provision is made for the co-operation of the two Associations in matters affecting their mutual interests, and arrangements are made for the acquisition by each of the Associations of a considerable holding in the share capital of the other."   As with the Dyers' Association the heads of branches were to receive commissions on their profits.   The issued capital amounted to £1,820,000—£620,000 in 4 per cent. debentures and £1,200,000 in ordinary shares, the vendors taking £191,130 in debentures and £370,000 in ordinary shares. The total purchase money was £1,779,092, of which £906,937 was goodwill, or eight and a third years' purchase of £109,384, the average profit of the preceding five years after deducting depreciation.   A commission of 2½ per cent. on the purchase money was paid by the vendors to Mr. Scott Lings, the promoter of the company, out of which he had to defray the preliminary expenses.   There were forty-five directors, of whom seven formed an executive board.   A 7 per cent. dividend was prophesied.   Differences from the Bradford Dyers' Association are at once noticeable—the heavy amount paid for goodwill is noteworthy, and further whereas the Bradford Association dealt with a compact district the members of the British Cotton and Wool Dyers' Association were scattered over the West Riding and Lancashire and across the Border to Selkirk and Hawick and north to Glasgow and Paisley.   Trouble was not long in coming, and it came to stay as the following table succinctly shows ; it gives the net trading profit after allowing for depreciation and office and professional charges :—

15 months to	31/3/01	.	.	.	.	£69,854
Year to	31/3/02	.	.	.	.	58,946
,,	31/3/03	.	.	.	.	103,868
,,	31/3/04	.	.	.	.	70,406
,,	31/3/05	.	.	.	.	46,971
,,	31/3/06	.	.	.	.	83,671

The amount required to pay the promised 7 per cent. on the ordinary shares was £84,000. It may at once be said that the circumstances in which the "Slubbers" found themselves were quite unprecedented. The extra cost of coal alone in 1900 accounted for an additional charge of £15,000, while the higher price of cotton and the diminished consumption of cotton and wool, all told heavily on the fortunes of the Association. In 1900-1 alone 25 per cent. less material was dyed, which meant not only a loss of profit but an increase of standing charges on what work actually was done. Even when the cotton industry improved it did not react to the advantage of the Cotton and Wool Dyers, for the betterment was mainly in the grey trade to meet an exceptional demand from the East.

But there were other reasons which caused immense dissatisfaction among the shareholders, and they showed themselves as early as the annual meeting[1] in 1901 when the chairman admitted that "if the directors had known the character and standing of some of the concerns before they had been included in the prospectus they would have been left out in the cold". This rather went to prove that not much examination had been made of the results of Mr. Scott Lings' labours. The natural result was a heavy burdening of the accounts with the cost of closed branches. On the other hand the case for inclusion was well put by Mr. Dixon, one of the managing directors of the Fine Cotton Spinners' Association, who at the same meeting said in defence of the directors: "Mention had been made about the closing of works, but whatever might be thought he could assure them that that policy, rightly and wisely pursued in relation to some of the smaller works, was the right one, for they could make more money from one well-conducted firm than from four or five not well adapted. Some seemed to object that certain small firms

[1] *Financial Times*, 20th June, 1901.

had been bought, but in forming a big association like that they were bound to a large extent to take the bad with the good.   It was all very well to say the firm was a bad one, but if not included it would be outside, quoting against them and stopping them making the profit they otherwise would do." On this one can only observe that a cautious business man will consider carefully the " extent " to which he will adulterate good firms with bad, and may be pardoned if after all he comes to the conclusion that the method followed by Messrs. Coats of combining strengths is the better.   On 31st March, 1906, the capital value of closed works stood at £149,378.

Even more serious was the terrible burden of goodwill, which, including that for new businesses purchased, amounted, according to the auditors' report for 1902-3, to £1,008,125, or more than half the issued capital.   When profits were not forthcoming the shareholders wasted much indignation on the individuals whom they alleged to be responsible for the over-capitalisation, but not much sympathy can be felt for investors who did not study their prospectuses enough to see that over-capitalisation was staring them in the face.   Yet the directors laboured hard at improving their organisation.   Six additional firms were bought up, including an American company doing a good mercerising trade.   Thirteen small branches were closed and their business transferred to other branches.   An arrangement was made in the course of 1901 by which the association undertook all the mercerisation work upon yarns made by the Fine Cotton Spinners' Association for mercerised fabrics; previously many of the fine-spinning firms had done their own mercerising, but the British Cotton and Wool Dyers' Association had made a specialty of this work.   Central offices were secured, and a central buying department for dyes, etc., was opened, enabling the business to be conducted with smaller stocks; stock was reduced, owing to this cause, from £125,201 in 1900-1 to £91,423 in 1901-2.   Before the amalgamation several of the firms had done a merchanting business in yarn, buying it in the grey state and selling it dyed; this was ex-tended, and late in 1902 a central yarn buying department was opened with good results.   Later a yarn merchanting branch was opened in America. In the internal management of the business a hint was taken from American practice. "The. managing directors," said the chairman at the annual meeting in May, 1902, "some months ago constituted a system of weekly meetings of the branch managers in the various sections of the association's trade, whereby each separate section, the slubbing dyers, the Yorkshire cotton dyers, the Lancashire cotton dyers, and the Scotch dyers, met and conferred together, and exchanged ideas as to the working of the respective sections. This was leading to better results." Much new machinery had been put in the works, and, lastly, the managing directors were reduced from four to three.

All these reforms were excellent, but against bad trade and over-capitalisation they were of little avail and shareholders whose property was quoted at about 6s. 9d. per £1 share might be pardoned for losing their tempers. Shareholders' committees were appointed and succeeded in getting the vendors to agree that £130,000 of loans made by them in 1900 should be left with the association for ten years to be paid off at 10 per cent. per annum. Over 80 per cent. of this loan was afterwards converted into second mortgage debentures. In 1904 proposals were made to reduce the capital, but they did not come to anything. The "executive board," however, was reduced to four members, thus making, like all small committees, for efficiency. At last, however, the good cotton year, 1905, had its effect even on the melancholy "Slubbers," and for 1905-6, not only was £30,000 transferred to a newly started reserve fund, but for the first time a dividend on the ordinary capital was paid. It was not large, only 2½ per cent., but still it was a dividend. The capital is now £1,891,864.

The great difference between the Bradford Dyers and the British Cotton and Wool Dyers is that the former dye finished cloth, and so can establish proprietary names and make them known to their customers, while the latter dye yarns which pass into a great variety of cloths. Consequently it pays the Bradford Dyers to send travellers to the Far East to spread the knowledge of their specialities, while any manufacturer can easily set up his own plant to dye his own yarns. Of course the British Cotton and Wool Dyers' Association has a practical monopoly of mercerising, and with its labour-saving machinery it is superior, in the bulk trade, to the manufacturer who dyes his own yarn.   But it is a handmaid to the main cotton and wool industries, and too far removed from the ultimate consumer to exercise any influence on him.   It must, therefore, always be a dependent trade, able to gain profit only in good times by doing a large trade at a low price.   This must be its nature whether in a combination or in separate firms, and the advantage of a combination is in its economies and in its greater ability to devote money to that scientific investigation upon which cheapness depends.

The Yorkshire Indigo, Scarlet, and Colour Dyers (Limited), of Huddersfield, floated in July, 1899, was a combination of eleven firms representing "nearly all the Yorkshire dyeing businesses known to be engaged in indigo and scarlet dyeing of wool and cloth manufactured for uniforms, liveries, etc., and used by the British, Indian, Colonial, and Foreign Governments, in the Army, Navy, Post Office, and Civil Service Departments, and by the constabulary, railway, and other institutions.   The firms have also carried on a general colour-dyeing business.   The company will be in a position to manufacture and supply most of its own dye-wares, and will take over the drysaltery, dye-ware, and chemical business of Pickles, Smithson, & Pickles, Limited, which is one of the best known and most important of its kind."   A kind of monopoly of ability and opportunity was claimed for the company, for, still quoting the prospectus, "it is believed for the under-stated reasons that the position of the company will render successful competition almost impracticable.   (1) Indigo wool and piece-dyeing is almost exclusively carried on in Yorkshire.   The several dye-houses taken over are conveniently situated in the centres where the goods are manufactured, and they possess many facilities which it would be difficult to reproduce.   (2) The dyes used in the processes of indigo and scarlet dyeing are of a very expensive character, and exceptional skill and technical knowledge are required to manipulate them profitably.   (3) The number of competent managers and foremen is limited, and the services of those hitherto employed by the several firms will be retained by the company. (4) Manufacturers are indisposed to risk changing from dyers who have been accustomed to deal satisfactorily with their particular goods, and this is especially the case with indigo and scarlet dyeing. (5) The successful conduct of this branch of the dyeing industry necessitates the command of ample capital." After providing for repairs, maintenance, and depreciation the average profit of the preceding three years had been £30,179. £450,000 of capital was issued in equal proportions of 4½ per cent. debentures, 5½ per cent. preference shares, and ordinary shares, the vendors taking one-third of each class. The amount of goodwill cannot be separated from the rest of the purchase money, but no promotion fees were paid, and an 8 per cent. dividend was promised. In comparison with the Bradford Dyers' Association, where the total purchase money was 12.72 times the average annual profit, in this case the purchase money was 14.36 times the profit.

For the first three years the company was successful, acquired some additional businesses, and paid its 8 per cent. Then the strain of bad times, for all trade was then depressed, became too much, and the ordinary dividend, after dropping to 3½ for 1902-3, failed altogether for the next three years, and in fact £4,000 had to be withdrawn from reserve to complete payment of the preference dividend for the year ending 30th June, 1905. One chief cause of loss has been the adoption of khaki as the colour for military uniforms, while in the early years not only was the high price of coal a hindrance, but in their second annual report the directors spoke of exceptionally heavy expenditure on renewals, extensions, and improvements. The closing of some of the businesses is under contemplation.

The English Velvet and Cord Dyers' Association has a somewhat curious history. It was incorporated in April, 1899, for the purpose of amalgamating fourteen firms—nine other businesses being subsequently acquired—engaged in "the dyeing, bleaching, printing, embossing, finishing, etc., of velvets velveteens, cords, moles, etc., and the amalgamated companies and firms comprise a very large proportion of the cotton velvet dyeing trade in this country, and also a considerable portion of the corduroy dyeing industry. The larger of the associated businesses are old established, and are located in Manchester, Salford, and the immediate neighbourhood, or in Yorkshire, and are conveniently situated for dealing with the cloth in an economical manner." To continue quoting from the prospectus issued in April, 1903: " The association was originally formed as a private company, and it was determined that before any issue was made to the public, the results of amalgamation should be tested by actual working. The first two years' working showed that, though substantial profits had been earned, the concern had in the first instance been over-capitalised." The original purchase price was reduced from £1,026,450 to £748,752 by the cancellation of preferred and ordinary shares, and when put before the public the capital was £711,744—£209,475 in 4 per cent. debentures, £211,886 in 5 per cent. cum.-preference shares, and £290,083 in ordinary shares, the vendors retaining one-third of each class. The average profit for the three years that the association had been at work was £65,956, or, after providing for depreciation, £50,406. Goodwill stood at £153,007, or three years' purchase of profits. "Large economies have been effected," continued the prospectus, " to effect which some of the works have been closed, and the businesses have been transferred to other branches." There were nineteen directors—six of them " managing "—somewhat of a crowd for a concern not of huge magnitude. For 1903 the gross trading profit was £54,065, a drop of £11,900, but still 6 per cent. was paid ; in the next two years the inevitable grip of bad times was felt, and the dividend was halved. With regard to price policy there is to be noted a circular issued after the amalgamation prescribing to the customers that they must " undertake not to buy goods which have been dyed outside the association, or to directly or indirectly support outside competition ".

Not much information has appeared in the public press about the Leeds and District Worsted Dyers' Association, but it is a modest concern with a capital of £226,000, formed in 1900 by the amalgamation of ten firms, and its dividend returns show it to have been fairly successful, though it, too, suffered from the lack of general prosperity in 1904-5.

While many of the textile combinations have not justified the hopes with which they were founded, there has been in the textile industry only one actual tragedy, the collapse of the Yorkshire Woolcombers' Association. Woolcombing is the initial process of the worsted industry and it has always been divided into two branches—the commission combers who worked for merchants on commission, and the topmakers, or wool merchants, who owned combing machinery and did all or part of their own combing. About 1893 an association including the principal firms in the Bradford district was formed to stop undercutting, but in 1895 it broke up owing to the withdrawal of Messrs. Holden, Burnley, & Co. and Messrs. Isaac Holden & Sons, the two largest concerns in the trade, and "unnecessary competition" once more became rampant. Early in 1899 a meeting of woolcombers was held at Bradford to consider amalgamation ; the two Holden companies would not come in, but expressed their readiness to adhere to a "satisfactory schedule of prices". It was decided to proceed with the plan, and Mr. Scott Lings, who had gained considerable reputation from his organisation of the Fine Cotton Spinners' Association, was called in as promoter. Primarily the object was to combine the commission combers, but afterwards it was thought advisable to bring in a majority of the topmakers who owned combs. The association was registered in August, 1899, and was floated with a capitalisation of £1,931,800—£750,000 4 per cent. debentures, £650,000 5 per cent. preferred ordinary shares, and £531,800 deferred ordinary shares—the vendors taking all the deferred ordinary and one-third of the other issues. At first thirty-eight businesses were acquired—thirty commission combers and eight topmakers ; later two commission businesses and one topmaker's were purchased, making the total forty-one. After providing for repairs, maintenance, and depreciation, the average annual profits were certified to be £98,939, and £13,124 was added for the profits derivable from increases of plant since the make-up of the accounts. The basis upon which the undertakings was acquired was "as to the commission combers a valuation of the assets, with an allowance for goodwill dependent upon profits computed upon an average of the last four years, and as to the combing branch of the topmakers' businesses now acquired, the average profit-earning capacity of the respective businesses computed on the average of the last three years". The total purchase money was £1,825,653, leaving £106,147 provided by the issue for working capital. A 5 per cent. dividend was predicted. Mr. Scott Lings got 2½ per cent. commission, out of which he had to pay the accountants, Messrs. Glossop, Craven, & Tebbs, for their services.

The career of this association was brief and inglorious. For the year to 30th June, 1900, the gross earnings were £104,573; for 1900-1, £44,462; 1901-2, £63,318. In 1899-1900 5 per cent. was paid on the preferred ordinary shares and nothing on the deferred; in the following year after paying debenture interest and providing £23,277 for depreciation there was a debit balance of £16,813; and in 1901-2 the debit balance was increased to £18,074, including a loss of £2,853 by forgeries of scrip. In November, 1902, a receiver was appointed by certain of the directors who had become guarantors for a bank overdraft of £60,000. The debenture holders then put in a receiver to safeguard their interests. Negotiations followed for a reconstruction of the company on the basis of a substantial refund by the vendors, but they broke down and a writ for restitution of moneys was issued by the directors against one of their number. A committee of investigation was appointed by the shareholders but that came to nought. At last legal proceedings were taken by Messrs. J. & P. Coats, holders of £50,000 debentures, and certain others (representing altogether £70,000 in debentures and £35,000 in preferred ordinary shares) against seven of the director vendors, claiming damages owing to misrepresentations in the prospectus. The case was tried in the autumn of 1904 and resulted in a verdict for the plaintiffs.

The causes of this collapse were two—bad trade and overcapitalisation. In 1899 prices had been raised to a fictitious height owing to speculation based on the expectance of a scarcity of fine wool on account of the drought in Australia in the preceding three years. A restriction of business naturally ensued and prices began to fall so rapidly that everybody kept out of the fine wool business, fearing they should not be able to realise the money they paid for raw material. All along the line, from wool merchants to manufacturers, no one would have anything to do with fine wool products, and a sympathetic depreciation attacked other sorts of wool. The year 1901 was still bad and the association's turnover for 1900-1 was £100,000 less than for the previous year, but in 1902 prices were on a safe level and demand awakened again, only, however, to be followed by another bad year. The great rivals of the association, Messrs. Isaac Holden & Sons (capital £652,500), who were working on the same combing prices, paid no dividend for 1900, 2½ per cent. in 1901, and 7 per cent. in 1902, making it apparent that there were other reasons for the failure than bad trade. The high price of coal and other materials accounted for something, and there was an unfortunate experience with an expensive patent for extracting burrs from wool. Much was done to improve the organisation. A centralised system of book-keeping was adopted, enabling the executive to work on two banking accounts and exercise a close control over the expenditure. Eleven plants were closed and their business transferred to other branches. The efficiency of the machinery was improved by liberal expenditure on renewals and improvements, partly met by the bank over-draft already mentioned. In 1901 the directorate was reduced by eleven from the original number of twenty-six. Distrust of the association was responsible for a considerable loss of trade, for the outside topmakers naturally did not care to send their "tops" to be combed by a concern containing many of their rivals. This distrust was accentuated by the unjust suspicion that the association was responsible for the rise in prices notified in a circular issued in September, 1900, and signed by eight other combing firms and companies as well as by the association. Further, it was openly charged by Mr. Ayrton, one of the directors, that some of the topmakers had been disloyal to the association in not sending the same quantity of wool to be combed as they had treated at their own plants before they sold them to the association; of course, the state of trade was some excuse for this.

When everything else has been said, over-capitalisation still remains the main cause of the downfall of the Woolcombers'

Association. Three kinds of concerns came into the union—
those which "should never have been allowed into the association," as Mr. Ayrton said at the general meeting in 1902, and
had to be closed down; those which were unable to compete
with their rivals, and were the cause of much expenditure in
bringing them up to date; and a comparatively small number
of efficient firms. During the legal proceedings instituted by
Messrs. J. & P. Coats, full disclosure was made of the circumstances attendant on the flotation, and they are full of instruction. Mr. Ralph Neville, K.C., one of the counsel for the
defence, properly enough put the blame on the public for being
taken in: "May I say—and it is just an instance of what effect
a prospectus really has in the minds of the public—how it is
conceivable that all the preference shares should have been
subscribed for ten times over and the debentures three times
over with that statement in the prospectus, when they were
buying a commercial business at the top of a boom, to give a
return of 5 per cent. I do not know. It is absolutely inconceiv-
able, but still they did. . . . Of course it really was because a
lot of ignorant people, who knew nothing about business or anything of the kind, had heard of the great success of the Fine
Cotton Spinners' Association, and they thought it was the day
of trusts; that all the trusts were going to do as well; the bottom
had not come out of the American trusts at that time." Yet
it was not entirely greed which inspired the investors, it was
also reliance on the names of men holding prominent positions
in the trade which figured on the directorate. The average
investor does not look behind a prospectus, but behind this prospectus were the contracts, and these if examined might have
given pause to many who sent in applications. By the contracts commission combers were to receive the 'fair value' of
their works, and for goodwill one-tenth of that sum plus or
minus the aggregate net profit or loss of the four years preceding the date of the last balance-sheet, with full power to Mr.
William Glossop to make any additions or deductions necessary to bring out the fair average profit. The topmakers were
to receive as purchase money twelve and a half times the net
average profits of the three years preceding the date of the last

balance-sheet ; these profits were to be calculated on the basis
of Messrs. Isaac Holden & Sons' prices and not on those actually
charged by the combing branch to the merchanting branch of
the same topmaker.

At the time the businesses were bought, the vendors, as one
of them said in court, " bound themselves morally not to ask
each other what was paid for the businesses," for if the proposal
came to nought the information so gained might be used for
purposes of competition. Thus the public were deprived of
that protection they had a right to expect from the directors,
and the whole matter of purchase was left in the hands of one
man who naturally would want to ensure success of the consolidation by bringing in as many concerns as possible. Four
cases of commission combers were mentioned in court, involving £51,557 purchase money, in which nothing was added for
goodwill, showing that the losses from four years' trading were
so large as to extinguish one-tenth of the value of the assets.
Altogether thirty commission combers sold 565 combs for
£914,794, and eight topmakers sold 151 combs for £880,562 ;
from this it would appear that either much of commission business included was worth little, or that the topmakers were
exacting a very good price. Both conclusions are justified.
The topmakers were entitled to a higher price than the commission combers, for they were selling an assured business and
undertook to send all their wool to the same combs as before,
while the commission men had to hunt for trade. The bottom
fact of the transaction was that the association was founded on
the top of a boom. Men would not sell except on terms which
allowed them to capitalise their expectation of continued good
trade, and since they were selling as individuals to themselves
as an association their duty to the investing public was overlooked. In one case a business was bought on the basis of
running night and day, though it had not run at night since
1895. Another works was bought by the vendor early in 1899
for £5,509, and after having £700 spent on it was sold to the
association for £40,387 ; in this case the annual profits were
from £3,600 to £4,300, so that the vendor made a very good
bargain for himself when he bought the combs, and it is

fair to add that these particular combs earned $4\frac{1}{2}$ per cent. on their purchase price during the life of the association. In a third case, purchase was based on too short a period of running, and the calculation was vitiated by the omission of some and the over- or under-estimate of other items, but still the works returned nearly 5 per cent. on their price for the owner was well able to keep them fully supplied with wool. All these cases, and many others, show the necessity of viewing a prospectus almost with suspicion, and of requiring strict proof of all the statements therein.

Late in 1904 the association was reconstructed as Woolcombers, Limited, with a capital of £585,000—£325,000 in $4\frac{1}{2}$ per cent. debentures, £210,000 in 7 per cent. preferred shares, and £50,000 ordinary shares. Four of the original vendors guaranteed the interest on the debenture stock for ten years, and that the net profits of their works after providing for depreciation should, during the next ten years, amount in the aggregate to £30,350 annually. In return they were to receive half of the net profit earned in any year at their respective branches above the amount guaranteed by them. The prospectus showed the results of the trading since the original inception of the association as under, profits being taken less administrative expenses, but before deduction of debenture and loan interest, directors' remuneration, income tax, or depreciation :—

Year to 30th June, 1900	.	.	.	.	.	.	£92,024
,,	1901	.	.	.	.	.	29,719
,,	1902	.	.	.	.	.	52,445
,,	1903	.	.	.	.	.	62,468
,,	1904	.	.	.	.	.	22,410

In 1905 the preference dividend was paid and in 1906 a dividend of 5 per cent. on the ordinary shares.

In the minor branches of the textile industry there are several small combinations. The United Velvet Cutters' Association (March, 1900), was a union of four firms (one of which was already an amalgamation of two firms) at Rochdale, Manchester, Warrington, etc., engaged in velvet cutting or the production of the pile on velvets and cords. These firms were the principal ones in the trade, doing three-fourths of the business and employing the majority of the workmen. " The consolidation of these businesses," to quote the prospectus, " must reduce unnecessary competition, besides economising working arrangements, which will enable one staff to obtain orders, instead of employing separate ones for each firm, and will effect considerable saving in the collection and re-delivery of goods." The average annual profits for the previous six years were £10,084. The purchase money was £126,705 ; land, buildings, plant, machinery, and utensils being valued at £61,041 ; book debts were not included in the sale, and the value of stock of materials was not given. The capitalisation of goodwill was, therefore, somewhere about six years' profits. Provision was made in the prospectus for the purchase of a fifth firm at £12,000. The capital issued was £140,000, and has since been raised to £200,000 for the purchase of other businesses. Reports as to working are not obtainable, the capital being almost all held by the vendors.

The Extract Wool and Merino Company, also dating from 1900, is an amalgamation of seven firms in the heavy woollen district engaged in extracting wool and merino from rags by the carbonisation of the cotton contained therein. This was a rapidly growing industry for the consumption of shoddy and mungo so produced grew from an average of 104,000,000 lb. in 1875-99 to 132,000,000 lb. in 1895-99, and to 145,000,000 lb. in 1900-4 ; 1904 alone showing 180,000,000 lb. (*Tariff Commission, Report on Woollen Industry, Section* 1514). The special advantages of combination were represented to be the ability to take on large contracts, and the power to buy rags in very large quantities instead of in small lots as the separate firms had done. The issued capital was £270,000, on which the vendors guaranteed for the first year 7 per cent. The prospectus forecast was not quite fulfilled, but still 6 per cent. was paid for the first three years. In 1903-4 £2,000 had to be withdrawn from reserve, but in the following year prosperity returned. One works has been resold to the vendors and the capital is now £201,186. Another creation of 1900 was J. & J. Baldwin & Partners, Limited, an amalgamation of five businesses engaged in the production of fingering, knitting, and other wools. The purchase price was £669,391, of which £59,747 was for goodwill, patents, etc., equivalent to about a year and a half's profits. Shares and debentures amounted to £751,895, the vendors taking three-tenths of the ordinary stock, and a 7 per cent. dividend on the ordinary shares was anticipated. The fortunes of this concern have been of a fluctuating description.

The English Fustian Manufacturing Co. was established in 1900 to unite all the firms in Todmorden and a majority of those in Hebden Bridge, representing altogether 80 per cent. of the trade of the two districts. The capital of £500,000 was mainly subscribed by firms in the syndicate.

After 1900 the combination movement in textiles received a prolonged check. The scant success which, from the investor's point of view, had attended many of the amalgamations, frightened away the public, and not till November, 1904, was another enterprise of this kind put on the market. This was Mitchells, Ashworth, Stansfield, & Co., of Waterfoot, formed to take over eight businesses of felt manufacturers and merchants at Waterfoot, Manchester, Edenfield, and London. Three of these firms had originally agreed to amalgamate, and then the others were acquired " with the view of making the amalgamation as complete and effective as possible ". The works of two of the firms were to be closed. The average annual profits were certified to be £44,418 on the basis of three and two-thirds years' trading. The purchase price was £674,656, including £40,300 for goodwill and £90,500 for patent rights ; the price of the two largest firms, Mitchell Brothers and Richard Ashworth, was £327,566 and £173,363, respectively, the others running from £9,000 to £54,000. This was clearly a case of the large firms combining, and then absorbing the small to extinguish competition. The capital is £674,646, all the preferred and ordinary shares being taken by the vendors, and only £200,000 5 per cent. debentures offered for public subscription.

The combination movement in the textile industries developed with great and increasing vigour in the five years, 1896-1900, and out of the seventeen amalgamations achieved eleven originated in the last two years. But no complete notion can be formed of the way in which the idea of combination appeared to possess people, reaching almost to the height of a mania, without some little consideration of the consolidations which were proposed, but did not actually come into being. In 1898 Mr. Crewdson, of English Sewing Cotton Co. fame, circularised the Belfast flax spinners, some forty firms, regarding their willingness to join an amalgamation capitalised at £4,000,000, but they were more addicted to price cutting than combining. The jute manufacturers of Dundee were also reported to be considering the formation of a large combination with a capital of £2,000,000. More serious efforts were made to combine the worsted spinners of the Bradford district, a meeting being held in the end of January, 1900, under the chairmanship of Mr. Scott Lings—for some years the most active spirit in the combination movement. One hundred and six firms were represented, and a committee was formed to devise a scheme which would bring three-fourths of the trade into the union. A capital of £18,000,000 was talked about but in the end the necessary support was not forthcoming. What, if it had come off, would have been unique among " trusts " was a combination proposed among the velvet weavers, cutters, dyers, and merchants. " All told," said the *Textile Mercury* (2nd December, 1899), " there are about seventy firms, and it may safely be asserted that seven of them could produce all that the public requires of them at the present time." Negotiations proceeded throughout 1898 and 1899, but the interests involved were too diverse for reconciliation. The dyeing and velvet-cutting sections afterwards fused on their own account. An amalgamation of the manufacturers of elastic cords, braids, and webs at Leicester, Coventry, Derby, etc., with a capital of £1,000,000 was another of the projects of 1900. Still another much-discussed scheme of the same year was a union of the lace and muslin curtain manufacturers of Ayrshire and Nottingham. There were some thirty firms in the trade and the capital was to be £2,000,000, but the large firm of Messrs. Morton, of Darvel, N.B., held out, and the plan collapsed. A further argument against the proposal was that there were too many small makers who worked with one or two looms in hired rooms; they could not possibly be admitted, and yet their competition might threaten the success of a concern suspected of aiming at monopoly. The Nottingham Lace Dressers had had for some time an association which suffered from members secretly giving preferential treatment, and so in 1900 it was "understood" that a combination had been formed of all the firms in Nottingham, except half a dozen, with whom working arrangements had been concluded. The capital was to be £1,000,000, but this project, too, has gone to the limbo of unissued prospectuses. Combination has also been proposed several times in the Scotch tweed industry, but despite the pressure of Yorkshire competition mutual jealousies have been too strong for joint action.

CHAPTER VII.

THE CHEMICAL INDUSTRIES.

THE salt industry, like many another, was marked by high prices in the early seventies, followed by an equally pronounced slump. A great development of the alkali industry about 1870 caused an equivalent expansion in the demand for salt, and the price of common salt (which is the standard, all other grades moving in relation thereto) was 12s. 4d. per ton at works in 1872, 14s. 8d. in 1873, and 10s. in 1874. Then it fell to 4s. 9d. in 1881, and at last in 1885 a combination of salt producers was formed to restrict output and put up prices, but with only feeble effect. Mr. Falk, President of the Chamber of Commerce for Cheshire and Worcester, said in his "Salt Circular" for 1887 (quoted in *Times*, 24th September, 1888): "Implacable competition among a small section of the largest makers has brought prices below all records, salt being freely offered at 50 per cent. below cost. All the large chemical contracts for 1888 have been taken at ruinous prices. Nor has there been any more extensive demand for the article below cost. The total export proves a considerable decrease on the average. The principle of association has been violated again and again, and with more disastrous results than ever yet known. Nothing but a new form of general consolidation can resuscitate the trade." "The highest price of common salt during the last ten years," said the prospectus of the Salt Union, "has been 7s. per ton at the works, and the lowest 2s. 3d.; the average price about 5s. 6d. per ton. . . . For East Indian salt the highest price has been 13s. f.o.b., and the lowest 6s. 3d. f.o.b."

The situation had become intolerable, and a London syndicate in the summer of 1888 took in hand the engineering of the "new form of general consolidation" which culminated in October in the formation of the Salt Union, an amalgamation of sixty-four firms, including all those in Cheshire, one in Middlesbrough, and four in Ireland. The total purchase price was £3,704,519, the vendors bearing all charges up to allotment, except legal charges and stamp duties on incorporation. The capital was £4,000,000—£1,000,000 in 4½ per cent. debentures, £1,000,000 in 7 per cent. £10 preference shares, and £2,000,000 (of which the vendors took £900,000) in £10 ordinary shares. The management was entrusted to fourteen directors, with committees of the vendors acting from time to time in the various districts under the direction of the board. This was the first great English amalgamation and its magnitude was set forth with considerable pomp of enumeration. "The object of the company," to quote the prospectus, "is to consolidate the undertakings of the salt proprietors in the United Kingdom, with a view of ending the reckless competition which injuriously affects the salt industry without conferring any adequate advantage on the public. The properties to be acquired or controlled by the company are of great extent and magnitude. Some of the salt firms have been established upwards of a century; their salt brands are known throughout the civilised world; and the benefit of their personal business connections will for the most part be preserved. The properties include freehold and leasehold salt, brine, and other lands, brine shafts, works, buildings, salt pans, railway sidings, tramways and lines into works; steamers, boats, flats, barges, gasworks, locomotives, railway trucks and vans, quays, landing stages, timber yards, fitting shops, warehouses, horses, ponies, vehicles, cottages for workmen, brickyards, railway and river communications, and factories for making most of the articles required in the trade, rendering the aggregate property one of the largest and most complete in the kingdom."

The output of salt in 1887, including salt in brine used at chemical works, was 2,206,951 tons, of which 1,769,719 tons came from Cheshire, 252,000 tons from Worcestershire, 136,267 tons from Durham and North Yorkshire, 43,155 tons from Ireland, and 5,810 tons from Staffordshire. The directors reckoned an output of 2,000,000 tons from their works, or 90·6 per cent. of the whole. On this they reckoned to make an increased average profit of 5s. a ton, which, after payment of all prior charges, would leave 20 per cent. for ordinary dividends and reserve. Not that the union sought to make a monopoly! On the contrary, the chairman said at the first statutory meeting: "All that the company aspired to was to occupy such a commanding and controlling position in the trade as to enable them to secure for the industry the three conditions without which no industry could flourish in this country or elsewhere, . . . the proper supply of the requirements of the community, . . . the obtaining of good wages for the workpeople, . . . and the third condition, without which neither of the others would have any value, was the providing of an adequate and remunerative opportunity for the investment of capital." The four thousand shareholders, doubtless, to a man agreed with such well-turned sentiments, especially the last.

Meanwhile, the consumers of salt had been rushing in to place their orders in anticipation of the rise with the effect of making the advance more rapid and pronounced. By November, 1888, common salt had risen from 2s. 6d. per ton to 9s., and lump salt for export from 8s. to 15s.; in the spring of 1889 common salt was quoted at 10s. 6d. New properties were acquired in 1889, Bell Bros.' salt works at Middlesbrough, Runcorn Soap and Alkali Co., Wharton Railway and River Salt Works, and other minor properties. Of these Bell Bros.' works were the most important, for it was the competition of Middlesbrough which had brought down prices since 1880, and that port was an excellent centre of distribution for the fishing industry of the East Coast and the Baltic trade. An attempt was made to form an American Salt Trust in 1889, and the Salt Union made arrangements with the promoters for safeguarding their mutual interests; these included the appointment of three members on the English advisory board of the trust. The American company, however, did not proceed to allotment, but early in 1891 the union made an agreement with the American producers on the basis that the union was to pay an agreed sum to them for each ton it exported to the

Northern Atlantic States in excess of 150,000 tons per annum, and to receive the same amount on any deficiency. These apparent attempts at an international trust did not increase the popularity of the union.

The annual consumption of salt for domestic purposes was estimated in 1888 to be forty pounds per head of the population, and therefore the contemplated extra profit of 5s. a ton was equal to about a penny per head yearly. Either this sum would have to come out of the pockets of the middlemen or retailers, or the retail price of a halfpenny a pound for refined salt (93s. 4d. per ton) would have to be modified in some way, such as selling in smaller packets, which would probably extract an even greater sum from the consumer. More serious was the probable effect on industries where purchases were necessarily made in bulk ; 5s. additional profit on the 715,000 tons so consumed meant an additional tax on industry of £180,000 per annum. In Germany salt was produced at the average price of 4s. 8d. per ton, and her advantage in the chemical trades would be seriously increased by the policy of the Salt Union. Discontent soon manifested itself. The resources of the two principal salt-beds of Cheshire, Northwich and Winsford, were estimated at 2,800,000,000 tons, and to monopolise them was absurdly impossible. Mr. Garner started immediately to equip large new works at Winsford. The chemical manufacturers of Widnes acquired the salt-fields at Fleetwood in order to cover their requirements. The discovery of new salt deposits at Barrow was announced, and the German producers made inquiries about the possibility of exporting. Abroad the competition of solar salt in the Mediterranean, in India, in America, and elsewhere had to be faced.

In 1889 the net profit, after deducting maintenance, commissions, etc., was £474,990, although large contracts for a large tonnage had been made at low prices by individual producers before the union was formed. The following year this factor did not affect the trade, and there was also a recovery in the national exports of salt which in 1888 had been 898,671 tons, in 1889, 666,757 tons, and in 1890, 726,021 tons. Nevertheless, profits fell to £306,447, and instead of the 10 per cent. of the previous year only 7 could be paid on ordinary shares. Worse was still to come. Eighty per cent. of the cost of salt was coal, and the prices of 1887 and 1888—4s. 10d. and 5s. 1d. at the pit head being the average prices in those years for the United Kingdom—have never been repeated; as for the other constituent of cost, labour, 1889 began a general upward movement in wages. At the same time the production of salt all the world over was stimulated by the high prices, and with increased production came increased competition and lower profits. The over-capitalisation of the company now became evident. The ordinary dividend was 5 per cent. in 1891 and 1892, and in the latter year deliveries had dropped from the 2,000,000 tons of the prospectus to 1,354,000; in 1893 came a further drop to 3 per cent., in 1894 to 2½ per cent., in 1895 to 2 per cent. and in 1896 to 1 per cent.—after that a great silence.

In 1898 deliveries fell to 967,000 tons and profits to £37,341, while both in that year and in 1899 no preference dividend was paid, and at the end of 1899 the £10 ordinary shares were quoted at 1⅞. The high price of coal stimulated efforts at an agreement among the producers. Negotiations in 1898 were not successful, but subsequently, according to the Union's Report for 1899, "an association for regulating salt prices was formed, which is working fairly satisfactorily". Later it appears to have broken down, but in 1901 another combination of the salt manufacturers of the kingdom was arranged to bring prices once more to a remunerative level. Deliveries rose from 853,000 tons in 1900 to 925,000 in 1902, but still no dividend could be paid although for the last-mentioned year profits were £110,093. The burden of dead capital could no longer be borne, and in 1902 the capitalisation was reduced to £2,600,000 from £4,200,000 by writing down the £10 preferred shares to £6 and the £10 ordinary to £4. Still only 5 per cent. could be paid on the preferred shares, and as the arrangement with the other manufacturers though renewed was continued on a lower level of prices the outlook was not cloudless.

The offices were moved from London to Liverpool, a "works committee" of directors met in Cheshire once a week to give a close supervision to the business, the manufacture of sulphate of ammonia was undertaken, a gas producer plant was installed, and numerous other economies were adopted. A new agreement with the other salt makers was made in 1903, which " enabled them to meet the competition of new outsiders at a minimum amount of loss". Nevertheless, deliveries kept on dropping:—1903, 898,000 tons; 1904, 890,000 tons; 1905, 861,000 tons. Net profits fell from £99,619 in 1903 to £68,399 in 1905. The chairman said at the annual meeting in March, 1906: "The principal cause of the diminution in profits was that the combination into which they entered with outside makers had come to an end (30th June, 1905). It was not a good one for the Union, but it was the best under the circumstances. The arrangement was that each outside maker was limited to a certain amount of tonnage and the Salt Union was to take the balance. The Union, however, felt that they were not receiving fair play and made an effort to regain what they thought were their rights. They were quite willing to enter into that combination again if their rights were fairly treated, that was to say, if the trade would not allow of all the pans being worked there should be a *pro rata* diminution in each case. The ending of the combination had commenced a war of prices, and the fight had continued up to the present time. The union hoped that common-sense would at last intervene, and that the outside makers would see that it would be more profitable to work half or two-thirds of their pans at a profit than work the whole at a loss."[1]   The decline in deliveries was due to a dock strike at Liverpool, which made it difficult to get remunerative freights to India and had caused a falling off of 77,000 tons in shipments to Asia. It was added that since 1898 £100,000 had been spent on additions to plant out of revenue, including the producer gas plant and a new vacuum evaporation plant, and £115,000 in preference dividends. Further economies in administration in continuance of the policy of concentration and retrenchment were expected.

At last in the autumn of 1906 peace was restored to the industry by the creation of the North-Western Salt Company, a limited liability company which was to act as sales depart-

[1] *Times*, 17th March, 1906.

ment for the salt trade. It had a subscribed capital of £10,000, and included practically all the British makers as well as the Salt Union. Its functions included the regulation of output, prices, and distribution, a central office being established for the conduct of selling business. Here we see a kartell of the most effective German type of sales association. Naturally, its first action was to raise prices. Beginning with an over-capitalised attempt to secure a monopoly and force up prices, the salt trade has after eighteen years of bitter and unremunerative competition unified itself into a national trust, but history shows that only moderation in price policy can secure any permanency to the new arrangement. The average export price of salt in 1888, a year of great disorganisation in the industry, was 10·81s. per ton, but after the formation of the Salt Union it was raised to 16·15s. in 1889 and to 17·98s. in 1890. From this point it fell to 13·36s. in 1898 owing to the greatly stimulated competition. Attempts at combination now began and the export price has been : 1899, 14·23s.; 1900, 16·71s.; 1901, 16·50s.; 1902, 16·51s.; 1903, 16·15s.; 1904, 16·36s.; 1905, 14·97s.; 1906, 14·22s. The fluctuations give evidence of the wavering effectiveness of the combinations, 1901, 1903, and 1905 being years of collapse. Hitherto each effort to raise prices seems to have created fresh competition.

The calamitous history of the Salt Union formed for long the staple warning against attempts to introduce the " un-English " device of monopoly into British trade, and the morals drawn from its failure were amply reinforced by the similar ill-success of the United Alkali Company. The origin of this company was also to be found in over-competition and un-successful attempts to reconcile conflicting interests. " Some seven years ago," said Mr. Brock at the statutory meeting of the company in February, 1891, " the manufacturers of bleaching powder tired of the warfare they had been carrying on among themselves for several years. They had accordingly deter-mined to unite in a voluntary association, reduce the quantity made, and raise the price. After six years' working this arrange-ment came to an end from causes inherent in a mere voluntary agreement, and the old warfare began again with its resulting loss." [1]   Immediately after the dissolution of the combination on 31st December, 1889, the price of bleaching powder fell £2 a ton.   Soon it was rumoured that a syndicate was at work trying to amalgamate the chief manufacturers, and a great rise in prices followed, bleaching powder advancing from £5 a ton to £6 in October, 1890, and caustic soda from £7 to £11 5s. Gradually the syndicate proceeded towards success, although the paper-makers, large consumers of bleaching powder, threatened to start their own works.   The scientific position was peculiar, for most of the British works adopted the Le Blanc process for making alkali, utilising the surplus chlorine to make bleaching powder, and as the supply of chlorine was in excess of the demand for "bleach" there was always a tendency to over-production.   On the other hand, the ammonia or Solvay process was cheaper for making carbonate of soda, but the chlorine from the salt used went to waste.

The *Times*, in its Money Article of 29th August, 1890, issued a weighty warning: " It did not seem to us very probable that this audacious scheme would come to anything, for it was notorious in business circles that the great majority of the works in question were equipped with plant for producing soda by the Le Blanc process, which has been for some years superseded by the Solvay process in which ammonia is used. Most of the Le Blanc works have, indeed, been carried on at a loss for a year or two past, and those which have contrived to make profits were only able to do so because the ammonia works had not until quite recently been able to produce bleaching powder cheaply.   Now, however, that difficulty has been got over, and the single article which could still be produced profitably by the Le Blanc works is being manufactured by their rivals.   Under these circumstances it is natural enough that the proprietors of the Le Blanc works should have tried to establish an association on the lines of the Salt Union, in the hope that the public might be induced to purchase their works.   It is, we think, surprising that any responsible persons outside the trade should have been found to take up this scheme. . . . The want of caution of the ordinary investor is well known, but we hardly

[1] *Times*, 5th February, 1891.

think that even the most careless person will be inclined to put money in the proposed Chemical Union when he knows the facts regarding it which we have already mentioned." All these allegations were vigorously denied by the Le Blanc makers.

In the autumn of 1890 the company was registered, and orders for chemicals were placed in abundance for 1891 at the union prices, which were on the basis of the average of the preceding six years, that is, the old combination prices. The prospectus was published in February, 1891, and it then appeared that the capitalisation was £8,500,000—£2,500,000 in 5 per cent. debentures, £3,000,000 in 7 per cent. £10 preference shares, and £3,000,000 in £10 ordinary shares. The vendors subscribed for £2,128,070 debentures, £2,340,030 preferred, and £2,697,350 ordinary shares, being forced to this heavy subscription by the disastrous effect of the Baring crisis on the money market. The *Times*, still obdurate, said : " We do not see that the public have anything to gain by assisting them " (5th February, 1891), but the public were impressed by the evident belief of the vendors in the value of their property and the flotation was a success. Forty-eight firms were included, of which three were salt makers ; fourteen were situated at Widnes, nine at St. Helens, nine on Tyneside, four in Scotland, three in Ireland, three at Runcorn, two in Flint, and one at Bristol ; the salt works were two at Port Clarence and one at Fleetwood. The price for the properties and patents was £6,851,500, which was arrived at " by a sub-committee of eight acting under the direction of a committee of thirteen, appointed by the manufacturers, and after careful consideration by such sub-committee of the producing power and position of the works, and of the reports made by two or more members of the committee or directors who in each case have examined the works ". No promotion money or goodwill was included ; and, in addition, manufactured stock was to be taken at a fair market value and raw materials at cost ; the book debts were not transferred. Again an impressive list of products was detailed, sounding almost like a chemical encyclopædia ; 700,000 tons of vitriol were made annually and nearly all used in the works in the decomposition of 600,000 tons of salt ; the output included bleaching powder, 150,000 tons ; caustic soda, 180,000 tons ; soda ash, 140,000 tons ; soda crystals, 140,000 tons ; sulphate of soda, 60,000 tons—besides plant for the treatment of 100,000 tons of copper ores, and for the production of artificial manures, soap, glycerine, caustic potash, sulphate of ammonia, bicarbonate of soda, etc. Altogether, according to the chairman, taking the four heavy chemicals the three ammonia process firms made 115,000 tons and the company 565,000 tons, or 83 per cent., and, taking the total output the company made 90 per cent. The works acquired included nearly the whole of the Le Blanc works in the United Kingdom and, despite the assertions of their critics, the directors maintained that " the Le Blanc process is the only process by which bleaching powder and other chlorine products in conjunction with caustic soda are economically manufactured ".

For the fourteen months ending 31st December, 1891, the net profit was £695,000, and 5 per cent. was paid on the ordinary shares. For the next five years the record stands, profit being taken before payment of interest on debentures :—

	Net Profit.	Ordinary Dividend.
1892	£863,107	6 per cent.
1893	496,895	5 ,,
1894	339,117	nil.
1895	368,092	1 per cent.
1896	408,903	2 ,,

A reserve of £517,000 was also accumulated. Since 1896 no dividend has been paid on ordinary shares, and nothing was added to reserve till 1901, when a transfer of £50,000 was made. The course of net profits before deducting debenture interest has been as follows (*Financial Times*, 23rd March, 1906):—

	Net Profit.
1897	£334,196
1898	319,096
1899	319,599
1900	331,270
1901	352,146
1902	369,457
1903	330,833
1904	349,053
1905	426,440

Reserves, etc., amount to £960,000, of which £750,000 is hypothecated to writing down assets.

Alkalies include soda ash and caustic soda, used in the manufacture of soap, paper, and glass ; soda crystals for domestic washing purposes ; and bicarbonate of soda, used for baking and in the manufacture of ærated waters, drugs, etc. They are thus in constantly increasing consumption, but they are just those chemicals in which the ammonia process has the advantage of cheapness. According to Mr. Alfred Mond, of Brunner, Mond, & Co., in his contribution to *British Industries Under Free Trade* (edited by Harold Cox—Fisher Unwin, 1903), the consumption of alkalies in the United Kingdom increased 24·2 per cent. in 1881-85, 31·2 per cent. in 1886-90, 4·7 per cent. in 1891-95, and 19·8 per cent. in 1896-1900. Exports averaged in 1891-95, 301,879 tons; in 1896-1900, 210,543 tons ; and in 1901-5, 217,463 tons; in 1900 they were at their minimum of 182,857 tons, from which they have risen steadily to 236,060 tons in 1905. The British production of alkalies rose 43·3 per cent. between 1879 and 1883, 4·6 per cent. in 1884-88, 10·3 per cent. in 1889-93, and declined 6·1 per cent., 1894-98, and to 7·6 per cent. in 1902. The decline in exports was largely due to the heavy American tariff of 1897 and to the policy of the European countries in protecting their chemical industries. The net result of the changes in the direction of trade is that the production of alkalies is to-day very much what it was at the inception of the United Alkali Co., and as successful rivals have grown up and developed the burden of the changes fell on the "chemical trust".

The bleaching powder trade has also undergone a good deal of transformation. The use of wood pulp in the paper industry, especially the increasing use of wood pulp bleached with sulphurous acid, has deprived the bleaching industry of one of its great customers. The importation of wood pulp rose from 156,609 tons in 1891 to 576,153 tons in 1905. Simultaneously exports fell from 70,355 tons in 1891-95, to 62,005 tons in 1896-1900, and to 47,463 tons in 1901-5. The domestic consumption of bleaching powder decreased 29·2 per cent. between 1891 and 1895, and rose 32·8 per cent. in 1896-1900—a slight net decrease. The loss caused by this change affected the United Alkali Co. all the more seriously as bleach-

ing powder was its *pièce de résistance*, and when about 1898
electrolytic methods of manufacturing bleach came into commercial use the situation became almost desperate.   The new
method, which was largely taken up in Germany, allowed 90
per cent. of the chlorine to be extracted from the salt, instead
of only 50 per cent. by the old Le Blanc method, and this
triumph of science naturally led to over-supply of the market
and a collapse of prices.   The course of average export prices
has been as follows:—

								Per Ton.
1895	.	.	.	.	.	.	.	£7·09
1896	.	.	.	.	.	.	.	6·84
1897	.	.	.	.	.	.	.	6·35
1898	.	.	.	.	.	.	.	5·51
1899	.	.	.	.	.	.	.	4·94
1900	.	.	.	.	.	.	.	5·83
1901	.	.	.	.	.	.	.	6·62
1902	.	.	.	.	.	.	.	6·14
1903	.	.	.	.	.	.	.	3·89
1904	.	.	.	.	.	.	.	4·09
1905	.	.	.	.	.	.	.	4·10

This table sufficiently explains the variation in the company's net profits.

As in the salt industry, attempts were made to counteract
the destruction of profits by alliances.   From 1900 an agreement
between British and Continental makers restricted output and
governed prices with satisfactory results, though not enough to
yield a dividend to the ordinary shareholders of the United
Alkali Co., but towards the end of 1902 a large German firm
made a big cut to secure the following year's contracts.   The
combination went to pieces and a disastrous fall in values
followed.   The agreement had been renewed from year to
year, but at each renewal the German makers, having to dispose of their heavy electrolytic output, demanded a larger
share of the trade; this was granted for 1901 and 1902, but for
1903 they sought to obtain a guaranteed minimum export to
the United Kingdom, to exclude British makers from Germany and Switzerland, and to be allowed to sell both in
England and in the United States at a lower price than English
makers; it was plain that there was no benefit in maintaining
the arrangement.   The war of prices brought profit to no one,
and in the summer of 1903 a temporary arrangement was
made which led to an improvement in values from £2 per ton

to £4 or £5. This arrangement appears to have been made permanent, for Messrs. S. W. Royse & Co. in their report on the heavy chemical trade for 1904, said that "production has been well controlled to meet market requirements," and of 1905 they had to chronicle a "great steadiness of values," with a rise in contracts for 1906 to £4 12s. 6d. a ton. The United Alkali Co. acquired additional salt lands about 1899 and copper properties in Spain in 1903 and 1904, in order to secure its supply of salt and pyrites, two of its chief raw materials. Four additional chemical works have been absorbed since its foundation, its staff of workpeople numbers 12,000 men, and its output of finished products exceeds 1,000,000 tons annually. Its capital is now £8,733,670, and the burden of the original over-capitalisation is so high that, despite the scientific know-ledge of the managers and the skill displayed in the develop-ment of new branches, such as artificial manures and cyanide, a dividend on the ordinary shares is not yet at hand. The scientific reconstruction of the business has been carried out at the expense of dividends, but it was necessary for self-preservation.

Fortunately for the credit of the British chemical industry, we can point to one great company, not only a giant but a profit-making giant, Brunner, Mond, & Co., of Winnington and Northwich, which manufactures alkali by the ammonia process.   Established in 1881 with a capital of £200,000, it had at the end of 1906 a capitalisation of £2,789,650. It ab-sorbed Murgatroyd's Ammonia, Soda, and Salt Syndicate (ex-cept the salt business) in 1895, the Cheshire Alkali and Salt Co. in 1897, Bow, Thompson, & Co. (for £350,440) and the salt works of Bell Bros. in 1900. It also owns mines in North Wales, a holding of £11,429 in the Power Gas Corporation ("Mond Gas"), and a further holding in the South Staffordshire Mond Gas Co.   Its financial history for the last six years is as follows :—

Year to 31st March,	Net Profit.	Ordinary Dividend.
1901 . . .	£417,878	35 per cent.
,, 1902 . . .	480,430	32½ ,,
,, 1903 . . .	524,260	30 ,,
,, 1904 . . .	548,500	30 ,,
,, 1905 . . .	612,530	35 ,,
,, 1906 . . .	704,469	35 ,,

And in the same time £509,000 has been written off to reserve, etc. In 1906 out of the reserve fund of £1,000,000 a special dividend was paid to the holders of ordinary shares of 33⅓ per cent. on the amount paid on such shares. Countries with no history, we are told, are happy, and similarly companies which are prosperous publish little material for the economic student. The prosperity of Brunner, Mond, & Co. is due to the combination of remarkable business ability and scientific knowledge in the directors.

The English companies working electrolytic processes are neither so large nor, having suffered from the "bleach" war, so prosperous. The Castner Kellner Alkali Co. (capital £674,988) has had a ten years' existence, and in 1900 acquired the Aluminium Co.; it paid 4 per cent. in 1904-5 and 6 per cent. in 1905-6, and its average dividend has been 5⅛ per cent.

Borax and nitrate of soda are two important chemical products produced abroad largely with English capital and, although to a less extent British industries than those branches so far dealt with, deserve a brief consideration. Borax Consolidated was formed in January, 1899, to put an end to competition which had reduced prices 50 per cent., when the companies found, as one of their chairmen put it, that "there were other ways of doing away with competition besides 'snuffing out'". Twelve companies owning factories in England, France, Austria, and the United States, and all the most important mines and sources of production of crude borax entered the amalgamation; other properties were acquired later. The capital was £2,200,000—the vendors taking all the £600,000 ordinary shares and one-third of the debentures and preferred. "The policy of the managers," said the chairman of the Borax Company, "was to increase the consumption of borax in every possible way by fixing a moderate and reasonable price rather than by raising it." And the chairman at the fourth ordinary meeting in February, 1902, added: "The low prices to which it has been our policy to reduce some of our products in some places, serve to stimulate consumption and encourage new uses, while at the same time they tend to discourage competition—for I may say we have ever in mind the necessity of being able to produce both our crude and our refined material at such prices as will render competition unremunerative. Of course you will easily understand that the success of this company in the three years of its existence has led to attempts in this direction, but the advantages which this company enjoys of possessing enormous quantities of the best and cheapest crude material has obtained for it a position which it will be difficult to assail." [1]   The policy somewhat resembles the plan of differential prices adopted by American trusts to crush local competition and so much denounced in the United States, but the defence is certainly effective.

No combination is so effective as one which owns the sources of supply of the raw material for a commodity in general demand, and Borax Consolidated owes its prosperity to being in that position. Its dividend record is refreshing :—

Period to 30th September, 1899 .	.	.	.	.	12½ per cent.
Year to „ 1900 .	.	.	.	.	17½ „
„ „ 1901 .	.	.	.	.	17½ „
„ „ 1902 .	.	.	.	.	17½ „
„ „ 1903 .	.	.	.	.	17½ „
„ „ 1904 .	.	.	.	.	17½ „
„ „ 1905 .	.	.	.	.	17½ „

The exports of Chilian nitrate were in 1870, 136,287 tons; in 1880, 225,559 tons; in 1890, 1,050,119 tons; and in 1899, 1,380,002 tons. Such an expansion of supplies led to a great fall in prices. As early as 1890 combination was proposed, but though the English companies agreed the interests of the coast producers could not be reconciled, and, though a temporary plan was adopted later, it was not till after ten years that effective action was taken. The *Economist* (27th October, 1900) thus described what took place : " Combination between the various English and Chilian nitrate producers was suggested, and a plan was put into operation whereby all the producers agreed to make only a certain quota each. This for a time helped matters, until one or two new companies that were not in the combination were brought out, which knocked the scheme on the head. Since then several attempts have been made to again form the combination, but without success until recently, when the secretary of the Nitrate Association in Chili went

[1] *Financial Times*, 8th February, 1902.

quietly to work, by approaching the various companies and getting them to agree as to the quota they would accept, without letting them know what the others had agreed upon. By this means he minimised the risks of jealousy between the different makers, which had been the cause of the attempts at combination previously falling through. On Saturday last the scheme was accepted and signed at Iquique, and the English companies have also since accepted it. The recent output has been about 33,000,000 quintals per annum, while the demand has only been for about 32,000,000 quintals, but the combination has fixed the output at 31,273,000 quintals for five years from 1st April, 1901. It is understood that the Chilian Government has lent its aid in bringing about the combination, and, if that be so, what has hitherto proved an obstacle has been removed. Chili collects an export duty on every quintal of nitrate sent out of the country, and any restriction in the value of export would of course be against the interest of the Government. . . . The fact that Chili is understood to be working in harmony with the combination is thus noteworthy; but perhaps the Government thinks that an ultimate gain by an increased value of the State nitrate grounds may prove sufficient compensation for an immediate loss."

Chili has a monopoly of nitrate grounds, and at the time when the combination was formed about three-fourths of them were being worked, one half by British companies, the remainder being of low quality or disadvantageously situated. The life of the fields was put at about fifty years, but in 1902 and later new fields of good quality were explored so that the possibility of fresh competition was not excluded. The benefits of the combination were soon shown. Mr. Thomson Aikman in his first half-yearly report for 1902 said: "Nitrate of soda for the first time for several years shows a considerable falling off in consumption, equivalent for the twelve months just ended to over 12 per cent., while the average price has been almost an identical percentage higher, although now fallen to below the previous twelve months' average". Variations in the area under cultivation in Europe for sugar beet accounted for variations in the demand, and the supply was regulated accordingly, with allowance for the admission of new producers. Thus, quoting from Mr. Aikman's report for 1904: "The Producers' Combination, in May last, declared the maximum shipment for the year ending 31st March, 1905, at 36,000,000 quintals (1,630,000 tons); they allocated on the same basis as last year the individual shipping quotas to the various existing producers, making an aggregate of 37,500,000, and have since given to new producers over 1,000,000 further. . . . The uncertainty of labour in the nitrate producing districts, the total supply of which appears to be inadequate to meet the requirements of all the oficinas now working, has had a more potent effect in restricting production than the fairly liberal quotas granted to each. A producing capacity of about 200,000 tons has been added to the figures of last year, but the individual authorised quotas of old oficinas were fixed at the same figures. During the next twelve months new oficinas equal to a producing capacity of a further 200,000 to 250,000 tons will probably commence working. . . . Cost of production continues considerably higher than before the combination, but the advance of over 30 per cent. in f.o.b. price which has taken place since its operation, added to the consequent conserving of grounds, has rendered the industry so highly remunerative to producers and producing companies that it seems highly probable a means will be found of continuing its beneficial operations after March, 1906, when present agreement terminates."

A considerable amount of negotiation was required before the combination was renewed in 1906, and the currency of the new agreement was reduced to three years. There was a greater number of new manufacturers and some of the old companies put forward claims for larger quotas. The reconciliation of all these claims was a matter of no slight difficulty—it is always the crucial point of a "pool"—but the old combination had been too profitable for a relapse into competition to be tolerated, and in the end the necessary adjustments were made.

In the dye-ware and colour industry there is no concern which can be compared with the great German companies, but still three small combinations are to be noted:—

		Capital.	Year Ending	1899.	1900.	1901.	1902.	1903.	1904.	1905.	1906.
1898	British Dye-woods and Chemicals Co.	£ 570,000	30th June	2	3	nil.	2	nil.	nil.	nil.	nil.
1899	United Indigo and Chemical Co.	240,000	,,	—	6	4	nil.	nil.	nil.	nil.	nil.
1900	Yorkshire Dye-ware and Chemical Co.	294,000	,,	—	—	nil.	nil.	nil.	nil.	nil.	nil.

The British Dye-woods and Chemicals Co. was an amalgamation of four Scotch firms which showed an aggregate annual profit of £45,200. Their expectation that they would be "able largely to reduce competition and to effect many important economies in their purchases as well as in the production and distribution of their goods" was not proof against the low prices, and for the first five years and a half profits only averaged £22,400 a year. In 1901 an investigation committee was appointed which effected numerous economies and concentrated to some extent the work of the different branches. For 19_5-0, after deducting depreciation, there was a net profit of £15,971, out of which the full dividend was paid on the preferred shares up to 30th June, 1905, and 1 per cent. on account of 1905-6.

The other two companies may be taken as attempts on the part of the dye-ware firms to defend themselves against the dyeing combines whose superior economic power might otherwise be too great in the matter of purchasing. The United Indigo Co. (headquarters Manchester) was a combination of eight North of England firms, which showed profits "considerably more than sufficient to pay 8 per cent. dividend on the ordinary shares, independently of the economies and advantages expected to result from this amalgamation". Thanks to khaki and synthetic indigo in three years the company's sales of indigo declined 50 per cent. There is still an important drysaltery business, and the arrears of preference dividend are small. An investigation committee was appointed in 1903, and at the meeting to receive its report the chairman said that "none of the amalgamated firms had sought combination; the negotiations, therefore, were conducted quite independently of the vendors, and individually they did not know how many firms

were approached to join.   Some of the vendors were unknown
to each other until brought together by the promoter, and with
the knowledge they then had the vendors were impressed by
the firms brought before them, but they did not fix the bases of
purchase of the businesses.   Reliable valuers, accountants, and
lawyers were called in, and contracts carried out accordingly"
(*Financial Times*, 25th February, 1904).   A case, in fact, of
consolidation promoted from the outside.

The Yorkshire Dye-ware and Chemical Co. combined a
dozen firms, and of its issued capital all the ordinary shares
were held by the vendors.   The depression in the textile industry naturally affected the subsidiary trades, and that to some
extent explains the disastrous career of the company.

The Government recently tried to place our manufacturing
industries which use alcohol on the same footing as Germany,
and so avoid a repetition of the history of the colour industry,
but according to a correspondent of the *Times* (6th October,
1906), a combination stands in the way.   He said: "The
first result of the Revenue Act, 1906, which has just come into
force, has been the formation of a convention among makers of
methylated spirit.   The Revenue Act provided for the use by
manufacturers of a special methylated spirit on which the Board
of Inland Revenue grants a rebate of 5d. per gallon.   The
makers of this spirit, however, are only quoting at 4d. per
gallon below the old price, instead of 5d. as anticipated, which
looks as though manufacturers who use spirit are not getting
full advantage of the Government concessions.   Before the new
regulations came into force the spirit dealers did not quote uniform prices, but, curiously enough, the 'cutting' which has
hitherto existed has come to a sudden stop simultaneously with
the new Excise regulations.   The methylators do not attribute
their unanimity to the Government concessions, but to other
causes.   Should the convention follow the example of the other
trusts, it is quite possible that the price of industrial spirit will
not remain at its present level; or in other words, there is a
possibility that manufacturers will not be benefited by the
Revenue Act to the extent the Government intended.   The
price of methylated spirit, of the kind which could be used for

motor cars if it were cheap enough, remains unchanged for the present. In Germany, where the use of duty-free alcohol for manufacturing and motive purposes has been allowed for many years, the spirit industry has also come into the hands of a trust, with the result that the advantages which should accrue from the use of an untaxed spirit are becoming smaller and smaller. Had competition in the English market in industrial alcohol continued there was every possibility of our manufacturers being able to produce certain articles as cheaply as the Germans, but there are distinct signs that competition is at an end."

In the manufacture of explosives the Nobel Dynamite Trust Company first occupies our attention on account of its seniority. It was created in 1886 to unite the interests of the four dynamite companies, and the reasons for its existence were thus explained by the chairman at the thirteenth annual meeting in June, 1899 (*Economist*, 3rd June, 1899): "For some years prior to the formation of the trust company a strong competition existed in the sale of explosives between the German companies and the Glasgow company. This was seen to be so ruinous that after a time the directors of the German companies and those of the Glasgow company, through the intervention of the late Mr. Nobel, met on numerous occasions, both here and on the Continent, to discuss the position. . . . These meetings resulted in an amicable agreement, but, after a time—perhaps about a couple of years or so—it became necessary, for certain causes which I need not mention in detail, that a still closer bond of union should be made between the companies if we were to get the best results from our arrangement. Hence the formation of the trust company, which I believe was made on lines which, although perfectly familiar now, were then of a novel character. . . . It was a fundamental part of the arrangement that each of the companies was to retain its autonomy, and the business carried on by it was in every respect to be as if no trust company was in existence." The trust company was in fact a " holding company" with a board of directors elected by the boards of the manufacturing companies. In 1897, 1898, and 1902 fresh capital was issued to provide for further purchases of shares in dynamite and explosives companies and to finance the subordinate companies, and the capital is now £2,785,400. The details of these subsidiary companies scattered over the whole world are not published. The report for 1901-2 referred to the " Continental powder companies with which the companies are linked by a pooling agreement," showing that the whole international trade was regulated. But the report for 1905-6 announced that in June, 1905, the United Kingdom Price Convention was broken up, and that " prices in this country and in several of the extra-European markets have reached a level at which there is no longer any profit". The trade in blasting explosives is passing through a severe crisis owing to the partial substitution of gelatine compounds for dynamite, but, nevertheless, owing partly to the increased demand for war material, partly to the reduction in cost produced by the increased output, the profits for 1905-6 were the largest on record —£328,681. In the twenty years of its existence the company has distributed in ordinary dividends over £3,750,000, or an average of nearly 10 per cent. per annum, and has accumulated a reserve of £320,000 in addition to £750,000 accumulated by the subsidiary companies.

Curtis & Harvey, Ltd., was an amalgamation of eight leading firms and companies manufacturing and trading in black, smokeless, military, sporting, and blasting powders. They owned fifteen works which with stock, etc., were valued at £820,142, and the company was capitalised at £850,000, of which the share capital, £450,000, was taken by the vendors. With subsequent additions the capital now amounts to £916,000. " For trade reasons," the directors in issuing their prospectus did " not consider it desirable to make any statement as to profits other than that on the present basis they are amply sufficient to secure the debenture interest, without taking into account the increase which will result by economy of administration and reduction of competing agencies." Since the formation of the company in 1898 it has only paid ordinary dividends of 5 per cent. in 1901, 2½ per cent. in 1904, and 2½ per cent. in 1905.

Kynoch, Ltd., was the name taken in 1897 by G. Kynoch

& Co., Ltd., on reconstruction of the company in order to make expansion of its business easier. They were then manufacturers of explosives and munitions of war, sporting ammunition, and blasting explosives, but many subsidiary businesses have been added, some directly connected with the main business, as their soap works started to secure the supply of glycerine needed in their explosives works, others quite unconnected. At their Lion Works, Witton, Birmingham, military and sporting ammunition, steel shells, soap, and candles are made, and there are rolling mills and the general offices ; at the Holford Works, Perry Barr, Birmingham, military ammunition and gas and oil engines are manufactured ; at Lodge Road, Birmingham, there are metal rolling mills ; at the Endurance Works, Stirchley, Birmingham (acquired 1900), steel shells are made ; Hadley & Shorthouse, Birmingham (absorbed 1901-2), turn out cut and wire nails, and brass and copper sheets and tubing ; at Kynochtown, at the mouth of the Thames (purchased 1901-2), there are cordite, gun-cotton, gunpowder, and cartridge works ; there are also gunpowder works at Barnsley, chemical and explosives works at Arklow, and a building estate at Corringham in Essex. The Inchicore Paper Mills, near Dublin, were bought in 1901-2, and the Clondalkin Paper Mills in 1906. The ruling idea of the directors appears to have been that while increasing their main business they should, on the principle of " not having all their eggs in one basket," seize every opportunity of acquiring any business out of which a profit could be made. The company thus in a way imitates in manufactures the department stores of retail trade. Success has justified the policy, for the share and loan capital has grown from £495,000 in 1897 to £1,370,370 in 1906, and a dividend of 10 per cent. has been regularly paid on the ordinary shares in addition to various bonuses. The average profits of the five years to 31st March, 1906, have been £91,828, compared with £64,060 in the four years after reconstruction.

Mr. Arthur Chamberlain has said that it was to get free from the " ring " of glycerine makers that Kynoch's started soap making, of which glycerine is a by-product. The association, to use a politer word, has controlled the price of glycerine for some years past, as it has, to some extent, the price of soap, but values are said to be to-day at a low level.

The month of October, 1906, was enlivened by the formation of what was soon popularly known as "the Great Soap Trust," in which the moving spirits were Messrs. Lever Brothers. This firm started making soap at Warrington at the rate of twenty tons a week in 1886, and two years later it moved to Port Sunlight, near Birkenhead, where a model town was built which in 1899 had 3,000 inhabitants. This town, like Bourneville, can be fearlessly compared with the best specimens of much-lauded American philanthropy. In 1899 the output was 2,400 tons per week. An office was opened at Sydney in 1888 for the collection of copra, or dry cocoa-nut kernel, in the Polynesian islands and a mill was erected there in 1895 for crushing out the oil. The company also possesses a mill at Vicksburg, on the Mississippi, for extracting oil from cotton-seed, and another mill was opened at Port Sunlight in 1897 to utilise Egyptian seed. The business is thus in close touch with the raw materials, and in particular it is free from the British Oil and Cake Mills, Ltd., which controls so much of the seed oil trade. To this, as well as to the business enterprise of its founder, is the strength of the undertaking due. Foreign tariffs are circumvented by a mill built in Switzerland in 1897 and another at Mannheim in 1898. It consolidated its position in 1889, when it had a capital of £2,000,000 and was paying dividends of 10 and 12½ per cent., by adding to its household and toilet soaps a new branch through the purchase of the American firm of Brooke & Co. (capital £250,000), whose "Monkey Brand" was well known for cleansing wood and metal articles. Since then it has paid 15 per cent. annually. Its issued and paid-up capital is £3,850,000, in addition to which £2,000,000 B preference shares were created in July, 1906, but it is not known how much was subscribed.

There has not for a long time been absolutely free competition in the soap trade. "We have had a working arrangement in the trade for the past thirty years," said Mr. W. H. Lever, M.P., in an article in the *Daily Chronicle* of 22nd October, 1906. "Hitherto our amalgamation, called the Soap Manufacturers' Association, has agreed when prices should be renewed and lowered. Now the work of that association will be extended, and the sole reason for this is the increasing competition between us." Outside and associated makers competed furiously together, using such devices as house-to-house distribution of free samples, prize competitions, prizes for the collection of soap wrappers and coupons, extensive newspaper advertising. In fact, for some years the soap trade indulged in a perfect orgie of advertisement, and Lever Brothers were prominent in the debauch. Capacity for such extensive expenditure was rudely checked by the rise in the price of raw materials. " Perhaps the reason," said Mr. Lever, "why our closer association has come about at the present moment, rather than at any other time, is the high price of raw material, which has made it impossible to continue fighting each other in the way we have been doing without a material rise in the price of soap to the public. . . . The increase lately in this price has meant £300,000 a year to one firm in the amalgamation. Take the case, for instance, of cocoa-nut oil. We have had it as low as 18s. 6d. a hundredweight. A fair normal price is 24s. per hundredweight. To-day's price is 33s. It is going into butter and not into soap. We have our own oil mill at Sydney where we crush the copra that is made in the islands in the Pacific. The product of that mill is at such a price that it pays us better to send it to Hamburg, where it is made into butter." "This rise," said Mr. R. E. Markel, director of Joseph Crosfield & Sons, in a letter to the *Times* of 29th October, 1906, "was already trenching on the fund for wages and salaries, not to speak of profits or bonuses. The common danger naturally brought manufacturers together; and, in seeking a basis which should give greater permanence to their agreements, they were impressed with the enormous advantages to be gained for each and all in the substitution of friendly co-operation for indiscriminate competition over the whole field of production and distribution." "We have gone into the figures," said the *Times Financial Supplement*, 29th October, 1906, "and are satisfied that the average advance in the ingredients of soap has been during the past year not less than 30 per cent."

The firms and companies which agreed to the amalgamation were Lever Brothers, Port Sunlight (capital £3,850,000) ; Vinolia Company, London (£250,000); Joseph Crosfield & Sons, Warrington (£800,000); Joseph Watson & Sons, Leeds (£500,000); Christopher Thomas & Brothers, Bristol (£300,000) ; Ogston & Tennant, Glasgow ; W. Gossage & Sons, Widnes ; Tyson, Richmond, & Jones, Liverpool ; Hodgson & Simpson, Wakefield ; Edward Cook & Sons, London ; J. Barrington & Company, Dublin—eleven in all, and the capital was alleged to be £12,000,000, though this was probably a pure guess. These businesses were not fused together in the sense that they were to lose their identity. Mr. Markel, in the letter already quoted, describes the amalgamation as " a friendly arrangement for co-operation and especially for the interchange of commercial, technical, and scientific information and experience. Far from contemplating the absorption of constituent concerns, the agreement provides for their separate existence and safeguards their individuality. Thus, while there will be a central board to direct the commercial policy there is no idea of interfering with the internal arrangements of the various firms. All the wholesome benefits of a trust will in this way be secured without any sacrifice of incentive or of individual enterprise." The organisation would appear to be something between an English amalgamation and a German kartell, leaving to the members freedom in manufacturing but placing the selling part of the business under common control and dividing up the markets. Mr. Lever said : " One firm will take charge of Scotland and will act as agents for the other firms in that part of the country. A Bristol firm will do the same for the West of England. From this it will be seen that all we are doing is to introduce practical business-like arrangements into our concerns. We shall reduce friction, save labour in handling the products of the various firms concerned, and altogether be in a better position to serve the public than we were before."

Mr. Markel set forth in eloquent words the policy of the trust : " For, let there be no doubt about this, the combine has immense possibilities in which the whole nation will indirectly share. Let me briefly indicate these. In the first place I would premise that we produce not merely soap but a very large number of chemicals ; the combine is in fact a soap and chemical combine. The industry is dependent for a large number of its most essential materials on foreign supplies. Hitherto it has been at the mercy of these markets, the most fluctuating in the world. One of its first objects will be to rid itself of this dependence by cultivating land suitable for various oil-producing seeds. In other words the combined resources of the trade will enable it to do for itself something analogous to what the Cotton Growing Association is doing for the Lanca-shire cotton trade. Surely there can be no objection to this ? As an incident in the production of oils for its soap it will be able to manufacture on a large scale the special hard fats required for candles, chocolate, and other purposes, as well as lubricating oils and oils used in industries, such as the paint and varnish industries. Co-operation will also enable us gradually to make ourselves independent in the matter of many fine chemicals, such as colours and synthetic perfumes, which hitherto we have been compelled to import. Further, the com-bine contemplates embarking on the production of quite a number of new articles, which it believes will give it predom-inance in industries practically new to England. Under these circumstances, viewing the immense resources of the combine— financial, technical, and scientific—is it too much to hope that, directed with an enlightened policy by the combined experi-ence of all the manufacturers, it will succeed in winning for England not merely in soap but in its allied industries a practi-cal monopoly in all the open markets ? Think what this means, the sole supply of soap and a large number of other chemicals to more than three-fifths of the inhabitants of the world."

One would imagine that such noble aims would have won the approval of the world, but, sad to say, a storm of obloquy burst on the heads of Mr. Lever and his associates. To a great extent it was their own fault. With a carelessness which threw some doubt on the business capacity of which they boasted, they allowed their scheme to become public property before it was brought to a conclusion. Secondly, they antagonised the retailers by raising the price of soap to them 20s. to 25s. a ton, while keeping the retail prices at their former figures, and then by striking an ounce off the nominal pound bar of soap they sought an additional recoupment of 7 per cent. from the customer. The householder did not care much about the grocer, but heartily disliked what he thought was a mean trick, even although the manufacturer was still bearing himself the bulk of the increased cost. The grocers were furious. Saying nothing about their own numerous agreements to hold up the prices of proprietary articles and their frequent attempts to boycott and destroy the co-operative stores, they held meetings of their associations all over the country and passed resolutions pledging themselves to push non-trust soaps. Taking advantage of the public excitement they put up the price of trust soaps a halfpenny a pound, so that if they had to handle the unclean thing they would at least have a handsome profit. The outside makers very smartly joined in the hue and cry; it was plainly good business to do so, and no doubt they reaped a good harvest. The London grocers discussed plans for making their own soap co-operatively, and Messrs. J. C. & J. Field placed before their customers a scheme for establishing a subsidiary company with a capital of £90,000 to manufacture soap for the trade. Kynoch, Ltd., issued £100,000 of debentures to enable them to take advantage of "the unexpected opportunities in the soap trade," and the old-established firm of John Knight was converted into a public company with an issued capital of £370,000 to provide £45,000 for immediate developments. It would have mattered little to the "trust" what the grocers or housewives said, had not almost the whole newspaper press united in attacking it and its policy. Competition not only meant low prices—it also meant increased adulteration—but it also meant plenty of advertising, as the following excerpt from the *Daily Mail* of 22nd October, 1906, shows :—

"The *Daily Mail* stated that the estimated 'loss in newspaper advertising through the formation of the soap combine will approximate to £200,000'. The point was immediately referred by the *Newspaper Owner* to a leading firm of advertising agents, with the startling result that the head of that firm put the figure at nearer £500,000 than £200,000. From another source we are informed that a cocoa trust is already looming on the horizon ; while the devastating effects of the tobacco trust on newspaper advertisement columns is still a chastening memory to the publisher. Meanwhile, tobacco and soap are up in price, and cocoa may follow. That is where the public comes in, and it is here, also, that the newspaper editor should find his text. Newspaper advertising means competition ; competition means fair prices to the public. Trusts, in the great staple household commodities, mean artificially maintained prices, and should be strenuously fought in their incipient stages alike by the public and the Press.—*Newspaper Owner.*"

The panic fear of a "trust" on the grossest American principles was quite unjustified. At most the combination controlled two-thirds of the output, while outside were fifty firms, including popular makers like Pears', Knight & Sons, Hudson, Fels, and great companies like the United Alkali Co., Kynoch's, Price's Candle Co., etc., which made soap as a by-product. All of these would gladly seize any opportunity of extending their trade such as might be offered by a trust aiming at high prices and monopoly. In its fright, or love of excitement, the public leant a ready ear to the most ridiculous rumours, that 700 men were dismissed from Lever's, that a union with the Beef Trust was being operated, that the trust was speculating in tallow for the purpose of bringing their rivals to their knees, and so on. Yet all the turmoil plainly showed that the trust idea was not popular with the consumer, and that, having learned some of the American lessons, he did not put much faith in the philanthropy of combined manufacturers. After a few weeks the amalgamated firms recognised their folly, and restored prices to their original level and the pound to its original size, but the mischief had already been done. Next time an amalgamation is arranged in a British industry the secret will be a little better kept by its promoters. The trust came into existence on 1st November ; on 23rd November the following circular was issued to the press :—

"The working arrangement entered into between the leading soap makers of the United Kingdom has been received with such great disfavour by the trade and the public as to make it unworkable, and as it is clearly the first consideration to endeavour to satisfy the trade and the public, it has been decided to terminate the working arrangement from to-day, 23rd November.

"Each firm will, therefore, continue to conduct from this day its own business, as was done prior to the negotiations being entered upon, and entirely separate from each other.

"The working arrangement between the leading soap makers is now, therefore, absolutely and finally dissolved."

So ended, at least for the time, a combination which promised to achieve a useful improvement in the trade, but was almost unique in the manner in which it was engineered and fought. Simultaneously to announce a combination of firms, making an article of general consumption, to raise the price, and to forecast a reduction in advertising, could not but antagonise the consumer, the shopkeepers, and the Press, and showed an extraordinary misunderstanding of the business situation.

CHAPTER VIII.

GRAIN-MILLING.

THE grain-milling trade of England has undergone a complete revolution in the course of the last thirty years, and the consequence of the change has been that for some time past millers have found the present organisation of the trade quite unsuited to modern conditions, and have been trying with no little vehemence to work out a new form of organisation which will remove all existing evils. Students of organisation problems will, therefore, find this trade an exceedingly interesting one to study, and fortunately there is much more information available than is usually at public disposal in the matter of the internal affairs of a great industry. The National Association of British and Irish Millers, whose objects are "by all available and legitimate means to protect and promote the milling interest in all its branches" and to "adopt the best means to promote the formation of local associations in all parts of the country, to be affiliated with this association," has since its foundation in 1878 worked arduously to achieve the aims so set forth. More particularly during the last seven or eight years it has dealt with the problems of organisation and has been served by presidents who have striven hard to regulate their trade. From the reports of the various meetings, conferences, and conventions, and also from the pages of the *Miller* and the *Millers' Gazette*, two excellent trade papers, as well as from private sources, this chapter has been compiled.

The President of the Board of Agriculture stated in the House of Commons (21st May, 1903) that about "thirty years ago there were probably about 15,000 corn and flour mills in the United Kingdom ; now there are about 9,000, including about 1,000 first-class roller mills and 3,000 with a more or less complete roller system". This reduction shows how much milling like other trades has been concentrated. The magnitude of some of the firms now in business may be grasped by consideration of the fact that out of 2,858,363 quarters of wheat imported into Hull in 1901 all but 97,224 quarters went to fifteen firms, the large milling companies, Messrs. J. Rank, Limited, and H. Leetham & Sons, Limited, taking, respectively, 522,267 and 352,143 quarters. A respectable share of the milling industry is in the hands of co-operators. The two mills of the English Co-operative Wholesale Society, at Dunston and Silvertown, manufactured to the value of £1,364,527 in 1905. In addition the output of the Scottish Wholesale Society's mills at the Chancelot, Junction, and Regent Mills in the same year was £863,210. There are also eight other corn mills owned by federations of co-operative societies whose capital in 1905 was £347,071 and sales £1,364,527. All this large production being co-operative does not affect the competitive market otherwise than by making the struggle among private millers for the rest of the trade proportionately keener. It is not possible to calculate the share of the industry which is in the hands of joint-stock companies as so many are private or family concerns. There are, however, at least fourteen public companies with an authorised capital of £3,440,000, of which £3,322,248 is paid up ; including debentures (£897,482) the total share and loan capital is £4,219,730. The largest of these companies is Messrs. Spillers & Bakers, Limited (capital £950,000), Henry Leetham & Sons, Limited (£750,000), making a good second. In most cases particulars as to profits are not available, but the following figures as to the ordinary dividends paid by Spillers & Bakers show the fluctuating character of the trade :—

Year to 28/2/92	.	.	.	.	.	.	6 per cent.
,, 93	.	.	.	.	.	.	nil.
,, 94	.	.	.	.	.	.	2½ per cent.
,, 95	.	.	.	.	.	.	5 ,,
,, 96	.	.	.	.	.	.	10 ,,
,, 97	.	.	.	.	.	.	10 ,,
,, 98	.	.	.	.	.	.	15 ,,
,, 99	.	.	.	.	.	.	5 ,,
,, 00	.	.	.	.	.	.	5 ,,
,, 01	.	.	.	.	.	.	10 ,,
,, 02	.	.	.	.	.	.	10 ,,
,, 03	.	.	.	.	.	.	10 ,,
,, 04	.	.	.	.	.	.	10 ,,
,, 05	.	.	.	.	.	.	10 ,,

Grain-milling was once a native rural industry, but it has gradually lost that character owing to the increasing dependence of the United Kingdom on foreign countries for the supply of wheat and to the greater use of rolling-mill machinery. In 1854, our import of wheat was 14,870,000 cwt.; in 1870-74 it averaged 39,562,000 cwt.; in 1880-84, 57,619,000 cwt.; in 1890-94, 65,455,000 cwt.; and in 1901-5, it averaged 86,849,000 cwt. The natural result has been a concentration of the industry in the large port districts, London, Liverpool, Hull, and the Bristol Channel. Mr. Wm. Nicholls, a prominent miller, said at the Buxton Conference of the National Millers' Association in February, 1901 : " The position of to-day was that three sections of the United Kingdom manufactured about one-third of the total output of the United Kingdom. They had Liverpool taking the lead with 450 sacks an hour ; they had Hull and York with their output of 350 sacks an hour ; and they had the Bristol Channel with an output of 350 sacks an hour ; and the total output of the United Kingdom was about 3,500 sacks an hour." The production of flour in London in 1901 was put at 35,000 sacks per week, and the consumption at 100,000 sacks per week. The rest of the production is divided among the numerous small country millers. Of them Mr. Nicholls said : " The English wheat miller, if properly situated at the present day, was quite as able to compete and make a profit as the port millers, because if his native supply was within his district, he was enabled to secure that at relatively low prices, and the farmers of his district had a certain loyal feeling towards this local miller, and they worked together perhaps for the common good. If the English miller had to pay freight and charges, he of course was handicapped in the degree to which he had to pay these charges. This remark applied to the supply of material and also to the location of his trade. The English wheat miller, if he desired to cultivate a baker's trade, was quite able to do so with the addition of foreign wheat, foreign flour, or flour supplied by his larger coast competitors." This last remark refers to the " mixing miller " who mixes American with British flour to produce a grade of flour more suited than pure English flour to make bread agreeable to English tastes.

It is a charge against him that he encourages the importation of foreign flour instead of buying from the port millers flour made from foreign wheat. We have, speaking broadly, a differentiation of the milling industry into two classes with diverse interests, port millers working on foreign wheat, and country millers grinding mainly, though not quite entirely, home-grown wheat.

The part played by machinery has been very important. Mr. S. Leetham, the president, said at the annual meeting of the National Association on 3rd May, 1901 : " Twenty years ago our trade was threatened with extinction owing to the pressure of foreign competition ; this was due entirely to the fact that our machinery had become obsolete, and that the Americans with greater perspicuity and alertness of mind had the insight to scrap theirs as soon as they realised it was out of date. Our convictions came, as they generally do, rather late, but we mastered the position, and to-day, without any aid from the State, we stand able to meet legitimate foreign competition. I think you will agree that I am not exaggerating when I say that, so far as the mechanical details of British mills are concerned, we are well able to hold our own against the world." The output of English flour mills thirty years ago, when they were mostly of the old type, was stated by the President of the Board of Agriculture to have been 52,000,000 cwt. annually ; it was in 1903 about 76,000,000 cwt. On the other hand, it must be pointed out that up to 1899 the total imports of flour grew more rapidly than the imports of wheat, and more rapidly also than the growth of population, though the rate of the seventies has been far from maintained. The average annual import of flour in 1870-74 was 5,124,000 cwt. ; in 1880-84, 13,280,000 cwt. ; in 1890-94, 18,829,000 cwt.; and in 1901-5, 17,848,000 cwt. The importation of flour from the United States reached its maximum of 19,467,000 cwt. in 1892, and has since then seriously fallen off. Many other factors besides the efficiency of British millers must be taken into consideration—the demands of other countries, the home consumption in the States, the policy of selling surplus flour below cost, and the practice of the American railways which favour the transport of wheat rather than flour. In 1902 our import of American flour fell off considerably and our import of wheat rose proportionally, the change being caused apparently by the differential duty on flour—now removed.

The adoption of rolling-milling on a large scale cheapened production, but the output of the port mills soon grew beyond the needs of their immediate districts. This was a necessary result of large scale production and became acute about 1896. "We see," said Mr. Baker at the Convention of 1899, "that we can make an extra 1,000 or 2,000 sacks of flour at a small cost, and we look about for an outlet for it; every man is quite justified in doing this, but what is wrong is sending it into a district, and knocking down the price in that locality." Curiously enough he did not see that the arrival of a large additional supply of flour in a district would of itself depress prices, even though no attempt at cutting was made by the vendor. According to Mr. Nicholls in the address already quoted, there is considerable local over-production in the Liverpool district and not quite so much in Hull, while the Bristol Channel mills about meet their requirements. Liverpool and Hull both competed vigorously in the Bristol Channel district, while the last did not invade the territory of the two former. Other millers said that the Plymouth district was the "dumping ground" for the surplus produce of Hull, Liverpool, and Cardiff. Here then we have keen competition between the port millers and the country millers whose territories they invade, and further competition between the different port districts for the right to oust the country miller. The Bristol millers, again, complained that in 1899-1900 inland millers having a plentiful supply of good English wheat invaded the Bristol district and undersold the town millers. Not only do we observe from all this overlapping a violent competition reducing prices and profits throughout the whole industry, but also a permanent and growing discrepancy of interests between the port and country millers. The country millers blame the port millers for depressing prices by over-production, but the port millers retort that there can be no national over-production so long as so much flour is imported from abroad.

A further evil of this competition is the growing practice of selling forward. Thirty or forty years ago this practice did not exist, though as a matter of convenience deliveries were sometimes delayed for short periods. Large milling firms in close connection with the import grain trade naturally came to adopt the practices of that trade and bought their wheat for future delivery, covering their risk by similarly selling their flour forward. The economic advantage of such a system is that it gives the miller security, though profits may be smaller owing to the greater equality of prices. Large bakers, also, who have a good knowledge of the tendency of prices, can profit by buying their flour for future delivery. Reckless forward selling for extended periods—six, nine, or even twelve months—without consideration of the financial standing of the purchaser, is a very different affair. A weak buyer, if the markets turn against him, can rid himself of his contract simply by not paying for what has been already delivered; a stronger man can purchase for his immediate requirements at the lower prices and delay acceptance of deliveries under his contract until the market again turns in his favour. In both cases the miller suffers. As flour prices move more slowly and at longer intervals than wheat prices, the opportunity of making profits as the wheat market changes is lost when flour is sold forward. At the Buxton conference in 1901 Mr. Leetham gave a vivid picture of the way in which trade is dislocated by inordinate competition :—" The price of wheat advances, and the miller has a large stock, and now is the chance to conserve his connection, forsooth—perhaps to increase it. We all seem to think that the best way of securing business is to sell lots of flour forward, and so make sure of a certain amount of trade. Is the explanation for this mode of procedure to be attributed to the fact that we love the peace of mind which comes from absolute security, forgetting altogether the premium we have to pay for this mode of insurance? One great motive which induces us to indulge in this insidious custom is certainly the knowledge that unless our flour is placed forward, all the buyers will be filled up by competitors and both mill and travellers will be short of work. You will notice I have said placed forward—not sold forward—for in many instances the flour buyer is unaware that he has (to use a phrase unfortunately well known in the milling trade) 'been kept right'; he is kept in sublime ignorance of this altruistic action on the part of the miller or his traveller until the price nominally advances, and then he learns, perhaps to his surprise, how the matter stands. The contract is of course accepted, because when all the millers are sold forward, it matters little to them where the nominal price stands, and with an unanimity worthy of a better cause they bolster up the advanced price until a fair proportion of buyers are again in the market.   It will be found that when it was the universal practice of millers, or their sons, to conduct the selling of their own flour, very little was sold forward except to the best men, who kept themselves posted in the daily fluctuations of wheat, and then in quantities commensurate with their trade and finances; but when the travelling system perforce was introduced, the greater scramble for the orders, not only of the best men, but the others, brought out in evidence the inborn selfishness of the trade, each thinking that by securing the orders for a few weeks ahead he was doing his competitor out of his fair share of the trade, and so, all blind to their real interests and those of their customers, reckless booking went on, but as every competitor had also done the same, the public only got the advantage. . . . Whilst the system prevails, millers have to permanently keep large stocks, upon which they have to pay warehouse expenses, interest, and other charges.   They have to bolster up an artificial price, to satisfy their customers, at times out of all relation to the real price of wheat, and their loss under this head of the current orders of some of the best men means loss of valuable permanent trade. . . . It is here that much misunderstanding arises with our competitors, and what seems to be a high tempting price on paper, consequent on the artificial price being advanced inordinately, is often the means of a rude awakening, when to the few buyers in the market outside competitors take the advantage of the few available orders; instead of the miller gaining even a little advantage by the rise just at this point, he has either to continue his policy of bolster and lose the current sales, or drop his price, so that the advance has in many cases done him more harm than good."

To sell flour forward at a low price after an advance in the price of wheat and then to keep up "spot" prices at an artificially high level to give a fictitious value to contracts is certainly the acme of folly. Mr. Leetham at the annual meeting of the National Association in 1901 pointed the way out of the absurdity : "With more frequent fluctuations in the price of flour the conditions under which flour would be sold would more nearly approach those of wheat. . . . With the necessary fluctuations in the price of flour there would be less extended forward selling, for the simple reason that the rise and fall would oftener occur ; this would mean more frequent spot-buying, and what is of infinitely more importance, less anxiety on the part of millers to book forward ; for if we know that flour buyers will be in the market every few weeks the wild rush to book forward will disappear." The conference of 1900, after a full discussion of the evils of unrestricted competition, came to the conclusion "that the fluctuation of the price in accordance with wheat was a desirable thing," and "that forward sales on a proper basis were not an objectionable thing". A proper basis was stated by the large millers to be two or three months. The conference passed, therefore, no restrictive rules, but accepted the policy that forward selling and overlapping should be dealt with by local associations for the fixing of prices. Committees were appointed to initiate such associations in the following districts :—

Berks and District.	Lincolnshire.
Bristol, Gloucester, and Bath.	London.
Derby and Notts.	Midlands.
Devon and Cornwall.	North-Eastern Counties.
Dorset.	North-Western Counties.
Eastern Counties.	Northants and Bedfordshire.
Hants, Cambs, and Peterboro'.	Potteries and District.
Kent and Sussex.	Shropshire and Hereford.
Leicester and District.	Southampton District and Portsmouth.

There were already in existence in these districts the

Kent Flour Millers' Association, the London Flour Millers' Association, the North-Eastern Association, the North-Western Association, the East Midlands Association, and the Potteries Association.

Associations were indeed no new thing in the milling industry. The Sheffield Association was formed about 1873, the London Association in 1878, the Kent Association in 1897. At first they concerned themselves with regulating the conditions of sale—were Konditionen-kartelle, to use Dr. Grunzel's classification. Thus the Kent Association abolished Christmas boxes; the London Association fixed the period of delivery at within four months from the date of sale and the time of payment at one month after date of delivery. The National Association itself was active in this direction and in 1898 drew up a National Sale Note, which was accepted by the National Association of Bakers and Confectioners and was afterwards adopted by many of the local associations. It included the following conditions : " The delivery of the flour must be made in reasonable quantities, and the contract completed within three months from date of sale, or sooner if specified on Bought Note. Tender shall be satisfied by a letter from seller to buyer, stating that the flour is ready for delivery. Payment must be made within one month from date of delivery, or by cash on or before delivery, at seller's option. The flour delivered must be of an average quality of the seller's grade as named in the contract." Provision was also made for lawful cancelment of the contract and for the adjudication of disputes by two arbitrators appointed by the Millers' and Bakers' Associations.

Such a degree of regulation was not sufficient to cure the raging competition. It was felt that some means must be found to limit the rivalry of districts with each other and to harmonise the interests of the port and inland millers. Mr. Leetham suggested that a local association would be able to maintain the balance of power by planting a mill of its own in a rival district and so carrying the war into the enemy's country. But the enthusiasm with which the regulation of prices was adopted in 1900 was due to the fact that there were then in existence associations operating in this way very successfully. The

London Flour Millers' Association, consisting of sixteen firms, fixes at its weekly meeting the prices of two standard grades, "London Whites" and "Town Households," and these are published in the daily press. They are, however, standard and not compulsory minimum prices. The rules are of the simplest and contain no penalties for breach, nor is there any information as to how far the official prices are observed.

One of the most interesting of all the price associations was the North-Eastern Millers' Association formed at the end of 1899. It covered the country from Newcastle to Grimsby, and included forty millers, leaving five or six outside, among the members being the two large Hull firms of Leetham and Rank. Some years before there had been an association which for a time had raised prices a shilling a sack, but it broke up under the competition of outsiders. Six local associations, which previously had had occasional understandings, now amalgamated on the basis of the mutual recognition of each other's prices. In each district there was a committee. Any member of a committee desiring an alteration in the price of flour had to communicate with the district secretary, either by letter or telegram, and he in turn communicated immediately with the other committee men. Any alteration arrived at by vote of the majority was at once telegraphed to all millers and salesmen in the district. Each member and each salesman had every evening to send to the district secretary full particulars of all contracts made that day. A monetary deposit, reckoned according to the capacity of the mills, was required to cover penalties for breaches of the rules. After nine months' working it was found that this method of fixing prices did not enable the members fully to cope with outsiders, and in order to give a greater amount of freedom the rules were altered so that no change could be made in prices if in a committee of eight two were adverse to change. The terms and conditions of sale were also regulated, and fixed differences between the prices of various grades of flour were established.

At first the members were satisfied, and Mr. Rank said that although the outsiders were taking local trade at 3d. and 6d. a sack below association prices, yet the members were not making any less money. But circumstances speedily altered ; competition from Liverpool came in and other evils made themselves felt. Mr. Rank, at the annual meeting of the National Association on 3rd May, 1901, summed up the situation in words which conclusively show the innate weaknesses of price associations : " In arranging for fixed prices, it will be seen that the worst equipped and most unfavourably situated mills must be considered, and must, of course, make a profit ; therefore the larger mills must perforce work at such a margin of profit as shall, and indeed does, invite outside competition. . . . The miller whose word is his bond has to suffer, whilst some seem to be seeking every means for evading or overriding the spirit of the agreement. They give way to things that are both demoralising to themselves and to their travellers. Millers have in some cases substituted a better class of flour, which has been invoiced and charged at the price of the grade below it. They have wilfully and systematically allowed some people more discount than the rule permitted ; they have allowed cartage to customers when they themselves (the millers) have performed the cartage, and have offered to invoice flour at the net price after deducting the rebate, and then again allow the rebate, as though it had not been taken off, when the invoice was settled ; and a very common form of underselling has been the invoicing of rough stuff, such as maize, oats, barley, and meals, etc., at such prices as showed a distinct loss." The result was the practical break-up of the association, for though it continued nominally in existence, the clauses respecting prices, terms, and conditions were suspended. Prices fell to an unprofitable level, and, for instance, the Cleveland Flour Mills made a loss of £2,655 in 1901.

The policy of imposing fines was much contested, for it was pointed out that they not only led to friction but also were ineffective, since a member who had made up his mind to break from the policy of his association would certainly have too much at stake to care about a mere fine. The Liverpool Association imposed no penalties, and yet found it could trust to the honour of its members. The fixing of prices, also, was achieved indirectly; the members met together weekly and each named his minimum price, and in two years' working, 1900-1, they honourably observed the terms they quoted and could trade in safety, knowing the extent of competition they would have to meet. Here again we note that the regular meeting together of the persons engaged in any trade for the discussion of trade conditions naturally tends to an informal regulation of prices through the communication of views as to the state of the market.

The formation of associations at first went on briskly. In 1901 price organisations were set up in Birmingham and district (with 80 per cent. of the millers), the East Midland Association (apparently reconstituted), Devon and Cornwall, and the Southern District (for Hants, Wilts, Sussex, and Dorset); early in 1902 the Notts and Derby Association was formed. The Kent Association grew to include 90 per cent. of the millers in the county. The rules of the Southern District Association may be taken as typical. Discounts, cartages, charges for sacks were regulated; a contract note was to be prepared; no member was to send to a buyer, in anticipation of a rise in price, a contract note where no sale had been made; the price of the standard grade, " fines," was to be fixed by the majority of a committee of five every Friday. Each member was to deposit a promissory note payable on demand of £10 if his sales did not exceed 200 sacks per week, and so progressively up to £50 for sales exceeding 1,000 sacks. No penalty was provided for breach of the price rule, but for offences against the other regulations a money penalty could be enforced by the council, subject to an appeal to the association, and recovered from the member's deposit. Both at Birmingham and in the Southern Association the rules were dropped in the spring of 1902, because the port millers would not promise to observe the regulations. In fact on this rock all attempts at fixing prices seemed fated to shatter. The conference of 1900 had suggested that no alteration should be made in prices against the opposition of one port and one inland miller, but even this compromise was of no avail. The *Miller* of May, 1902, had to confess that local associations were " at present languishing and not progressing as rapidly as we should wish ".

The Budget of 1902 with its duties on grain and flour interfered with the natural course of prices, and afforded an opportunity for action in which all interests were harmonious. The South Wales and Gloucester, Potteries, North-Western, Liverpool, and London Associations arranged that undelivered portions of contracts made before 15th April should be charged with an additional rate of fivepence per cwt., and this resolution was also adopted by the council of the National Association. The bakers protested, and a conference of the National Associations of the two trades was arranged, and a compromise arrived at of a rise of sixpence per sack of 280 lb. from 1st May. This was, however, practically the last effort of the milling trade at price regulation.

The four years, 1899-1902, in which the association movement was active in the milling industry were low price years, the average price of " Town Made White " flour being 26s. 7½d. ; in 1893-96 the average was 24s., for 1897, 30s., and for 1898, 33s. Besides, imports were steadily rising and in 1899-1901 reached their maximum. The brief gleam of prosperity in 1897-98 only made the succeeding depression more keenly felt. But with 1903 came a change. The increase of the home demand of the United States and the growth of a profitable export of wheat to China, coupled with the stationary character of the wheat crop, put an end to the dumping of surplus flour in British markets. The *Miller* of August, 1904, was able to say that " the British flour trade is rapidly becoming the monopoly of the British flour miller. For nigh on two years foreign competition has ceased to injure us." This favourable state of trade was reflected in prices, " Town Made Whites " averaging 27s. for 1903, 28s. 6d. for 1904 and 1905, increases made more important by the change in the nature of the imports. Comparing 1903 with 1899, 21,500,000 cwt. more wheat and 2,300,000 cwt. less flour were imported in the former year. It is not surprising that with the return of prosperity the movement towards combination should have died out in a trade so difficult to organise. To-day the topics which interest flour millers are the national sale note, the bankruptcy laws, the grading of wheat, and technical education.

There are, nevertheless, indications that the subject is only in the background. Mr. J. B. Clark, a well-known authority, writing in the *Miller* of March, 1906, said: "At the present time nearly every miller is crowded out with common flour; but as this common flour is made of a thousand and one wheat mixtures and another thousand and one flour divides and percentages, the system is unheard of and impossible whereby such accumulation can be classified and sold under the slightest chance of giving any satisfaction whatever anywhere. There is no trouble with the highest grades—they are unapproachable." A similar state of things had existed before in the milling trade, and Mr. Nicholls in 1901 suggested that the National Association should form a department to which millers making excess grades should send their flour for distribution among its members, this Clearing House acting as the selling agent, but the proposal was not adopted. An organisation of this kind had actually been tried in the West of England in 1894, but without success. Later in 1901 a proposal was made to form a regular sales association in the form of a limited company through which the members would sell all their flour, but it never got beyond the suggestion stage. Mr. Clark's solution is roughly on the same lines: " 1. All millers should be members of the National Association. 2. At certain centres there should be a warehouse, where surplus flour could be received. 3. These warehouses should be provided with machines for blending or mixing flours in various and varying percentages. 4. All flours received would be tested by an expert on arrival. 5. Mills in the districts should be visited weekly or monthly by a travelling expert miller, flours inspected, and prices arranged according to the brand of flour which it was desirable to sell. 6. A highly competent man should be retained to do the blending so that the cost of salaries and general upkeep could be covered by the process." And he adds: " For the past two or three years we as a trade have been free from attack, and during that time we have taken care to improve our modes of manufacture so that nobody can touch us in quality of output. The year 1906 is witnessing a return of the dumping of the *inferior* grades, and we must be prepared to combat that also. The millers of these islands are all fighting individually, and, as a consequence, against each other, and the result is to let the foreigner in."

The value of such plans is not in their immediate feasibility but in the evidence which they afford of the direction in which the mind of the trade is turning. That the grain-milling industry is capable, under certain circumstances, of closer co-operation is shown by the continued activity of the London price association, whose weekly announcements of the price of flour are made with the utmost regularity, and by the less ambitious but still effective working of the Kent, Liverpool, and some other associations. In one case, the Corn Millers' Association of the North of Ireland, not only prices but output have been successfully regulated. Twenty-three maize or Indian corn millers formed this association in 1900. Two officials were appointed, the Millers' Accountant and the Referee. The accountant was to ascertain the total quantity of yellow meal delivered by each of the parties in the two years, 1st November, 1897, to 31st October, 1899, and on the basis of this information the referee was to fix the total deliveries and the proportionate share of each member during the currency of the agreement. The accountant was also to ascertain the weekly deliveries of each member during the continuance of the agreement. Adherence to the contract was secured by a system of pooling profits : " Each of the parties hereto will, during the continuance of this agreement, pay a sum of 10s. per ton on the yellow meal which the Millers' Accountant may so find he has delivered in each week . . . and the money so payable will be divided monthly amongst the parties in . . . the proportion that each party's deliveries for the two years mentioned bears to the total deliveries of all the parties thereto for the same period." In this way no member can derive any profit from over-production, while he gains by slight under-production, which also tends to maintain prices. But "if the deliveries of yellow meal by any of the parties hereto shall during any month fall more than 10 per cent. below his or their proper proportion of the current deliveries, or if the weekly deliveries of any of the parties hereto shall be stopped or become reduced to the extent of 10 per cent. through suspension of payment, bankruptcy, or compounding with creditors, or strikes, or lockouts, or any other cause, or through a desire no longer to be bound by the terms of this agreement," a meeting of the members must be held, and, subject to an appeal to the referee, a two-thirds' majority of those present can decide what shall be done. The accountant is to be allowed free access to all necessary documents and books, and the expenses of carrying out the agreement are borne by the parties in the proportions of their legal deliveries. Meetings of the parties may be called by any of them subject to five days' notice. The term of the agreement is one year. The referee has final power to decide when there has been a breach of the agreement and may inflict penalties up to £200 for each offence, such penalties being divisible among the parties as the referee may decide.

This agreement is still in force, having been renewed from year to year. When it was adopted there was no profit in the trade. Through its action better conditions have been established, with the result that fresh competition has sprung up. Nevertheless no one has broken from the agreement, and while the members are satisfied there have been few complaints from traders. The members meet in Belfast every Friday and arrange prices without, however, absolutely fixing them. The success of this association is all the more noticeable when it is compared with the general failure of the looser forms of organisation.

Despite the slender and ephemeral success—if even so mild a phrase is not too strong—of associations, British millers have seldom slackened in their desire to find an organisation for their industry which would liberate them from the thraldom of competition. The consolidation movement which has affected so many other industries has not left milling entirely untouched. Even in the end of 1888 it was proposed to federate all the mills between the Tweed and the Humber into the North-Eastern Milling Company, Limited, but sufficient support was wanting. When the Convention of the National Association of Millers met at Llandudno in June, 1901, Mr. Scott Lings, the promoter of several textile combinations, was invited to address the members on the subject of amalgamation. He proposed the formation of a " holding company " which would " acquire a substantial control of the interests in the various individual firms composing the trade ". Each of the combining firms would transfer to the central company the same proportion of their shares and take its shares in lieu. Harmony of interests would thus be secured by the pooling of the profits of each firm on the agreed proportion of shares. The powers of the directors of the central company could vary with the degree of independence proposed to be left to the several firms. They might simply have power to convene the members from time to time to decide upon lines of policy, or they might have larger powers—buy the raw material for all the mills, act as a sales agency for the whole product, and undertake the financing operations for all the members. He warned them against the danger of dismissing too many managers who might set up as rivals, and against trying to change the ordinary course of trade ; he also urged the importance of training up men who would act in future years as directors. It was agreed to circulate the scheme among the members for their opinion, but out of 240 firms and associations who were communicated with only thirty sent replies, and of these only four supported Mr. Scott Lings' proposal.

Such a scheme was obviously fanciful. To combine some 9,000 millers, large and small, of whom the majority were inland millers who only competed with their immediate neighbours, and whose only common bond was hatred of the invading port miller, was simply absurd. Even to bring the 1,000 rolling mills into line would be a gigantic task. With the large port millers the case is different, for their circumstances, interests, and perils are all of the same character. What they have to fear most is the competition of each other within the same district, and the competition of port millers in other districts. The natural development, therefore, would be the amalgamation of firms in the same port, and then perhaps the union of the several ports. Such a combination would dominate the flour market and could either easily beat down the competition of the small inland millers or leave them in peace to deal with their local wheat. Faint indications of such a development are not wanting. In the Bristol Channel district the New Cardiff Milling Company agreed in March, 1903, to an amalgamation with the Phœnix Milling Company in order to form a new company; plant, mills, etc., were to be taken over at £85,000, stock at current market prices, and book debts at a valuation. The Phœnix Company is already controlled by Spillers & Bakers, Limited, a company formed in 1890 by the union of Spiller & Company, of Cardiff, and W. Baker & Sons, of Bristol, so that we may here see the beginning of a concentration of the Bristol Channel trade round that firm. Johnston, Mooney, & O'Brien, Limited, is a Dublin company formed in 1889 by the union of three baking and milling businesses; capital, £175,000. The Avondale Bread Company of Birmingham (paid-up capital, £15,944) was formed in 1899 by the union of the Vale of Evesham Flour Mills Company and the Avondale Bread Company. In the spring of 1903 it was rumoured that a consolidation of the London flour mills was in contemplation, but the report was false. The experience of other countries shows that large amalgamations of milling firms are not impossible.

The National Association of Millers has attempted for some years to regulate the conditions of purchase so as to insure the purity of the grain bought. In 1898 they asked the London Corn Trade Association to insert a clause in contracts requiring the shipper to make an allowance when the percentage of foreign matter in Black Sea, Danubian, and Indian wheats was more than 3 per cent. In barley contracts in the Bristol Channel district a " 3 per cent. dirt clause " brought down the percentage of extraneous matter from 10 per cent.; for beans a 5 per cent. allowance was made; and in linseed at Hull 3 per cent. Despite these precedents the London Corn Trade Association refused to alter the principle of arbitration in matters of dispute. The percentage system was proposed to meet f.a.q. (fair average quality) contracts, but purchases were also made on "inspection certificate," "adopted standards," "natural weight basis," or "about as per sample". The millers in 1899 again asked that when purchases were made by sample the buyer should be entitled to require that an analysis should be

15 *

made of the sealed bought sample and of samples from the bulk deliveries, any excess of dirt to be allowed for. Again the Corn Trade Association would not interfere with the arbitrators, and the millers after repeated rebuffs decided in the spring of 1902 that they would try to get representatives elected on to the executive of the Corn Trade Association and in that plan they have at last succeeded. It is interesting to quote, out of the controversy, a letter from the secretary of the London Corn Trade Association showing how f.a.q. standard samples are made up : " I am directed by my committee to inform you that all samples received by this association are submitted to them whether sold as f.a.q. or superior thereto, and that out of those samples they exclude any that in their opinion are undoubtedly too good or too bad ; so that your correspondents who think that all wheat sold as superior is excluded from the standards are mistaken in that supposition, and those who think that decidedly inferior wheat is necessarily admitted because it is sold on f.a.q. contracts, are also wrong. The admixture is also made proportionately to the quantities represented, and every effort is made to obtain samples of all shipments, whether to the Continent or the United Kingdom."

Finally, the Council of the National Association in 1902 prepared a thorough scheme for teaching flour milling technology, and proposed to co-operate with local committees for that purpose in Bristol, Birmingham, Cardiff, Dublin, Edinburgh, Glasgow, London, Newcastle, Plymouth, Stockton, and York; at Gloucester, Liverpool, and Hull classes already existed. In thus caring for the technical training of millers the National Association has probably found its most useful and most promising sphere of activity. The Irish Flour Millers' Association, formed late in 1902, with twenty-two members, has cognate aims, for its immediate purpose is to disabuse the public of their prejudice against Irish flour.

CHAPTER IX.

TOBACCO AND LIQUOR TRADES.

THE tobacco trade has been the theatre of one of the keenest struggles ever fought out between British and American business men, a fight which resulted in the complete defeat of the foreigner. The first shot in the fight was the purchase of the young and prosperous business of Ogden's, Limited, by the American Tobacco Company in September, 1901. Ogden's profits had been in 1898-99, £26,854, in 1899-1900, £46,500, and in 1900-1, £38,330, and their cigarettes were among the most popular brands. The American company at once made it plain that they were going to do things on a large scale, for they offered £2 10s. for the £1 ordinary shares, 25s. for the £1 preference shares, and ten guineas premium on the debentures, and practically all the issued capital was acquired, the price paid for the business being £818,000 of which £218,000 represented goodwill. At the meeting of shareholders to confirm the sale on 20th September, 1901, the chairman did his best to create an American terror: "The American Tobacco Company," he said,[1] "make no secret of the fact that they desire to obtain a large share of the tobacco trade both of England and of the Continent. . . . Whilst we have only an issued capital in debentures and shares to the amount of £460,000 their capital is fifty millions sterling, or in other words for every £1 of capital issued by us they have £100, so that the contest in a cutting competition, whenever it came, would be unequal. Further, we had to take into consideration the fact that out of their profits the American Tobacco Company have set aside for the purpose of the active business efforts they intend to make of capturing the English and European trade a sum of six millions sterling."

[1] *Financial Times*, 21st September, 1901.

The reply of the British manufacturers was prompt. Within a month thirteen of the leading tobacco firms issued a circular announcing the amalgamation of their businesses under the name of The Imperial Tobacco Company (of Great Britain and Ireland), Limited, and adding " we wish our customers to be assured that if they remain loyal to British commerce we shall stand by them, and that, in the arrangements which are now being made for carrying out the amalgamation, the interests of the retail trade will be carefully borne in mind. As soon as our arrangements are completed a further communication will be addressed to you, and we venture to hope that meanwhile our respective customers will continue the confidence hitherto reposed in us." The prospectus, issued in February, 1902, gave the following particulars as to purchase money :—

W. D. & H. O. Wills, Bristol	£6,992,221
Lambert & Butler, London	754,306
Adkin & Sons, London	146,497
Hignett's Tobacco Co., London	54,183
Franklyn, Davey, & Co., Bristol	473,555
Edwards, Ringer, & Bigg, Bristol	372,603
John Player & Sons, Nottingham	601,456
Hignett Bros. & Co., Liverpool	477,038
William Clarke & Son, Liverpool	403,582
Richmond Cavendish Co., Liverpool	319,805
Stephen Mitchell & Son, Glasgow	701,000
F. & J. Smith, Glasgow	525,803
D. & J. Macdonald, Glasgow	134,973
Total	£11,957,022

Of that sum £8,518,097 was paid for goodwill, trade marks, licences, proprietary brands, etc., of which £7,666,288 was the price of goodwill alone, or 7·2 years' profits. The annual average profits of the combined companies for the last three years was certified to be £1,062,922, before charging interest and directors' fees, but after deducting working expenses and depreciation. The capital issued was £14,518,097—£1,500,000 in 4¼ per cent. debentures, £4,500,000 in 5½ per cent. cumulative preference shares, £4,259,049 preferred ordinary shares, and £4,259,048 deferred ordinary shares. The vendors took one-third of the debenture and cumulative preference issues, and all the preferred and deferred ordinary shares, these last two classes having been issued against the goodwill, brands, etc. For working capital and extensions £2,561,075 was available out of the proceeds.

With the transfer of the respective businesses to the Imperial Tobacco Company on 1st November, 1901, the fight with the American Trust began in earnest. Besides the two and a half millions just mentioned, the Imperial Company had two other weapons. The first was a bonus scheme for giving to the retailers "a yearly sum regulated by the amount of home trade profits distributed as dividends upon the ordinary shares, which will be apportioned amongst the participating customers by way of percentage upon their purchases of proprietary goods, as compared with the total amount of such goods sold by the company during the year". The other was the acquisition of Salmon & Gluckstein, by the conversion of the latter's capital of £450,000 into 10 per cent. preference shares on which the Imperial Company guaranteed the dividend, while a new issue of £100,000 (£10,000 paid up) in ordinary shares was made to be allotted to the Imperial Company, carrying control and surplus profits. Salmon & Gluckstein had a flourishing retail business with 140 shops, mainly in London, and their dividends had grown from $7\frac{1}{2}$ per cent. in 1895 to $10\frac{1}{2}$ per cent. in 1900. They had also a few months earlier made a tentative arrangement to manufacture goods on cheap terms for the retailers' alliance, which of course they now gave up, thus relieving the Imperial Company of some competition. The Imperial Company thus obtained a splendid nucleus organisation for the distribution of their goods which they could extend if they got into trouble with the retailers; through their branch William Clarke & Son they already possessed numerous retail shops in Ireland.

This entrance of the manufacturers into the retail trade contained some germs of weakness, for the 20,000 tobacconists in the United Kingdom naturally regarded it as a menace to their interests. Before the coming of the Americans the United Kingdom Tobacco Dealers' Alliance was formed to secure a minimum profit of 20 per cent. on tobaccos and 25 per cent. on cigarettes; out of this, of course, working expenses, generally estimated at $12\frac{1}{2}$ per cent. on the turnover, had to be met. They were also negotiating with Salmon & Gluckstein, who offered to manufacture for them on the basis of charging them 3 per cent. over cost, thus making each tobacconist virtually his own manufacturer. The retailers now appeared to be able to play off the American and Imperial Companies against one another, or to push against them both the interests of Gallaher's, Murray's, Bell's, Cope's, or others of the still independent makers, or to run their own scheme against all. But they were too numerous a body to come to a common mind, and Messrs. Salmon & Gluckstein gave up their plan on account of the friction and delay. Meanwhile Ogden's, as agents for the American tobacco trust, made a bold bid to capture the smoking public by reducing the prices of American cigarettes 35 to 45 per cent., while the retailers were offered for a short time free gifts of cigarettes. This astute offer shattered against the offended patriotism of the British people, who were incensed at an impudent attempt to capture British trade and boycotted the foreign intruder. Of course there was a considerable expansion in Ogden's business, it was a glorious time for the shoeblack and the messenger boy, but many tobacconists reported a transfer of trade from American to British goods. It was the same patriotism which helped on the flotation of the Imperial Company to raise the subscription for the million of debentures to £5,000,000.

A further element of strength in the Imperial position was that they owned a large number of the most esteemed and best advertised brands. There are 20,000 brands in the tobacco trade, to such an extent are individual tastes catered for, and the backbone of the business is the man who has his favourite brand and will not be lured from it by cuts in price. These in great numbers were with the Imperial Company.

Now began a war of circulars. In March, 1902, the Imperial Company offered a bonus to all retailers who signed an agreement containing " among others, a provision not to stock or sell without the consent of the Imperial Tobacco Company any proprietary goods manufactured or sold by the American Tobacco Company, or Ogden's, Limited, or the British Tobacco Company, Limited, recently promoted by the American Tobacco Company, or any person, firm, or company objected to by the company in writing ". £50,000 was set aside for the first half-year's bonus, and afterwards a sum equal to one-fifth of the amount earned on the home trade towards ordinary dividend, whether preferred or deferred. "It is not the wish of the Imperial Tobacco Company," said their circular, "to interfere with the sale of goods by the other manufacturers carrying on business and competing for trade in an ordinary manner." This agreement was to be signed by 24th March. Ogden's retorted with telegrams to all the retailers urging them not to sign, followed by a circular in these terms : " Commencing 2nd April, 1902, we will for the next four years distribute to such of our customers in the United Kingdom as purchase direct from us our entire net profits on the goods sold by us in the United Kingdom. In addition to the above we will, commencing 2nd April, 1902, for the next four years distribute to such of our customers in the United Kingdom as purchase direct from us the sum of £200,000 per annum. The distribution of net profits will be made as soon after 2nd April, 1903, and annually there- after, as the accounts can be audited, and will be in proportion to the purchases made during the year. The distribution as to the £200,000 per year will be made every three months, the first distribution to take place as soon after 2nd July, 1902, as accounts can be audited, and will be in proportion to the pur- chases during the three months' period. To participate in this offer we do not ask you to boycott the goods of any other manufacturer."

This extraordinary offer astounded every one. " There is no parallel to this magnanimity," said the *Times*, " except perhaps in the case of that friend of country yokels who sells sovereigns for sixpences." And all the press waxed eloquent over the virtuous indignation which the American trust showered on the boycotting circular of their rival. The British combine, with some astuteness, and probably some malicious selection of the date, gave on 1st April all the leading newspapers a page adver- tisement of excerpts from their own comments on the Ameri- can invasion—an exceedingly effective advertisement. But the boycotting clause gave trouble, and both in London and Birmingham the retailers at crowded meetings refused to sign. So the Imperial Company modified their agreement by a fresh circular: "We have," they said, "no intention of exercising our power in an arbitrary or unreasonable manner, and, in order to relieve customers of all apprehension on this point, we promise that so long as a customer does not display in his windows the goods of Ogden's, Limited, or the American Tobacco Company or their allies, we will not exercise our power of prohibition without first giving three months' notice, and the customer shall in that event have the option of withdrawing from the agreement. . . . We have not the slightest intention of interfering with the sale of goods produced by other British manufacturers, and we trust that they will co-operate with us in defence of common interests. Of course, there is no objection on our part to the display of their goods in any manner you think fit."

This skilful retreat evoked a fresh circular from Ogden's, but having already given everything they had nothing more to offer, and could only protest that they at least had not entered the retail trade. Meanwhile both antagonists had forgotten the wholesale tobacconists who now met and formed the Wholesale Tobacconists' Protection Association, refused to sign either agreement, and "respectfully asked that such terms will be arranged as will ensure our receiving 5 per cent. above what we have to allow on all proprietary goods". Ogden's and the independent manufacturers came to a satisfactory understanding with the wholesalers, but the details of the negotiations with the Imperial Company were not divulged. Ogden's also agreed to guarantee the retailers their 20 and 25 per cent. rates of profit, and introduced a wonderful coupon scheme by which smokers could obtain bicycles, watches, and other presents.

Meanwhile the Imperial Tobacco Company went on its way undismayed, without reducing its prices. Two more firms were acquired—W. & F. Faulkner, of London, and W. A. & A. C. Churchman, of London, Ipswich, and Norwich. Competition also began in the colonial markets, and report credited the Imperial Company with the intention of invading the preserves of the American Tobacco Trust and joining hands with its still existing competitors. At last the end came with an official statement in September, 1902: "The business of Ogden's, Limited, has been transferred to the Imperial Tobacco Company, and the export businesses of the Imperial Company, Ogden's, Limited, and the American Tobacco Company and its allies have been amalgamated, and a joint company is in course of formation under the name of the British-American Tobacco Company, Limited. The result is that the Imperial Company will, as between the hitherto competing parties, be left in possession of the trade of the United Kingdom, while the American Company is not to be disturbed in the United States or Cuba, and the British-American Company will compete for the trade in other parts of the world." The purchase price of Ogden's was £3,000,000, of which £1,500,000 represented goodwill, and over £1,000,000 stocks of tobacco; the goodwill was paid for by ordinary shares. The capital of the British-American Company was £6,000,000 (called up £5,220,021), and the Imperial Company nominated six of its eighteen directors.

Thus Ogden's passed from the scene, leaving behind it a rich crop of lawsuits over its famous bonus promises. The litigation did not end till August, 1906, when final decision was given upholding the validity of the agreement, and Ogden's settled their liability by a compromise payment of five quarters' bonus. In the course of the legal proceedings some interesting figures were disclosed. Before the American purchase of Ogden's the sales and the gross profit, after deducting discount, were as follows (*Tobacco*, June, 1906):—

		Sales.	Gross Profit.
Year to 31st May, 1899	. .	£678,471	18·55 per cent. of Sales
,, 1900	.	973,076	20·00 ,,
,, 1901	. .	1,419,131	18·37 ,,
Six months to 30th Nov., 1901		900,772	17·81 ,,

After the purchase there was a great increase of business, but an immense cost.

		Sales.	Gross Profit.
Four months to 31st Mar., 1902		£593,083	5·89 per cent. of Sales
Three ,, 30th June, ,,		541,838	3·59 ,,
Three ,, 30th Sept., ,,		718,725	5·40 ,,

The loss during this period of ten months was, according to the accountants, about £376,500. Advertising alone in June, 1902, cost £114,920. The moral is obvious. The Imperial Company for its first year of trading showed a profit of £42,000 above that shown in its prospectus, and the addition to its ranks of three companies besides those already mentioned, making the number of businesses absorbed nineteen. The contrast between American and British methods of business is, to say the least, striking.

The good fortune of the Imperial Company has never slackened as the following details show:—

	Net Trading Profit.	Placed to Reserve.	Dividend on Deferred Ordinary.
Year to 31st October, 1902	£1,105,576	£150,000	*nil.*
,, 1903	1,259,672	150,000	4 per cent.
,, 1904	1,452,146	200,000	6 ,,
,, 1905	1,705,647	250,000	8 ,,

Its share and loan capital is now £17,545,165, and its assets are £20,072,193, of which goodwill and patents account for £9,562,000. Ogden's had about 4,300 and the Imperial about 7,000 customers who had signed their respective agreements. Once the war was over a new agreement was substituted, requiring the signatories to conform in every respect to the company's prices and terms, and not to supply any person not so conforming; the company's payment to be at the old rate, *i.e.*, one-fifth of the ordinary dividend arising from home trade. Their schedule of prices fixes the retail price so that there can be no undercutting. The retailers were still hankering after the 20 and 25 per cent. rates of profit, conceded by the independent manufacturers, and a meeting of the Tobacconists' Alliance pledged its members "to stock and display the goods of the independent manufacturers and, as far as possible, place with them their orders for loose tobaccos, cigars, and cigarettes". At the same time 18,000 retailers have signed the agreement, showing, at least, a modified trust in the Imperial Company, and a very sound distrust of their own strength.

In 1903 the Imperial Company acquired a large interest in Klingenstein & Co., cigar importers. In the following year the largest distributing business in Australia was amalgamated with the distributing branch of Wills as Kronheimer, Ltd., thus strengthening the British and American Tobacco Company which had already bought up the two American firms exporting plug tobacco to Australia. The two largest Australian tobacco manufacturers were already united in the British Australasian

Tobacco Company (capital £1,200,000), and they as well as two other Australian companies took shares in Kronheimer, Ltd. The working of the combination was the subject of a Royal Commission which by a majority of four to one recommended the nationalisation of the industry. The evidence, as well as the two reports, is of a highly contradictory character, and may be studied in No. 26 of the publications of the Commonwealth for 1906. The Imperial directors in their report for 1905-6 set aside £100,000 as the nucleus of a pension fund for their employees. It also disclosed the fact that one of the boasted advantages of a trust, its power to control the prices of raw material, was of doubtful validity. The buyers being reduced in number through amalgamations were able at first to come to an agreement and reduce prices, but later on the farmers discovering the "pool" combined in turn, stored their tobacco, and with the help of the banks held it for the rise. One after another the great tobacco districts have organised themselves with profitable results to the growers, and *Tobacco* in its issue of January, 1906, gives from the American press an exciting account of how the "Night Riders" in some districts intimidate the "independent" farmers and prevent them from selling to the trust agents.

Great as is the position of the Imperial Tobacco Company—doing, as the chairman claimed in 1904 "rather over 50 per cent." of the whole trade—it is doubtful if it has seriously affected the position of its more solid British competitors. In fact by causing several of them to put their houses in order and to strengthen themselves by alliances it has increased their ability to compete. Thus Cope Brothers amalgamated in 1902 with Lloyds of London, and in 1905 bought up a Nottingham house; its capital is £426,400. R. & J. Hill in 1904 absorbed H. Archer & Co.—capital £281,000. In both these cases the results have justified the action taken. On the other hand the attempt to form the National Provincial Tobacco Company of four firms with a capital of £500,000 broke down in 1903. The large private company, Gallaher's of Belfast, probably the largest of the independents, has certainly not been hurt, nor has any other firm in possession of a favourite and well-advertised brand. That was the great weapon of the Imperial Company in its fight with the American trust, and it is the great defence of the independents. There have been some complaints against the Imperial Company of underselling, but they only appear exaggerated accounts of ordinary competition.

The relations between the Imperial Company and the retailers have certainly not given complete satisfaction to the latter, but there is every reason to believe that they have been treated more generously than their strength could command. The cigar and cigarette manufacturers and the wholesale tobacconists are fairly well organised, but the retailers are not locally organised in a manner proportionate to the fuss they made in the early days of the "tobacco war," and seem to have very little power to maintain prices. The Tobacco Dealers' Alliance has striven hard to secure an organisation for the supply of the retailers, and in September, 1904, it was reported that five firms had been selected to manufacture special brands exclusively for the Alliance. The United Tobacconists' Association, now eleven years in existence, and with strong branches at Dublin and Birmingham, appears from the reports in *Tobacco* to pay 20 per cent dividend, but the extent of this co-operative effort does not appear to be great. At present the manufacturer, through his scheduled price, is the agent whereby retail prices are maintained, for it is to his advantage that the retailer should have a permanent interest in the sale of his goods. The Imperial Tobacco Company claims that by its schedule of prices it protects the retailer against underselling and secures him a "legitimate profit" upon every article sold. The view of the trade is shown by the following extract from *Tobacco* of February, 1906: "As one of the most powerful weapons in the trade, the schedule has emerged from criticism into approval. While it was being forged and when it first came into use it was regarded by many retailers as interfering with liberty. Why should a manufacturer dictate to the retailer what he should sell at? was asked. Gradually the position was reversed, and at present any objectionable feature which a compulsory minimum retail price may bring with it is considered to be compensated for by uniformity of price, which is the direct

outcome of schedules." Of course the undercutter is boycotted
by the manufacturer.

The retailers made great complaints during the war of the
tyranny of the " trusts," in the light of which the resolutions
governing the action of the United Kingdom Tobacco Dealers'
Alliance read rather queerly. The governing committee was
empowered " to enter into agreements with manufacturers or
manufacturers' associations or combinations, by which non-
members of the Alliance be charged a price at least 10 per
cent. on all tobacco and 12½ per cent. on packet and loose
cigarettes higher than the highest price charged to any
member ". The members bound themselves "to sell only at
such prices as shall be fixed from time to time by the governing committee," and " to purchase, sell, and deal only and
exclusively from and in the goods of those manufacturers who
agree with the Alliance ". It is not necessary to suppose that
this scheme was carried out in its entirety; it bears futility
written large all over it.

At one period the Imperial Tobacco Company appears to
have thought of trying conclusions with the co-operative movement, but discreetly withdrew. " Two or three years ago,"
says the *Co-operative News* of 24th March, 1906, the Imperial
Tobacco Trust Company desired the English Wholesale
Society to observe certain conditions in the sale of the trust's
tobaccos, otherwise supplies would be cut off. The Wholesale
Society could not see their way to fall in with the views of the
Imperial Tobacco Trust Company, and there the matter evi-
dently ended. At any rate the English Wholesale Society
continued to send orders to the trust company, and none of
them came back unfulfilled." As the English Wholesale
Society manufactures tobacco on its own account, and has an
output of 2¾ million pounds of tobacco, 21 million cigarettes,
and 2½ million cigars, it would only regard a boycott as a good
opportunity of extending its own business.

While the main attack on the British tobacco trade failed,
the American Tobacco Trust succeeded in capturing the Cuban
cigar trade, through its subsidiary, the Havana Tobacco Company, which first of all acquired the Havana Commercial

Company and then bought up a controlling interest in Henry Clay & Bock, buying 90 per cent. of the £10 ordinary shares at £17, and paying £14 for the £10 preferred shares. The English directors at first opposed the surrender of the company, but ultimately had to yield at the end of 1902 to the power of the purse.

Matches go with tobacco, and the story of the submission of Bryant & May to their American rivals forms a suitable pendant to the tobacco war. The Diamond Match Company of America invaded England about 1896 and founded the Diamond Match Company of Liverpool. In 1901 the Liverpool company was "absorbed" by Bryant & May, but the absorption was of a curious character. The capital of Bryant & May was £400,000; that of the Diamond Match Company was £580,000; the latter company was to receive £80,000 in Bryant & May shares, to be converted, along with the existing £400,000, into cumulative preference shares with a dividend of 14 per cent.; in addition, £400,000 in deferred shares were to be issued to the Diamond Match Company, thus giving it the control while the English shareholders were to be pensioned off in luxurious ease. The shareholders in Bryant & May were obviously staggered by the proposal, but Mr. Barber of the Diamond Company put the situation before them with brutal clearness. " The machinery now being used in Bryant & May's factory was the invention of men who had been in the employ of the Diamond Company since its inception, but that machinery was discarded by that company fifteen or sixteen years ago, and they had gradually been improving on it. He did not think there was a year when the Diamond Company of America had not expended at least $50,000 in experiments in improving their machinery. . . . In fact in this direction they had spent altogether fully $1,000,000, with the result that they had machinery for the manufacture of matches that could not be competed with by any machinery in the world. . . . In the North of England they had driven the cheaper matches out of the market, and had competed successfully with Bryant & May; but they had not a factory in the south, and it had been a question with them whether they should build a factory here or make a proposition to Bryant & May. They did not want the waste incident to competition, and accordingly they put forward a scheme of amalgamation." [1] The English company had been caught napping, and had to surrender to the superior business skill of their rivals. The extent to which concentration has gone in the trade may be gauged by the remark of the managing director of R. Bell & Co. at the annual meeting in March, 1905, that whereas ten years ago there were forty match manufacturers, there were then only nine. This is partly due, of course, to foreign competition.

It will be quite in accordance with the fitness of things if we next proceed to the whisky trade, which suffers severely from over-production, and where the distillers have had for years to adopt a policy of restriction. The Distillers Company—a combination of six Scotch firms formed in 1877—absorbed two other distillery companies in 1902; in 1903 another distillery was bought, and in 1905 it acquired a half share in the United Distilleries Company of Dublin. The company thus dominates the grain whisky trade of Scotland, leaving six independent companies outside, and its Irish purchase was made to prevent its policy of restriction being spoiled by the Irish distillers. Its capital is now £2,169,350 and it pays a regular 10 per cent.

With regard to beer, it is a matter of common knowledge how all the large brewing companies for long pursued a policy of buying up public-houses and converting them into "tied" houses, and it is equally notorious to what straits some of them have been brought by their reckless competition in this respect. In some towns, like Liverpool, for example, the control of the retail trade is very complete, practically all the houses being in the hands of the brewers. This exploitation of a state-granted monopoly and the resulting interference with the tastes and desires of the public have aroused no little opposition, and one of the most popular adjuncts of temperance reform is the freeing of the tied houses.

Three hundred and seven British brewing companies are listed in Burdett's *Official Intelligence* for 1906; of these,

[1] *Financial Times*, 16th July, 1901.

16

270 with individual capitals of less than £1,000,000 aggregate
£88,630,000 ; twenty-one of £1,000,000 and upwards but under
£2,000,000 amount to £26,640,000 ; and sixteen of £2,000,000
and over amount to £70,572,000. The companies with less
than £1,000,000 capital are mostly local breweries with a local
trade and reputation, and there has been a good deal of concentration amongst them leading to local amalgamations such
as the Bristol United Breweries (capital £745,000), of four firms,
Chester Breweries (capital £680,000), of five firms, and many
other cases. The complete analysis of this class is as follows :—

				Total Capital.
174 companies of single firms	.	. . .	.	£52,378,000
51	„	two „	. . . .	15,581,000
27	„	three „	. . . .	10,644,000
9	„	four „	. . . .	4,808,000
3	„	five „	. . . .	1,853,000
1	„	six „	. . . .	265,000
3	„	seven „	. . . .	1,552,000
1	„	eight „	. . . .	891,000
1	„	nine „	. . . .	651,000
270				£88,623,000

The combinations of two firms are very often amalgamations of a brewery with a wine and spirit business.

The next class of companies with capitals of less than
£2,000,000 includes nine amalgamations :—

	Components.	Capital.
Newcastle Breweries . . .	8	£1,000,000
Bentley's Yorkshire Breweries .	7	1,071,000
Wilson's Breweries . . .	6	1,714,000
Benskin's Watford Breweries . .	5	1,394,000
Manchester Breweries . . .	4	1,137,000
Style & Winch	4	1,206,000
Phipps & Co.	2	1,127,000
Smith's Tadcaster Breweries . .	2	1,200,000
Threlfall's Breweries . . .	2	1,825,000

The local concentration is again prominent.
Reclassifying the giants of the trade we get the following :—

4	£2,000,000 and under £3,000,000	£9,394,700
3	3,000,000 „ 4,000,000	10,168,400
6	4,000,000 „ 5,000,000	24,859,000
1	5,000,000 „ 6,000,000	5,440,000
1	6,000,000	6,000,000
1	over £6,000,000	14,710,000
16		£70,572,100

Up to the end of 1905 three of these had absorbed other businesses: Charrington's, with a capital of £4,025,000, includes two firms; Whitbread's, with a capital of £4,289,000, includes four, and Watney, Combe, & Reid, whose capital is £14,710,000, was a combination in 1898 of Watney & Co., Combe & Co., and Reid's Brewery. In 1905, however, the shareholders of the last-named company resolved to reduce their huge capitalisation by £2,389,000 in deferred shares, and that should properly be deducted.

In 1906 Samuel Allsopp & Sons, whose capital of £5,085,000 had been written down from £6,515,000, acquired the businesses of the Burton Brewery Co. and Salt & Co. on unusual terms. The selling companies were to transfer their assets, properties, and business connection to a trust company in exchange for £1,357,000 in securities, shares, and cash for allocation among the persons interested. Simultaneously the trust company was to lease the properties to Allsopp's for a rental of £70,000 and certain other payments for a term of years within which the mortgages, loan, and preference share capital of the trust company would be repaid and Allsopp's become actual owners. But the trust company retained powers of re-entry on non-payment of rent.

The large brewery companies compete among themselves and against the local breweries for all the trade that is not tied, and one result has been the disappearance of 213 businesses by amalgamation. Fifty-two per cent. of the capital is owned by 12 per cent. of the companies. Of course private brewing firms have not been taken into account.

CHAPTER X.

THE RETAIL TRADES.

THE retail trades appear to be the last stronghold of competition. No barriers beset the entrance to them, only a moderate capital is required for starting, and, given brains and a fair amount of luck, a large business may grow up out of very small beginnings. Nor has any great scientific knowledge hitherto been deemed necessary, though grocers and ironmongers are now giving considerable attention to technical education suitable for their trades. The trade mortality is consequently considerable; 940 grocers alone succumb every year. Out of this strenuous competition the large business has developed just as it has in manufacture, economies attending on large-scale distribution as well as on large-scale production. Every town has its notable businesses, great in proportion to the size of the town. In London they become gigantic—like Maple & Co. with £2,620,200—but that is only because London is larger and wealthier than other towns; the same principle of growth may be observed in a village. Persons with small incomes are compelled to buy their household supplies in small quantities and often on credit, and thus the retail traders of each locality and, to a less extent, of each district in a town, enjoy a certain limited monopoly. But facilities of travel and transport are constantly reducing that advantage and giving the large shop in a big town more and more customers at a distance among those classes which are able to pay ready money. The success of the Civil Service Supply Association and the Army and Navy Stores has led to a host of imitators, and the large department shops like "Whiteley's" (capital £1,800,100), Spiers & Pond's (capital £2,206,000), Harrod's (capital £738,550), offer to the shopper such economies of time and trouble that they are even more dangerous to the small retailer than the large single shop. Many a country shopkeeper has reason to blaspheme the parcels post and cheap railway carriage for bringing his mammoth competitors to his very door. The danger is multiplied when the large shop sets up branches all over the town or all over the country, and gives to each advantages of large common stock and joint buying which renders it superior to its local rivals. This development may be seen in the grocery shop of the country town which sends out salesmen with light spring-carts, not only to supply the outlying country folk but to take away the business of the village shop ; or if the village is of a fair size a branch of the town shop may be set up. From this to Lipton's, Ltd., with a capital of £2,500,000 and three or four hundred town and country branches is only a matter of degree. The druggist, grocery, provision, meat, milk. restaurant, and tobacco businesses afford numerous examples, " Lipton's," the Home and Colonial Stores (capital £1,200,000), Hudson's, in groceries and provisions; Spiers & Pond, Slater's (£455,000), Lockhart's (£228,795), A.B.C. (£192,954), and Lyons' (£1,256,000), in restaurants; Express Dairy Co. (£125,000), Maypole Dairy Co. (£923,000), in milk ; Salmon & Gluckstein, A. Baker & Co. (£200,000), in tobacco ; " Boots " (£1,348,500 in five companies), in drugs ; Nelson's (£601,434) and Eastman's (£1,126,490), in the meat trade, are familiar and successful instances.

Against such large masses of capital the small trader struggles in vain. To "deal at the stores" is a certain mark of gentility, and the small shopkeeper must rely on the working and lower middle classes who do their shopping on a Saturday night. Even there he does not escape the competition of the grocery stores—the branches of Lipton's and the Home and Colonial, or of Barrow's Stores and Joseph Burton & Sons in the Midlands—which cater for all classes. Competition is thus brought down very fine. "Certain local firms," said a speaker at a meeting of grocers in Glasgow reported in the *Grocer* for 15th September, 1906, "who had from fifty to sixty shops were content with a weekly profit from each branch of ten shillings to a pound, thus giving them an income of something like £50 per week." Nor do the perils of the retailer end there. He must still over the great industrial districts of England and Scotland face the competition of the co-operative stores whose supreme attraction is that profits go into the pockets of the customer. In 1905 there were 1,457 co-operative societies doing a retail business of £61,086,991, and the effect of their withdrawal of this large amount from private trading is increased when it is borne in mind that it is not spread over the whole country but concentrated in certain districts.

The weapon of the retailer is cheapness. The customer seldom possesses any expert knowledge of the goods he wishes to buy, and must either trust to reputation or secure what advantage there may be in the lowest price. As to the vast majority of people the saving of small sums is a matter of importance the retailer in many trades caters for such persons recklessly. Thus in the drapery trades we have everything cut down to something three farthings, season sales to clear out stocks at fabulous reductions, sales of " bankrupt stocks," and similar devices. The customer having a free choice of supplies exercises an economic pressure on the retailer, which he in turn transfers to the wholesaler, and the latter to the manufacturer. The manufacturer cannot cut prices indefinitely without running down to his cost of production and risking a strike if he tries to save on wages. He seeks a way out of the difficulty by trying to dispense with one or more of the middlemen and attempting to get into touch either with the shopkeeper or the actual consumer. Sewing machines and bicycles are sold direct by the maker to the user without any intermediary. In the boot trade large makers or factors have opened their own retail branches—like Manfield's, or Abbott's, or Randall's, or Dick's, or Lilley & Skinner's. This trade gives us two noteworthy amalgamations: in 1903 Freeman, Hardy, & Wills, of Leicester, boot and shoe manufacturers and retailers, purchased the old-established retail business of Messrs. Rabbits, of London, thus raising their capital to £525,000 (now £575,000), and making their number of retail shops about 400. Next year the Public Benefit Boot Co. (formed in 1897 to acquire two businesses), capital £350,000, and Lennard's, Ltd., capital £150,000, both retail boot companies, amalgamated. So long, however, as the manufacturing capacity of the trade continues to be about one-third in excess of what is required to meet the demand, so long will the boot trade be unfitted for combination of any kind. The wholesale provision and grocery trade also yields some instances of the search for strength through amalgamation. Thus in 1898 Cooper, Cooper, & Johnson (capital £340,000) united the business of tea grower, dealer, and retailer, but with conspicuous lack of success; in 1899 D. Hughes, Evans, & Co. (capital £120,000) joined together a wholesale provision business and twenty-six retail shops in London; in 1906 Messrs. Lovell & Christmas (capital £560,000), of London and Manchester, a wholesale provision house started in 1851 and paying 10 per cent., amalgamated with Messrs. Geo. Wall & Co., Ltd., of Liverpool, and Wall & Co., of Manchester. The combined companies in this last case have large interests in Argentina, France, Denmark, Australia, and Canada and their present capital is £900,000.

Where the manufacturer cannot dispense with the shopkeeper as a distributor he tries to reduce him to an entirely subordinate position by making his shop a "tied house," a device practised in the strawplait industry and very common in the liquor trade. But this method of securing exclusive customers, though common enough, as we have already seen, in many industries as a method of binding wholesale houses, is not well adapted to the ordinary retail trades. A more effective way is to appeal through advertisements directly to the consumer. Soaps, teas, coffees, drugs, and a host of other articles are made up by the makers in packages suitable for retail trade, and the merits of the respective proprietary brands are kept prominently before the public by eloquent announcements in the newspapers, pictorial appeals on the hoardings, distribution of free samples, the gift of prizes for the collection of coupons issued with the goods, and similar devices. In this way a demand for the particular article is created, the retailer must stock it, and as the cost of handling it is less than that of other articles which he must prepare, weigh, and pack himself, he is under a constant temptation to cut the price of proprietary goods and use them as "leading lines" to attract trade to his shop.

At last the retail traders have seen that the traditional methods of trading do not always bring prosperity, and locally in every branch they are organising themselves into associations, which again are federated into district and national associations. In various degrees of strength we find such organisations among chemists, tobacconists, grocers, ironmongers, bakers, saddlers, stationers. Usually they seek to deal mainly with those general trade matters in which the individual is powerless such as legislation, railway rates, and legal business. They have also made strenuous efforts to cripple the co-operative movement, an enterprise in which they have gained more notoriety than success. From the nature of their trades they have only a limited power of dealing with prices, but the attempts at regulation increase in frequency and intensity.

Chemists and druggists, having a quasi-professional status, and with the entrance to their trade guarded by apprenticeship and examination, are by far the most strongly organised of the retail trades. There are some nine or ten thousand chemists, and these are generally organised into local associations which have partly a scientific character ; indeed the scientific organisation of the trade is strong and highly creditable to the members. Proverbially a profitable business, it has nevertheless suffered severely from the competition of the "stores" and limited drug companies, and has lost trade to doctors who do their own dispensing. The lucrative trade in much advertised patent medicines and similar proprietary articles ceased to be gainful when grocers and stores took them up and pushed them as "leading lines" at cut prices. The owner of a patented article must, however, make it worth the retailer's while to push the article ; if the price is cut too low, the shopkeeper will substitute either a rival article or one of his own composition on which he can get at least a decent profit. Consequently, we get the device of the protected price. Price cutting was especially severe in the eighties owing to the activity of the "stores". Messrs. Burroughs, Welcome, & Co. claim to have been the first to try to protect the retailer, and they were soon followed by others. Thus in the trade papers of 1894 we find manufacturers' advertisements, of which the following is a sample: "If you buy two dozen 1s. size ' ,' and sign our agreement not to sell to any person whatever below the present cutting price of 10½d. per bottle, we will charge you 9s. 6d. per dozen, and will allow you as a bonus for non-further cutting 2s. on every dozen. This will leave you a profit of 3d. per bottle at the cutting price of 10½d., or 40 per cent. on your outlay. . . . If any one, after having signed our agreement, infringes the same, we will proceed against him according to the terms of the agreement for the recovery of the bonus given to him, as well as for damages, costs, etc., and an injunction will be applied for to restrain him from repeating his breach of contract. Besides this, we shall refuse to supply him with goods, except at the full price of 9s. 6d. net, without bonus, so that he could not make any reasonable profit by selling under 10½d. per bottle."

The advantages of such a plan alike to the manufacturer and retailer were evident, but it was equally plain that the wholesale houses, among whom cutting was equally keen, could not conduct their business on the basis of a multitude of individual agreements. The Proprietary Articles Trade Association was therefore established in January, 1896, to unite the interests of manufacturers, wholesale dealers, and retailers. Its objects are: "(a) The discussion of matters of common interest to the branches of the trades represented, with a view to decision, and, if necessary, concerted action. (b) The taking of such steps as the association may be advised are legal to deal with extreme cutting of prices, and to give advice and render assistance to its members in preventing substitution. (c) The doing of such other things as may appear to be of benefit to the trade." It is governed by a council of thirty members, ten from each section, the three sections forming three committees to deal with matters particularly affecting their branches of the trade, subject to ratification of their decisions by the council. Manufacturers and wholesale vendors pay an annual subscription of five guineas, retailers five shillings. The association has an official organ, the *Anti-Cutting Record*, with a monthly circu-

lation of 10,500 copies. According to the annual report for
1905-6, after ten years' activity 214 manufacturers and 3,647
retailers paid subscriptions in 1905, compared with 81 manufacturers and 1,989 retailers in 1902. There are also twenty-
two wholesale members, "practically all the leading wholesale
patent medicine houses in the country, and there is hardly room
for any improvement". A protected list of proprietary articles
was drawn up, the owners of which agreed to supply them only
on condition that they were retailed at specified prices. At
first the plan of campaign adopted was a strenuous boycott, but
as success attended the association it found it could afford to
pursue a milder policy. The *Year Book* of the association for
1906 thus describes the course of action taken:—

"The proprietors pledged themselves not to supply their
goods to any one on the P.A.T.A. 'stop list,' and any trader
who persisted in cutting any one of the articles was placed on
that 'stop list'. This plan worked well, and the list" (of
protected articles) "slowly but steadily increased, and by the end
of December, 1897, it comprised 142 articles. In 1898 it was
found that the proprietors of certain very important articles
would join the association provided they were at liberty to
supply any of their own customers who agreed to maintain
their prices, even although the customers were cutting some
article on the P.A.T.A. list. It was found that the list had
grown sufficiently, and that the scheme had so worked as to
allow this difficulty to be met, and the proprietors were allowed
to join the association upon these terms, the essence of the
revised scheme being that if a firm persisted in cutting any one
article on the list his name was added to the 'stop-list,' and
he could not then obtain supplies of any of the goods on the
list without going direct to the proprietor, buying in bottom
quantities, and giving an individual agreement to maintain the
prices. That this has worked well is proved by the extent of
the list published in this *Year Book*, and we think that no one
who knows the trade will quarrel with the statement that
cutting of any P.A.T.A. article is an isolated and rare circumstance."

The *Year Book* continues: "When a manufacturer wishes

to protect the price of a proprietary article through the agency of the P.A.T.A., it is necessary that he should join the Manufacturers' Section. The application for membership must be accompanied by cheque, value £5 5s., in prepayment of the first year's subscription, and must be made, in the first instance, to the secretary, who lays such applications before the council at the beginning of each month. Full particulars as to prices, profits assured, etc., should be sent. The council insist on the rate of profit to both the retail and wholesale trades being adequate; 20 to 25 per cent., when the goods are purchased from wholesalers in ordinary quantities, is the retail rate recommended by the council for medicinal articles. Other particulars may be had on request. If the application is passed, the articles are placed upon the protected list, and the executive undertake all the protection work in connection with them. That list is sent in the *Anti-Cutting Record* to all chemists in business in the Kingdom and to a large number of grocers and others holding patent medicine licences. The advantages of assuring profit through the P.A.T.A., as compared with private plans, are (1) that the articles are kept constantly before the trade; (2) that, other things being equal, most retailers give the preference to P.A.T.A. goods; (3) that the wholesale houses are all acting in conjunction with this association, whereas they are, almost without exception, opposed to private plans as giving too much trouble; (4) that the P.A.T.A. method is much the less expensive; and (5) that it is much more effective all round. It is more effective because it has numerous friends and private inquiry agents in every town; because the executive have accumulated information respecting hostile cutters and those who supply them which no individual firm can possess; because a power can be brought to bear upon such cutters which can be exercised by no one proprietor; and because the machinery for protection is all ready to hand and in working order. Every wholesale house has signed an undertaking to withhold supplies of P.A.T.A. goods from cutters on the 'stop list'; and any cutter refusing to conform with P.A.T.A. proprietors' prices is liable to be placed on the 'stop list' and to be kept there as long as the proprietors order."

The *Year Book* contains a list of 215 firms who own, control, or are agents for many hundreds of articles, the details of which occupy forty-six octavo pages in the protected list. As regards ordinary trade the association can show remarkable success. The report for 1905-6 says: "With the very large accession to the protected list of articles of extensive sale, there has naturally been an increase in the work entailed by reported cases of cutting. The council are glad to report that whilst the reported cases of cutting have been numerous, the cases where the association has been defied are rare. The council have now no fear of their ability to ultimately bring any offender into line. In this connection it is fitting that every credit should be given to the members of the wholesale trade who so loyally support the council in their efforts to prevent supplies of articles on its list reaching cutters." The action of the association in maintaining prices is no doubt assisted by the fact that just as ignorant patients have a prejudice in favour of medicine which is black and evil-tasting, so is there a general notion that eighteenpence, half a crown, and so on, according to size of the bottle, are the traditionally respectable prices of medicinal goods. The year 1905 was distinguished by the inception of a war against co-operative societies. With that persistent misunderstanding of the nature of dividend on purchases which characterises all retailers, the association decided that the quarterly or half-yearly dividend paid on its trading by a co-operative store was, like a bonus given by a private trader, an illegitimate reduction of the protected minimum price. A notice was prefixed to the protected list to the effect that: "Dealers in the articles included in the following list are respectfully informed that the articles referred to are supplied to the trade only upon condition that they be not resold below the prices therein stipulated, and that no bonus or dividend on the purchase money or rebate in cash or goods be given unless the value of such bonus, etc., be charged to the customer in addition to the P.A.T.A. minimum price of the article". All the 215 owners of or agents for protected articles agreed to impose this condition, and nearly all the Chemists' and Grocers' Associations in the country also accorded their support.

The reply of the co-operators was equally decisive. They refused to submit to the dictation of the chemists and proceeded to manufacture substitutes at the works of the English Wholesale Society. Like every other attack on the co-operative movement this boycott only served to stimulate the loyalty of store members. The *Co-operative News* of 23rd June, 1906, reported that "a representative of the *News* had a conversation on Tuesday with the gentleman who has charge of the department of the Wholesale Society which is affected by the step taken by the P.A.T.A., and was informed that the societies had stood loyally by the Wholesale Society throughout the whole business. The official named one of the articles for which the society was on the 'stop list,' and said, 'in this article alone we have turned out during the last three months as much as we did in the whole of the previous twelvemonths'". The *Co-operative News* for 1st September, 1906, contained a list of fifty-eight popular proprietary articles (eighteen of them not on the protected list) and in parallel columns the substitutes manufactured at the English Wholesale Society's drug works at Pelaw, Newcastle-on-Tyne. The standing advertisement of the Scottish Wholesale Society: " Support your own industries—buy at your own shop and employ your own capital," is a very powerful appeal, and the efforts of the chemists' associations to bring the co-operators into line are as little likely to meet with success as their efforts to persuade Parliament to prohibit the sale of drugs by companies.

An interesting example of how price maintenance may in certain circumstances partly defeat its own ends is shown in the following extract from the catalogue of the Civil Service Supply Association : " Pressure from traders combined in an association for the purpose of keeping up the retail prices of proprietary articles has caused certain manufacturers to fix minimum prices below which their articles must not be sold. Whilst the Civil Service Supply Association, for the convenience of its members, continues in some cases to supply those goods at the prices fixed by the makers—prices frequently much higher than the committee of management would desire to charge—the extra profits derived from the sale of those articles are utilised in reducing the prices of the great variety of other goods in which there is and can be no limitation of price." The Civil Service Supply Association has proprietary drugs of its own, whose sale is doubtless stimulated by this notice.

The association now proposes to deal with "substitution," or the pushing of some more profitable article in place of that asked for. "The retailer," says the *Year Book*, "has a right to persuade the customer to take something else, and each man must settle his business policy in this respect for himself. But a different consideration arises where the proprietor has added his article to the P.A.T.A. By so doing he recognises the retailer's right to a profit, and he takes upon himself the burden of securing that profit for the retailer. Common fairness dictates that the least he has a right to expect is that when his article is asked for it will be handed over the counter without any attempt to sell anything in its place." "Cases of substitution in relation to P.A.T.A. goods," says the report for 1905-6, "have been investigated, and the Council will in future deal with such cases as they do with those of cutting." Such removal of competition is not likely to make for moderation in prices.

The Chemists' Proprietary Articles Trade Association has been described in detail because it is so strong and active a body. It is the pattern upon which all similar organisations model themselves, and an equal measure of success they fondly hope to attain. The assistance of the very able and active officers of the P.A.T.A. has been extended to the grocery, saddlery, and stationery trades, for they are not only defenders of their own interests but also propagandists of an idea.

The Stationers' Proprietary Articles Trade Association, formed in 1905, held its first annual meeting in May, 1906, when it was able to announce that it included seventeen manufacturers, sixteen wholesale houses, and 884 retailers. Its protected list included 600 items, two-thirds of which had the full face value as minimum selling prices. All the London houses publishing diaries, except one, had agreed to "protect" the selling prices of their 1908 diaries; conferences had been held with the publishers of calendars and the makers of writing ink; and negotiations were going to be opened with the manufacturers of pens, pencils, etc. There had been some underselling, but it had been stopped without it being necessary to put any trader on the stop list. As it is estimated that there are about 20,000 retail stationers in the kingdom, it is plain that, despite a promising beginning, the association has still "a long row to hoe".

The Saddlers' and Harness Makers' Proprietary Articles Trade Association was established in September, 1905, and issued its first protected list in February, 1906, the council exhibiting much satisfaction because the list covered fifteen pages compared with seventeen in the first list of the chemists. After a year's working the association numbered twenty makers, including most of the leading houses, nineteen wholesale vendors, and 316 out of 5,000 retailers. Since the issue of the list some fifty or sixty houses, mostly outside the saddlery trade—the Civil Service Supply Association, Army and Navy Stores, Spiers & Pond, etc.—agreed to raise their prices to the prescribed level, and only two firms had refused and had been placed on the "stop list". This association exhibits quite a militant spirit. Said the chairman at the first annual meeting: "It was only fair to refuse to handle the goods of firms who did not belong to their association. This had been well driven home in London and in all the large provincial cities. There was one firm whose goods were being kept out of their shops, and he hoped would continue to be so kept until they came into line with other makers" (*Saddlers' Gazette*, August, 1906).

Like all the retail trades except the chemists, organisation in the grocery trade consists mainly of gaps. There is a Federation of Grocers' Associations which has grown in sixteen years from 25 to 124 associations, leaving thirty or forty associations outside, but even now it only includes about 14,000 members out of some 70,000 in the trade. The local associations are also grouped into district federations governed by councils, such as the Midland, Metropolitan, and South Wales Councils. The annual conference of the federation in July, 1906, dealt with Sunday trading, house duty, the American canned meats scandal, compensation for accidents, weights and

measures, margarine, milk-blended butter. The topics occupy-
ing the attention of the Midland and Metropolitan Councils in
the same month were inspection, building bye-laws, compensation, milk-blended butter, and railway rates; the Midland
Council also discussed the appointment of a solicitor and an
analyst, and a scheme of technical instruction for grocers'
assistants. The fifth annual report (for 1905-6) of the Eastbourne Grocers' Association gave as the list of subjects which
had occupied their attention during the preceding twelvemonth:
"The sale of proprietary articles, the supplying of goods by
manufacturers to hotels and customers direct, selling prices of
bacon, Sunday closing of shops, selling price of butter, cheese,
sugar, etc., weight of mince-meat in jars, combined buying, the
adulteration of butter, the sale of margarine, traffic in empty
biscuit tins and jam jars". These summaries sufficiently ex-
plain the general business of the associations. At some places,
such as Workington and Reading, plans for combined buying
have been adopted, while Eastbourne established a grocery exchange where members could sell goods overstocked or unsuitable for their district, but not much use has been made of it.

No class of shopkeepers is so much exposed to the competition of stores, multiple shops, and co-operative societies as the
grocers who at every turn must be beaten by the low prices
which the superior buying advantages of their rivals make
possible. Thus at a meeting at Glasgow in September, 1906,
it was reported that one multiple shop was selling Danish
butter at 1s. 2d. per lb. against 1s. 4d., the lowest at which an
ordinary shopkeeper could make a decent profit; another
"stores" was selling best sugar at 2d. per lb. instead of 2½d.
The grocer must "cut," make "leading lines" to attract trade,
or even adopt less reputable means of securing some profit.
"They sold hams and bacon without profit," said a sorrowful
Glasgow man at a previous meeting; "they might make it up
by selling 6d. margarine at 8d. or 10d. a lb., or even as butter,
but that was not legitimate or honest business." Over all the
great bulk articles of his business the grocer and provision
dealer cannot hope to control prices; it would be very easy for
a company to dump down a new shop in a profitable district,

and the temptation would be too great to be resisted. The grocers fully recognise that generally the company shops are the chief enemies to be feared in the matter of price-cutting, but those who have observed the improved service introduced by and on account of those shops, compared with the insufficient and inefficient service previously rendered in many places by the individual shopkeeper, knows that the case is not concluded by the grocer's version. A local association deems itself fortunate if it can keep retail prices moving in response to wholesale prices, and if the pages of the *Grocer* be examined, say during the autumn of 1906, it will be found that there was a persistent and generally successful effort all over the country to raise the price of sugar, ham, bacon, cheese, soap, etc., on account of the advances in the price of raw materials. The means adopted vary according to the strength of the association. In Glasgow, for example, where combination was young and weak, "there was," a speaker said, "to be no naming of prices. What they wanted was the retailers to advance their prices in proportion to the advance that had taken place in the wholesale market. . . . The wholesale trade agreed to deal directly with retailers, and remonstrate with them on the folly of selling without profit" (*Grocer*, 11th August, 1906).

Sometimes the rise takes the form of an increase made by the shopkeepers without any attempt at uniformity either in the amounts added or in the actual prices. Thus at Birmingham a resolution was carried "that an advertisement should be inserted in the local papers recommending an advance in the prices of ham and bacon" (*Grocer*, 21st July, 1906), and at Liverpool "it was decided to advertise that people must be prepared to pay higher prices for bacon and butter" (*Grocer*, 4th August, 1906). The next step is to fix the amount of increase —at Oldbury "it was resolved to raise the price of bacon ½d. per lb." (*Grocer*, 14th July). Finally, a minimum price is fixed ; thus at Wolverhampton two resolutions were adopted, "that an advertisement be inserted in the local papers intimating that the association had decided to advance the price of provisions 1d. per lb.," and "that the association circularise the trade recommending that the minimum prices for drafts (bacon)

17

should be 8d., hams, 1s., and finest Canadian cheese, 8d. per lb."
(*Grocer*, 28th July, 1906). Generally, an association must rely
on moral suasion to back up its resolutions. The Kettering
Association "have been working with companies which have
local shops in reference to the price of loaf sugar. The minimum for some time has been 2¼d., but they found that some
of the companies were now selling at 2d. It was decided to
approach them, pointing out that they considered this was not
necessary, and asking whether they would agree to maintain the
minimum price of 2¼d." (*Grocer*, 21st July, 1906). The chairman of the Birkenhead Association said that "since the retailers increased the price of sugar some months ago there had
been occasional signs of a collapse, but they had succeeded in
preventing any falling away. Last week there was some misapprehension, and some grocers seemed like reducing prices,
but luckily with the aid of the secretary he was able to prevent
it" (*Grocer*, 7th July, 1906). Apart from persuasion the only
way to meet underselling is by underselling; thus at Leicester
"the honorary secretary was instructed to circularise the trade
in Leicester and district to the effect that tea was being sold in
the town at less than a shilling per lb., and that they would be
free to take what steps they chose to protect themselves"
(*Grocer*, 21st July, 1906).

A varying amount of success attends the efforts of these
associations. Thus at Warrington the attempt to fix the price
of sugar broke down in July, 1906, but the Leicester Association in its annual report (*Grocer*, 21st July, 1906) could say :
" In maintaining a legitimate margin on sugar the association
has helped to secure for some of its members a profit of pounds
per week for months, while others have had their donations
repaid over and over again through the same cause. Had
there been no association, competition would probably have
kept traders at the old suicidal policy of selling sugars at a
loss. Prices, too, have been fixed on lard, cheese, and bacon,
having a beneficial effect in sustaining a living profit."

A special association of some interest is the Retailers'
Sugar Association (London and Suburban) established in 1904,
which publishes the prices of sugar weekly in the *Grocer*, and

receives a large amount of support from the company shops. In the second annual report the secretary said : " Over 10,000 letters and circulars have been despatched in connection with five changes in the minimum retail prices of sugar during the year. Over 3,000 calls have been made, and 250 journeys taken to inquire into and rectify cutting." It meets undercutting by local selling at prices quite unremunerative; thus at a meeting (*Grocer*, 15th September, 1906) " a very strong feeling was expressed in regard to the small shopkeeper who undersold, and it was resolved that where any member of the association was forced to cut under such circumstances he should sell at least ½d. per lb. under the current prices of the association ".

With regard to proprietary articles the grocer occupies a different position. Owing to keen competition among members of the trade and abundant advertising on the part of the manufacturers he is compelled to handle many special descriptions of goods which he would not otherwise be disposed to sell. His point of view is therefore that expressed by the chairman of the Proprietary Articles Committee at the annual trade conference (*Grocer*, 14th July, 1906): " The basis of the movement which they had set on foot was that in selling a proprietary article they were selling something which did not particularly advertise them as traders, but particularly advertised the manufacturers, the packer, or the importer of the proprietary article. If then they did not advertise their own business, the man whom they did advertise was under some obligation to them, and the obligation that he had to fulfil was to make terms which were satisfactory to the retail dealer. It was their business to refuse absolutely to sell for any one who would not give them a fair remuneration for their labour and the time involved in selling such an article. When a minimum price had been fixed no one should go behind it, and if the trade all round would agree to stand by that, he could assure them that they would not be long in realising their object."

The annual conference of 1900 passed the following resolution : " That this conference, being impressed with the unsatisfactory position in which retailers find themselves placed through the attitude taken by a section of the trade in retailing proprietary articles at prices which in many cases barely cover the ordinary working expenses, urges that it be an instruction to the General Purposes Committee to ask the most prominent manufacturers of cocoas, starch, blue, mustard, soaps, meat extract, condensed milk, baking-powder, cornflour, sauces, and such other firms as it may be deemed expedient, to co-operate with them in devising means whereby a minimum profit of 15 per cent. (calculated on sales) may be secured to the retailers; and, further, that in consideration of manufacturers acceding to this request, the General Purposes Committee will notify to all affiliated associations the names of such firms, and recommend the subscribers to give prominence to the articles so protected, and that all bonus or dividend paying companies shall add the amount of any bonus or dividend paid to such retail price."

This policy of protected prices maintained by a boycott of cutters on the part of the manufacturers has been steadily followed during the past six years. The Grocers' Federation instituted a Proprietary Articles Committee and recommended that each association should do the same, but only thirty have done so. No protected list has yet been issued, but soaps, cocoas, and a variety of other articles are sold at retail prices fixed by the manufacturer. In the trade advertisements we see such phrases as : " Prices are efficiently protected from cutting "; " all brands are sold at fixed prices to the public so that there is no cutting"; "costs you 1s., sells at 1s. 4d."; " leaving 3d. per lb. clear profit". The trade associations are, however, by no means so able to deal with cutters as the chemists' associations are. For one thing it is much easier to become a grocer than a chemist—it requires less training and capital—and for another there are far more grocers than chemists. Messrs. Cadbury, writing to a correspondent who complained that their 6d. packets were being sold at 5½d., said : " The grocers themselves fixed 5½d. as the correct selling price of our cocoa, and some years ago we had the utmost difficulty to secure this price to the trade, as several grocers were then inclined to sell our 6d. packet at 5¼d. or even 5d. . . . When the time comes that the grocery fraternity will unite in fixing price limits that will leave a substantial margin of profit, it will be to the mutual advantage of both the trade and ourselves, and we should gladly do our share to support such an action " (*Grocer*, 11th January, 1902). Messrs. Lever made the same point in the debate on the price of soap : " All our experience of minimum retail selling prices has been that the manufacturers are powerless, except in those cases where by cutting the cutter's margin of profit practically disappears. The price of soap has advanced 1s. to 1s. 3d. per cwt. Your proposed advances are from 2s. to 3s. Cutters who are not members of your associations throughout the country would not follow the advance, and we should have no means of forcing them to do so, because those declining to follow would be too numerous for us to deal with " (*Grocer*, 8th September, 1906). In addition the proprietary articles sold by grocers may be easily replaced by other proprietary articles of the same class, or by teas, soaps, cocoas, etc., which are sold unbranded.

The grocery trade has for many years exhibited a strong hostility to the co-operative stores, and has instituted many boycotting operations against them which have not only ended in ignominious failure but led to an actual increase of co-operative sales. Undeterred by these experiences, the grocers' associations are now attempting, with some slight measure of success, to induce manufacturers to boycott the stores, and the endeavour is being carried on with great energy in conjunction with the chemists' associations. As an illustration the following letter of the Mazawattee Tea Company to the Bradford grocers may be quoted : " Whilst I am exceedingly pleased that your association agrees with the circular which has been sent out, *re* our not supplying our cocoa to co-operative societies in places where there are grocers' associations, and where the members of these associations promise to keep our goods to the front and not to cut the prices below those distinctly marked on the tins, I regret being unable to go so far as to say we will not supply co-operative stores in any part of the kingdom. . . . I would add that we have given our word not to supply the Wholesale Co-operative Society, and also to stop the supplies of any local wholesale firm who may supply indirectly the co-operative stores

about which we have pledged ourselves down to associations"
(*Grocer*, 11th January, 1902). Side by side with this we may
place a resolution of the Leeds Association which "further expresses its oft-repeated determination not to take up any new
article which, whilst fixing a minimum selling price, does not
provide that this shall be an absolute minimum subject to
no deductions" (*Grocer*, 1st September, 1906).

It is, of course, on firms bringing out a new article that
grocers can most easily exercise compulsion, and through them,
indirectly, on firms owning old-established proprietary goods.
The Co-operative Wholesale Societies, however, manufacture
their own soaps, cocoas, etc., and pack their own teas, and what
they lose as agents they will, through the loyalty of their
members, gain as makers so that the boycott has little terror
for them. The retail traders of St. Helens, always prominent
in the fight against the co-operators, have paid them the unusual
compliment of copying their methods. The St. Helens and
District United Traders' Profit Sharing Association, including
most of the traders in the town, was started in July, 1906.
Each customer receives an identification card entitling him to
trade at any of the associated shops; with his purchases he
gets paper checks, which he exchanges periodically for receipts
at the head office of the association. Every Monday the
retailer pays to the head office the dividend on his profit-sharing
sales, and also a commission of 3d. in the £, and every quarter
the head office pays the customers dividend at the rate of 2s.
in the £; or alternatively the customer may take his dividend
at once in the shape of a discount of 10 per cent.

The violent discussion about soap prices which occupied
the autumn of 1906 throws some light on the conflicting interests of manufacturer, retailer, and customer. Messrs. Lever
announced in the middle of August that owing to a rise of £3
per ton in the price of raw materials they were compelled to
advance the price of soap to the grocer from 1s. to 1s. 3d. per
cwt., bearing the rest of the additional cost themselves. As
this brought down grocers' profits by 5 per cent. to 12½ per cent.
on their outlay there was a considerable outcry. Messrs. Lever
refused to raise the retail price, as a halfpenny extra per tablet

meant £4 13s. 4d. per ton on unscented soap and £6 per ton on scented soap. The grocers retorted that it was the expense of advertising which really impelled the firm to make the change, to which the reply was that such expense was only incurred on new brands and not on the established soaps now being raised. The grocers resolved to advance the prices of soap themselves, and as the public was much excited by fears of a soap trust the grocers could avoid the odium of such an action, the blame for which would be thrown on the makers. Messrs. Lever further committed the tactical blunder of proposing to substitute a 15 oz. for the pound tablet, a step from which the public outcry compelled them to retreat. Wherever they were strong the grocers met and raised the price of trust soaps a halfpenny a pound, resolving also to push the sale of the soaps made by manufacturers known not to be favourable to the combination then being engineered. Whether the increase could have been maintained is open to doubt. The chairman of the Birmingham meeting said: " A rise of a halfpenny would on the return show a profit of about 25 per cent. Could it be expected that such a rise would be at once universal ? Such a profit, without any loss on handling and needing the employment of only a small capital, would be a great attraction to the hardware store dealers, the hucksters, the oil and colour merchants, and chemists. It would also be giving the whip-hand to the co-operative stores " (*Grocer*, 13th October, 1906).

Lastly, a word must be said about the efforts of the grocers' associations to repress certain forms of trading which aggravate competition. One of these is "stamp trading," where the customer receives from the grocer stamps proportionate to the amount of his purchases which he can afterwards exchange for china or other goods at the local office of the stamp trading syndicate. While this attracts some trade to the shopkeeper-member it is equivalent to a tax of 5 per cent. on his turnover. At Reading, for instance, the associations of butchers, china dealers, ironmongers, and grocers sent out circulars opposing the proposed introduction of stamp trading as a burden and a cause of friction, and their action was successful. Coupon trading, a form of advertisement much practised by soap firms, is the sending out with each package a coupon which, when a certain number have been collected, entitles the purchaser to a prize in toilet soaps, bicycles, jewellery, etc. Ultimately, of course, the customer or the retailer must pay for this generosity, and therefore the general feeling of the trade is one of pronounced hostility to coupons. On the same footing is placed direct trading by manufacturers with hotels on lower terms, and the Proprietary Articles Committee proudly reported that in the case of one firm they had " obtained an undertaking from the firm that in future this direct trading should not be practised ".

The London Coffee House and Restaurant Keepers' Trade Society, formed in 1900, must claim a moment's attention. The fourpenny plate of meat was raised to fivepence, and at a meeting in January, 1901, it was decided "that on and after the 17th day of January, 1901, no halfpenny cup of tea, coffee, or cocoa be sold after 7.30 A.M.," but this was not extended to the off-trade. The competition of coffee stalls was bitterly lamented, and a strong desire was manifested to get them shut up at 5 A.M. instead of 9 A.M. Combination for trade regulation in the interests of those combining is far-reaching in its attractions!

CHAPTER XI.

THE bakery trade has to face much the same sort of competition as other retail trades. Not only is there an over-supply of small bakers in every town and district, but the competition of large company shops like those of the Aerated Bread Company and Lyons & Company which advertise their bread through their restaurant business must be faced. There are also large bread factories which not only sell bread and flour retail, but supply grocers, provision dealers, and other shopkeepers. The latter often make a "leading line" of bread and flour, selling them at very low prices in order to attract customers to their shops and dispose of their other goods at rates high enough to cover the loss on bread. A bakery is also now almost an indispensable adjunct of a co-operative store, and is often on a large scale; the bakery of the Royal Arsenal Co-operative Society, Woolwich, turns out nearly 4,500,000 two-pound loaves yearly, equivalent to nearly £51,000, and the United Baking Society of Glasgow, a federation of co-operative stores, has a trade of £482,500. The Dunston flour mill of the English Co-operative Wholesale Society incurred a very heavy loss immediately after its starting because its managers would not join in an attempt to put up the price of flour, and similarly the co-operative stores in carrying out their policy of keeping bread at a uniform price have often stopped the endeavours of bakers in their locality to raise the price of bread. The stratification of the baking trade shows us all kinds of undertakings from the small shop, often with an underground bakehouse, up to the large limited liability company, like Huntley & Palmer or Peek, Frean, & Company,

which manufactures biscuits wholesale.   There is another line
of development according to the class of trade from the baker
who caters for a purely working-class constituency to the West
End confectioner who does a purely luxury trade.   The conditions of competition are thus not uniform, bakers who deal
mainly in specialities being free from much of the harassment
which besets those doing a common trade.

Here may be noted one combination, Callard, Stewart, &
Watt, Limited—a company formed in 1896 to unite the old-established West End businesses of Messrs. Stewart & Company,
Messrs. Callard & Callard, Messrs. Callard & Company, and
Messrs. T. Watt & Sons.   One of their establishments was
founded nearly two hundred years ago and is supposed to be
the oldest baker's shop in London.   Their capital is £240,000,
and they have paid dividends ranging from 8 to 17 per cent.

The organisation of the baking trade closely resembles that
of the other retail trades.   There are local associations, district
federations, and a National Association which holds an annual
exhibition and conference.   These deal with the ordinary
subjects of interest to business men, but price-fixing is unquestionably the one which most attracts the members.   The
chairman of the Berwick Master Bakers' Association, in apolo-
gising for the small attendance at the annual meeting in March,
1906, said : "There will still be found bakers (too many) who
never thought it necessary to attend any meeting of the trade
unless it was for the purpose of advancing the price or opposing
any proposed reduction".   The strength of the local associations varies partly according to the nature of the competition
to be met, partly according to the ease with which customers
can travel to other districts for supplies.   Ipswich has a strong
and flourishing association which maintains the price of bread
at a "fair" level, but at Norwich, where there is reported to
be a grocer with a large bread factory and a co-operative
society which sells over a million and a half quartern loaves
annually, the association is very weak.   The Brixton and
Camberwell Associations constantly report "bad business,"
especially on the confines of their territories where non-associated bakers can compete ; here the competition is plainly fos-

tered by cheap trams. Of the Manchester Wholesale Bakers' Association the *British Baker* (18th May, 1906) reported that "it is hardly necessary to say that the whole policy of the Wholesale Association since its inception has been one of prices, and it has done more useful work for the trade than could possibly be estimated in this particular direction". As an instance of indirect price-fixing we may note the agreement of the West Bromwich bakers in July, 1906, to supply only twelve loaves to the dozen.

The competition of the grocers is the standing theme of discussion at bakers' meetings, and persuasion and force are alternately used for its removal. After two years' negotiations with the bakers the Manchester, Salford, and District Grocers' Association resolved : " That we accept the proposed basis of 6d. per dozen on 'seconds' bread, and in view of the basis of profit we undertake to render our assistance to secure the minimum price " (*British Baker*, 12th October, 1906). Plymouth was the scene of a fierce fight described by a correspondent of the *British Baker* (20th July, 1906) : " Some two or three years since two or three third-rate grocers prevailed on a certain baker to bake bread for them at a price to enable them to sell at a penny under the regular trade figure, the usual plea being that they were going to fight the co-operative society, but as a matter of fact to produce a 'leading article' for their own business. For a time they cut into some members of the trade rather badly. Eventually the local association tacitly consented to allow the bakers nearest the cutting shop to meet it by making two qualities of bread, best and seconds ; the latter to be at the grocers' figure. Some of the grocers thereupon began negotiations for the rental of an unused Government bakery, which hitherto had been used in baking bread for the army. A few of the leading bakers hearing of this stepped in and instructed one of their number to try to secure the premises first, which he did, and up to a week or two since (Midsummer) they have paid the rent and kept the bakery idle. The effect of those actions was 'to nip the movement in the bud,' and the sale of the cheap bread is gradually decreasing."

For the better protection of a living profit the bakers have called in the millers to their assistance, especially in South Wales and the West of England where the spirit of combination is strong. The Swansea Bakers' Association in 1896 failed by their individual action to secure the co-operation of the millers, but when the separate associations federated the balance of power was altered and the millers recognised that recalcitrancy on their part might lead to an increased trade in foreign flour. In 1901 the Federation of Master Bakers', Confectioners', and Millers' Associations of South Wales and the West of England was formed with 700 members in Bristol, Cardiff, Swansea, Barry, Penarth, and Newport. Bristol seceded in 1905 and set up a Master Bakers', Millers', and Flour Merchants' Association of its own, with 200 baker members out of a total of 270, to regulate the price of bread in the town. The federation has now 500 baker members and includes thirteen affiliated associations, its area extending from Exeter to Swansea.

A sales note was accepted by the millers and bakers in the following terms: "(A) The buyer undertakes not to sell any bread or flour at a less price than that for the time being fixed by the Master Bakers' Association of the district in which the buyer resides. In the event of any breach by the buyer of the above undertaking the buyer agrees that the seller shall have the right of determining this contract, or to sell out against the buyer, and of refusing to deliver the balance then undelivered of the contract quantity of flour, and that the exercise of this option shall not affect the sellers' right to recover the price of the flour delivered under this contract. (B) Messrs.
may require cash before delivery, or limit credit to a period of seven days, if the purchaser sells any flour supplied under this or any other contract made by him with them at a gross profit of less than 3d. per score on Messrs.   's price of the day, or sells bread made from such flour at a gross profit of less than 9s. per sack, it being hereby admitted by the purchaser that each sack of flour produces ninety-two 4 lb. loaves ; and any breach of the above conditions may be deemed a failure in the due performance of this contract, and shall further give

Messrs.   the right, at their option, of cancelling this contract in respect of any goods undelivered thereunder."

In this way the underseller was deprived of his power to enter into a contract for a lengthy period and so secure his supplies. The result was prompt and satisfactory, for after a few months the president of the federation was able to say at the Bakers' Exhibition in September, 1902, that he "did not believe that in Cardiff, Swansea, and Barry there were more than three men who sold below the federation minimum price. One man sold a light loaf and another gave something away with his bread;" only one firm of millers held aloof. In October, 1902, Clause B of the above sale note was abandoned because it was "unworkable and impracticable, and does not carry out the main idea for which the federation was formed —namely, to prevent unfair competition". Clause A, which has been passed as legal by Mr. Eldon Bankes, K.C., was retained as the basis of contracts.

In imitation of the Welsh associations the Bournemouth and District Master Bakers' and Millers' Association was established in November, 1902, and soon achieved fame by the stringency of its rules, the most important of which ran as follows: "9. The committee shall meet at least once in every month, or oftener, if necessary, to receive the official price of fines flour, and to determine the retail price of bread and flour accordingly, such official price to be received from three millers, members of the association. 10. The minimum gross profits on bread shall be not less than 5s. per sack. The basis of calculation to be ninety-two quarterns to the sack. 11. The allowance to wholesale customers shall not exceed 6d. net per twelve 4 lb. loaves and *pro rata* for flour. 12. (*a*) No member of this association shall sell bread or flour retail under the price fixed for the time being by the committee, who shall instruct the secretary to issue notice to all members of any alteration in the price. (*b*) The trade shall refuse to supply any bread or flour seller who fails to comply with the rules of the association. 13. No member shall buy from, or sell to, any person who breaks the rules of the association." The committee was also given powers to expel members guilty of breach of the rules. The policy of "exclusive dealing" soon created an uproar. The Liverpool millers were invited to join in a similar arrangement, but replied that "while prepared to consider any cases of underselling" they must "decline to become members of any association having an exclusive dealing clause as a basis of membership," and some of the Bournemouth millers followed suit. The council of the National Association of Millers also, in January, 1903, endorsed the Liverpool resolution.

The bakers now bent all their energies to securing the adoption of a sale note on the model of that adopted by the South Wales Federation. The Cardiff Association introduced the following note which was adopted at Norwich, West Bromwich, the Potteries, Bootle, Plymouth, and in the course of 1906 was accepted also by forty-seven millers at Manchester (practically all those supplying the district), and at Liverpool. It ran: "The buyer undertakes not to sell any bread or flour at a less price than for the time being fixed by the Master Bakers' Association of the district in which the buyer carries on business; and any breach by the buyer of the above undertaking shall be deemed a failure of due fulfilment, giving a right to cancel the contract in respect of any undelivered goods, or to sell out such goods against the buyer as hereinafter provided. Failing due fulfilment of this contract, sellers reserve the power to cancel or sell out against buyer, and buyer will pay all loss and expenses on resale as liquidated damages, in addition to paying for all goods previously delivered." A clause identical with that formerly known as Clause B, but guaranteeing a gross profit of 10s. per sack was adopted at Neath and accepted in principle by Messrs. Spillers & Bakers and the Cardiff and Channel Mills. Peace has, however, not yet been arranged with the South Wales grocers who claimed that as they handled three times as much flour as the bakers they were entitled to a voice in the fixing of prices.

The ironmongery trade also has its local associations, its district federations, and the Ironmongers' Federated Association. The National Association was formed in 1900 by forty associations with 600 members. Organisation seems to be strongest in Lancashire where the country federation is very

active, and the Preston Association is particularly strong.
Following on the action of Preston new price lists were adopted
in the autumn of 1906 for wire-netting and corrugated sheets,
following on increases of price by the manufacturers. In October
the Preston Association undertook to draw up a price list for
hollow ware based upon the prices of the five chief makers. On
account of the number of makers and grades this was admittedly
a difficult task, but it was hoped that if the prices of first and
second grades could be maintained the lower grades could be
neglected. Opposition to the supply of gas and electric fittings
by municipalities occupies a great deal of the attention of the
association, but perhaps their chief hostility is reserved for those
manufacturers who supply customers direct. The Federated
Association appealed in the summer of 1906 to the Commercial
Travellers' Association for their help in this matter, pointing
out that the increase of direct trading must mean the diminished
employment of travellers, but they met with a refusal. The
association policy is to urge all members to deal only with those
manufacturers who will undertake to sell only to the trade.
For this purpose the National Association has published for
circulation among ironmongers an " In Accord List " of makers
pledged to sell only to the trade ; the first attempt in this
direction was made in 1881, but twenty-five years had to pass
before it could be realised.

Proprietary articles play a large part in the trade politics,
and the phrase " price maintenance " is as sacred to an ironmonger as " protected prices " to a chemist. " Every one in the
hardware trade," said the *Hardware Trade Journal* (24th
August, 1906), " could name scores of good articles that have
been ruined by price-cutting. Many an excellent line has been
brought upon the market and had a fair success until the price-
cutter has taken it up and made it impossible for any tradesman
to take any further interest in it. Price maintenance is primarily
designed to stop this evil and to allow a good article to remain
upon the market indefinitely, and to give the retailer a permanent interest in stocking and selling it." This community of
interest between maker and seller obtains a fairly wide recognition. Thus in the *Hardware Trade Journal* for 31st August,

1906, we find a circular of the Gramophone and Typewriter Company to the effect that "from 1st September onwards we intend to pay carriage on all goods to firm order to any part of the United Kingdom, provided the dealer is stocking and handling no disc machines or records other than those of our manufacture"; and the Chicago Flexible Shaft Company wrote that "the new model clipping machine which we are bringing out this season is to be price maintained, and we undertake not to supply any ironmonger who cuts the price below the retail figure of 32s. 6d." In the issue of the same paper for 21st September, 1906, a meeting of the Bournemouth Association is reported, at which "the honorary secretary placed before the meeting correspondence which had taken place between himself and Brades of Birmingham, as to cutting the price of their shovels by two local traders, not associationists. Following a visit to the tradesmen concerned by the firm's representative they had signed an agreement to raise their price 2d. per shovel." A member of the association also got into trouble for selling two lawn-mowers to the borough corporation below the minimum price; he compromised by giving his profits to the Boscombe Hospital.

The following letter from Mr. R. H. Smith, of the Ironmongers' Federated Association, to the *Hardware Trade Journal* (12th October, 1906) is instructive as to trade methods : " I have pleasure in informing you that a meeting took place on the 4th inst. between the following lawn-mower makers, *viz.* : Thos. Green & Son, Ltd., Ransomes, Sims, & Jefferies, Ltd., and Alexander Shanks & Son, Ltd., on the one hand, and a deputation of the Ironmongers' Federation. . . . At this meeting it was agreed that the lawn-mower makers should continue for the next year the existing arrangement relating to the selling prices of their mowers, *viz.*, a maximum discount of 15 per cent. for cash from list prices; and the following fresh arrangements were made : (1) *Re* Jobbing Gardeners. The lawn-mower manufacturers agree not to supply jobbing gardeners direct, except in districts where they are not represented by an ironmonger or other *bonâ-fide* trade agent. The makers authorise their agents to allow to jobbing gardeners any discount up to

25 per cent. in cases where they buy for re-sale ; (2) *Re* Lawn-
mower Repairs. The makers agree to print the following in
their catalogues : ' Machines requiring repair can be collected
and sent on to us by local ironmongers '. In respect of the above
the deputation agreed to make the following recommendation
to the trade : In consideration of their agreeing to continue
the present arrangement relating to ' price maintenance,' and
of the further concessions they have now made as above, the
Central Board of the Ironmongers' Federated Association agree
to repeat, and strongly emphasise, the recommendation to their
members to stock and push the sale of the manufactures of the
makers represented at this meeting, *viz. :* Thos. Green & Son,
Ltd., Ransomes, Sims, & Jefferies, Ltd., Alexander Shanks &
Son, Ltd." These are not the only lawn-mower firms which
maintain prices for we find the Chadborn and Coldwell Manufacturing Company writing to the Southport Association :
" You may take it that we are absolutely pledged to the principle of price maintenance, and you may depend upon it that
we shall supply our machines to no firm that is guilty of offering to supply our lawn-mowers at less than the minimum sale
price established by us ".

Agricultural implements are not sold direct by the makers
to farmers, but through agents who are very often ironmongers.
The usual extreme competition broke out among the agents,
who naturally cut the prices of articles which they only kept
on sample, neither making them, nor canvassing for them, nor
packing them, but only forwarding orders by post, and this in
due course led to combination among the agents to get the
business back on to a profitable footing, especially in the West
of England and Cornwall. About 1899 the National Federation of Agricultural Implement Dealers was formed, its members being county or district associations. The object of all
these associations was to fix, with the help of the makers,
minimum retailing selling prices and maximum discounts, and
to boycott all agents and firms not members. The boycott had
been tried in individual cases twenty years earlier but now the
scale of activity was higher, as, for example, in 1899 forty-two
firms of makers were induced to refuse supplies to a farmers'

18

co-operative society. The combine was brought under the notice of the Central Chamber of Agriculture, and the very wise advice was given to the farmers that they should follow the example of their Irish brethren and themselves combine. Some of the Irish agricultural co-operative societies, it was pointed out in the debate, imported their implements direct from Canada, and another speaker said that two years ago the Cromwell Co-operative Societies had discounts of 45 per cent. quoted to them when they wanted to purchase agricultural machines.

In 1900 there were only some 170 members of the federation, but three years later it included 120 makers and 900 agents. The makers were bound to deal only with the associated agents and the agents only with the associated makers; outside the ranks of the federation a rigid boycott was maintained throughout the twenty-six counties in which local associations operated. No agent was allowed to sell a binder except at £7 profit, or a mower below £3 profit. On other implements, machinery, and fittings the agent was allowed by the makers 30 per cent. discount and 5 per cent. additional for cash in a month, but was prohibited from giving more than 10 per cent. discount off list prices. Formerly a farmer could get a very good discount for ready cash, but now he was deprived of this advantage. Not only were farmers' expenses seriously increased by the combine, but a man was especially hard hit when, on commencing farming work, he had to spend a large sum in equipping his farm. Prices were much lower in non-associated districts, a binder, for instance, costing £30 in Scotland and £32 in England. The Wilts and Hants farmers successfully carried on a counter-boycott, and when in July, 1903, the action of the federation was again brought before the Central Chamber of Agriculture, a resolution was proposed urging "all agriculturists to show their disapproval by dealing only with those makers and agents who are not members of the Implement Combine, and that in order to carry out the foregoing resolution the Central Chamber advertise the names of those firms who are outside the National Implement Federation". This proposal, however, was smothered.   The obvious remedy for the farmers is to form co-operative societies, which the makers could not afford to ignore, but English farmers have until quite lately shown remarkably little aptitude or liking for joint action.

The prices of photographic materials are all "protected"; for many years there has been no cutting possible in plates, papers, cameras, etc., which are all sold at their face price. A great deal of the trade in such goods consists of novelties which may or may not be improvements but are always being substituted for the older examples of their class, and there is a large and increasing number of manufacturers.   The makers are therefore under every inducement to compete among themselves, using every form of advertisement to ingratiate themselves with the public ; in this campaign established reputation is a great factor.   The goodwill of the retailers is ensured by handsome discounts off the fixed list retail prices—generally 20 to 25 per cent. for plates, 33⅓ per cent. for papers, 15 to 30 per cent. for other goods.   An extra 5 per cent. is often allowed on large orders and 2½ or 5 per cent. for cash in a month.   The discounts are detailed in the price lists issued to dealers only by the manufacturers, which also specify the retail prices, and the invoice bears some such note as : "Any photographic goods included in this invoice are sold to you, and discount allowed thereon, on condition that they are resold by you and your customers on the following terms. . . . Retail, not under manufacturer's list prices.   Wholesale, as per Plate and Paper Makers' Association rules.   Or on manufacturers' conditions, whichever may apply. . . . Acceptance of these goods will be considered as acceptance of these terms.   If you do not agree, please return the goods.   Any breach of these terms will render you liable to legal proceedings."   For all this the public finds the cash.   Kodak, Ltd., introduced an American practice in 1901, the granting of preferential discounts to those dealers who were able to declare that over a given period they had supplied no other make of roll-film apparatus or material than that made by the company, but abandoned it after two years' trial on account of the disfavour with which it was received.   This was probably only a step in an attempt by the

18 *

Eastman Kodak Co. of America to capture British trade, and may be put on the same level as its efforts to absorb the Ilford Co. (capital £380,000) in 1903, which was defeated by the shareholders of the latter who were not at all disturbed by the great capital—£4,948,000—of Kodak. Competition in the photographic trade is far from being extinct, but it is confined to quality and does not take the form of price-cutting by retailers.

In May, 1902, the Association of the Publishers of Private Christmas Greeting Cards was formed "to protect the trade in private Christmas Greeting Cards against the discount system, of which retailers have so frequently complained in recent years". The prices of these cards to the public were to be fixed by the publishers and wholesale dealers, and were not to be cut by the retailer, who was to make his profit out of the rebate allowed him by the publisher not exceeding $33\frac{1}{3}$ per cent. off list prices. The stationers were informed that "no books of cards published by any member of this association will be supplied to you until you have joined the association as a retail member". Thirty-eight firms joined the association, including practically all the largest publishers of private Christmas cards.

From art to books! The autumn of 1906 was enlivened by a book war, which really turned on no higher matters of principle than were involved in protecting the price of a lawn-mower, a toilet soap, or a box of "Morrison's Pills". The magnitude of the forces at strife and their large capitals—and also the advertisements they had to dispose of—aroused an extraordinary amount of interest. Unlike most trade disputes it was conducted in public, *The Times*, though one of the parties concerned, throwing open its columns to friend and foe alike, while the other newspapers reported the progress of the fight and interviewed the antagonists indiscriminately. There was, therefore, a vaster amount of material placed before the student than he usually has at his disposal, but at the same time an enormous mass of entirely irrelevant matter. The leading parties to the strife were the Publishers' Association, consisting of some seventy of the leading publishers in the country, the Booksellers' Association, similarly representative of the retail trade, and *The Times* Book Club, a library and bookshop from which "over 81,000" persons were, according to the manager, "entitled to purchase books". The publishers and booksellers had already been at war in 1852, and *The Times*, with perhaps a kind of maliciousness which was not unnatural, reprinted the story in pamphlet form. At that time the publishers sought to prevent the booksellers from selling books at a greater discount than 10 per cent., and after the dispute had been submitted to the arbitration of Lord Chief Justice Campbell, Dean Milman, and George Grote a decision was given in favour of the booksellers.

Lord Campbell said: "Such regulations seem *prima facie* to be indefensible, and contrary to the freedom which ought to prevail in commercial transactions. Although the owner of property may put what price he pleases upon it when selling it, the condition that the purchaser, after the property has been transferred to him and he has paid the purchase money, shall not resell it under a certain price, derogates from the rights of ownership, which, as purchaser, he has acquired. . . . We are reminded of the peculiarity, that the publisher names the price at which the book is to be sold to the customer (which may be considered the maximum price), whereas the manufacturer in other trades entirely leaves the price to be paid by the customer to be fixed by the retail dealer. Some complain of this proceeding of the publisher as a grievance. But, admitting the expediency of the publisher continuing to name a retail price at which the book is said to be published, this can only be as a guide, and cannot hinder the making of a fair bargain between the retail dealer and the customer." This passage shows how remote are those ideas about "freedom in commercial transactions" from the practice of to-day. Fifty years of keen competition and the development of proprietary articles have altered the opinions of retailers. Indeed, were it not irreverent, we might say that books were the earliest proprietary articles. In each book the publisher possesses a complete monopoly, subject only to the limited competition of books dealing with the same subject, and he can make the price what he pleases unless, what seldom happens, he is dealing with a strong and determined author.

Free competition being secured, the booksellers proceeded to compete and the rate of discount went up until, except in remote country towns, the uniform rate was 25 per cent. to the ordinary customer, while public libraries, which gave large and regular orders involving little trouble and no risk, got sometimes as much as 40 per cent. The booksellers had now enough of competition and began to long for a "living profit". On books with a large sale a small profit, when aggregated, might be sufficient, but the case was different with books with a limited circulation but which practically must be bought by libraries and serious persons. These were, therefore, attacked first, and with the help of the publishers segregated into a class of net books. This was in 1899, and thenceforth seventy-five firms of publishers issued the following "terms and conditions of supply of net books to retail publishers" : "We the undersigned several firms of publishers, being desirous as far as possible of ensuring that books published at net prices (such books being hereinafter referred to as net books) shall not be sold to the public (including school libraries and institutions) at less than such net prices, hereby inform you that henceforth we shall only invoice and supply to you net books published by us or any of us on our usual trade terms provided you on your part agree not to sell any net book published by us or any of us at less than the net price at which it is published. If you agree to these terms please sign and return the form of acceptance appended hereto. If you do not agree to these terms we shall not allow you our usual trade terms on net books, and shall only invoice and supply them to you at the net prices at which they are published, and in the event of you selling any net book published by us or any of us below the net price at which it is published we shall each require you to pay for all net books invoiced and supplied to you (and which have not already been paid for) at the full net prices at which they are published. The above does not apply to *bonâ-fide* remainders and dead stock."

This is an exact parallel to our proprietary articles where the grocer must promise "not to cut the prices distinctly marked on the tin". The grocer and the bookseller occupy equivalent positions, the author perhaps compares with the inventor, and the publisher with the manufacturer. Whatever code of ethics we apply to the one case we must apply to the other.

Books sold to the public at 25 per cent. discount are supplied by the publisher to the bookseller at prices which allow the latter a gross profit of about 10 per cent. if he buys in single copies or about 24 per cent. if he subscribes, that is orders the book on speculation before publication, taking the risk of unsold copies. On net books the bookseller would be able to make gross profits of about 26 per cent. on single copies or 36 per cent. on larger orders. These profits are subject to the cost of carriage, and to the bookseller's office expenses. In 1901, 2,322 books out of 7,997 were sold net and the vogue of the net book is still increasing.

In September, 1905, *The Times* opened its Book Club giving to all 'annual subscribers to *The Times* the right of membership free of charge and the privilege of receiving three books at a time. This was not philanthropy. *The Times* was quite frank : " Last year we spent £40,000 in making known the merits of *The Times*, and by this means enlarged our circulation so much that advertisers found it worth their while to increase by more than one-half our revenue from the advertising columns of *The Times*. That £40,000 was well invested. We now make an offer to subscribers that cannot.fail to double our present circulation, and we are prepared to spend £100,000 upon the project which will achieve that result." To the library *The Times* added a bookselling business, not only for new books at ordinary booksellers' rates which the reader could buy after reading, but also for second-hand books from their library for sale to their subscribers. " Clean and uninjured copies, virtually as good as new, their condition indicating that they have been in circulation for about a month," were to be sold at 35 per cent. off the published price in the case of ordinary books and 20 per cent. in the case of net books, greater discounts being granted in the case of books showing three and six months' wear. *The Times* signed the ordinary net contract, and in turn asked the publishers for a five years' contract for supply of their books which was agreed to by sixteen ; for an undertaking to spend on advertising in *The Times* 15 per cent.

of the amount spent by *The Times* with them—to this forty-eight consented, but were afterwards voluntarily released ; for an agreement not to supply their books to any similar newspaper book club for five years, to which twenty-five agreed, but it was dropped.

The booksellers were soon alert, and although the publishers had already accepted the " definition of a second-hand book as being one which has been used by more than two subscribers and is returned in such a state that it cannot be sold as a new book," these terms were capable of varied interpretation, especially when *The Times* was issuing flamboyant advertisements in which various books published quite recently were offered at prices far below the published price. At the urgent request of the booksellers the publishers drafted a new agreement forbidding the sale of second-hand net books under price for six months after publication ; to this *The Times* refused to agree. The additions to the old agreement were :—

" Not to offer for sale or sell any second-hand copy of any such net book at less than the published price within six months of publication.

" Not to treat as unsaleable or dead stock any new copy or copies of any. such net book within twelve months of the date of your latest purchase of any copy or copies thereof, and then only such copy or copies of such latest purchase as shall remain in your hands.

" Not to offer for sale or sell or cause to be sold at a price below the published price any such dead stock as aforesaid without having first offered such dead stock to the publisher thereof at cost price, or at the proposed reduced price, whichever shall be the lower ; and after such dead stock shall have been returned to the publisher, or with his assent sold off under the published price, not to offer for sale or sell or cause to be sold any further copy or copies of the same book below the published price."

And wholesale booksellers were required " Not to sell any such net book at less than the full net price at which it is published to any customer who shall offer for sale or sell or cause to be sold any such net book contrary to the several conditions of supply above set forth ".

Then burst forth a shower of letters, advertisements, circulars, and interviews. The booksellers and publishers were thoroughly united and determined to win. *The Times* was stubborn not to give way. The next shot was the withdrawal of all advertisements from *The Times* by the publishers. *The Times* replied to the boycott with a boycott of its own. " With certain publishing houses," ran the circular, " we have written contracts, still in force, under which they are obliged to supply books to us at trade prices. Some of the others have already refused to sell us any further books at the discount they give to the smallest bookseller's shop. . . . Our subscribers . . . can, in selecting the books they draw from our library, as well as in buying books, discriminate in favour of those publishers who continue to supply *The Times* with books upon the ordinary terms, and they can, so far as possible, refrain from compelling us to purchase for their use books issued by those publishers who try hardest to keep books from us " ; and six publishers were placed on the black list.

Now, every one in the fight had a good case. The publishers had to stand by the booksellers for they were indispensable as distributing agents ; of course the interest of the manufacturer in the retailer is always that he should do the maximum of service even if he has to be guaranteed a living profit. The booksellers could be pardoned for seeking to destroy *The Times* Book Club. In its first year it claimed to have made 1,771,166 issues and to have sold 309,911 new and 31,554 second-hand books, all of which seemed so much trade taken away from the genuine bookseller by a rival who was only in the book business as a side-show. *The Times*, on the other hand, asserted that it bought a much larger number of copies of every book than an ordinary library did, and took more care of them ; they were therefore bound to drop out of demand at an earlier date and in better condition than with other libraries. It claimed that it was not fair to prohibit selling second-hand while there was a market for the book, and maintained, and truly, that a great part of the bookselling business which it did was not taken away from the booksellers but was a new demand created by its method of allowing books to be read before purchase. In reply to a circular sent to the members, it was ascertained that 95·6 per cent. of those who replied and had bought books second-hand from the club would not have bought those books from a bookseller.

All the rest of the controversy was outside the subjects considered in this volume. The fear that *The Times* Book Club would become a great book trust and the criticism of its " American " methods were very much exaggerated. On the other hand, the denunciations of the publishers for exacting exorbitant profits were unjust, since they treated the publisher as a mere agent and neglected his most important function, that of financing the author. The interest of the public is in cheap and good literature. The interest of author, publisher, printer, bookbinder, and bookseller is in getting each the largest possible profit consistent with good service from the others, and at least in getting a living profit. Broadly speaking, demand increases in proportion to cheapness, but that is subject to limitations in the case of books. Broadly speaking, also, books are dearer than they might be, considering their cost of production, but no other method of financing the poor or not yet successful author has yet been devised than that of making successful books pay for unsuccessful. The committee of the Authors' Society entered the fray on the side of the publishers in the fear that " mere cheapness " meant bad books and starving authors, but they were answered by other and popular authors who protested that their interests lay in the largest circulation, which, in the end, was bound to bring the greatest profit and reputation.

Judged by such ethics as apply to business it does not seem necessary that in any branch of the retail trade the interests of the consumer should be considered more than is necessary to keep him as a customer. Judged by any higher standard it does not seem plain how the present system can be maintained and at the same time the interests of producer, distributor, and consumer harmonised. In the case of the book war it is by no means clear on which side the final interests of literature lie—but then literature is as difficult to define as "second-hand". The general aspects of the question of retail prices will be discussed later, but as all trade disputes which are purely a trial of strength between different methods seriously disturb business, the immediate interests of the outsider are best served by a compromise which binds all parties and allows the opposing methods to be tested by their efficiency and not by mere weight of capital.

CHAPTER XII.

THE TRANSPORT INDUSTRIES.

THE circumstances of land transport are such that the determination of rates of carriage is governed by conditions which do not exist in manufacturing or retail industries, and therefore it has been excluded from detailed consideration in this volume. Free competition is impossible on tramways, except so far as it is provided by omnibuses, and on railways it is restricted by the policy of Parliament. Every railway has a certain limited area adjacent to its line within which it is free to tax the traffic what it will bear subject to the supervision of the Railway Commissioners, but Parliament has permitted competitive railways with different routes to be built between important centres in order to prevent the monopoly of large districts. Severe competition was for a long time practised between these points until the railways saw the advantage of having fixed rates. Representatives of the companies interested meet monthly in "conferences"—the English and Scotch Traffic Rates Conference, the English and Irish Traffic Rates Conference, for trade between England and Scotland and England and Ireland respectively, and the Normanton Conference for most of the English traffic—and discuss, and if necessary alter, the rates between competitive points. This abolition of competition led in its turn to the control of rates by the Railway Commissioners in a way which, though only moderately effective, at least expresses the public interest. Fixed rates diverted competition from prices to facilities, and much wasteful expenditure was incurred in the competitive search for traffic, collection of goods, and providing facilities in excess of what was required by the trade of a district. At last the

London and North-Western Railway took the initiative, and, after concluding an agreement with the Lancashire and York-shire Railway which worked beneficially, followed it up by another with the Midland Railway with a view to more economic working.

The competition of omnibus companies is freer, though it is ultimately limited by police regulation of traffic. There are brief sharp bouts of competition and then the companies settle down to provide competing facilities at common rates over the same route. On many of the routes the different omnibus pro-prietors are united in "associations" and pool their earnings, sharing them per omnibus. In 1900 the Associated Omnibus Company was formed, with an issued capital of £135,000, to acquire three businesses, and has had a generally successful career. Several attempts have been made, but without result, to amalgamate the two great London companies, the London General Omnibus Company and the London Road Car Com-pany. Now, with the advent of the motor-bus and of numerous motor-bus companies, there has been an increase of competition and four of the London companies united in December, 1906, to form the Vanguard Motor Omnibus Company with an authorised capital of £1,000,000.

In ocean traffic we can have complete freedom of competi-tion. The ship is tied neither to port nor trade but can go wherever cargo and profit call. Normally, payment for services of a ship are fixed purely from considerations of supply and demand, and this circumstance brings shipping alone of trans-port services into line with our manufacturing industries. The shipping industry would seem to be the inexpugnable strong-hold of free competition, and in fact there is probably more competition there than in any other of our great industries. But to this statement there are important limitations.

There are two classes of ships, the " tramp " and the " liner ". " The tramp," to quote Mr. Walter Runciman, M.P. (*British Industries Under Free Trade*, p. 130), " goes everywhere, competes for everything against everybody, cuts into any trade—British, foreign, or colonial—whenever he can see a profit ; and he is similarly subject to attacks with no means of defence except his own efficiency." The capital invested in these ships is estimated by the same authority at about £120,000,000. Practically all the bulk cargoes are carried in tramps—coals, grain, timber, cotton, ores, sugar, petroleum, nitrates—all the goods which are transported in such quantities that a ship can be hired or "chartered" for the purpose. Chartering is done either for the voyage or for a period of time, sometimes several years, and all the conditions of service, except price, have been determined for each great trade by the shippers and shipowners in joint conferences and expressed in the contract of hire, or "charter party". There are also a large number of shipowners' associations which deal with legal, labour, political, and other general questions affecting the industry. To this extent the trade is regulated and causes of friction removed so that competition moves more smoothly. But the tramp shipowner has always before his eyes the imminence of new competition. Every spurt of prosperity results in fresh orders to the shipbuilding yards and always for tramp cargo steamers ; in times of depression the shipbuilder will take orders at very low rates, or will build on speculation, or take payment in shares. Small companies owning a few ships, or even only one, hunt up capital all over the country, and once started must compete à outrance on penalty of falling into the hands of a receiver. Freight rates depend solely on the amount of cargo to be carried and the number of ships at hand to carry it. Consequently, they fluctuate violently and at short intervals. *Fairplay* for 28th December, 1905, gave particulars of sixty-four cargo steamer companies with a paid-up share capital of £8,577,424. In 1905 the aggregate profit was £762,698, and an average dividend of 3·33 per cent. was paid ; £238,505 only was written off for depreciation, although the minimum adequate amount, reckoned at 5 per cent. on the original cost of steamers, was £740,901. Truly a paradise of competition !

Although all the conditions are so adverse it is not surprising that some efforts have been made at regulation of rates. The Sailing Ship Owners' International Union was formed at Paris in December, 1903, to regulate freights for sailing vessels of 1,000 tons and over on the return voyage from Australia and the Pacific Coast of America to Europe. The immediate cause of the combination was the heavy bounties paid to French ships which made it possible for them to accept terms which left non-bounty-fed vessels no profit. The object was rather to prevent extreme cutting of rates than to raise them to a profitable level, and the most that has been achieved in the bad freight period that has lasted since its formation has been the reduction of losses to a reasonable figure. As only 1,800,000 tons, or 17 per cent., of the total British tonnage consisted of sailing ships at the time the union was formed, and its regulations applied only to a small fraction of that, it is plain that the union is of very little importance to British shipowners. Still 75 per cent. of the total British, German, and French sailing ship tonnage was included in 1904 and 87 per cent. in 1905.

In June, 1905, another and more important attempt at rate fixing was made by the constitution of the Baltic and White Sea Conference. The conference was international, the meetings to be held in annual rotation in the different countries concerned, while the offices were to be permanently in Copenhagen. The minimum rates for the export of lumber from ports in these seas was fixed for the next quarter, when another meeting was to be held, but freights for the next season could be concluded provided they were not under the rates fixed. Altogether 1,048 steamships of an aggregate of 1,612,000 tons were concerned in this combination, which has been " more or less successful " according to *Fairplay*. Such success, however limited, has given rise to aspirations for further union. " This has certainly been a step in the right direction," wrote *Fairplay* on 28th December, 1905, " but whether it is possible to formulate a similar combination from other directions, such as the River Plate, for instance, it is almost impossible to say. At the same time, if owners could be brought together more frequently and conferences held, no harm could result, while it is just possible that the united intelligence of owners represented at such meetings might result in some common action being taken to secure rates of freight being brought up to, and maintained at, a living basis. There is no doubt that the severe competition that has gone on amongst tramp owners of recent years has been of a suicidal nature, for millions upon millions of tons of cargo have been carried at a loss by owners sooner than step out of the front rank."

As for the liner, " her route is cut and dried," as Kipling says. She sails between fixed ports, on regular days, cargo or no cargo, and all arrangements are made and advertised for months before hand. Liners vary from the "ocean greyhound" carrying mainly passengers and their baggage, through "intermediate" boats of slower speed and carrying both cargo and passengers, to pure cargo boats. There is no exact line of demarcation between the liner and the tramp, for new trades are always growing up to that degree of magnitude which demands a regular service. There is no estimate of the capital invested in liner tonnage, but the number of *Fairplay* already quoted from gave a list of twenty-one liner companies with a total share capital of £20,215,645, debenture and other loan capital £10,744,015, and dividend for 1905 on share capital 4·38 per cent. Only six of those companies had a share capital below £500,000, while eight exceeded £1,000,000. It thus appears that competition would be more difficult because the business unit is so much larger, and it would cost so much to duplicate a service. Nevertheless, as the low dividend shown proves, rates of freight are still governed by tramp competition, always on the look-out for a profitable trade however brief in duration. A certain amount of common action is almost forced upon the shipowners trading regularly between certain ports, as we have already seen is the case with iron-masters, coal-owners, and all persons whose business is done openly in the market, on the floor of the exchange. Common knowledge always leads to agreement, especially at moments when there is business enough for all, and this indicates the advantage of more lasting methods of regulation. To-day most of our great liner routes are governed by shipping conferences, often international in character, known to the trader as "shipping rings".

The classic example of a conference is the Hankow Tea Conference which led to the famous Mogul case. The ports of Hankow and Shanghai were the headquarters of the China tea trade during its short but lucrative season, and were served by vessels regularly employed on the China and Japan lines, and by vessels generally trading to Australia and elsewhere and seeking trade at Hankow only while freights were abundant there. The former class included the Peninsular & Oriental Steam Navigation Co., the Orient Steam Navigation Co., the Messageries Maritimes Co., the Glen, Castle, Shire, and Ben Lines, and in 1879 and 1883 "conferences" were held to limit the tonnage sent to Hankow. In the spring of 1884 another conference was held, and the following circular issued: "Shanghai, 10th May, 1884. To those exporters who confine their shipments of tea and general cargo from China to Europe (not including the Mediterranean and Black Sea Ports) to the P. & O.S.N. Company's, M.M. Company's, O.S.N. Company's, Glen, Castle, Shire, and Ben Lines, and to the S.S. *Oopack* and *Ningchow*, we shall be happy to allow a rebate of 5 per cent. on the freights charged. Exporters claiming the returns will be required to sign a declaration that they have not made or been interested in any shipments of tea or general cargo to Europe (excepting the ports above-named) other than by the above lines. Shipments by S.S. *Albany, Pathan,* and *Ghazee* on their present voyages will not prejudice claims for returns. Each line to be responsible for its own returns only, which will be payable half-yearly, commencing the 30th of October next. Shipments by an outside steamer at any of the ports in China or at Hong-Kong will exclude the firm making such shipments from participation in the return during the whole six monthly period within which they have been made, even although its other branches may have given entire support to the above lines. The foregoing agreement on our part to be in force from present date till the 30th April, 1886."

The Mogul Steamship Co. were admitted to the benefit of the arrangement in respect of the homeward voyage of their vessels the *Pathan* and *Ghazee,* as mentioned, but on desiring to participate in 1885 the boycott was put into force, a sharp rate war ensued, and as one of the incidents of the campaign the associated companies withdrew agencies from firms acting for the Mogul Co. In May, 1885, an action was brought against the British companies in the conference for damages arising out of their alleged illegal conspiracy and for an injunction to restrain them from continuing the said wrongful acts. Decision was finally given by the House of Lords in December, 1891, against the Mogul Co., Lord Chancellor Halsbury saying: "I have been unable to discover anything done by the members of the associated body of traders other than an offer of reduced freights to persons who would deal exclusively with them ; and if this is unlawful it seems to me that the greater part of commercial dealings, where there is rivalry in trade, must be equally unlawful."

The whole strength of the conference system lies in the device of a 5 or 10 per cent. rebate which is held by the ship-owner for six months, and is forfeited if inside that period a single ounce of freight is shipped by an independent vessel. A large shipper has always too much at stake to afford disobedience, and the control of the shipping companies is firmly riveted on our over-sea trade. British traders have frequently complained that this system has led to preferential rates in favour of Continental shippers. For example it was alleged that the P. & O. Co. was charging in 1894 10s. per ton on iron from Antwerp to Bombay or Calcutta and 15s. 9d. from London. Sir Thomas Sutherland, the chairman of the incriminated company, at the annual meeting in December, 1897, denied that there was any competition in iron between London and Antwerp since the heavy cost of railway carriage made Glasgow and Liverpool the natural ports of shipment. The rate of 10s. was, he said, due to German competition at Hamburg and Bremen, and the company reduced their rate from Middlesbrough to meet it. But his real defence was this: "Now what I desire to point out emphatically in this connection is that if we had not carried a ton of this foreign cargo, every particle of it would have been conveyed by German ships. Our abstention would not have made the slightest difference to the British trader. But while we kept our necessary interest as shipowners in the foreign trade, we at the same time lowered our Middlesbrough tariff to the foreign level." One slight error in his argument is the assumption that German competition would have forced rates so low if the P. & O. Co. had not also been in the trade, which is not necessarily true. But the point is good that as a ship-owner he had to consider his foreign as well as his British trade. As a shipowner it did not matter to him where his freights came from, so long as in developing one trade he did not inflict such injury on the other as would ultimately result in loss to himself by bringing loss on his fellow-countrymen. And how far any particular course of action may tend in this direction is always the matter at issue between shippers and shipowners. Shippers, it must also be remembered, are mainly concerned with low freights, however obtained, irrespective of loss to the shipowners, tempered only by consideration for possible increased cost after some competitors have been forced to abandon the shipping industry. Neither party is altruist, though each expects the other to be.

This same charge of giving preference to the foreigner was brought by the Leeds Chamber of Commerce and other bodies in 1902 against the South African Shipping Conference. To this Sir Donald Currie, chairman of the Union Castle Line, in a letter to Sir A. Hime, Premier of Natal, on 25th August, 1902, replied: "There is not the slightest foundation for the charge so frequently and so recklessly made that we have followed this course. The rates of freight from all Continental ports are the same as from British ports, and we have in all our agreements with German and other lines stipulated for this in the interests of British merchants and shipowners. It is quite true that from the interior of Germany through to South Africa goods can be forwarded at reduced German railway rates, provided the goods are shipped by steamers under the German flag; but this regulation is wholly outside of our power to remedy. The Government of Germany have not only granted a large annual subsidy to the German South and East African Mail Line, but they have supplemented this by additional aid and support from their State railways, and by granting an allowance on all inland traffic forwarded by these German steamers. There is no favour shown to British steamers loading in German ports—on the contrary, they are absolutely opposed and prejudiced by the German State rail-ways." Probably British shippers would reply that the ship-owners should reduce the rates from British ports by an amount equivalent to the German railway allowance, but the German lines would probably meet this by another cut, or the German Government might still further reduce its railway rates, or the German lines might even carry the war into the enemy's camp by cutting rates from British ports. A rate war is always a happy time for merchants, but a prolonged and bitter struggle between such mighty antagonists as modern shipping com-panies are is not to be lightly undertaken by any company, especially if one of the parties has a great, resolute, and enter-prising Government at its back. To ask the shipowners to bear the whole brunt of the fray is not fair.

The case is altered when a "ring" has ships plying between two exporting countries and an importing country at similar freight rates, and an outsider comes in and cuts the rates from one of the exporting countries only. Sir Donald Currie also wrote: "In regard to traffic from America, which it has been said is advantaged by lower rates than from England, the fact is that the rates were assimilated, as far as this was possible in dealing with goods dissimilar in character; but so little to the advantage of American shippers has this been done that the opposition now carried on from New York to South Africa is actually justified by shippers of American goods, who complain that British lines have been charging higher rates, and not lower rates, from New York than from Great Britain". The Houston and Prince Lines, in June, 1902, cut into the "ring's" monopoly, quoting 15s. per ton lower rates, and specially reducing the rates from the United States. One circular, quoted in the *Iron and Coal Trades Review* (29th August, 1902), stated that the agents of the independent lines "will at all times make rates which will enable the American merchants and manufacturers to compete with those of Europe". Rates from New York to South Africa were 10s. per ton, while those from British ports varied from 25s. to 42s. 6d., according to the class of goods. There was nothing new in this discrepancy; it had occurred before in the South African trade in a war with the Hansa Line, and frequently in other trade routes when conference steamers happened to be serving ports where competition prevailed as well as those in which the combination rates hold good. Thus, in 1898, cotton goods were shipped from America, *viâ* Liverpool, to Shanghai, for 25s. 6d. per ton, while the rate from Liverpool was 40s., and the rate on machinery from America to China was 40 per cent. less than from Liverpool. Bar iron from Belgium to Hong-Kong cost 12s. 6d. per ton and from British ports 18s.

There is no doubt that in such circumstances foreign manufacturers receive an advantage over British. "The result," said Mr. Birchenough, in his *Report on British Trade in South Africa* (Cd. 1844-1903), "has been to give a great stimulus to American trade and to introduce into the South African market manufactures which would not otherwise have found their way there for years. . . . No single circumstance has proved so favourable to the rapid growth of American trade with South Africa as these low freights, and we owe them to the action of British shipping companies." Indirectly these low rates helped towards the overstocking of South Africa with goods to the injury of all sound trade since.

Whether we attribute the blame for low "war rates" to the conference or to the independent lines will depend upon the view we take of the previously existing rates. The merchants' case was that the conference had abused its monopoly by keeping rates high, proportionately higher than anywhere else in the world, and that it had kept them high while they had fallen elsewhere. "To this," to quote again Mr. Birchenough, "the conference replies that their rates are necessarily higher than other rates owing to the peculiarity of the South African trade. They get practically no return cargo, and the outward freight has really to carry the cost of the double journey. They do not rely either upon their mail privileges or upon their monopoly. They provide a fleet of 250 vessels, representing a million of tonnage, and give a first-rate and quite regular service. Steamers are out of date in nine or ten years, and have to be replaced. They spare no expense to keep up a high standard of ships, and man them exclusively with British

seamen.   If they employed Lascars they might no doubt run
their boats more cheaply.   Taking all these facts into consideration, their charges are not unreasonable.   The best proof is
that the conference does not make abnormal profits; indeed,
no other trading company in South Africa would be willing to
work for so small a return."   That is the case for the conference, and, *mutatis mutandis*, it is the case for all conferences.
Mr. Birchenough concluded that "in the absence of free competition it seems impossible to decide what is a reasonable
freight charge to South Africa".   It is only reasonable, however, to expect that conference rates will always be above
competitive rates, but whether they are beyond what is counterbalanced by the advantages of regular service, stability of
charge, and equal treatment of all shippers, will be generally
beyond the power of a critic to say.   In the South African
case they were high enough to make it worth the while of the
six companies in the conference to fight the Houston-Prince
combination for about eighteen months; though no doubt the
fight was partly due to resentment at interference—"we do not
require the assistance of this gentleman's steamers," said the
conference letter to Sir A. Hime.   They were high enough
also to allow the admission of Mr. Houston to the "ring" when
the war ended.   And, finally, when a conference was held
between the shipowners and representatives of the South
African Governments in 1905, Sir Donald Currie complained
that credit had not been given to the shipowners, although "in
the last three years we had reduced rates of freight upon fifty-
two descriptions of goods to an extent ranging from 2s. 6d. to
12s. 6d. per ton," and expressed his willingness to make further
reductions of 8 or 9 per cent. on certain classes of goods.

Another complaint relates to the tyrannical action of the
conferences, especially in their rigid enforcement of the rebate
regulations.   To this the associated shipowners reply that they
can only provide the conveniences of regular and abundant
supply of shipping at steady rates common to all shippers if
they are guaranteed some continuity of their business, and this
they can only secure by binding their customers to them by
material bonds too expensive to break.   But the charges of

tyranny go beyond the forfeiture of rebates. The Leeds Chamber of Commerce alleged that "shippers in the home trade, who make use of any competing line, are threatened with higher rates, . . . and it would appear, moreover, that customers in South Africa of firms making any use of such competing lines are threatened with similar penalties". Messrs. Townsend & Mellor in a letter in the *Liverpool Daily Post*, of 10th January, 1903, gave some striking evidence on these points summing up as follows : " The conference lines have directly or indirectly penalised shippers by refusing to carry goods, except at double rates, for any shipper who has shipped by the Houston Line. They have threatened consignees of cargo by Houston steamers at the various South African ports that their receiving cargo by Houston steamers would cause them to be charged double rates on all cargo received by such consignees by conference steamers, notwithstanding the fact that the consignees did not control the shipments, the subject of offence. The conference have refused to receive goods from shipping and cartage agents, on the ground that such agents had, although under the instructions of their principals, shipped by, or carted goods to, the Houston Line." Finally Mr. Birch-enough says : " I am inclined to think that the methods of the ' ring ' in enforcing their monopoly by means of threats and punishments to individual shippers have been characterised by a want of tact and moderation, which is far more responsible for the exacerbation of public feeling than either the scale of their charges or any want of satisfaction with the excellence and regularity of the service ".

So much space has been given to the South African Con-ference, not because it is worse than other similar organisa-tions, but because, thanks to the large share of public attention occupied by everything South African, it has been dragged into publicity. From it we learn that under favourable circum-stances a conference can become a very powerful monopoly, keeping up rates and enforcing its decrees with a good deal of high-handedness. The merchants are helpless because only a very strong competitor can take the risks of a fight with the " ring," and if he becomes really dangerous he can be bought off by admission. Joint action to establish a rival line always breaks down on account of the great expense and risk involved, and the want of mutual confidence among the merchants.

The ordinary comparison with railway conferences, which is often made by shipowners, that the lines simply agree as to rates and compete in providing facilities breaks down because over the railways the State has set up the Railway Commission as a regulator, and shipowners have never professed their desire for the creation of a similar body. In November, 1906, a strong Royal Commission was appointed to inquire into the whole system of conferences and rebates and their effects on British trade, and it is to be hoped that its deliberations will end in the settlement of one of the most grievous of industrial disputes.

Conferences exist in the homeward journeys from the Plate, from Singapore, from China, from Calcutta; in the Australian shipping trade; in the New Zealand Cape trade; in the Atlantic, the Mediterranean, and many other trades. The Singapore Conference has also been charged with favouring foreign countries: " It costs 56s. per ton to ship tapioca to Leith or Belfast and 50s. to Glasgow against 42s. 6d. to St. Nazaire, Dunkirk, Rotterdam, Venice, Fiume, etc. Again, as an example, it is possible to ship to Havre and (or) Marseilles, direct or indirect, at one, and that the lowest, rate; but we cannot obtain option of London and (or) Liverpool except at 5s. extra. Again, it is allowed by the conference to charter sailing vessels for Marseilles, but not for the United Kingdom ! " (" Impericum " in *Liverpool Daily Post*, 16th January, 1903). The protests of the New Zealand Government against the high rates on the Cape trade and their threats to establish a State-owned line are well known. Representatives of twelve British and foreign companies met in conference at Ostend in September, 1902, and raised outward freights to South American ports to compensate for the losses in the homeward trips owing to lack of cargo.

The case of the Atlantic trade is peculiar, and has been very fully discussed by Mr. J. Russell Smith in the *Political Science Quarterly* for June, 1906. Combination in this trade is made difficult by its great size, for it employs about 3,000,000 tons of shipping trading from a great number of American to a great number of European ports, and by the necessity of obtaining a properly mixed cargo of light and heavy goods to ensure proper buoyancy of the ship. A vessel partly laden with light goods may require, for safe navigation, a part cargo of heavy goods, and having got good rates on the high value cargo will be prepared to take the heavy cargo on very low terms. Grain has always been in demand as ballast, and, as it is generally carried in chartered vessels, the liner is brought into direct competition with the tramp. The introduction of water ballast has, however, considerably modified this necessity. Another impediment to joint action has been the fact that the trade is carried on by all the European nations. Since 1868 there has been a Transatlantic Shipping Conference which dealt with bills of lading and similar questions. " In 1902," says Mr. Russell Smith, " this conference, with operating headquarters in New York, was made the mechanism for the carrying out of a minimum freight agreement to the United Kingdom which was made in Liverpool and planned for the relief of all interests. The transatlantic carriers were suffering from a rate depression which in twelve months had cut their earnings from exceptional prosperity to hopeless loss. At one time this agreement included forty-six lines and services." The rate depression was due to the great output of new shipping in 1898-1901.

This agreement was particularly feeble and only governed "articles essentially requisite as ballast cargo". The withdrawal of any one member, for which a fortnight's notice was required, dissolved the agreement, and rates were as a rule only struck from week to week. " From time to time difficulties arose and concessions in rates would be granted, permitting the carriers from a certain port or ports to cut the rate a certain amount to secure a prescribed maximum amount of named articles of freight in order to get ballast, after which the usual rates were resumed. The converse of this was also practised when certain ports refused to carry certain commodities for a period so that other ports might get their share

This refusal to carry was brought about by the mere quotation of a rate sufficiently high to drive the freight to the ports agreed upon. . . . The agreement covered only named articles ; the list was occasionally changed, or the rates on single commodities altered. At times the desire to compete would be gratified by withdrawing the agreement on a certain article or articles for a named period."

It was a considerable achievement to work an agreement in such a trade at all, and shows how strong was the desire to escape from competition. After two years' operation it was destroyed by the differential railway rates from the interior of America to the sea-board which had to be equalised by adjustment of the ocean rates. A Baltimore line " refused to submit to sea differentials that absolutely wiped out the advantage of the land differential". The general agreement broke down in February, 1904, but " the London traders met immediately and continued the agreement so far as it affected them, and their agreement is still in operation. The Glasgow traders and various other traders after the general break gathered themselves together as before and made and informally maintained their agreements." West-bound trade is mainly in high-value goods which must go by the quickest route and can bear a high freight rate. The London carriers have had since 1901 an agreement with a classification of the higher grade manufactures into seven classes, covering 10 per cent. of the trade. " On the other 90 per cent., the agreeing London carriers feel that they must be free to meet the market, which sets the rate for all freight moving in great quantities."

In the spring of 1902 fourteen British, American, German, French, and Dutch lines came to an agreement fixing and raising the rates for saloon passengers travelling to America. The Cunard withdrew in June, 1903, and in 1904 there was a prolonged and costly war in steerage rates arising out of a quarrel between the German lines and the Cunard as to the Continental emigrant traffic. Formerly the Cunard Line had a monopoly of the Scandinavian business and left to the Hamburg-America and North-German Lloyd companies all the emigration from Russia and the north of Austria and Hungary, except a small agreed proportion. When the Cunard made an agreement with the Hungarian Government to run an emigration service from Fiume this was regarded as an unwarrantable intrusion into German preserves. War was declared, rival services being started to compete with the Cunard for the Scandinavian and Hungarian traffic. The American-English companies who were bound to the Germans by the Morgan Agreement were summoned to the fray, and the steerage rates were reduced to 30s. For about eight months the fight raged and vast sums were lost, showing once more that there is no competition so violent as that between great business units. The Cunard Company, however, came out of the fight rather better than its rivals, and when peace was signed in January, 1905, they were allowed to continue undisturbed their contract with the Hungarian Government. The Atlantic Passenger Conference finally broke up in the spring of the same year owing to disputes with the Cunard Company as to the dates of sailing of the rival companies' ships. This time, however, a rate war did not ensue.

The strenuous nature of maritime competition has naturally led to a certain amount of combination intended to strengthen the competitive power of the amalgamating units. The close connection of shipping and steel interests in Furness, Withy, & Co. and of shipping and oil interests in the Shell Transport and Trading Co. have already been dealt with. Another example of the same kind of union is the formation of the firm of Elders & Fyffe's in 1901, uniting the fruit businesses carried on by Messrs. Elder, Dempster, & Co. and Fyffe, Hudson, & Co., and providing a market for the banana business developed by the former in return for a subsidy of £40,000 a year granted by the Jamaican Government to them in connection with their Imperial West Indian Mail Service. These are combinations of shipping and trading interests. Pure shipping combinations are exemplified by the following. The Wilson's & Furness Leyland Line combined three firms in 1896, with a capital of £510,000. It passed under the control of Frederick Leyland & Co. in 1900, who at the same time acquired the West India and Pacific Steamship Co.; capital of F. Leyland & Co., £3,300,000. The Atlantic business of F. Leyland & Co. was sold to Mr. Pierpont

Morgan in 1901, and Mr. Ellerman, the chairman, then organised the Ellerman Lines by amalgamating the remaining business of F. Leyland & Co. in the Peninsular and Mediterranean trade; the City Line to India (founded in 1840 by Messrs. George Smith & Sons, of Glasgow); the Hall Line to India; Papayanni & Co. in the Mediterranean trade; the Westcott and Laurance Line from Antwerp to the Levant; Palgrave, Murphy, & Co. trading to Oporto; and the Ellerman-Harrison joint line to the Cape. This was a considerable extinction of competition, and the capital of the union was £770,000.

The Bucknall Steamship Lines, Ltd., established in 1900, united the interest of Messrs. Bucknall Bros. (who were managers of the Steamship Lines), the British and Colonial Steam Navigation Co., and the Bucentaur Steamship Co., with an issued capital of £1,850,000. This union was one of convenience of management, for the lines were complementary rather than competitive. William France, Fenwick, & Co., formed in 1901, with a capital of £450,000, united three firms engaged in carrying coal to London. Of all these amalgamations the Union-Castle Line, which in 1900 amalgamated, with a capital of £2,000,000, the two famous steamship companies in the Cape trade, is the only one which possesses anything like a dominance in its trade. The curious point about their union is that the mail contracts which they shared on competitive terms expressly forbade amalgamation, and it was only after the Cape Government agreed to the grant of a joint contract that it was possible to put an end to the "continual rivalry, friction, and opposition," as the chairman described their relations.

The Booth Steamship Co., capital £1,000,000, united two interests in the Brazil trade in 1901. The China Mutual Steam Navigation Co. was sold in 1902 to Mr. Alfred Holt, of Liverpool, who also had a line to China. The Canadian Pacific Railway Co., which had its own fleet in the Pacific, completed, in 1903, its connection with Europe by purchasing the Beaver Line of Liverpool. In the same year Thomas Wilson, Sons, & Co., a private limited company, with a capital of £2,000,000, acquired the fleet of Messrs. Bailey & Leetham, their friendly rivals in the Hull-Hamburg trade, and in 1906 they came to an agreement with the North-Eastern Railway whereby the services between Hull and Hamburg, Antwerp, Ghent, and Dunkirk were to be run by the parties on joint agreement, each taking an equal financial interest. The Lancashire and Yorkshire Railway had already a service from Goole and the Great Central Railway one from Grimsby, the object being to secure the advantage of through booking of goods, and the intervention of the railway serving Hull was thus imperative. Lastly, the Royal Mail Steam Packet Company, once the most conservative of all companies, acquired as from 1st January, 1906, the whole of the interest of the Pacific Steam Navigation Co. in the Orient-Pacific Line to Australia, hitherto jointly worked by that company and the Orient Steamship Company.

Except in the case of the Union-Castle Line and Ellerman Lines it is impossible to say whether combination has greatly strengthened the firms combining; at all events it has not enabled them to control the vagaries of the freight market. The International Mercantile Marine Company, otherwise the " Atlantic Shipping Trust," was, on the other hand, a deliberate attempt to extirpate competition and fix rates. Its formation in the spring of 1902 was doubtless connected with the efforts already described to govern the east-bound Atlantic trade by a conference, and was perhaps more directly a result of the condominium established over the chief American railway lines. It was hoped that by means of through rates east-bound goods would be secured for the railways and the shipping lines under their control. Mr. Pierpont Morgan had already bought the Leyland Line at £14 10s. per £10 ordinary share, reselling all except the Atlantic business to Mr. Ellerman, but the announcement in April, 1902, that he had secured control of the historic White Star Line was an immense shock to the British public. Gradually the details trickled out. The lines acquired by the American syndicate were the White Star Line of the Oceanic Steam Navigation Co. (capital £750,000), the Leyland Line of Frederick Leyland & Co. (capital £3,114,350), the Atlantic Transport Company (£1,000,000), itself a combination of several small companies, the American Line, which had acquired the old Inman Line, and the Dominion Line. The purchase money of the White Star Line and the Dominion Line was ten times their net profits for 1900, and at the same rate for the businesses of Ismay, Imrie, & Co., and Richards, Mills, & Co., the respective managers of the two lines. The interests acquired in the Leyland Line were valued at $11,736,000, and in the American and American Transport Lines at $34,158,000, subject to bonds for $19,686,000. One-fourth of the purchase money of the White Star and Dominion Lines was to be paid in cash and three-quarters in preferred shares of the new company, with a bonus of 37½ per cent. in common stock.

The total capital issued was $170,000,000 or £34,000,000 —$50,000,000 in 4½ per cent. bonds, $60,000,000 in 6 per cent. preferred stock, and $60,000,000 in common stock. The over-capitalisation was glaring even after writing off the common stock as gambling counters. The book value of the Cunard Line was under £15 per ton, and even if the whole fleet bought was worth that, which it was not, that would only have amounted to £16,200,000, to which of course should be added a good sum for other assets, investments, wharves, etc., taken over. The year 1900, which was taken as the basis of the transactions, was a year of exceptionally high freights owing to the demand of the British Government for ships for transport purposes—for instance the Cunard Company doubled its average profits—and to purchase on the basis of the returns for that year was to risk future disappointment. If it be true as stated (*Financial Times*, 6th January, 1903) that the White Star shareholders received per £1,000 share £14,213, of which £4,143 was in cash, they made an uncommonly good bargain for themselves.

It was plain that if the combination was to earn decent profits it must not only control but raise rates, and it proceeded to negotiate a series of alliances with other interests. An agreement was made with Messrs. Harland & Wolff, the great shipbuilders of Belfast, who had built the White Star Line, whereby the Morgan syndicate agreed to give the Irish firm their European building or repairing, but without limitation of their power to place orders in American yards. Subject to being kept continuously employed Messrs Harland & Wolff agreed to work exclusively for the syndicate, "and in any case not to accept orders from parties who are competitors of the purchasers in any trade at the time carried on by them without first obtaining the purchasers' consent"; but this was not to apply to the Hamburg-America Company. Work was to be done on terms of 5 per cent. commission on the cost of new ships, including "a due proportion of fixed expenses and establishment charges," and 10 to 15 per cent. for repairs. As Messrs. Harland & Wolff owned 51 per cent. of the Holland-America Line its friendly co-operation was secured. More important was the agreement with the Hamburg-America and North German Lloyd Companies. Briefly, the German companies and the American syndicate bound themselves to observe the present division of the Atlantic trade and not to poach on each other's territory or to start new enterprises until they had been considered by the standing joint committee, whose duty it was to keep all the parties in touch with each other, and with permission of mutual participation. If one of the parties temporarily required more ships it was to apply to the other before chartering from outside firms. The saloon passenger traffic was to be regulated by arranging a "pool". Finally, the German companies were to pay to the syndicate the dividends on 20,000,000 marks, or one-quarter of their capital, and the syndicate was to pay to the German companies 6 per cent. on the same amount, that is, upon at least 20,000,000 marks. The last provision meant that the syndicate were to guarantee the German companies 6 per cent. on one-quarter of their capital, distinctly an advantageous arrangement for them, since the average dividend of the Hamburg-America Company for the previous ten years was just over 5 per cent., and of the North German Lloyd $4\frac{1}{4}$ per cent. Both parties also bound themselves not to try to buy up each other.

The importance of the International Mercantile Marine Company was partly commercial, partly political. Its commercial importance consisted partly in its assumed power to control rates, and alternatively in its increased competitive strength. We have already seen that the former did not in reality, and could not, exist owing to the irregularity in the volume of the Atlantic shipping business and the nature of the goods carried. As a competitor it failed both to cajole and to coerce the Cunard Company (capital £2,000,000) into union, while its alliance with the German companies proved, like so many alliances, a source of weakness, by dragging it into a costly rate war which involved it in actual loss while the Cunard had only to pass its ordinary dividend. Competitive strength depends very greatly on the policy of providing liberally for insurance, depreciation, etc., so that the fleet may always be maintained at a high modern standard. Conservative practice is to devote 60 per cent. of the net earnings to these purposes, and the Cunard Company in the twenty years 1885-1904 allocated £3,980,000 to depreciation, etc., and only paid £912,000 in ordinary dividends. A further source of strength would be the savings accruing from combination. Prof. Meade in his article on "The Capitalisation of the International Mercantile Marine Company" (reprinted in *Trusts, Pools, and Corporations*, edited by Prof. Ripley; Ginn & Company, Boston) says: "Shortly after the Mercantile Marine Company was organised, the statement was made, unofficially, but apparently on good authority, by the Wall Street *Journal*, that the average net earnings of the different fleets for four years was $6,107,675. The same authority stated that the estimated savings in the cost of operation for the year were $10,000,000." This would make the tonnage earnings nearly twice the average amount earned by its three greatest competitors, the Cunard and the German Companies, and was obviously pure exaggeration.

The working of the International Mercantile Marine Company, so far as regards the American, Red Star, White Star, Dominion, and Atlantic Transport Lines, is shown below: the accounts of the Leyland and National Lines are published separately.

	1903. $	1904. $	1905. $
Gross earnings . . .	31,037,420	28,846,993	33,362,918
„ expenses . . .	27,036,898	27,040,586	27,456,174
Net earnings . . .	4,002,522	1,806,407	5,906,744
Charges for bonds, loans, and income tax . . .	3,645,227	3,845,557	3,880,055
Result for year . . .	355,295	2,039,150*	2,890,848†

* Loss.   † After deducting $236,643 for trade agreements for 1904.

The profits of the Leyland Line for 1905 were £88,418 and of the National Line £12,076, all of which was written off to depreciation. No allocation was made for depreciation in 1903 and 1904, but in 1905, after wiping out the debit balance for the previous year ($1,537,748), $2,000,000 were appropriated for that purpose. This was only 1·66 per cent. of the cost of the properties. Nothing also is written off investments or on account of the accumulated losses (after providing for depreciation) of the Leyland and National Lines. " The preference stock of the company is quoted at 28¾, the common stock at 10½, and the bonds at 75½. Taking the cost of the fleet as shown in the accounts, it works at about £40 per ton gross, of course, an absurd value. To bring the fleet down to a saleable price, a process which in the case of property controlled by American millionaires is absolutely unnecessary, it would require to write off a sum approaching £20,000,000 sterling, and this on a reasonable system of book-keeping, as understood by British auditors, would have to be done before dividends could be declared. A noticeable feature in connection with this American corporation is the fact that the 4½ per cent. gold bonds, which are supposed to be a first charge on the entire property of the company, stand at a discount of 25 per cent., and at that price yield a return of 6 per cent. Now the 3½ per cent. debenture stock of the P. & O. Co. stands at 102, yielding 3½ per cent. against 6 per cent. on the parallel stock of the American combine. From this it would appear that whatever else our Yankee friends may teach us, they have yet something to learn in the matter of securing public belief in the financial stability of their maritime business" (*Fairplay*, 5th July, 1906).

The bad results of 1904 were due to the rate war, which cut down the North German Lloyd dividend from 6 to 2 per cent. and caused the Hamburg-America Company severe losses, which were fortunately made good by the profits of its other trade. In 1905 rates were maintained at a remunerative level, and as the German companies paid satisfactory dividends, substantial payments were received from them under the agreements. As a trading undertaking the company has been inferior to the

20

Cunard Company whose gross receipts averaged in 1903 and 1904 about £7·2 per gross ton, compared with about £6 per ton in each year earned by the International Company. As a controlling power it has equally been a failure. Its total capital is now $175,954,773, and with preference interest unpaid for three years there is little prospect of the holders of common stock ever getting anything.

The sale of the White Star Company created a kind of panic, not so much because so many ships were sold but because it seemed to be the sale of a trade route with the goodwill attached. As the magnitude of the outstanding companies came to be realised the public mind was appeased, and when Mr. Ismay, of the White Star Line, was made president of the Combination in 1904 it was felt that British prestige was restored. Politically there was some fear lest the vessels belonging to the company which received Admiralty subsidies should no longer be at the disposal of the British Government, but an agreement was signed in August, 1903, continuing the ships of the company on the same footing in regard to the Government as theretofore, prohibiting transfer of the ships flying the British flag to a foreign registry without consent of the Board of Trade, and requiring half the new tonnage built to be of British registry. The agreement was to remain in force for twenty years, but to be terminable at any time if the associated companies should " pursue a policy injurious to the interests of the British mercantile marine or of British trade ". The practical value of this agreement does not appear to be great so long as the control lies in American hands.

Of great significance, on the other hand, was the compact entered into between the Government and the Cunard Company. The company adopted a new clause in their articles of association :—" It is to be regarded as a cardinal principle of the company that it is to be and remain under British control, and accordingly—(A) No foreigner shall be qualified to hold office as a director of the company, or to be employed as one of the principal officers of the company. (B) No share in the company shall be held by or in trust for, or be in any way under the control of any foreigner or foreign corporation or any corporation under foreign control." Two new vessels of 24 to 25 knots speed were to be built in the United Kingdom, and they, as well as the whole Cunard fleet, were to be at the disposal of the Admiralty to charter or purchase on reasonable rates ; no vessel over 17 knots was to be sold without Admiralty consent, or to be chartered without giving the Government first refusal, or in any case for more than six months. The officers and three-fourths of the crews were to be British subjects, and the officers and half of the crews of the two new vessels were to belong to the Royal Naval Reserve and Royal Naval Fleet Reserve. Freight rates were not to be unduly raised or to give a preference against British subjects. In return the Government was to advance £2,600,000 at 2¾ per cent., and to pay, besides the mail subsidies, a subsidy of £150,000 for all other services for twenty years. The capital of the company was increased by £20, the new share being allotted to the Government. The charter of the P. & O. Co. was renewed a few months later, and contained the same exclusion of foreigners from the directors and officers, and the amount of stock which could be held by foreigners was limited to one-fourth of the whole. Similar provisions were also introduced into the new charter of the Royal Mail Steam Packet Company.

There was a good deal of criticism of this partnership between the Government and a particular shipping company, but it was necessary if the two new ships were to be built. It was also generally felt that a demonstration of the British determination to retain the command of the ocean trade, even at the cost of Government intervention, was both a necessary and a good thing. The wider policy of State participation in commerce does not claim discussion here, but the stipulation for reasonable rates, not discriminatory against British subjects, must be brought into prominence as an entirely new development of State control of industry.

CHAPTER XIII.

MISCELLANEOUS INDUSTRIES.

THE paper trade has its trade organisation like every other industry—the British Paper Makers' Association—for ordinary trade purposes, but apart from that there have been several attempts to consolidate the various units. In 1889 a Paper Syndicate was proposed but the scheme collapsed. When the trade seemed to be threatened by the formation of the United Alkali Company there were several proposals that the paper makers should start co-operative factories for the manufacture of their own bleaching powder, but nothing came of them. In November, 1889, the British Paper Makers' Association held a meeting at which it was resolved that, owing to the rise in the price of coal and raw materials, an advance in the price of paper was imperative. On account of the great variety of papers a uniform advance was not possible; obviously each fraction of the industry was to be taxed according to its capacity for bearing a rise. This is an interesting instance of a trade organisation being diverted in a case of emergency to the work of price regulation which was not contemplated on its establishment. There was some talk a year later of forming a combination, but as the *World's Paper Trade Review* (28th September, 1900), said: "There are so many in the trade who look upon failure as a foregone conclusion, that the project does not seem to have been seriously considered. There are mills in England that favour combination, but certain Scotch mills withhold their support, and in order to obtain a consensus of opinion a meeting is announced for 4th October. Hitherto the mills in question have failed to work unanimously in order to enforce higher prices, and therefore it seems very unlikely that the combination idea will be supported." It ended in talk, and, indeed, it is plain that there is not that harmony in the industry which is indispensable for joint action.

On the other hand one of the derivative paper industries, the manufacture of wall-papers, has been consolidated into a great amalgamation, the Wall-Paper Manufacturers, Ltd., which in February, 1900, united thirty-one firms engaged in the manufacture of wall-papers and raised decorative materials, such as anaglypta, etc. Working agreements were also made with three other firms, so that altogether about 98 per cent. of the trade of the Kingdom was included. Among the properties taken over were two paper mills, thus securing in part the supply of raw material. A syndicate " to put an end to vexatious rivalry between the leading firms " had been formed in 1899, and it was its successful working which led up to amalgamation. Valuation of the businesses bought was conducted on more scientific lines than has usually been the case with large combines, three accountants being appointed, one to represent the purchasing company, one to act for the vendors, and the third as umpire. Four small businesses were bought for £74,577 cash, and all the others for shares and debentures in such a way that a vendor received sufficient debentures to yield in interest one-fifth of his net earnings, preference shares to yield one-fourth, and the balance in ordinary and deferred shares. The total purchase consideration was £4,216,045, of which stocks, etc., amounted to £545,735 and book debts to £393,873, the balance, which was not separately certified, representing land, buildings, plant, goodwill, etc. No goodwill was paid in respect of four undertakings whose profits did not exceed 5 per cent. on their capital. The profits, partly estimated, for 1897 were £199,030, or 4·72 per cent. of the purchase money. The authorised capital was £4,200,000—£1,000,000 in 4 per cent. debentures, £1,000,000 in 5 per cent. cumulative preference shares, £1,100,000 in ordinary shares, and £1,100,000 in deferred shares. The deferred shares were " issued to apportion to each vendor his share of profit after 10 per cent. has been paid on the ordinary shares." £986,113 debentures and the same amount of preference stock were offered for public subscription, less one-third taken by the vendors. The total subscribed capital is £4,183,468. The financial results of the company are shown in the following table, profit being taken after allowance for depreciation and all other charges except debenture interest :—

	Net Profit.	Ordinary Dividend.
Year to 31/8/00	£183,006	8 per cent.
,, 31/8/01	223,811	8 ,,
,, 31/8/02	230,915	8 ,,
,, 31/8/03	246,335	8 ,,
,, 31/8/04	239,047	8 ,,
,, 31/8/05	243,227*	8 ,,
,, 31/8/06	228,908*	8 ,,

* Inclusive of about £2,700 for income tax.

The profit is uniformly larger than was shown in the prospectus except in the first year when £20,000 was set aside as a special depreciation for closed works. So far nothing has been paid on deferred stock, the directors preferring to have the company in a sound financial condition and to build up a large reserve rather than pay high dividends on the ordinary and deferred shares.

The company has practically a monopoly of the home trade, though one small rival concern, the Free Wall-Paper Co., was started in 1900; its capital is now £28,813. In 1905 the Lincrusta business of Frederick Walton & Co. was purchased. Its position was strengthened by a ten years' agreement with the dealers, the nature of which may be seen from the following circular printed in the *Daily Mail* of 23rd October, 1906 :—

"THE WALL-PAPER MANUFACTURERS, LTD.

"125 HIGH HOLBORN,

"LONDON, W.C., 17th October, 1906.

"Gentlemen,—In view of the fact that certain manufacturers are pressing for orders, permit us respectfully to remind you that by the terms of your agreement with this company you have engaged not to 'stock nor cut up patterns, nor issue in your pattern books, nor sell for stock any paper-hangings or any raised materials other than those manufactured by the company'.

"We have reason to believe that some of our customers, either from negligence or under the advice of interested parties, have been induced to commit small breaches of Clause 18 of the agreement.

" In those cases which have come to our knowledge, we have, in bringing the matter to our customers' notice, obtained from them formal recognition of their obligations, and a promise to comply with them in the future; and we have instructed our solicitors to commence proceedings and enforce the payment of damages against any of those who commit breaches of the agreement.

" In the general interest, and at the request of a large body of agreement customers, we are writing this letter to all, and take the liberty of bringing the matter to your attention, so as to avoid any chance of misapprehension.

" Yours truly,
" THE WALL-PAPER MANUFACTURERS, LTD."

Certain low grade qualities of paper ceased to be manufactured, but there does not seem to have been any attempt to force up prices. The chairman claimed in November, 1902, that "there is no question of the public having to pay higher prices owing to our combination. On the contrary, we are delivering goods to-day at lower prices than those at which any separate concern could produce them, and it is on our being able to do this that we rely to secure our prosperity in the future." Next year he said: " Notwithstanding the low prices which have ranged during the year, I am glad to inform you that the total turnover, both in money value and number of pieces, has exceeded that of any previous year, and it is my opinion that the results shown could not have been maintained but for the economies in manufacture which, as a combine, we have been able to effect". And at the 1904 meeting: " We have never made the slightest attempt to bolster up prices; on the contrary they are lower now than I have ever known them during my many years' connection with the trade." On the other hand the company tried to strengthen its position by commencing in 1905 the construction at Greenhithe of a new paper mill, which the board hoped would be "the finest paper-making mill in the world". This will give a better control over the main raw material.

There still remained foreign competition. Again quoting the chairman at the 1902 meeting: " The trade is aware that during the last three years attempts have been made by foreign manufacturers to export their goods here. These attempts have been persevered in with great energy and ability, especially by an American firm, and it is no matter of surprise with me that this firm has decided to abandon this market, and I unhesitatingly give expression to my conviction that it will never answer the purpose of any foreign manufacturers to produce goods for this market in our widths and lengths, which, as is well known, are unsuitable for their home trade". Our imports of paper-hangings are first recorded in 1905 as 2,418 tons (1906, 2,848 tons), but in *Kontradiktorische Verhandlungen über Deutsche Kartelle*, Heft 11 (Franz Siemenroth, Berlin, 1906), which deals with the wall-paper kartells, we find the following exports from Germany to Great Britain :—

	Tons.
1898	171·3
1899	192·9
1900	552·6
1901	1014·8
1902	1036·5
1903	1513·7
1904	1538·6
1905 (nine months)	1278·8

The value of the 1904 exports was about £61,500. In the same time our exports to Germany fell off from 243 tons in 1898 to 67 in 1904.

In 1902 the Wall-Paper Manufacturers made an investment in the large German company, Iven & Company, one of the largest and best managed of the German wall-paper concerns and a competitor of the kartell. Thereby hangs a curious tale. Herr Langhammer of the wall-paper kartell said (*Kontradiktorische Verhandlungen*, Heft 11, p. 104): "It is no accident that this factory has passed into English hands"—this was not quite true—" and that is of interest to us in Germany. You know the character of the English merchants and manufacturers ; they have not gone into it for the fun of the thing. It was this way. We German producers were competing more and more strongly with the English makers. They had formed themselves into a kartell and its continuance was endangered by our competition. The firm of Iven & Company had taken the strongest part in that competition and had built up a very

large and important business in England.   I have information
from people in England who were interested in the matter to
the effect that the amount of this firm's exports to England
was extraordinarily large.   From the correspondence which I
had with the manager of the English syndicate it is clear that
they first tried to limit the German exports by prohibiting the
English dealers from importing any quantity they wanted of
German goods. . . . In order to attain their end better they
had to knock their largest competitor on the head, and that
was our colleague, Herr Ivens, who had a large trade with
England.   The best way of knocking him on the head was for
the English with their large capital to take a share in the
firm.   They particularly bound the firm down not to send any
more wall-paper to England.   Gentlemen, you can see from
that that the English are very smart and clever people.   I
know, from what an English manufacturer told me, that they
also had the intention of securing an influence on the German
organisation.   They wanted ultimately to prescribe to the
German makers who were in the kartell that they should
export no more German goods to England, or at least only a
limited quantity.   The English have not succeeded in this so
far, but by their action they have immensely increased the
over-production in Germany."

British exports of wall-paper rose from an average of
3,771 tons in 1896-1900 to 4,440 tons in 1906, but the growth
of imports seems to have been a source of inconvenience to the
Wall-Paper Manufacturers' Association for a meeting of representatives of the company, the National Association of Painters
and Decorators of England and Wales, and the wall-paper
merchants for the purpose of maintaining prices and preventing
unfair competition was reported in the *Daily Chronicle* of 7th
February, 1907.

In 1898 an association of British Rubber Manufacturers
was formed in consequence of severe competition.   Its object
was to regulate prices and output with a penalty clause for
breach of the rules.   This is a trade in which there is considerable international competition, but owing to the steadily
increasing demand the association has succeeded in raising the

prices of manufactured goods proportionately to the rapidly rising price of raw rubber. The output does not now need to be restricted.

The British Oil and Cake Mills, which dates from July, 1899, amalgamated seventeen of the leading firms engaged in oil and cake manufacture and oil refining. " The business of oil seed crushing in this country is one of great magnitude. The consumption of oil cake for sheep and cattle food is steadily increasing, and the oils find a ready sale. Linseed oil is largely used in the manufacture of paints, varnishes, soaps, oil and floorcloth, while cotton-seed oil, in addition to being used in considerable quantities in the manufacture of soap, is in demand for edible and other purposes. The manufacturing power of the company will at once comprise twenty-eight mills and twelve oil refineries, the mills having an aggregate crushing capacity of not less than 500,000 tons of seed per annum, being, according to the Board of Trade returns for 1898, upwards of one-half of the total annual importation of oil seeds into the United Kingdom. . . . As considerable quantities of foreign oil, cakes, and other kindred products are imported annually for consumption into this country, this company intends to make their purchase and supply a special feature of its business. It is not the intention of the directors to attempt to create a monopoly or to raise prices. Desiring the co-operation of all interested in agriculture, they propose to give for the 'customers of each mill favourable consideration in the allotment of shares, with a view to their having a direct interest in the profits of the company " (Prospectus).

The profits of the several firms were taken out for various periods from two to five years, and aggregated an average of £101,489 before charging interest, directors' fees, and depreciation. The total assets, exclusive of goodwill, were valued at £1,067,500, and the purchase price was fixed by the vendor-promoters, who were reselling at a profit, at £1,368,000, with a further sum ascertained by valuation for the stock in trade and movable plant. £1,750,000 capital was issued—£550,000 in 4¼ per cent. debentures ; £600,000 in 5½ per cent. cumulative preference shares ; and £600,000 in ordinary shares ; the vendors took £125,000 debentures and one-third of the preference and of the ordinary stock. An 8 per cent. ordinary dividend was forecasted. A table of the financial results follows, showing the net profits after debiting every expense save income tax and debenture and mortgage interest :—

	Net Profit.	Ordinary Dividend.
Year to 30/6/00	£113,074	7 per cent.
,, 30/6/01	58,907	*nil.*
,, 30/6/02	120,155	6 per cent.
,, 30/6/03	84,544	5 ,,
,, 30/6/04	109,891	5 ,,
Six months to 31/12/04 . . .	45,331	5 ,,
Year to 31/12/05	62,851	*nil.*
,, 31/12/06	97,090	4 per cent.

The concentration of buying from which the company expected so much proved insufficient to deal with severe fluctuations. About October, 1900, there were sensational reports as to the linseed crop in Argentina, and "to give some idea of the panic," said the chairman at the annual meeting in August, 1901, "on 1st January linseed oil was £30 15s. per ton in London, and on 8th March it had fallen to £21 10s. The raw Calcutta linseed had fallen from 61s. 3d. per quarter in October to 44s. 3d. on 28th February. River Plate linseed had fallen from 52s. on 29th January to 36s. per quarter on 6th March. He regarded these circumstances as unprecedented." The natural consequence of such violent changes was dislocation of trade and severe depreciation of stocks, ending in a nil dividend. Again, in the last three months of 1904 it was "not possible, considering the cost of raw material, to obtain a remunerative profit from crushing," and in 1905 it "had been quite impossible to foretell the course of the market or to make any profit on linseed," although costs of manufacture were lower and the mills better equipped than ever before. The 8 per cent. dividend which figured in the prospectus took no account of depreciation and very little of reserve, only £17,252 being available for central office expenses, directors' fees, and reserve. From £20,000 to £30,000 a year has been provided for depreciation, and £18,000 to £25,000 for reserve, showing that the directors have been more conservative than the vendors.

The good returns since the amalgamation are to be attri-

buted to the directors' policy of consolidation and the economies
resulting from improved methods of manufacture. The Groves
Mill at Hull was bought in 1902 and completely equipped with
the latest machinery, and in 1903 the Eagle Mills, belonging to
Mr. Rank, of Hull, were purchased. These latter also were
new mills, " the finest and largest of the kind in the United
Kingdom ". Mr. Rank had become a very severe competitor
and threatened to take the seed crushing trade of Hull from
the company, so that it was with some relief that the directors
accepted his offer to sell. A good deal of complaint was made
of the " dumping " of foreign oil cake, but at least it has not
increased materially since the formation of the amalgamation.
During the five years ending with 1899 imports averaged
350,904 tons, and during the following six 362,295 tons. The
company has also by no means a monopoly of the home production, for there must be some 30 or 40 per cent. of the trade
done by independent millers.

The electrical industry is, in all its branches except tele-
graphy, one of our newest industries, and has been severely
hampered in its development by defective patent laws, restrictive legislation, unhealthy stock exchange finance, lack of scientific education among manufacturers, and disputes as to the
proper sphere of municipal action. Fortunately we are not
here called upon to apportion the respective amounts of blame
among these several causes. The incandescent electric lamp
industry, according to Mr. E. Garcke, is in a " fairly flourishing
condition ". It was, during its earlier years, protected by
patents which ensured a monopoly to the holders. Now there
is a considerable competition among a variety of lamps. The
Edison & Swan United Electric Light Company was formed in
1883 to amalgamate the Edison Electric Light Company and
the Swan United Electric Company with a capital of £471,298
in A and B shares, now raised to £781,064, after two write-offs
of capital in 1904 and 1905. On the A shares no dividend was
paid till 1888-89, but in 1892-93 all arrears of the cumulative
7 per cent. dividend were wiped off; from 1893-94 to 1900-1
the dividend averaged 5¼, and since then nothing has been paid
except 2½ per cent. in 1904-5 and 4⅛ in 1905-6. On B shares

no dividend has been paid since 1892-93 when 3 per cent. was distributed.

The cable industry is also a flourishing branch of the electrical industry and is of earlier origin than any of the others. Part of the prosperity, at least, appears to be due to the fact that the nine leading manufacturers formed the Cable Makers' Association. An anonymous correspondent of *The Times* (*Engineering Supplement*, 24th October, 1906), wrote : " The whole cable business is in the hands of the English Cable Syndicate, much to the detriment of the English ratepayers. The municipalities do not call for foreign tenders, in consequence of which the profits of the cable companies are so large that they can easily keep all foreign competition out of England by supplying private firms or central station companies at prices against which no foreign maker can compete, even apart from the fact that the English manufacturer always has got the advantage of freight." Of these charges the editorial note mildly said " we believe they are not deserved".

In the spring of 1902 the British Insulated Wire Company, of Prescot, and the Telegraph Manufacturing Company, of Helsby, near Warrington, were amalgamated under the style of British Insulated and Helsby Cables with a capital of £1,500,000. The union was due to the fact that the Telegraph Manufacturing Company was proposing to undertake the manufacture of heavy cables for town lighting, traction work, and power, which would have brought it into competition with the British company. Abroad they competed vigorously. " There we are in South Africa, where trade is reviving," said the chairman of the Telegraph Company, " simply knocking at each other's heads and losing profits, whereas had we been one we should have benefited considerably. When we do get to be one we ought to have that benefit. The same thing applies in Australia and some foreign countries." The joint profits allowed of a 10 per cent. ordinary dividend, but only 8 per cent. has since been paid. The accounts of the company disclose a feature which is characteristic of the electrical industry both at home and abroad, namely, heavy investments in other electrical undertakings. It is a common occurrence for a cable or electric manufacturing company to obtain a heavy order for supplies to an electric lighting or power company and to accept shares in the company in part payment. This method of financing has obvious advantages and disadvantages, but the points which affect us here are that it requires large capital in the hands of the manufacturer and facilitates competition even when there is an agreement as to prices, for the giver of the order will always be tempted to accept the tender which postpones payment most, even if it entails some over-capitalisation of the undertaking. Of the other cable companies an amalgamation was actually negotiated between W. T. Henley's Telegraph Works Company and Callender's Cable and Construction Company in 1902, but at the last moment it broke down. Callender's, however, in 1903, absorbed the Anchor Cable Company, and in 1906 they, " with others, acquired an interest in the St. Helens' Cable Works. That," said the chairman, " would help this company in many ways and give them a commanding position in the electrical trade not only in Great Britain but elsewhere." The capital of W. T. Henley's Company is £550,000, and its ordinary dividend has averaged 18 per cent. ; the capital of Callender's Company is £675,000, and its dividends range from 12½ to 15 per cent.

The manufacture of other electrical apparatus is of quite modern growth. Mr. Emil Garcke describes the industry in the following terms (*Times, Engineering Supplement*, 10th October, 1906) :—

" Ten years ago, and nearly twenty years after the inception of the industry, there were only twenty-four manufacturing companies registered in the United Kingdom, having an aggregate subscribed capital of £6,596,000. Now there are 290 companies, with £40,324,000 subscribed capital. These figures, however, include companies formed in this country as agencies of foreign firms. . . . The field is occupied mainly by large firms in strenuous competition with each other as well as with foreign manufacturers. . . . It is exceedingly difficult for large manufacturers to obtain competitive orders on a remunerative basis. . . . In 1900-1 forty-three companies made an average profit of 7·5 per cent. on a subscribed capital of

£11,921,000, whilst last year ninety companies earned an average of only 5·11 per cent. on a subscribed capital of £28,930,000." The British Electric Traction Company, which is intimately concerned with the flotation of subsidiary companies for local power and traction schemes, acquired the Brush Engineering Company in 1902, because, as the chairman said, "it is very advisable that we should have control of some manufacturing works not only for the purpose of supplying our various associated undertakings with the apparatus required for establishing the undertakings, but facilities are required by us for carrying out repairs and making replacements". Among the larger companies are the British Westinghouse Electric and Manufacturing Company, of Manchester, capital £4,291,353 ; the British Thomson-Houston Company, of Rugby, capital £1,012,000 ; Messrs. Siemens Bros., of London and Manchester, and Dick, Kerr & Co. The last-mentioned company dates from 1890 and originated at Kilmarnock ; in 1902 it absorbed the English Electrical Manufacturing Company of Preston. Its capital is now £847,580, and it has paid dividends ranging from 10 to 30 per cent.

"A British Manufacturer" writing in *The Times, Engineering Supplement* of 10th October, 1906, proposed the formation of a kartell of British electrical manufacturers. A minimum price rate was to be fixed, and profits at this rate were to be pooled after deduction of cost, the cost price of each product being standardised by a committee. The pooled profits were to be divided among the members in predetermined proportions based on the sales of each firm for the preceding three or five years. Underselling was to be punished by a penalty "consisting of the difference between the price received and the fixed minimum price rate". The writer admitted that "in a free trade country, high prices or under-production would merely throw the trade into the hands of foreign rivals," and therefore the committee "would issue a forecast of the approximate aggregate output required to satisfy the coming demand," and each member knowing his allotted percentage would know "to a nail" what to produce. The scheme met with little favour. Another firm to whom the scheme was submitted wrote: "If we had protection in this country, it is possible that we might do something in the way suggested in this letter, but we have found from experience that it is absolutely impossible to attempt any combination, as things are, to keep prices up on the lines suggested by your correspondent. We are all suffering at present from over-production, and until this is rectified, either by manufacturers restricting their output or going out of the trade altogether, we shall continue to suffer." The suggestion was, however, not entirely fruitless, for, said the *Engineering Supplement* on 14th November, "two meetings of representatives of electrical firms have, we understand, already taken place, when discussions were held as to the advisability of concerted measures for the benefit of the British electrical industry".

The special sphere of the joint-stock company in modern times has been the exploitation of new industries whether originating in patents or in the development of foreign sources of raw material. The risk necessarily incident to all such undertakings is minimised by being distributed among a number of small speculators who risk their savings under more or less adventurous leadership for the sake of a large prospective gain. Particularly in the working of foreign propositions the original pioneer companies are often moderately capitalised and genuinely prosperous, but they are soon followed by a swarm of others whose prospectuses are full of large figures and decorated with a "gilt front-page". The boom speedily swamps the industry with over-production, and a general collapse ends in wholesale reconstruction or in combination, and the industry has to climb slowly and painfully out of the swamp into which the financiers had cast it. Nitrates, tea-planting, rubber plantations, jarrah wood are all familiar examples. The nitrate companies ended in a combination to regulate output, the jarrah-wood companies terminated in an amalgamation. The merits of jarrah wood for street-paving purposes first attracted the attention of English capitalists in 1897, and very quickly nine companies were formed with a share capital of £2,205,000. The market was quickly glutted and prices were cut recklessly. Only two of the companies ever paid a dividend, and one of these paid for only one year. The only successful company, Millars' Karri and Jarrah Forests, took in hand the task of clearing away the over-capitalised wrecks, and after three years' negotiations amalgamated eight of the companies in August, 1902, as Millars' Karri and Jarrah Company, and the issued capital now outstanding is £1,636,581. Of this sum £1,260,000 was in preferred and ordinary shares, so that nearly half the original share capital was wiped out.

The labour of taking over the companies and making all necessary adjustments lasted well into 1903 and involved some troublesome litigation. By getting rid of seven boards of directors and a large portion of the office staff a saving of from £10,000 to £15,000 a year was expected. Besides the works in Australia where 3,200 men were employed, the company had sawmills at Purfleet-on-the-Thames, and in 1903 undertook exploration work in the forests of North Borneo. While the company had a monopoly of the West Australian trade it was still in competition with timber coming from all over the world, and although the public contracts on which the company depended were good when got, they required some getting. " It sounds an easy thing," said the chairman (31st December, 1903), " to say you have secured a contract for 300,000 sleepers here or there, but no shareholder who is not inside the company knows the amount of preparation and time that has to be brought to bear to the securing of the contract. Some negotiations are commenced, and even offers are made as long as twelve months before the negotiations result in obtaining the order." The company also has suffered severely from an increase in the wharf and railway rates in West Australia, which were raised by the Government of that colony in 1902 by an amount equivalent to about a 5 per cent. dividend on the ordinary shares. At the annual meeting in August, 1906, the preference dividend was paid for the half-year to 30th June, 1905, and although the surplus of liquid assets for the year under review was £134,876 above the figure on 31st December, 1902, the development of the company's properties necessitated a resort to " banking finance ". The industry, in fact, has not yet recovered from the straits into which it was landed by the company promoter.

United Carlo Gatti, Stevenson, & Company is a company which has sometimes been abused as an " ice trust," although, fortunately, it presents few points of comparison with its American namesake. It was formed in July, 1901, " with the object of acquiring as a going concern the business of importers and wholesale distributors of ice, now carried on by Carlo Gatti & Stevenson (Limited) of 21 Villiers Street, Strand, and of acquiring and amalgamating therewith the business of importers and manufacturers of ice now carried on by Slaters (Limited) as a branch of their well-known business of general purveyors. Carlo Gatti & Stevenson (Limited) was formed as a private company in the year 1903, with the view of amalgamating the old-established ice businesses previously carried on by Mr. Carlo Gatti and the late Mr. George Stevenson." The ice trade of London had grown from 118,815 tons in 1891 to 205,390 tons in 1900, and of the latter amount the combining companies imported 154,000 tons, a proportion " more than maintained " in 1901. Possessing three-fourths of the trade the company expected to be able to secure more favourable terms from the Norwegian exporters and to save in the cost of distribution and administration. " This will," said the prospectus, " enable the company to supply the consumer at rates which will render competition practically harmless, and at the same time secure good profits to the shareholders." On this point it may at once be remarked that at a meeting of the master butchers of London, convened in the following December by the Butchers' Trade Society, the " trust " was accused of having " caused the price to go up from 18s. to 25s." The purchase money was £350,000, of which about £179,776 represented goodwill, being slightly over five years' purchase of the net profits estimated at £35,000 after allowing for saving from amalgamation. The capital is £379,660, of which the vendors took one-third, and a 10 per cent. ordinary dividend was anticipated.

The prospectus forecast was scarcely realised, the dividends paid being : 1901, 8 per cent. ; 1902, 6 per cent. ; 1903, 6 per

cent.; 1904, 6 per cent; 1905, 5 per cent. In 1904 the Provincial Consumers' Ice and Supply, Ltd., was formed with a
capital of £150,000 to acquire four businesses of ice-merchants
in Brighton, Portsmouth, and Southampton.

Meters, Limited, dating from 1898, is an amalgamation of
four Manchester and Oldham firms making gas and other indi-
cators. Its paid-up capital is now £469,013, and it has paid
from 5 to 6 per cent. dividend each year since its inception,
besides making good allotments to reserve.

The manufacture of umbrella furniture and ribs, etc., is a
trade which had suffered much from keen German competition
when in 1902 an amalgamation was achieved of five firms
which already had been members of trade associations for
some years past. Of these, Wright, Bindley, & Gell, who gave
their name to the new company, was registered in 1899 to
amalgamate a Birmingham and a Sheffield business, and paid
7½ per cent. per annum. The second largest, a Birmingham
firm, paid 8 per cent. regularly, and the other three were
smaller concerns. The directors of Wright, Bindley, & Gell
reported that " great savings will result under the scheme from
concentration in the selling department, as nearly all the concerns have at the present time separate agents, warehouses,
and stocks in each of the centres of trade; the principal
economies, however, will be made in the manufacturing department by allotting the different classes of work to the factories best suited for their production ". The issued capital is
£255,380, and the dividends paid have been: 1902-3, 6 per
cent.; 1903-4, 6 per cent.; 1904-5, 2½ per cent.; 1905-6, 4 per
cent.

R. Waygood & Co. was formed in 1900 as a public company to take over the business of R. Waygood & Co. which
had been established for over half a century, and its output of
lifts of all descriptions was, according to the prospectus, " believed to be the largest in Great Britain ". Its speciality was
industrial work, particularly electric cranes, and its capital was
£210,000. Two years later it achieved an Anglo-American
combination of considerable industrial importance by acquiring
the Otis Elevator Co., capital £20,000, which held the Euro-

pean patents of the Otis Elevator Co. of America, a combination of seven large firms, with a capital of £2,200,000 and 90 per cent. of the American trade. Its work was mainly in offices and hotels. The capital of the combined firms was £270,000, and no public issue was made. "The controlling influence in bringing about the combine," said Mr. Sellon, managing director of the Otis Company in an interview with the *Financial Times* (2nd September, 1902), "was really the fear of foreign houses coming into this country and seizing hold of the lift business. Such an event was rendered possible by the separate existence of two such firms as Waygood's and the Otis, both of which were in the same line, and yet each of which made a speciality of a branch that the other did not. Clearly, as a joint undertaking, the two would be infinitely stronger and in a much better position to combat foreign competition than if they continued to operate independently. Thus the ultimate consideration which determined the directors and shareholders of both companies in favour of fusion was that each company is able to supplement the other in important respects, Waygood's possessing excellent manufacturing facilities, while the Otis controls for the British Empire (except Canada) and Europe the patents, designs, and wide experience of the Otis Elevator Company of America. The British and American Otis companies are quite distinct organisations, having only the name in common, but the British concern is not only the proprietor of the American company's patents in the area mentioned, but has the immense resources of the latter at its back." How far this is a triumph of the "American invasion" must be left to the reader; it looks rather as if the American anthropophagi were eaten by the native; at all events the combination secured for itself prominence in the British lift trade. The dividends have been for 1902-3, 9 per cent.; 1903-4, 9 per cent.; 1904-5, 9 per cent.; 1905-6, 9 per cent. Waygood's during its two years of separate existence paid 10 and 7½ per cent., and the Otis Company 10 per cent. in the four years preceding amalgamation, so that it cannot be said that the combination has improved very much on the results of the companies when independent.

"To turn out a battleship complete" in every respect was the ambition of Vickers, Sons, & Maxim. To build and decorate hotels would be only a limited ambition for Waring & Gillow, an interesting example of an "efficiency combine". Formed in 1896 to unite the firms of S. J. Waring and Gillow & Co., furniture makers and decorators, it absorbed the old-established kindred business of Hampton & Sons in 1903, raising its issued capital to £2,205,000. In 1904 the company combined with the well-known contracting firm of J. G. White & Co. to form the Waring-White Building Company, and took half the share capital of their subsidiary. At that time the contracts in hand approached a million and a half sterling, and the company can claim to stand at the head of the decorating trade. Its capital is now £2,650,000. Six per cent. was paid on the preferred ordinary shares up to 1902 and 7 per cent. since then, but nothing on the £550,000 deferred shares issued to the vendors.

Building and decorating leads us gently to a series of trades which may be loosely connected together by the fact that they produce articles used in our homes for domestic purposes. Among them are several notable combinations. First comes Barry, Ostlere, & Shepherd, an amalgamation in 1899 of three Kirkcaldy firms of linoleum makers with a capital of £938,000 —purchase money £825,500. Control was also to be obtained of a French company with valuable works near Rouen. The capital has since been raised to £1,186,860, and all the ordinary stock is held by the directors. Its career has been one of fluctuations, the ordinary dividend for the year to 31st January, 1900, being 7½ per cent.; for 1900-1, 6 per cent.; 1901-2, 2½ per cent.; for 1902-3, nil; for 1903-4, 5 per cent.; for 1904-5, 5 per cent.; for 1905-6, 3 per cent. The high price of linseed in 1901-2 was a serious drawback, but since then with careful management results have improved despite the high cost of oil. New Walton inlaid linoleum works have been opened. The company exercises no sort of domination over the trade, and its results compare badly with those of some of the other companies.

Another combination of some domestic interest is the

Aberdeen Comb Works Company, also a flotation of 1899. Although small in size it included the three firms which, as the chief survivors after a severe competition under which many firms succumbed, made "considerably over 90 per cent. of all the horn combs made in the United Kingdom". The capital was £300,000—£125,000 in 4½ per cent. preference, £125,000 in 6 per cent. ordinary, and £50,000 in deferred shares; it has since been reduced to £287,500 by repayment of preference capital. The purchase money was £291,000, and the vendors took one-third of the preference and ordinary shares and all the deferred. Two of the businesses, employing 1,160 persons were in Aberdeen, and the third with 200 workpeople was in York. The York factory was closed and the whole of the manufacture concentrated at Aberdeen. For 1899 a dividend of 6 per cent was paid; 1900, 4 per cent.; 1901, 4 per cent.; 1902, 2 per cent.; 1903, 4½ per cent.; 1904, 4 per cent.; 1905, 4½ per cent. No dividend has been paid on the deferred shares. The Scottish Comb Company was started in opposition and for several years inflicted great loss on the Aberdeen Company which met the prices and retained its trade. "As soon as we heard that they were to start an opposition," said the chairman at the annual meeting[1] in March, 1904, "we sent for the organisers of it. We told them that our goods were sold on so small a margin of profit that to come in below us, as they would have to do, could only end in their ruin or in ours, possibly both, and we even went the length of holding out inducements to them to abstain from making so great a blunder. But all was useless. . . . Perhaps it is better that this fight has been encountered at this early stage of our existence, because we have shown clearly that while we were capable of earning a small dividend they were making very heavy losses." This unsuccessful rival was bought in 1903 for £7,250 cash. The economies of consolidation have been fully earned, for all the works have been concentrated at Hutcheon Street, Aberdeen, and two superfluous London warehouses have been closed as well as several overlapping agencies.

Still sticking to industries of domestic interest, Mansell,

[1] *Financial Times*, 19th March, 1904.

Hunt, Catty, & Co. claim a little attention, if only to show that there is no branch of trade so trifling as to escape the spirit of combination. The three leading firms manufacturing embossed and laced papers and fancy paper table decorations amalgamated in 1890; then bought up a Leeds firm and a London engineering house which made the special machinery used in the business ; in 1900 the National Lace Paper and Speciality Company of Brooklyn was acquired. All the business of the company is now concentrated in one factory at Hampstead. The capital is £95,000, and the average ordinary dividend has been close on 17 per cent. The annual net profits have nearly quadrupled since the company was started, and the average dividend for 1900-4 was 22½ per cent.

The International Sponge Importers only date from 1904, and have not yet emerged from the difficulties which beset a young amalgamation. The special advantage of the combination was expected to lie in economy of buying, especially through stoppage of the competition which previously existed between the three constitutent firms. Its capital is £291,908, and it paid 3 per cent. in 1904 and 1905. Higher net profits have been obtained by economies without raising prices, and an investment has been made in a chamois leather firm.

Loder & Nucoline was an amalgamation in 1887 of three firms with factories at Limehouse, Silvertown, and Liverpool, for making butter substitutes from cocoa-nut fat for use in the chocolate trade. As much cocoa-nut oil is used in the soap trade there was an opening for the manufacture of this new commodity as a by-product, and accordingly Messrs. Joseph Crosfield & Sons, soapmakers, of Warrington, erected large plant in 1902, and put on the market refined cocoa-nut butter. This is an example of how a good proprietary article trade can be cut into.

More noteworthy was the combination in 1903 of Messrs. J. & J. Colman (capital, £1,915,620) and Messrs. Keen, Robinson, & Company, of Norwich, the great mustard manufacturers. These were the two leading firms in the trade. No particulars are available about the union, and the businesses are still conducted in nominal independence. Another large combination was that of the Anglo-Swiss Condensed Milk Company and the Henri Nestlé Company, under the title of Nestlé & Anglo-Swiss Condensed Milk Company, with a capital of £1,800,000. These were the two leading producers of condensed milk, but they have not a monopoly.

CHAPTER XIV.

SURVEY AND CONCLUSIONS.

THE preceding chapters have disclosed three main lines of development within the combination movement—integration or vertical combination, as in the iron and steel industry; amalgamation or horizontal combination, as in the textile industries; and terminable associations, as in the retail trades. These lines are not to be regarded as independent, but as closely interwoven. The predominance of integration in the iron and steel trades is due to special features of the industry not elsewhere repeated. The costs of production of each higher stage are reduced by the utilisation of some energy which otherwise runs to waste in the lower stage—such as the use of molten iron in steel-making and the rolling of the hot ingot in the mills; in both cases there is loss if cold pig-iron has to be melted for steel and cold ingots have to be reheated for rolling. Mr. Axel Sahlin, of the Millom Works, told the Iron and Steel Institute: "As for the struggling independent blast furnace marketing a product of Bessemer iron, often through the agency of brokers, and the equally crippled maker of standard grade steel, who looks to the same intermediary and to the warrant yards for his raw material, I venture the prediction that many of these will soon be driven to the wall, unless they sensibly combine forces, each plant becoming a co-operating link in the unbroken chain of processes which turn the ore into merchantable steel" (*Journal of the Iron and Steel Institute*, 1901, vol. i., p. 163). There has thus been a special impulse in these industries towards the growth of the large self-sufficient unit, and it has been augmented by the policy of the Government in its contracts for armour-plates, ordnance, and battleships. Were these made solely in Government works then private firms and companies would have to depend on foreign orders, but the policy of utilising independent firms as semi-public arsenals has naturally led to their aggrandisement.

There does not appear any immediate prospect of an extension of horizontal amalgamation on a large scale in the iron industry, though as has been shown it has proceeded to some extent among immediate competitors. At the same time there is no impassable obstacle to this development, in such branches at least as the textile machinery makers, or in the ordnance companies where we have already the significant alliance of John Brown & Co. and Cammell, Laird, & Co. At present, however, we must correlate the evolution of those large efficiency combinations of integrated form with the almost universal prevalence of associations for the fixing of prices, the regulation of output, and the demarcation of territory. The reduction of numbers along the former line makes ever more possible combination along the latter, and in proportion as the strength of the units increases so does the possibility of securing trade by internecine competition diminish, and the necessity for combination to ensure lasting peace become more evident. We may thus expect, in no very remote future, to see the iron industry governed by loose federations of great powers, each large firm belonging to a number of associations according to the variety of its products ; and there is the final possibility that these may unite into a general union on the lines of the German Stahlwerksverband.

Over the great bulk of our industries horizontal amalgamation is the representative form of permanent combination, and our survey has shown that there is hardly any description of trade to which it is unsuited. It is equally easy to exaggerate and to undervalue the magnitude of this development. Great as is the extent to which industry has passed into the hands of large combinations, greater still is the domain still subject to the individual trader. But the encroachment on the realm of free competition steadily progresses, though not at the feverish speed of six or seven years ago. We have to reckon with the probability, to use no stronger term, though one might without exaggeration say the certainty, that we are in the early stages of the evolution of the form which industry will take in the future. Whether that be so or not, there are certain features of the movement to which some special attention must be directed.

The special reason for the formation of an amalgamation is always the existence of destructive competition, the result of a surplus of productive capacity. The industry as a whole is over-capitalised, and in the rush to secure enough trade to provide a dividend on each lump of capital prices go tumbling. One way out of such a state of things is to combine only the strong competitors, and trust to their superior efficiency and to the economies of concentrated manufacture to reduce the competition of outsiders to a negligible quantity. This was the method adopted by Messrs. J. & P. Coats, and in that instance it was completely successful. The case is similar with such unions as the Imperial Tobacco Co., the North British Locomotive Co., the Metropolitan Amalgamated Wagon Co., Guest, Keen, & Nettlefolds, and the alliances of Vickers and Beardmore, John Brown & Co. and Cammell, Laird, & Co. Yet the competition even of a decaying firm is not easy to crush out. It may be that the outside business is old-established and that the value of the plant and buildings has already been written off, thus reducing the standing charges. Or regard may be had only to the income remaining over cost, no interest being charged against capital. Thus one of the defendants in J. & P. Coats v. the Yorkshire Woolcombers' Association, while admitting that 5 per cent. would be a " fair thing" to allow for interest, said, "I did not debit any rate of interest against capital. . . . I was not paying interest on my capital. I was content to invest my capital and get the best interest out of it I could." As he would probably have lost more by shutting down and selling his business, his action was quite justified. Again we have seen that in the iron industry when a firm is driven into insolvency the receiver competes for business at any rate to attract trade and so make a better appearance when he comes to sell, thus dragging the successful competitors still further into the mire.

Under such circumstances an amalgamation must include

the weak as well as the strong; a certain amount of the over-capitalisation of the industry must be taken over by the new company, and the only problem is to keep it within moderate bounds. Much, therefore, will depend upon the way in which the properties to be acquired are valued. When this duty is left entirely in the hands of an accountant-promoter, as in the Woolcombers' Association, or to an accountant acting with a committee of the vendors, as in the English Sewing Cotton Company, especially when the accountant or promoter is paid by a commission on the purchase money, there is certain to be over-capitalisation, because the interests of the vendors will be solely or mainly considered. The safest plan is that adopted by the Wall-Paper Manufacturers where one accountant was appointed to represent the vendors, one to represent the purchasing company, and one to act as umpire in case of the other two disagreeing. It is not sufficient to value the assets accurately, regard must also be had to the possibility of machinery being reduced to the scrap heap by new processes or inventions or by the more favourable location of competing plants. Thus the plant of the Weardale Steel Company which was certified to be in excellent condition had within a few years to be scrapped and new works had to be built on the coast; the processes of the United Alkali Company were soon largely superseded by fresh inventions; and the Portland Cement Manufacturers have been seriously hampered by the cost of introducing new methods of manufacture. The task of reconciling the temporary interest of the vendor in getting a good price for what he sells and the permanent interest of the amalgamation in securing the properties at their real value to the industry is the hardest which can fall on the organisers, since it is next to impossible to say in which particular works the unnecessary capacity resides.

The value of a firm may in part be measured by its ability to earn actual profits, and this is not to be measured merely by the cost value of the plant and buildings, but by the reputation of the firm, its connection, its trade-marks and patents, all the elements which go to make up goodwill. This is an undoubted asset, but one of a particularly elusive character.

It is here to-day and gone to-morrow. The value of a concern making proprietary articles consists very largely of reputation, of goodwill, but it may be destroyed in a few weeks by a substitute which captures the fickle popular favour. On the other hand, the estimation of some old-established goods is so firmly rooted that it appears unshakable. So long as a firm is doing well it can carry a heavy amount of goodwill, but if things go unfavourably the potentiality of making future profits rapidly runs down to zero. A large amalgamation is at its formation particularly liable to over-capitalisation, for each individual vendor, knowing how necessary it is that he should be brought in if competition is to be really eliminated, can call on the purchasing company to stand and deliver. It is only in rare instances, mostly in the iron industries, that the parties agree to neglect goodwill for the sake of starting the new undertaking with the least possible burden. After all, the result in personal income is the same whether a high dividend is paid on a low capitalisation or a low dividend on a high capitalisation, but the difficulty of financing the company in bad times is immensely greater when the nominal capital is greatly in excess of the real assets. When the parties to the combination intend to continue in close personal connection with the business they will have regard to their permanent interests and amalgamate on the basis of their real assets, but if they are voluntarily retiring, and still more if they are being squeezed out, their object will be to take their profit immediately in a high price and as much as possible in cash. The interaction of these two classes of motive will largely determine the amount paid for goodwill and the ultimate over-capitalisation. The common opinion of business men appears to regard three years' purchase of net profits as a normally fair value of goodwill in most businesses. The Imperial Tobacco Company got eight years' purchase, but this was quite an exceptional instance, depending upon the great popularity of their numerous brands.

The necessary burden of over-capitalisation may be reduced by good management and conservative finance. Indeed we may, so long as it is not too great, regard it with equanimity as the price paid for the opportunity of organising the industry and extirpating waste. By concentrating office staff, banking, insurance, supervising and scientific establishments, the costs of management may be reduced ; by closing small, badly equipped, or unnecessary works, and transferring their business to others, and also by concentrating certain classes of work in particular mills specialised for the purpose, the machinery can be kept running full with much economy in manufacture ; by combining the selling businesses of the different firms savings can be made in travellers, agents, and advertisements, or with the same expenditure and staff the work of individuals can be specialised and the market more thoroughly exploited ; by the creation of a proper statistical department the weak points in the organisation can be promptly detected and a keen spirit of emulation maintained among the several branches. On the other hand these changes must be carried out judiciously and not too quickly, to avoid dislocation of trade. Where these improvements are attained the economies realised will enable the over-capitalisation to be written off, whether it takes the form of goodwill or closed works. The early years of an amalgamation should therefore be characterised by conservative finance, by generous allocations to depreciation, especially of goodwill, closed works, and patents, and by the building up of a substantial reserve, and they ought to be judged more by their conduct in these respects than by their dividends. A company which keeps on carrying in its books a heavy valuation of goodwill or closed works is in a weak position. Where an amalgamation has begun by virtually capitalising its prospective economies like the Calico Printers, the Bleachers, or the British Cotton and Wool Dyers, it is hard for it to get into a satisfactory position, as the Stock Exchange quotations show. But even in these cases it must be remembered that the trade has benefited by its improved organisation and the economies of concentration. The promoters dreamed, or induced the public to believe, that the cash value of the improvements could be paid for twice over, in the purchase money received by the vendors and in increased dividends to the investors. In those cases where subsequent economies are not sufficient to balance over-capitalisation a surgical operation ending in the drawing off of the watered capital may be required to put the company in a sound position from the Stock Exchange point of view.

Relief could soon be had from the burden of over-capitalisation if the combination had an effective power to raise prices, but we have already seen that the great movements of trade are beyond the control of any organisation however large. In 1903 the United States Steel Corporation, fortified by alliances with the other producers and protected by an effective tariff, had nevertheless to restrict its output by one-fourth, and where, as in the United Kingdom, there is no tariff, the power of organised capital is much more limited. At the same time it is safe to assume that British "trusts" keep prices on the whole somewhat above what they would be under free competition, but before attributing this to them as blame we must be sure that competition prices are healthy prices, an assumption which cannot be made. Close investigation between prices and costs before and after amalgamation would be necessary to determine this question, and needless to say the information is not at our disposal. Speaking broadly there have been very few complaints of price extortion on the part of our great amalgamations, and where made they have generally been supported only by the scantiest of evidence. When the Bradford merchants were at odds with the Bradford Dyers' Association they nevertheless admitted that the price policy of the great combine had been moderate.

An amalgamation must look to its permanent interests when it operates in a free trade country, and consequently cannot risk the creation of fresh competition by any violent enhancement of prices. The Salt Union neglected this obvious maxim of trade and came to grief. But in several smaller ways an amalgamation can manipulate prices to its profit. It can more rapidly take advantage of a rising market and offer a tougher opposition to a fall of prices than is possible when the industry is not organised. It can either cease the manufacture of unprofitable lines of goods or it can raise their prices to a paying level. It can retain for itself, at least for a longer time than under free competition, the savings arising from improved processes and economies in organisation, instead of passing them over at once to the consumer. It can recoup itself more quickly for a rise in the price of its raw materials. More than these things it cannot do with safety, and it is therefore driven to a variety of devices in order to secure its market. The Imperial Tobacco Company offers its customers a bonus and guaranteed retail prices, while the Bradford Dyers' Association offers special terms for a first preference in trade. The Wall-Paper Manufacturers bound the dealers to them by a ten years' agreement, but this is a two-edged weapon which may operate against the manufacturers, as the Portland Cement Manufacturers found, if the course of prices is contrary to what was expected. The institution of the Piece Dyeing Board also must be mentioned as a method of ensuring reasonable prices as between maker and merchant, but if both agree it can be utilised to raise prices against the ultimate purchaser. It appears to be a device of great value in the regulation of prices and in the steadying of industry, and there is every reason to conclude that it is capable of great extension.

With such limited powers over prices an amalgamation is thrown back on its own inherent capacities as an administrative method. Unless it can show that it is the cheapest and best mode of production it will fail, and it is our good fortune that this problem is being worked out in Britain free from complications of tariffs or secret railway agreements. Success, in a word, depends upon management. It is a far more difficult thing to run an amalgamation of twenty businesses than to run these businesses separately; more complex questions of business organisation arise, and the functions of the supreme governors of the undertaking are of a higher order. The manager of one out of many competing businesses has to take part in a scramble for trade, the manager of an amalgamation has to provide for the supply of a whole market. A huckster may run the former but a statesman is required for the latter. All these points have already been brought out in superabundance in the preceding chapters and need not be further laboured here. It is enough to refer to the organisation of the Associated Portland Cement Manufacturers or the Bradford Dyers or Fine Cotton Spinners, and above all to the classic report of the investigatory committee of the Calico Printers' Association.   Where brains enough cannot be found amalgamation will be a failure.   In the future men must be trained for the new duties under the new organisation, and between commercial universities on the one hand and on the other provision of means of advancement for the capable such as the Calico Printers provide, there is no reason why we should not get the men.   Rule of thumb is dead in the workshop, the day is with the engineer and the chemist with their methods of precision; in the counting-house and boardroom there is no longer a place for the huckster or gambler, the future is with the commercial statesman whether in a large individual business or a combination.

The short-term power of terminable associations over prices appears to be greater than that of the permanent amalgamations. For one thing the definite and immediate object of their formation is to bring about an advance, and since the length of their duration is doubtful it is expedient to exploit the early loyalty of the members and to utilise the brief space before fresh competition can be called into being.   An amalgamation is an open and confessed attempt to achieve domination; an association does not thrust itself upon the public gaze but works in secret.   Consequently, it is not surprising that the best grounded complaints of extortionate prices are directed against the coal " rings," the boiler-plate associations, and similar bodies. Some particulars of these have already been given.   Yet once more the warning must in justice be repeated that it is not fair to compare post-association prices with prices on the bankruptcy level.   Persons who have enjoyed the advantages of competition among their suppliers naturally resent a combination which deprives them of this source of profit, even though the continuance of competition threatened the existence of the industry.   The power which price associations, pools, and selling syndicates exert over prices is exactly of the same nature as that exercised by amalgamations—the swift seizure of an opportunity for a rise, resistance to a fall, and the transference of the increased cost of raw materials to the consumer.   There is no long-term control, and unless the short-term control is judiciously applied, it leads, as the iron associations show, to resentment on the part of buyers, to fresh competition, and to failure. When trade must be conducted at a fixed price large buyers lose the advantage which their large capital gives them over their competitors, and a tendency arises to meet combination with co-operation or integration. For example the Scotch shipbuilders established a co-operative factory to compete with the Rivet, Bolt, and Nut Co., but it failed; Messrs. Kynoch started a soap works to free themselves from the glycerine "ring"; and the London grocers proposed a co-operative soap company to fight the "soap trust". With a fixed price the large seller must also surrender his ability to quote lower than the small man and must seek the extra profit due to his size not from extra trade but by producing more cheaply. This inducement to improve his processes is, however, limited by uncertainty as to the continuance of the price. The one case in which association directly leads to economy is when territory is divided and the competitors are thereby saved the heavy expenses for railway transport consequent on invasion of distant markets.

Shipping conferences afford the only clear instance where a terminable association exercises anything like a permanent control over prices, and that is due to the almost prohibitive expense of equipping a rival service equivalent to that provided by the combined lines. If the service could be duplicated there would be a tremendous waste of capital, and yet nothing short of duplication is any permanent good to the merchants who want to be free. Perception of this fact has led to proposals to prohibit the rebate system. For these much is to be said, but, as Lord Halsbury very clearly saw in the Mogul case, interference with the right to compete would hardly stop there. Every argument launched against the policy of rebates—the policy of seeking to attach customers by giving exclusive privileges for exclusive patronage—strikes at many other trade methods. That school of thought which welcomes the increased control of the State over trade will of course have nothing to urge against the principle of subjecting the shipping industry to State supervision, though it might criticise this particular method. Those, on the other hand, who believe in the individualist basis of industry would do well to consider where interference with competition which is not contrary to law may lead them. It has already been indicated that there is a great deal to be said in defence of shipping conferences, and of the rebate policy as a means of guaranteeing that continuity of business on which the possibility of a full and regular service depends, while it is equally clear that a conference may, and sometimes does, fix its rates too high. The question, then, is not one of inherent wickedness, but of less or more, and so can be dealt with.

It is always a ticklish matter for an outsider to give advice to those actually engaged in an industry, but the temptation is irresistible to suggest that the difficulties of the shipping industry might be met by an extension of the conference idea. The Piece Dyeing Board, composed of dyers and merchants, decides when an increase in dyeing rates is permissible and also when a merchant has given the Bradford Dyers' Association enough trade to justify him in claiming their special terms. Shipping rates are not quite so simple a matter, but it does not seem that their fixing would be made any more difficult if the shippers were consulted through the port Chambers of Commerce. Even if the determination of the rates were finally left to the shipowners, still a frank talk with the shippers over proposed changes could only do good, and would be specially useful in the vexed matter of " preferential rates " to foreigners, a question which the abolition of rebates would not touch. The rigidity of the rebate system arouses more hostility than the rebates themselves, and it would conduce to smooth working if every case where forfeiture of rebates is incurred were submitted to arbitration. After the Bradford precedent a margin of elasticity should be allowed, and the infliction of penal rates, the bullying of agents and consignees, and similar methods of warfare should be forbidden by agreement. Shippers and shipowners seem to forget that ultimately the consumer can' be made to pay, if they would only agree.

The retail trades with their protected prices offer a peculiarly difficult problem. The shopkeeper asserts his right to a living profit and threatens to boycott the manufacturer who refuses his co-operation, while the manufacturer being dependent on the shopkeeper for distribution of his goods must submit. It is true that the shopkeeper is being hard pressed on all sides by department stores, by company shops, and by co-operative societies, but the greater part of retail trade is still in the hands of the small man. The manufacturer, therefore, although he is really only concerned with getting his own price and not with what the retailer gets, cannot yet rely on the stores and companies to make good the trade which he might lose through the displeasure of the shopkeeper. It is probable that large-scale distribution is winning every day, though for want of complete statistics it is impossible to say how far the shopkeeper may be losing ground or holding his own. Anyhow, it is too risky for the manufacturer to gamble on probabilities, and, besides, many of the stores and companies compete with the manufacturer by making or having made for them proprietary articles in substitution for his commodities.

The retailer proclaims his right to live by a trade which he himself chooses at a profit which he himself determines. This is somewhat like the extreme labour (miscalled socialist) assertion of the right to work at a trade chosen by the claimant for wages fixed by his trade union and paid by the State. In a communist state the equitable distribution of income is simple, being share and share alike ; in a socialist state, where the rule is " from each according to his ability, to each according to his needs," the problem is more difficult but still capable of solution. But what is the rule of equity in an individualist state, where the common welfare is assumed to arise from the clashing self-interest of individuals ? We may try to get at it through the workman's claim for a living wage—enough to maintain and educate himself and his family according to the standard of his class, to provide insurance against the uncertainty of the future, and to afford the possibility of rising in the social scale. This holds good so long as he is a necessary workman, the test being that he is actually employed. But the case becomes more difficult when he is in course of supersession by a new process, and when he is thrown out of work he loses his right of choice of a trade and must appeal to the State with quite other arguments. The difficulty with the retailer is that he is unable to prove that he is necessary to a community which may be equally well served by a co-operative store or a mutiple-shop company. The sole interest of a community which consists mainly of employed, and not of employing classes, is in good service, not in the maintenance of any special class to perform that service. The possibility that the enhanced profits of the employer might flow over to them in increased wages and salaries is too remote, and is quite as probable under some other system of organisation. The problem at present is not a moral one, but one of comparative strengths of competition. The retailer is within his rights in his efforts at self-preservation, but with society organised on its present basis no appeal to the pity of the community can be entertained. The same claim would have availed for the passing of a law for the destruction of power looms in the interests of the hand-weavers.

The special feature of the retailer's claim to a living profit is that it takes the form of a claim to a specific rate of profit on his turn-over irrespective of its rapidity, and thus he is led to reject the ordinary device of attracting trade by reducing prices in order to gain a larger income at a lower rate. For example, a shopkeeper who sells at a profit of 25 per cent. and turns over his capital four times a year doubles his capital annually, but if he sells at a profit of 20 per cent. and turns over his capital six times a year, he will make in twelve months a profit of £120 instead of £100. Even if allowance be made for increased shop expenses a surplus of profit will remain, for business charges will not increase proportionately. If quality be maintained the interest of the community is in cheapness, and his action, therefore, appears to be anti-social. Of course, profit will not indefinitely increase with the reduction of price, but the retailer takes it upon himself to declare arbitrarily when a reduction is no longer possible, although some larger business such as "the stores" has shown that with large-scale distribution it is possible. The maximum profit also may be produced by several combinations of profit per unit and total quantity sold, and while any one of these will satisfy the retailer the community regards as the best service that which produces the widest distribution of goods. At the same time there is no reason why the shopkeeper alone should bear the risk of experiment. The only equitable determination of price is made when the burden of mistake falls on those who ultimately profit, that is the consumers, and that can only be done through a co-operative society, which implies the preliminary elimination of the retailer.

The weakness of every form of combination in the United Kingdom is due to the free admission of foreign competition. If that can be removed their strength is enormously increased, and all the conditions of the problem are altered. Apart from tariffs this result may be attained in various ways. All the international interests may be gathered up into one British company, as in the case of Borax Consolidated, or the foreign interests may be partly extirpated by and partly brought into alliance with a British company, as in the case of J. & P. Coats, Ltd. Prices and output may be regulated in common, as in the Nitrate Combination, or territory may be divided, as in the International Rail Syndicate. Or while reserving certain territories for individual exploitation there may be co-operation in the development of others, as in the alliance of the Imperial Tobacco Company with the American Tobacco Trust. In one way or another the world's trade in rails, tubes, nails, screws, sewing-thread, bleaching powder, borax, nitrates, and tobacco is to a greater or less degree brought under international control, while, at least till lately, dynamite was so controlled, and repeated efforts have been made similarly to syndicate the whole steel trade. This development is due to several causes. Firstly, it has been demonstrated by abundant German experience that dumping does not pay and that it is more advantageous for a domestic trust or kartell that export trade should be so regulated as to yield the maximum of profit. Secondly, the experience of the iron and steel industries and the tobacco trade has shown that foreign invasion can best be met by combined effort.

" Capital had no country. By the operation of an economic law as inexorable as any of the laws of nature, capital would gravitate to those countries where it was most encouraged and least harrassed"—so spoke the chairman of F.

Leyland & Co. (*Times*, 8th May, 1901). In all industrial countries the attitude of the Governments towards capital is much the same, and the dangers which capitalists may have to meet in the future differ only, and that but to a slight degree, in their imminence. When, therefore, domestic industry is organised on all sides into combinations, and the great organisations stand face to face in amalgamations or kartells with the prospect before them of an ever fiercer fight for the world's trade, it is natural that capital should remember that its primary cause for existence is to produce profits. The risks of warfare are plain, and it is easier and more profitable to divide the spoils peaceably than to fight for them. In proportion, then, as the combination movement develops at home so may we expect it to be followed by international combination, not at once, indeed, but slowly and inevitably. The first phase of international control is the reserving of the home markets to the home producer, thus allowing to a domestic combination a greater control over prices.

The position of the British combinations in regard to the interests of the community may be summed up as not at present dangerous but containing, like every new development, great and unknown possibilities alike for good and for evil. Over prices their powers are not great but are growing. So far they have shown no increased power over their employees, and with a strong trade union they need not have. It would be indeed difficult to conceive of a " trust " more obdurate than Lord Penrhyn or more skilled and determined in warfare than the Federation of Engineering Employers. An amalgamation with hungry shareholders clamorous for dividends might well shrink from a strike which would mean the closure of all its works, while its officials might easily be less unwilling to confer with trade union officers than employers brought up in the belief that they could do what they liked with their own. Similarly there are no grounds for dread lest associated capital in this country should adopt some of the grosser methods of political control as practised in the United States. Yet organised interests have before now shown that they can exercise a great political power in a perfectly constitutional manner, and

there have even been instances in which they have been suspected of overstepping the bounds of strict propriety. " It is
undeniable," said the *Economist* of 12th August, 1899, " that
during the session just ended there has been an atmosphere of
money in the lobby and precincts of the House of Commons
scarcely known before. All manner of interests have gathered
there as they gather in Washington and in the various State
Legislatures of America." There is no cause for pessimism,
but there is every reason for watchfulness.

Nothing could be more fatal than in a panic to try to turn
back a great industrial movement. So far as can be seen the
great amalgamations are the best instruments of production yet
devised, and to break them up into their original components
would be foolish if it were not in most cases impossible. Crude
methods of suppression are always wrong, nor does it seem
sensible to search among legal principles relevant to a different
stage of industry for weapons to hamper and obstruct. Lord
Justice Bowen said in the Mogul case : " Nor is it the province
of the judges to mould and stretch the law of conspiracy in
order to keep pace with the calculations of political economy ".
Repressive legislation could only affect the outward form of
combination. Amalgamation cannot be prohibited without
forbidding the union of even two firms, while to make monopoly illegal would be fruitless where no formal monopoly exists,
and there is no way of determining the greater effectiveness for
evil of a merger including eighty per cent. of the trade over one
containing only fifty. No law can suppress the Gentlemen's
Agreement, where there are no rules, no constitution, no contract, but common action is effected verbally and informally,
and yet some of the most oppressive combinations have been
of that form. Neither combination nor agitation should be
driven underground, and it is significant that to-day complaints are generally raised in the United Kingdom, not against
the legally recognised amalgamations but against associations
which have no existence in the eyes of the law and work in
secret. To strike at the methods adopted by combinations is
not easy without at the same time repressing measures blame-
lessly adopted by the individual trader. Boycotting, dumping,

selling at a loss to crush competition, maintaining prices at the highest level which the market permits—these are no monopoly of combinations, but are weapons in everyday use by manufacturers, merchants, and shopkeepers. It would be indeed an extraordinary thing to strike at competition in the name of competition.

Not in these ways can we solve the problem how to retain the good in combination while avoiding its dangers. Where trust methods have been obviously illegal, or where they flourish behind an oppressive tariff, what to do is plain. But the case is different in the United Kingdom where the continuance of amalgamations and associations depends solely upon their efficiency as instruments of production and distribution. Too little attention has hitherto been given to this normal development of combination, and it has too often been lumped in the same condemnation with the most oppressive American trust or German kartell. While it has shown that it can weather bad times as well as flourish in good, it has not yet endured long enough to make it clear what general relations to the community it may develop or what may be the reciprocal duties of State and Combination. To take only two points, the alliance of the Government and the Cunard Company is a precedent which requires the gravest consideration, while the recognised difficulties of management of a gigantic business may necessitate important modifications of our provision of higher education. The point cannot be too much emphasised that we have not in this country to face the American problem or the German problem, but a problem of our own—the modification of society by a new organisation of industry, a more efficient method of production, evolving normally without artificial stimulus. Patience, not hostility, is our proper attitude. What is clear is that we need more study, more investigation, and above all, more discrimination.

APPENDIX I.

THE SOUTHERN DISTRICT MILLERS' ASSOCIATION.

(*The Miller*, August, 1901.)

RULES.

1. Area, Name, Place of Meeting (Hants, Wilts, Sussex, Dorset, —— Southampton).

2. *Terms of Payment.*—The following shall be the terms of payment for flour sold by members of the Association, for delivery within the district for the time being included in the Association area. A discount may be allowed at the rate of 3d. per sack of 280 lb. for payment within fourteen days from the date of invoice; 1½d. per sack for payment within one calendar month; after one month, net. Invoices shall be dated from day of delivery ex-store, or day of despatch from mill by rail or otherwise.

3. *Cartages.*—There may be allowed to customers doing their own haulage a rebate not exceeding the current charge of the railway or canal company or other carrier for such haulage.

4. *Sacks.*—All sacks in which flour is filled shall be : (*a*) Filled at gross weight and sold and paid for at the price of flour; or (*b*) filled at net weight and sold and paid for as sacks at not less than 4d. each for the five or four bushel sack, and at not less than 2d. each for the two and a half bushel sack; or (*c*) filled at net weight and not sold. In the last-mentioned case there may be allowed on the return of sellers' sacks in good condition a rebate at the rate of not exceeding 1d. per sack of 280 lb. An allowance of 2d. per sack of 280 lb. may be made to customers finding sacks or bags marked with their own name.

5. No member shall fill with flour sacks or bags which bear the trade mark or name of another member without his consent.

6. All sacks in which offals are sold shall be : (*a*) Provided by the buyer; or (*b*) charged at prices not below their actual value,

347

and at which they may be allowed for if returned in good condition; or (c) marked in seller's name to be returned.

7. No member shall purchase or make an allowance in respect of sacks or bags of any kind at prices beyond their actual value.

8. *Contract Notes, Sales, Deliveries, etc.*—A flour Contract Note shall be prepared and settled by the Council, and shall be used by all members of the Association in the following cases: (a) Where the quantity of flour exceeds twenty sacks of 280 lb.; (b) in all cases where the time of delivery is beyond fourteen days, or no time of delivery is stated.

9. No member shall, in anticipation of an advance in the price of flour or otherwise, send to any customer a Contract Note where no sale has in point of fact been made.

10. No member shall consent to the cancellation or variation of a contract with a buyer, except upon terms that the buyer shall pay to such member the full legal compensation for such cancellation or variation.

11. Where a buyer has one or more sales or contracts still open with any member, the Contract Note referred to in clause 8 shall be used in respect of any further sale or sales by such member to such buyer, and the rules applicable thereto shall apply.

12. Except as hereinafter provided, and in cases of contracts with public bodies, no Contract Note shall be entered into for delivery beyond three months from the date thereof; and in case of delivery not having been completed within such period by reason of the default of the buyer, the contract shall be enforced against the buyer.

13. The terms of sale of flour and offal shall be in accordance with the bye-laws and Sale Note of the Association, and no member shall sell or offer for sale otherwise within the Association area.

14. *Standard Grade and Regulation of Prices.*—For the purpose of fixing the standard price of flour there shall at present be one grade, called "Fines".

15. There shall be a Price Committee, consisting of five members of the Association appointed by the Council, who shall, every Friday, fix the standard price of Fines. Should any member of the Price Committee propose an alteration in the standard price on any other day, he shall communicate such desire by telegram or telephone to the secretary, who shall at once communicate with the other members of the committee by telegram or telephone, and on receipt of replies he shall take the decision of the majority as

to what alteration (if any) shall be made, and the secretary shall notify every member of the Association by that evening's post of such alteration.

16. *Procedure.*—Each member shall require purchasers to strictly observe and carry out the terms of the contracts entered into by them, and shall if and so far as may be required by the Council institute legal proceedings against the purchasers for any default in carrying out the terms of the contract, and any proceedings may be initiated by the Council as they think fit, either in the name of the Association (if possible) or in the name of the particular member, and in the latter event the member shall give every necessary authority to the Council to prosecute such proceedings. Any member may, as far as may be approved by the Council, make use of the name and authority of the Association to enforce, as against any buyer, the terms of the contracts or any of the rules or bye-laws of the Association, but upon giving to the Association such indemnity as the Council may require.

17. Any member may apply to the Council to be indemnified against costs or expenses of any legal proceedings, whether in respect of any contract or otherwise, and if the Council consider it a proper case for indemnity, he shall be indemnified accordingly.

18. *Deposits and Expenses.*—Each member of the Association shall deposit with the general secretary, in promissory notes, payable on demand, a sum computed on the basis of the amount of flour sold by him within the Association area, as follows:—

Not exceeding 200 sacks per week, £10   From 500-1000 sacks per week   £30
From 200-500   „   „   „   20   Over 1000   „   „   „   50

Such deposits may be made in cash, if preferred, and shall then be invested or deposited at a bank as the Council may determine. Each member shall have paid to him the amount of current interest upon his deposit.

19. Each member shall further pay his share of the current expenses in the proportion which the flour sold by him in the district bears to the whole amount of flour sold in the district by the members of the Association. He shall declare such amount to the secretary. The amount of such contribution shall be fixed by the secretary, and his determination shall be final.

20. *Secrecy as to Information Supplied to the Secretary.*—No member shall, on any pretext whatever, have access to any information furnished to the secretary or district secretaries by any other member for any purpose in reference to Rule 19, or in reference to the objects of the Association.

21. *Christmas Boxes, Gratuities, etc.* — No member shall, directly or indirectly, give or distribute any Christmas box, New Year's gift, or gratuity, or any gift whatever to any customer or customer's family or servant.

22. *Sales Through Agents.* — Each member selling goods through an agent, on commission or otherwise, shall notify the secretary to that effect, and any infraction of these bye-laws and regulations by such agent or salesman shall be an offence committed by the member for whom he so acts.

23. No salesman shall divide any commission with any customer or any manager, or servant, or family of such customer, and, in the event of his so doing, the member in whose employment he is shall be responsible for such offence.

24. *Employment of Salesmen.*—No member shall enter into negotiation to employ, or employ, a salesman within a period of six months from the termination of his engagement with any other member of the Association without the consent of such member, but such consent shall not be unreasonably withheld. Any difference under this bye-law shall be determined by the Council.

25. *Procedure as to Offences.*—In case, on the report of any member of the Association, or as the result of his own investigations or inquiries, it shall be brought to the knowledge of the secretary that any member has, or is supposed to have, failed to observe and perform any of the provisions and agreements of these presents, or other of the rules and regulations of the Association for the time being, such secretary shall forthwith communicate with such member in specified terms the nature of the charge, and such member shall forthwith furnish, or procure to be furnished, to such secretary all information which such secretary may require, and shall procure for his inspection, and permit him to inspect, all books, papers, and documents whatsoever relating to his business or to the matter under investigation, whether including any books, papers, and documents which may be in the possession of, or the property of, any clerk, salesman, traveller, agent, or servant of such member, and which relate to the business or to the matter under investigation, and such secretary shall be further at liberty to make inquiries and obtain information from the persons in the employment of, or connected in business with, such member. When, and as soon as such investigation has been concluded, such secretary shall report to the Council of the Association and to such member whether or not, in his judgment, the

charge brought against such member is or is not well founded, and if, in his judgment, such charge be well founded, a special meeting of the Council shall be called as soon as possible to consider the case. Full particulars of the charge shall be furnished at least seven days before such meeting to the member charged, and he shall be at liberty to attend personally, or by or with an authorised representative before the Council to meet the charge either with or without witnesses. If the majority of members present and voting at such special meeting resolve that the charge against such member is well founded, then either—

(*a*) The member shall, *ipso facto*, cease to be a member of the Association, and cease to have any further right of interest whatsoever in the funds of the Association, or his contribution thereto, or—

(*b*) If, in the opinion of the Council, it is a case where the powers of this sub-clause should be adopted, the amounts entered to the credit of such member in the books of the Association shall be reduced by a sum prescribed herein as the penalty for the offence, and, if no such sum be prescribed, by a sum to be fixed by such Council, and such member shall, for all purposes of the Association, be deemed to have contributed only the balance which will remain after such sums shall have been so deducted, and in that case such member shall be liable to make up his contribution to the proper amount at the date of the next following annual adjustment of the contributions of the members.

Provided always that in case the powers of sub-clause (*a*) are exercised, then the whole of the moneys standing to the account of such member; or if the powers of sub-clause (*b*) are exercised, then the amount deducted therefrom shall be entered to the credits of the other members of the Association in proportion to their then contributions to the funds of the Association, such proportions to be determined by the general secretary, whose decision shall be final, and such sums so added to the credit of any member shall be deemed part of the contributions of such member for the purpose of the future adjustments thereof, or the payments by or to such member necessary to effect any such adjustment, and accordingly each member shall be entitled to be repaid at the end of the year any excess of his contributions as so increased over the proper amount of his contributions for the next ensuing year, to be determined as hereinbefore provided.

26. Any member against whom any charge shall have been ascertained to be well founded under the preceding clause, shall

have the right of appeal to a meeting of the Association; such appeal shall be subject to the same procedure as the hearing before the Council.   A fee of two guineas shall be paid to the Association by way of deposit, to be repaid to the appellant or forfeited to the Association as the Association shall direct.   The Association shall have power to determine whether the costs shall be paid by the appellant or out of the funds of the Association, and may order any penalties already paid by an appellant to be repaid to him.

27. *Penalties.*—A penalty not exceeding the amount of the member's deposit may be enforced in respect of any offences against any of the following bye-laws :—

2, 3, 4, 5, 6, 7, 8, 9, 10, 11, 12, 13, 16, 21, 22, 23, 24.

28. Subject to the right of appeal mentioned in bye-law 26 hereof, and to bye-law 25, the amount of the penalty to be inflicted in any case shall be determined by the Council.

APPENDIX II.

AGREEMENT AS TO POOLING.

AN AGREEMENT made the — day of —— 1900, between the several Persons, Firms, and Companies, whose names are now or may hereafter be set out in the first column of the Schedule hereto.

Whereas the parties hereto are manufacturers of yellow meal, and for a long time past keen competition has existed in the said business, which has resulted in the cutting of prices, and with a view to ending this cutting and steadying prices, the parties hereto have decided to enter into this Agreement.

Now each of the parties hereto doth hereby mutually and severally covenant and agree with each of the other as follows :—

1. As soon as possible after this Agreement is signed the parties hereto shall, at a meeting to be called for the purpose, appoint a person to be called the Millers' Accountant, who shall have the powers and discharge the duties hereinafter mentioned. Any vacancy which may occur in the office shall be filled by the parties hereto, at a meeting specially convened for the purpose. The person appointed must be a duly qualified Chartered Accountant, and the appointment must be made by a resolution passed by a majority of at least two-thirds who may be lawfully present at a meeting of the parties hereto as aforesaid. The person so appointed may be removed at any time from the office by a resolution of at least two-thirds of the parties lawfully present at a meeting of the parties hereto, specially convened for the purpose. The person so appointed shall be remunerated on such terms as may be agreed on between him and the parties hereto, or any person or persons authorised by their resolution to enter into such agreement.

2. The Millers' Accountant shall forthwith after his appointment make such examination and take such steps as he may

think necessary for the purpose of enabling him to ascertain accurately what was the total quantity of yellow meal delivered by each of the parties hereto in each month for the two years beginning 1st November, 1897, and ending 31st October, 1899. He shall, as soon as he ascertains this, inform each of the parties in writing what he has ascertained such party's total monthly deliveries to have been, and what the total combined monthly deliveries of all the parties hereto have been during the same period. He shall also furnish this information to the Referee hereinafter mentioned, and the Referee shall thereupon fix what he considers would for the purposes of this Agreement be the proportion which each party's deliveries should bear to the total deliveries of all the parties hereto. The proportion so fixed shall bind each party hereto during the continuance of this Agreement, save and except that it shall be lawful for the Referee from time to time to reopen and reconsider and amend all or any of said proportions. In fixing such proportions the Referee shall have regard to all the circumstances and the primary object of this Agreement, and he shall be at liberty to take into account any circumstances connected with the trade, price of corn, production of meal and its price, and where any of the parties hereto shall not have been in business for two years ending 31st October, 1899, the Referee shall fix what proportion such party's deliveries are to be taken to bear to the total deliveries on such materials and such manner as in the circumstances he may think fair and equitable. The Referee shall communicate to each party hereto the proportion of such party fixed by him as aforesaid.

3. The Millers' Accountant shall also during the continuance of this Agreement take such steps as he may think necessary to ascertain accurately each week, beginning on the date fixed by the Referee under clause 13, the quantity of yellow meal delivered by each of the parties hereto during the preceding week. He shall forthwith communicate, in writing, to each of the parties hereto what he finds such party's deliveries to have amounted to, as well as what he finds the total deliveries of all the parties hereto to have been, and, subject to any variation which may be made on the same as the result of any appeal, each party shall be bound by whatever the Millers' Accountant finds his weekly delivery to have amounted to.

4. Each of the parties hereto will, during the continuance of this Agreement, pay a sum of 4s. per ton on the yellow meal which the Millers' Accountant may so find he has delivered in

each week beginning on the date fixed by the Referee under clause 13, and the money so payable will be divided monthly amongst the parties hereto in the proportions for the time being fixed as provided by clause 2, which is to be deemed for the purposes of this Agreement the proportion that each party's deliveries for the two years mentioned in said clause 2 bears to the total deliveries of all the parties thereto for the same period. The said sum of 4s. per ton may, at the Millers' Accountant's option, be settled as to all or part of same by contra account. It shall be part of the Millers' Accountant's duty to make out and furnish the monthly accounts, showing the amount payable to or to be paid by each of the parties hereto under the provisions of this Agreement, and a certificate of the Millers' Accountant as to the amount at any time payable by any of the parties hereto to the others, or any of them, shall be binding on all parties. The amount which may be so certified by the Millers' Accountant as payable by any of the parties hereto to the others, or any of them, shall be payable on demand and constitute a debt due by such person to the others or to such of them as the Accountant certifies it to be payable, and may be recovered as a debt in any Court of Law by the person or persons to whom it is so certified to be payable. No sum shall be payable under this clause until the Millers' Accountant has certified same to be payable.

5. None of the parties will, during the continuance of this Agreement, be engaged, directly or indirectly, in the manufacture of yellow meal with any person or persons not a party to and bound by this Agreement.

6. The quantity of yellow meal delivered by any of the parties hereto shall in all cases include yellow meal delivered by others for or on account of any of the parties hereto, as well as yellow meal delivered by any of the parties hereto as agents for or representing others or made for others from corn supplied by them, but where corn is ground for any of the parties hereto by any of the other parties hereto, the yellow meal delivered from such production shall be treated as part of the delivery of the person for whom the corn was ground.

7. The parties hereto may, by a resolution passed by a majority of at least two-thirds of the parties hereto present at a meeting of the parties hereto, specially convened for the purpose, increase, reduce, or abolish, on such terms and for such period as may be fixed by such resolution, the payment of 4s. per ton provided by the fourth clause, and may by such resolution provide

that such increase, reduction, or abolition is to apply only to yellow meal delivered to any specified town or district, or by or to any person or persons specified in said resolution.

8. If the deliveries of yellow meal by any of the parties hereto during any month fall more than 10 per cent. below his or their proper proportion of the current deliveries, or if the weekly deliveries of any of the parties hereto shall be stopped or become reduced to the extent of 10 per cent. through suspension of payment, bankruptcy, or compounding with creditors, or through breakdown of machinery, or fire, or injury to property, or strikes, or lock-out, or any other cause, or through a desire no longer to be bound by the terms of this Agreement, then and in any such case it shall be the duty of the Millers' Accountant to forthwith inform the Referee, who may after inquiring into the matter either then or subsequently convene a meeting of the parties hereto to consider the matter, and the decision of a two-thirds' majority of the parties hereto present at such meeting as to what in the circumstances ought to be done shall be binding on all the parties hereto, including the party or parties in default, save and except that any party aggrieved by the decision may require the matter to be referred to the Referee, and the decision of the Referee, who shall have power to do what he thinks just and equitable in the circumstances, will bind all the parties. It will be competent for the meeting or the Referee, as the case may be, to order the party or parties in default to pay to each of the other parties hereto or some of them any sum or sums of money they or he may fix or to reduce the proportion of the party in default in the distribution of said 4s. per ton, or to suspend or abolish the payment of such proportion for any time which may be fixed, or direct the payment of a higher sum than 4s. on such party's weekly deliveries, or the payment of a specified sum either in one or several payments.

9. The Millers' Accountant shall be allowed free access at all times to such of the books, documents, and records of each of the parties hereto as he may consider necessary to enable him to efficiently do the work and discharge the duties hereby relegated to him. It is to be a point of honour with the Millers' Accountant that he shall not communicate to any of the parties hereto, except as herein expressly provided for, any information in relation to the business of any of the parties hereto which he may learn in the course of his duties, except where same may be necessary in the enforcement of the provisions of this Agreement.

10. The expression "yellow meal" in this Agreement shall be

deemed to mean the product of mixed and/or yellow Indian corn, whether fine cut, coarse cut, or cracked or kibbled, or made from damaged or inferior corn.

11. A certificate under the hand of the Millers' Accountant that any of the parties hereto is indebted under the provisions of this Agreement to all or any of the other parties hereto shall be deemed to be final and conclusive evidence of the existence of the debt, and of the liability of the person therein stated to be the debtor to pay same, and such debtor shall pay the amount stated to be due by him to the person named in such certificate at the time mentioned in such certificate.

12. The costs of and incident to the preparation of this Agreement, and of carrying out and giving effect to its provisions, shall be borne and paid by the parties hereto in the same proportions in which they are to receive the said 4s. per ton.

13. This Agreement shall continue for one year certain from a date to be fixed by the Referee so soon as the proportions under clause 2 are fixed, and the date so fixed shall be endorsed by the Referee on this Agreement, and communicated to each of the parties hereto. This Agreement shall continue after the expiration of said year, unless and until terminated by any of the parties hereto giving to the Referee one month's notice, in writing, of his intention to terminate same.

14. At least five days' notice in writing shall be given to all the parties hereto of the holding of any meeting, and such notice shall specify the business to be transacted thereat, and such notice shall be deemed to be properly given if posted in Belfast at least five clear days before the date for holding such meeting, and addressed to the last-known address of the party hereto for whom it is intended. No business save what is specified in the notice convening the meeting shall be transacted at any meeting. Five of the parties hereto present in person or by representative at any meeting shall be deemed to form a quorum for the transaction of any business. Each party hereto may instead of attending any meeting personally send some duly authorised person to attend such meeting on his behalf, and to take part in the deliberations of such meeting and vote thereat.

15. The parties hereto will furnish and vouch such information and returns as may from time to time be required by the Millers' Accountant, or the Referee, and all such information and returns shall be true and correct.

16. Any of the parties hereto breaking any of the provisions of

this Agreement shall pay in respect of each breach as liquidated and ascertained damages the following sums, *viz.* :—

For every breach of clause	4	.	.	.	.	.	£200
,,	,,	,,	5	.	.	.	.	.	200
,,	,,	,,	9	.	.	.	.	.	200
,,	,,	,,	11	.	.	.	.	.	100
,,	,,	,,	13	.	.	.	.	.	200
,,	,,	,,	15	.	.	.	.	.	200

Such sums shall be paid at such times and in such sums, and shall be divided in such proportions between the parties hereto, or such of them as the Referee may decide, and the Referee shall also have power, if, after investigation, he thinks it right so to do, to remit altogether or reduce the damages payable and fixed as aforesaid.   The decision of the Referee that there has been a breach of any of the clauses of this Agreement shall be final and binding.   Any decision of the Referee under this clause shall be deemed to be an award, and capable of being enforced as such, and may be made a Rule or Order of any of Her Majesty's Superior Courts of Record in Ireland.   The payment of the aforesaid damages for breaches of any of the aforesaid clauses shall not be deemed a waiver or satisfaction of any sum of money payable under such clause, and the non-payment of which may be the breach complained of.   Such money may be awarded by the Referee, to be paid along with the aforesaid damages to the persons entitled to same, and be recoverable in the same way.

17. Any of the parties hereto may appeal from any decision of the Millers' Accountant to the Referee, and the Referee's decision shall be final and binding.   All disputes or differences which may arise amongst the parties hereto, or any of them, in relation to this Agreement, or anything herein contained or arising thereout, shall be referred to the Referee, and his decision shall be final and binding.

18. The Referee shall be —— of ——, and failing him the President for the time being of the Belfast Chamber of Commerce, unless he shall be a miller or in any way connected with the corn trade, in which case the Vice-President of the Chamber shall be the Referee.

19. Any of the parties hereto or the Millers' Accountant or the Referee may at any time call a meeting of the parties hereto.   All the meetings of the parties hereto must be held in Belfast, and between the hours of 11 A.M. and 5 P.M., and any meeting duly convened and constituted may be adjourned by a majority of two-thirds of those being parties hereto or authorised to attend on

behalf of any party hereto present at such meeting until another day.

20. In construing these presents, a firm, consisting of more than one person, shall be treated and dealt with for voting and all other purposes as one person.

Schedule referred to.
(Parties to the Agreement.) | (Their Signatures.) | (Addresses.)

NOTE.—The sum of 4s. per ton mentioned in the Agreement appears to have been since raised to 10s. per ton.

APPENDIX III.

THE CALICO PRINTERS' ASSOCIATION, LIMITED.

INCORPORATED UNDER THE COMPANIES ACTS, 1862 TO 1898.

SHARE CAPITAL £6,000,000
Divided into 6,000,000 Shares of £1 each.
5,000,000 of which are now to be issued as Ordinary Shares, and the Remainder
may be issued hereafter either as 5 per cent. Cumulative Preference Shares
or as Ordinary Shares.

4 per cent. Perpetual First Mortgage Debenture Stock £3,200,000

PRESENT ISSUE—

4 per cent. Perpetual First Mortgage Debenture Stock, which will
be issued in multiples of £1 ... ... £3,200,000
Ordinary Shares of £1 each 5,000,000

£8,200,000

Of the above issue £1,066,666 Debenture Stock and £1,595,170 Ordinary
Shares will be issued to the Vendors in part payment of Purchase Moneys, and
the remainder, *viz.* :—

£2,133,334 Debenture Stock
3,404,830 Ordinary Shares

are now offered for public subscription at par, payable as follows :—

	Shares. s. d.		Debenture Stock.
On Application	2 6	per share	10 per cent.
On Allotment	5 0	,,	25 ,,
On 1st March, 1900	5 0	,,	25 ,,
On 1st May, 1900	7 6	,,	40 ,,

The debenture stock will be registered in the books of the Company, and
the interest will be paid half-yearly on 1st February and 1st August in each year,
the first payment (calculated from the due date of each instalment) being made
on 1st August, 1900.

Interest at 5 per cent. per annum will be charged on instalments in arrear.

The debenture stock and the interest thereon will be secured by a specific
first mortgage to the trustees for the debenture stock holders of the freehold,
copyhold, and heritable properties now purchased by the Company and (subject
to necessary consents of landlords) the leasehold properties so purchased held in

England for terms having more than twenty-one years to run, or in Scotland for terms of thirty-one years or upwards from the date of the lease, and of the Company's beneficial interest in the French works now purchased by it, which will, for convenience, be retained in the French Registry in the name of a Trustee for the Company, and by a first floating charge on the undertaking, and other property present and future of the Company in England, and also (so far as may be consistent with the law of those countries) in Scotland, France, and elsewhere, but not including uncalled capital of the Company.

Power is reserved by the trust deed to create further debenture stock in addition to and ranking *pari passu* with the above £3,200,000 to a total not exceeding three-fourths of the nominal amount of the share capital of the Company for the time being, but no further amount of the stock beyond the present issue of £3,200,000 can be issued unless additional hereditaments are acquired, and then only to the extent of two-thirds of the value of such hereditaments, and of any fixed or loose plant and machinery in or about the same.

In case the Company is at any time wound up the stock is repayable at £120 per cent.

TRUSTEES FOR THE FIRST MORTGAGE DEBENTURE STOCK HOLDERS.

NEVILLE CLEGG (F. W. Grafton & Co.).
WILLIAM GRAHAM CRUM (Chairman of the Thornliebank Company, Limited).
EDWARD GORDON McCONNEL (Chairman of Edmund Potter & Co., Limited).

DIRECTORS.

FRANCIS FREDERICK GRAFTON (F. W. Grafton & Co.), Chairman.
JOHN HENRY GARTSIDE (Gartside & Co., of Manchester, Ltd.),
JAMES HYSLOP MACMILLAN (S. Schwabe & Co., Ltd.), }Vice-Chairmen.
CHARLES HENRY NEVILL (The Strines Printing Company),
LENNOX B. LEE (The Rossendale Printing Co.).
GEORGE McCONNEL (Edmund Potter & Co., Ltd.).
Z. HENRY HEYS (Z. Heys & Sons).
ROBERT McKECHNIE (James Black & Co., Ltd.).
(The above have been appointed the first Managing Directors of the Association.)
William Edmund Appleton (James Black & Co., Ltd.).
John William Arthur (Allan Arthur, Fletcher, & Co.).
Francis William Ashton (F. W. Ashton & Co., Ltd.).
C. H. Barlow (Robert Kay & Sons, Ltd.).
A. G. Barns-Graham (The Millfield Printing Co.).
John Barr (E. Potter & Co., Ltd.).
Thomas Bennett (J. Bennett & Sons, Ltd.).
Philip Ridgeway Bennett (J. Bennett & Sons, Ltd.).
George Bolden (Gartside & Co., of Manchester, Ltd.).
Lennard Bolden (Gartside & Co., of Manchester, Ltd.).
Robin Boral (S. Schwabe & Co., Ltd.).
Robert Boyd (T. Boyd & Co.).
Charles Timothy Bradbury (Gartside & Co., of Manchester, Ltd.).
Charles Brier (J. Brier & Sons).
Oliphant Arthur Brown (R. Dalglish, Falconer, & Co., Ltd.).
Abel Buckley (Hayfield Printing Co., Ltd.).
William Buckley (E. & J. Buckley, Ltd.).

Jonathan Hindle Calvert (J. H. Calvert & Bros., Ltd.).
Assheton Neville Clegg (F. W. Grafton & Co.).
Walter Graham Crum (Thornliebank Co., Ltd.).
Robert Dalglish (R. Dalglish, Falconer, & Co., Ltd.).
William Murray Dunlop (Black & Wingate, Ltd.).
W. R. R. Gemmell (Bingswood Printing Co., Ltd.).
Milner Gibson (Gibson & Costobadie).
William Gourlie (William Gourlie & Son).
Charles Gray (James Gray & Sons).
Charles Heape (Strines Printing Company).
John Helm (Bayley & Craven).
Zechariah George Heys (Z. Heys & Sons).
Robert Patterson Hewit (Hewit & Wingate).
Charles James Higginbotham (S. Higginbotham & Co., Ltd.).
Thomas Barrow Hudson (Bradshaw, Hammond, & Co., Ltd.).
John Jackson (Thornliebank Co., Ltd.).
Joshua Knowles (S. Knowles & Co., Ltd.).
Samuel Knowles (S. Knowles & Co., Ltd.).
Arthur Mervyn Langdon (Gartside & Co., of Manchester, Ltd.).
William Ambrose Laxton (F. Laxton & Co., Ltd.).
William Lees (Gartside & Co., of Manchester, Ltd.).
William Clare Lees (Gartside & Co., of Manchester, Ltd.).
A. Ronald Macgregor (A. R. Macgregor & Co.).
Charles Macnab (A. Macnab & Co.).
Alexander Miller (Inglis & Wakefield, Ltd.).
James Mills (James Mills & Co.).
Frederick R. Moir (Moir & Co., Ltd.).
Peter Moir (Thornliebank Co., Ltd.).
William Nassau Molesworth (J. L. Kennedy & Co., Ltd.).
Adam Murray (Adam Murray & Co.).
William Morell Neild (Hoyle's Prints, Ltd.).
John Fenton Newall (Rossendale Printing Co.).
John Jack Orr (S. Schwabe & Co., Ltd.).
John Cater Owen (E. Potter & Co., Ltd.).
Zechariah Pollard (The Gateside Printing Co.).
John Riley (Thornliebank Co., Ltd.).
John Robb (Inglis & Wakefield, Ltd.).
William Edward Rumney (Edward B. Rumney).
Thomas Russell (Springfield Printing Co.).
James Allan Sackville (Sackville & Swallow).
Ernest Charles Baber Saxby (Charles Saxby).
Andrew Corbet Scott (J. Black & Co., Ltd.).
William James Shimwell (E. Potter & Co., Ltd.).
Arnold Bryce Smith (Bryce Smith & Co.).
Norgrave James Bryce Smith (Whalley Abbey Printing Co., Ltd.).
Andrew Stewart (James Shaw & Co., Ltd.).
Alfred Charles Street (Edmund Potter & Co., Ltd.).
George Weyland Taylor (W. Rumney & Co., Ltd.).
Alfred Aitken Thom (Birkacre Printing Co., Ltd.).
James Walker (Robert Walker & Sons).
William Watson (William Watson & Co., Ltd.).

Alexander Russell Waters (John Waters & Co.).
Francis Venables Williams (F. W. Grafton & Co.).
George Williamson (Hardie, Starke, & Co.).
William Henry Wilson (Kinder Printing Co., Ltd.).
William Christopher Wood (Christopher Wood, Ltd.).
Arthur Wright (Wright & Whittaker).
Alfred Wyatt (S. Schwabe & Co., Ltd.).
Alexander Stephenson Young (W. Rumney & Co., Ltd.).

BANKERS.

Messrs. Cunliffes, Brooks, & Co.,
The Manchester and Liverpool District Banking Company, Ltd., ⎫
The Manchester and County Bank, Limited, ⎪ Manchester
Williams, Deacon, and Manchester and Salford Bank, Limited, ⎬ and
The Lancashire and Yorkshire Bank, Limited, ⎪ Branches.
The Union Bank of Manchester, Limited, ⎭
Messrs. Brooks & Co., 81 Lombard Street, London.
The London City and Midland Bank, Limited, London, and Branches.
The Bank of Scotland, Edinburgh, Glasgow, and Branches.
The British Linen Company Bank, Edinburgh, Glasgow, and Branches.
The Union Bank of Scotland, Limited, Glasgow, and Branches.

BROKERS.

Linton Clarke & Co., Bartholomew House, London, E.C.
Lumsden & Myers, 29 Cornhill, London, E.C.
Henry Cooke & Son, St. Ann's Churchyard, Manchester.
Aitken, Mackenzie, & Clapperton, 2 West Regent Street, Glasgow.

SOLICITORS.

Grundy, Kershaw, Samson, & Co., 31 Booth Street, Manchester, and 4 New
    Court, Lincoln's Inn, London, W.C.
H. E. Warner & Co., 10 Finsbury Circus, London, E.C.
Maclay, Murray, & Spens, 169 West George Street, Glasgow.
Moncrieff, Barr, Paterson, & Co., 45 West George Street, Glasgow.

AUDITORS.

Jones, Crewdson, & Youatt, 7 Norfolk Street, Manchester, and 17 Coleman
    Street, London, E.C.

SECRETARY (*pro tem.*)—David Knipe.

REGISTERED OFFICE—2 Charlotte Street, Manchester.

PROSPECTUS.

This Company has been formed primarily for the purpose of
acquiring and amalgamating the various Companies and Firms
engaged in the Calico Printing Industry.

The following have entered into contracts with this Association for the sale of their businesses :—

PRINTERS.

Name of Firm.	Location of Works.	Works First Established.	No. of Printing Machines.
Andrew & Sons, Geo.[1]	Nr. Manchester	1824	15
Ashton & Co., Ltd., F. W.	Nr. Manchester	1816	15
Bayley & Craven	Nr. Manchester	1806	12
Black & Co., Ltd., Jas.	Nr. Glasgow	1828	30
Bradshaw, Hammond, & Co., Ltd. ...	Nr. Manchester	1838	13
Bennett & Sons, Ltd., John ...	Nr. Manchester	1821	20
Bingswood Printing Co., Ltd. ...	Nr. Manchester	1873	11
Birkacre Co., Ltd.[2]	Nr. Manchester	1796	16
Buckley, Ltd., Ed. & Jos.	Nr. Manchester	1863	7
Brier & Sons, John	Nr. Manchester	1835	9
Boyd & Co., Thomas	Nr. Manchester	1825	19
Calvert & Bros., Ltd., J. H. ...	Nr. Manchester	1835	11
Dalglish, Falconer, & Co., Ltd. ...	Nr. Glasgow	1805	20
Dalmuir Printing Co., Ltd.	Nr. Glasgow	1891	6
Gartside & Co., of Manchester, Ltd.[3]	Nr. Manchester	1865	74
Gateside Printing Co., The	Nr. Glasgow	1881	6
Grafton & Co., F. W.	Nr. Manchester	1782	34
Gibson & Costobadie	Nr. Manchester	1800	16
Hayfield Printing Co., Ltd.	Nr. Manchester	1858	12
Hardie, Starke, & Co.	Nr. Glasgow	1830	7
Heys & Sons, Z.	Nr. Glasgow	1842	28
Higginbotham & Co., Ltd., S. ...	Nr. Glasgow	1800	19
Inglis & Wakefield, Ltd.	Nr. Glasgow	1841	23
Kay & Sons, Ltd., Robert	Nr. Manchester	1860	8
Kennedy & Co., Ltd., J. L.	Nr. Manchester	1850	16
Kinder Printing Co., Ltd.	Nr. Manchester	1849	17
Knowles & Co., Ltd., S.	Nr. Manchester	1820	19
Laxton & Co., Ltd., F.	Nr. Manchester	1853	8
Low Mill Bleaching and Printing Co., Ltd.	Nr. Manchester	1876	8
Macnab & Co.	Nr. Glasgow	1843	12
Macgregor & Co., A. R.	Nr. Glasgow	1868	4
Millfield Printing Co....	Nr. Glasgow	1895	6
Murray & Co., Adam...	Nr. Glasgow	1860	6
Potter & Co., Ltd., Edmund... ...	Nr. Manchester	1825	51
Rossendale Printing Co., The ...	Nr. Manchester	1790	24
Rumney, E. B.	Nr. Manchester	1750	18
Rumney & Co., Ltd., W.[4]	Nr. Manchester	1854	31
Saxby, Charles	Nr. Manchester	1794	9
Schwabe & Co., Ltd., S.	Nr. Manchester	1788	40
Springfield Printing Co.	Nr. Glasgow	1842	7
Strines Printing Co., The	Nr. Manchester	1794	20
Thornliebank Co., Ltd., The[5] ...	Nr. Glasgow	1798	45
Walker & Sons, Robert	Nr. Manchester	1845	7
Watson & Co., Ltd., William ...	Nr. Manchester	1889	13
Whalley Abbey Printing Co., Ltd. ...	Nr. Manchester	1860	25
Wood, Ltd., Christopher	Nr. Manchester	1847	13
			830

[1] Includes spinning and weaving business, and the greater part of the village of Compstall.

[2] Excludes market bleaching business.

[3] Includes spinning, weaving, coloured and black dyeing businesses and business of John Dalton & Co., and Waterside Mills, lately purchased.

[4] Includes spinning and weaving business.

[5] Includes nearly all the village of Thornliebank.

Name of Firm.		Location.	Established.
Allan Arthur, Fletcher, & Co.	...	Glasgow and Manchester	1873
Black & Wingate, Ltd.	... ...	Glasgow	1816
Bryce Smith & Co.	...	Manchester	1860
Gemmell & Harter	...	Manchester	1866
Gray & Sons, James	...	Glasgow	1888
Gourlie & Son, Wm.	...	Glasgow	1831
Hewit & Wingate	...	Glasgow and Manchester	1858
Hoyle's Prints, Ltd.	...	Manchester	1780
Mills & Co., James	...	Manchester	1887
Moir & Co., Ltd.	...	Glasgow	1894
Shaw & Co., Ltd., Jas. ...	...	Glasgow and Manchester	1840
Waters & Co., John	...	Glasgow	1883
Wright & Whittaker	...	Manchester	1895

The business of calico printing, from its magnitude and its capacity for indefinite variety of development, is one of the most important of the textile industries.

The art was introduced into Scotland in the early part of the eighteenth century, and was later carried into the North of England. Several of the concerns have been established considerably over a century, and their productions have attained a world-wide reputation and prestige.

Calico printing possesses the unique advantage of affording the cheapest means of ornamenting textile fabrics, and it is at the same time adaptable to almost every requirement. Whilst meeting the varied demands of fashion, a large proportion of the production is of a staple character, thus insuring steadiness of demand and cheapness of production.

The businesses acquired comprise about 85 per cent. of the calico printing industry in Great Britain. The strength of the Association is shown by the fact that it includes nearly every leading house of the trade, and that these supply goods not only to all branches of the home trade, but practically to every open market of the world. The businesses also deal with all sections of the trade, and include the production of every description of printed cotton, dress goods, furnitures, cretonnes, linings, flannelettes, and also of delaines and mixed fabrics. In addition, some of the businesses own large spinning and weaving plants.

The character of the business and the terms on which it is conducted are such as to render it unusually safe, bad debts being of infrequent occurrence and of relatively trivial amounts.

The purchases include the copyright of the whole of the registered designs of the vendors, representing the accumulated experience and skill of many years. The possession of these assures to the Association the widest powers of control, and the means of efficiently safeguarding their customers' interests in the future.

The magnitude and importance of the trade are well known. The average exports of printed calicoes for the five years ending 31st December, 1898, as shown by the Board of Trade returns, have been 977,000,000 yards, valued at £10,444,000 per annum, and the exports for the ten months ending October, 1899, were 885,000,000 yards, valued at £8,933,000. These figures do not include the vast outlet in the home trade of which no precise statistics are available, but with regard to this it is sufficient to mention that prints enter into the domestic economy of practically every household in the United Kingdom.

Though some of the firms included in this Association have been and are earning large profits, the results of the trading generally for the past few years have been of an unsatisfactory nature, attributable chiefly to internal competition and cutting of prices. The directors believe that amalgamation of interests and definite community of action promise the following advantages :—

1. The avoidance of undue or excessive competition and of the selling of goods below cost.

2. Large economies to be effected by the centralisation of buying and finance and concentration of production.

3. The prevention of overlapping upon the part of the firms constituting the Association.

In the past there has been an immense waste in sampling, engraving, and pattern distribution. This can be greatly reduced without detriment, and it is evident that large economies must ensue.

In regard to possible competition, the directors point out the following elements of security for the business of the Association :—

(a) That the magnitude of the operations will practically insure to them the first offer of all new inventions and discoveries relative to the trade, and also the best productions of the designer and engraver.

(b) That calico printing is in itself a difficult and complicated business, and that the best quality of work is obtainable, not so much by the skill of any one individual as by the combination of skilled workers under highly organised and experienced management.

(c) That owing to the very large savings which can be made in the expenses of production, all competition, whether in the home trade or in neutral foreign markets, will be met upon much more favourable terms than hitherto.

Certain markets are at present closed to English prints owing to hostile tariffs. It will in the future be possible to carry on works in foreign countries under most favourable conditions as regards designs, engraved rollers, etc., and in a way which was not practicable when such action depended solely upon the initiative of individual firms. The Association already owns a large works in France.

The valuation of the properties, plant, machinery, etc., has been made by the well-known firm of valuers, Messrs. Edward Rushton, Son, & Kenyon, and their valuation, a copy of which will be found below, amounts to	£4,750,233
In addition, the Association acquires—	
Book debts guaranteed by the Vendors and stock-in-trade amounting (subject to adjustment) to	1,895,587
Copper and other rollers valued, in the case of copper, on the basis of 8d. per lb. for rollers of the standard size, being 25 per cent. below current market price for new rollers (subject to adjustment according to the actual weights taken over) ...	894,715
The issue will also provide cash (subject to adjustment) available towards payment for the additions to property and machinery, and the designs, engraving, and sampling hereafter referred to	152,969
Making a total of	£7,693,504

The books of the various firms have been examined by Messrs. Jones, Crewdson, & Youatt, and their certificate is as follows :—

" MANCHESTER, 7th December, 1899.

" To the Chairman and Directors of the Calico Printers' Association, Limited.

" Gentlemen,—We have examined the accounts of the firms, with one small exception, who have entered into contracts for the sale of their businesses to your Association, and we beg to report thereon as follows :—

" Owing to the varying dates of stocktaking it is impossible to give the combined profits of any year separately, and we have therefore taken the aggregate figures over a period mainly of five years.

" For the above reason this period is not uniform, but the commencing date has in no case been taken prior to July, 1892, and is for the most part comprised within the years 1893 to 1898 inclusive.

" We find that the aggregate average results of the trading of the various firms, whose accounts we have examined, before charging income tax and interest upon partners' capital and loans, and after making necessary adjustments, and after deducting salaries of management in accordance with the contracts of sale, have been an annual average profit of £455,826 5s. 6d.

"From this sum should be deducted a proper and adequate provision for depreciation, and after consultation with your valuers, we consider that a yearly sum of £100,000 should be provided as a depreciation fund.

"The results are adversely affected by the diminished profits disclosed by a number of the firms during the later part of the period covered by our examination. These are due, in our opinion, to the unfavourable condition of the trade which prevailed during that time.

"(Signed)   JONES, CREWDSON, & YOUATT."

In regard to the Accountants' certificate, the directors point out :—

(1) That the years 1897 and 1898 were years of exceptional difficulty and depression in the calico printing trade.

(2) That no estimate based upon these years forms any criterion of the trade even under normal conditions.

The directors also desire to emphasise their opinion that as the outcome of the amalgamation far different and more profitable results may be confidently expected in the future than have been realised for many years past.

The purchase prices for the properties and assets acquired amount to the aggregate sum of £8,047,031, of which £1,066,666 is payable in fully-paid debenture stock and £1,595,170 in fully-paid ordinary shares, and the balance in cash, which latter is liable to be slightly increased or decreased by necessary adjustments of stock, book debts, and rollers.

The contracts for purchase in nearly every case provide that, in addition to the above purchase moneys, the Association shall pay in cash for (1) expenditure on additional property and machinery since the date of Messrs. Edward Rushton, Son, & Kenyon's valuations of each concern ; (2) for the value of designs, engraving, and sampling taken over, such value to be assessed by a committee appointed by the Board of the Association.

The businesses are bought equipped with working stock-in-trade, and free from liabilities.

The various businesses are to be taken over as going concerns with the benefit of the trading in most instances from the 30th September last, subject to payment of interest at 4 per cent. per annum on the purchase money, and the Association takes over all current contracts and engagements.

Those of the managing directors who are required to devote their whole time and attention to the business of the Association will each receive £1,000 per annum, and the managing directors collectively receive a commission on the profits which does not fall due until profits sufficient to pay a dividend of at least 5 per cent. on the ordinary shares have been earned. The other directors will, unless voted by the general body of shareholders, receive no remuneration except for the active management of branches, under the provisions of the contracts for purchase specified below.

The trustees for the debenture stock holders, in addition to their remuneration as trustees, will also receive, under the provisions of the contracts for purchase, remuneration for their share in the management of branches.

It is a matter of sincere regret to the directors that Mr. E. G. McConnel, who for many years has held the position of Chairman of Messrs. Edmund Potter & Co., Ltd., is unable, through ill-health, to join the Board. He will, however, be interested in the Company, and the directors will have the benefit of his experience and advice.

The Company buys in each case direct from the original owners of the businesses without the addition of any intermediate profit.

The vendors of the various businesses have provided a fund equivalent to 2 per cent. on their purchase price, which is to be paid to Mr. Ernest Crewdson, of 7 Norfolk Street, Manchester (who has negotiated the amalgamation), and is to be applied by him in his entire discretion and without liability to account in discharging all the preliminary expenses of the Association up to allotment other than costs of conveyance or examination of title, or stamps on conveyances, or agreements for sale or on any statement of loan capital, or trust deed for securing debenture stock, but including the remuneration to be fixed by Mr. Crewdson to be paid to himself or his firm of Jones, Crewdson, & Youatt.

The following contracts, all of which are dated the 2nd day of December, 1899, have been entered into by the following persons, firms, and companies, in each case with the Association, *viz.* . . . .

In the case of certain limited companies, where doubts have existed as to their powers, undertakings have been given by some of their directors or principal shareholders guaranteeing the performance of the contracts.

The trust deed for securing the debenture stock will be executed on the completion of the various purchases, and will be in the form of the printed draft referred to in an agreement dated the 8th of December, 1899, and made between the Company of the one part and the above-named trustees for the debenture stock holders of the other part, or such modified form as may be adopted in accordance with the terms of that agreement. Pending the execution of the trust deed, moneys payable by subscribers for the debenture stock will be paid to a separate account and applied in manner mentioned in the said agreement.

The above agreement and the printed draft trust deed referred to therein, the contracts for purchase specified above, prints of the Memorandum and Articles of Association of the Company, Messrs. Edward Rushton, Son, & Kenyon's valuation, and the certificate of Messrs. Jones, Crewdson, & Youatt, can be seen at the Manchester offices of Messrs. Grundy, Kershaw, Samson, & Co.

Stock Exchange settlements and quotations will be applied for in due course.

Applications for shares or for debenture stock should be made on the forms enclosed, and with the deposit forwarded to one of the bankers of the Company.

If no allotment is made the deposit will be returned in full, and where the number of shares or the amount of debenture stock allotted is less than that applied for, the balance will be applied towards the payment due on allotment, and any excess will be returned to the applicant.

Failure to pay any instalment on shares or debenture stock will render the previous payments liable to forfeiture.

Copies of the prospectus, with forms of application for shares and for debenture stock, can be obtained at the offices of the Company, or from the bankers, the brokers, the auditors, or the solicitors.

The following is a copy of Messrs. Edward Rushton, Son, & Kenyon's valuation :—

" 13 NORFOLK STREET,
" MANCHESTER, 7th December, 1899.
" To the Directors of the Calico Printers' Association, Limited.

" Gentlemen,—We have valued the properties of the firms who have signed contracts for the sale of their businesses to your Association.

" The works and estates comprise 34 freeholds, with about 1,730 acres of land, 9 long leaseholds of about 173 acres, and 15 shorter leaseholds (up to 99 years) of 325 acres or thereabouts, and the water rights connected with the works are very extensive and valuable.

" Several important Manchester warehouses, with the freehold sites, containing about 3,205 square yards, are included ; and also numerous residences, dwelling-houses, plots of valuable building land, and receivable chief rents.

"All the chief or ground rents, feus, and other burdens to which the various lands are subject have been deducted from the valuation, and in cases of leaseholds the rents payable have been considered.

"The plant and machinery includes 830 printing machines, 277,264 cotton spinning spindles, 6,656 power looms, hemming machinery, and packing plant, and in most instances is in first-class order, having been well maintained.

"The works buildings for the most part are well and sub-stantially built and arranged for economical and advantageous working.

"Our valuation as a going concern is as follows :—

Land, water rights, leasehold interests, and buildings	£2,315,988
Plant and machinery, utensils, office and warehouse furniture, horses, carts, etc.	2,434,245
Total Valuation	£4,750,233

" (Signed) EDWARD RUSHTON, SON, & KENYON."

Manchester, 8th December, 1899.

24 *

APPENDIX IV.

MANCHESTER, *9th September*, 1902.

TO THE SHAREHOLDERS OF

THE CALICO PRINTERS' ASSOCIATION, LIMITED.

DEAR SIR OR MADAM,

1. It will be within your recollection that at the adjourned general meeting of shareholders, held on 24th March last, it was decided to appoint a committee which should—

(1) Investigate the difficulties which had arisen between the vendors and the managing directors, as well as the system of management in the past.

(2) Draw up a scheme for the future management of the Association on lines likely to be successful.

2. It was agreed that the committee should be composed of an equal number of directors and of non-vendor shareholders.

The Board appointed the following directors to be members of the proposed committee :—

(1) BRADBURY, CHARLES TIMOTHY,	of Messrs.	Gartside & Co. (of Manchester), Ltd.
(2) CLEGG, ASSHETON NEVILLE,	,, ,,	F. W. Grafton & Co., Ltd.
(3) HIGGINBOTHAM, CHARLES JAMES,	,, ,,	S. Higginbotham & Co., Ltd.
(4) LEE, LENNOX BERTRAM,	,, ,,	The Rossendale Printing Co., Ltd.
(5) MCKECHNIE, ROBERT,	,, ,,	James Black & Co., Ltd.
(6) MACMILLAN, JAMES HYSLOP,	,, ,,	S. Schwabe & Co., Ltd.

They also on the recommendation of these six directors elected the following non-vendor shareholders :—

(1) HOLLINS, FRANK,	of Messrs.	Horrockses, Crewdson, & Co., Ltd.
(2) MATHER, SIR WILLIAM, M.P.,	,, ,,	Mather & Platt, Ltd.
(3) PARTINGTON, EDWARD,	,, ,,	Kellner-Partington Paper Pulp Co., Ltd.
(4) PHILIPPI, O. E.,	,, ,,	J. & P. Coats, Ltd.
(5) STANNING, JOHN,	,, ,,	The Bleachers' Association, Ltd.
(6) THOMSON, JOHN,	,, ,,	Stewart, Thomson, & Co.

The committee met for the first time on the 2nd of July, and held subsequent meetings from time to time up to the 21st of August.

INVESTIGATION.

3. In order to ascertain, so far as possible, the views of the 109 acting directors and vendors who are not members of the committee some were interviewed, and, it being impracticable to see more than a limited number, the others were informed that the committee would be glad to receive their views and suggestions in writing.

4. In response to this intimation more than fifty papers were handed in, some of them throwing considerable light upon the situation, dealing with many interesting details, and making valuable suggestions. The directors and vendors were also requested to state the names of those of their number whom they considered best qualified to control and direct the affairs of the Association in future, and by a large majority they designated the present Chairman, Mr. R. P. Hewit, two of the three managing directors (Mr. Buckley having expressed his intention of resigning on account of ill-health), and those other directors who are acting on the committee.

5. The investigations of the committee have led to the conclusion that the difficulties which have arisen between the vendors and the managing directors were, generally speaking, the unavoidable outcome of adequate provision not having been made for conducting the affairs of the Association on sound lines, and that the want of success and absence of satisfactory profits are also, to a considerable extent, attributable to the same cause.

6. When the Association was formed, suitable arrangements should have been made for working the business as one, and for increasing the efficiency and earning power of the numerous concerns of which it is composed. To accomplish this a central authority, having complete and effective control of all the businesses belonging to the Association, was indispensable, but it should have been constituted on lines enabling it to secure the confidence and loyal support of the directors and branch managers. It was not so constituted, and the best efforts of successive chairmen and managing directors have on that account been more or less paralysed. If their duties and sphere of influence had been defined and restricted, they would probably have met with less opposition. Many of the branches were, for a variety

of reasons, disinclined to carry out their instructions. Some of the reasons given were altogether bad, some inadequate; but in other cases the disinclination was justified. It was idle to expect that three or four men, however able, would be recognised by a large body of men of similar training and possessing similar knowledge and experience, to be the most competent judges of every question that would arise in connection with some sixty separate businesses. Even if they had been so regarded, it was well known that the time at their disposal was altogether insufficient to enable them to arrive at carefully considered decisions and that this compelled them to depute much of their work to permanent officials. This knowledge could not but increase the resistance, both active and passive, to instructions emanating from the head office. When the managing directors sought the advice of vendor managers, they found that the views of men, whom they were bound to consider equally competent to form an opinion, were in absolute conflict. This resulted, in a great measure, from the latter not being accustomed to take sufficiently into consideration the requirements of the Association as a whole, and from their judging most questions from the standpoint of the business with which they are connected.

7. There can be no doubt of the inherent difficulties of the situation having been aggravated by mistakes made by both sides, more particularly during the first eighteen months, but the want of harmonious co-operation between the board of management and the branch managers resulted chiefly from the absence of a carefully planned system of administration. There were frequent changes in the board of management, which prevented any continuity of policy; measures, which had been inaugurated and might have produced good results, were abandoned before they could bear fruit.

8. Many of the leading men in the Association, in particular those whose knowledge, experience, and successful management of their own businesses in the past entitle their views to special consideration, are in complete agreement with the committee in thinking that it was impossible for the present managing directors to overcome the difficulties of the situation, and that they have done exceedingly well under most trying circumstances. It must be borne in mind that the managing directors had no security of tenure and, in unison with the directors generally, were of opinion that the vendor managers were not amenable to their authority.

9. The committee does not share that opinion and does not

think that the service agreements with vendors, or the absence of any special service agreements, offer serious obstacles or enable any one in the Association to disregard the instructions of an executive appointed by the Board. The committee recommends that anybody not carrying out such instructions promptly and to the best of his ability, be notified that his services will be dispensed with and that no compensation will be given, it being left to his option to use any legal remedy he may have to obtain damages, should any be due, which the committee considers extremely doubtful.

SCHEME OF MANAGEMENT.

10. In drawing up a scheme for the management of the Association on lines likely to be successful, provision must be made :—

(I.) To secure to the fullest extent possible the many legitimate advantages which can be derived from the combination of a large number of manufacturers.

(II.) To counteract the disadvantages which are inseparable from the fundamental changes affecting the individual businesses forming the Association and from the transference of many responsibilities to a newly-constituted body lacking the specific experience required to deal successfully with entirely new conditions.

(III.) To establish as far as possible settled and stable relations between the various sections and individuals serving the Association, by making the new arrangements capable of being amended and perfected without their permanence being endangered.

It may not be inopportune to refer in some detail to the more important questions arising under these heads.

I.

11. The public was not asked to become interested in an aggregation of sixty-four disconnected businesses which would be worked by the vendors more or less independently of each other and on the same lines as previously. It is, on the contrary, clearly set out in the prospectus that the Association to which the public was asked to subscribe is one concern, consisting of a number of component parts, which would be controlled by a Central Authority, and that the business would be conducted on lines different from those followed in the past, this being necessary in order to secure a better return for the capital employed than had been obtained formerly.

12. Although it should hardly be necessary to emphasise this point, the committee considers it right to draw special attention to the matter, as it has been stated that some vendor managers resent interference with "their" works, that they claim to be allowed to work "their" business as formerly, and in accordance with their own ideas, as they know its requirements best.

13. Such unreasonable pretensions cannot be reconciled with the terms of the prospectus and the distinct representations made to the public in order to induce it to subscribe. It was stated that the object of the formation of the Association was to combine the businesses. This implies that as businesses with separate interests they would cease to exist, and that everything affecting them would be made subordinate to the interests of the Association as a corporate body, or in other words, to the interests of the shareholders. It must also be borne in mind that many of the businesses acquired by the Association had been by no means profitable. A certain number had been successful, some even doing a very remunerative business; but the aggregate profits were only sufficient to make a return of about 4 per cent. on the share capital of the Company. It is evident beyond doubt that the public subscribed on the strength of the statements contained in the prospectus as to the benefits to be obtained by combining the businesses and by working them differently in future. Every vendor manager whose name appears on that document is therefore under a personal obligation and in honour bound to use his most strenuous efforts to carry out the bargain made with the shareholders in strict conformity with the terms of the prospectus and to make the furtherance of the interests of the Association as a whole his sole aim.

14. It was asserted in the prospectus that, apart from the savings resulting from the avoidance of undue or excessive competition, large economies could be effected by :—

(a) Centralisation of buying and finance.

(b) Concentration of production.

(c) Prevention of " overlapping ".

(d) Reduction in expenses of production generally.

(e) Great reduction in cost of engraving, sampling, and pattern distribution.

15. The conviction that scattered individual effort will never secure these advantages makes the leading men in the Association unanimous in considering that a strong Central Authority is indispensable to its well-being, some having even expressed

a desire to see two or three managing directors invested with arbitrary and dictatorial powers. It is open to grave doubt whether such an arrangement as the last named would overcome the difficulties encountered in the past; but it is certain that, in in order to effect the economies enumerated under the five heads mentioned above, all the businesses belonging to the Association must be controlled and guided by a Central Authority, which has at its disposal all the information, intelligence, and expert knowledge which can be brought to bear upon such matters.

16. A statistical department is, of course, indispensable for the purpose of collecting information upon every matter concerning any one of the businesses belonging to the Association, and of furnishing such information at a moment's notice.

17. The representatives of three successful combinations have stated that without such help it is impossible to exercise any useful or even intelligent control and to obtain satisfactory results. Many of the directors and branch managers of the Association have arrived at a similar conclusion, and have expressed the belief that great benefit has already been derived from the statistical work carried on at the head office. It was not to be expected that this work, in many respects new to the officials to whom it was entrusted, would from the first be done in such a perfect manner as to escape criticism; but branch managers who formerly complained bitterly of the trouble, loss of time, and expense, caused by the imposition of additional clerical work and requests for detailed information, which an imperfect system of book-keeping made it difficult to supply, are now satisfied that these statistics are not only indispensable to the head office, but are exceedingly useful to the branches themselves for their own guidance.

II.

18. The disadvantages referred to under this head make themselves felt in most cases where a business is converted into a public company, and to a greater degree where a large number of businesses are combined and sold to the public. The necessity of meeting outside competition is no longer felt to the same extent, and the incentive to work the business economically in order to obtain an adequate return upon the capital employed is seriously lessened. Too much reliance is placed upon the possibility of obtaining higher prices, whereas it is in the case of a public company of the greatest importance to supervise every item of expenditure, to closely compare the cost of production and of

distribution with what it was formerly, and to reduce it wherever this can be done with safety. Only by these means can the interests of the shareholders be protected.

19. The opinion has sometimes been expressed that on account of the diversity and complexity of the work, and as success in the calico printing trade depends largely upon "individuality," upon the creative faculty and taste of the leading men, the businesses belonging to the Association cannot with advantage be placed under the control of a Central Authority, and that perfect freedom of action and absence of control are necessary to their well-being and the indispensable elements of success.

20. The committee does not share this opinion, and sees no reason to doubt that the business can be worked on the lines of the prospectus without unduly interfering with what is called "individuality," and believes that the advantages which it was stated would accrue from a consolidation of interests can be secured, and would greatly increase the profits.

21. The Association is in a position to secure additional advantages which the committee considers of special benefit. The best chemical and mechanical science can be employed to a greater extent than in the case of separate concerns, and men of thorough training in practical chemistry, as applied to calico printing, should be engaged on terms sufficiently liberal to attract the most capable. One of the greatest advantages of combination may be shown in improved quality of work all round, by reason of the power of the Association to command the highest skill and knowledge of the newest appliances and processes, and the best methods of distribution. The committee recommends that these matters have the immediate and constant attention of the Executive.

22. The new conditions under which the businesses are carried on render it necessary to prevent indifference and lethargy gaining ground, and suitable means must be devised for giving pecuniary recognition of good work done by individuals. If, however, "payment by results" were based upon the profits of the separate branches, there would be great danger of undue internal competition injuriously affecting the interests of the Association.

23. The profits have in the past been lessened to a serious extent by the branches competing with each other in a manner which is entirely inconsistent with the objects for which the combination was formed. It is difficult to say whether some of the branch managers have failed to realise the significance of

the change which·has taken place in the relations of their branch
to others in the combination, or have merely been unable to free
themselves from a trade jealousy, which, if allowed to continue,
would be a serious menace to the future prosperity of the business.

24. If managers and others were to receive bonuses or commissions computed upon the profits of the branches with which
they are identified, there would be great danger of their being
disposed, even to a greater extent than in the past, to consider
every question from a selfish point of view, and to be indifferent
as to how much other branches might be damaged.   It must also
be borne in mind that the earning power of the businesses belonging to the Association differs so much that the percentage of profit
furnishes no safe guide to the efficiency of the management.
There are concerns which, on account of the class of business
they do, would be considered to have produced very disappointing
results if they only yielded a profit of 7 or 8 per cent. on the
capital employed, whereas a similar percentage of profit could in
other businesses only be obtained by most strenuous efforts and
excellent management.   The rough and ready method of giving
a certain commission on profit would, therefore, operate most
unjustly.

25. It is stated in the prospectus that concentration of production, involving a suitable allocation of styles to the various works,
would greatly increase profits, and the committee considers this
very probable.   It would, however, be very difficult to make the
necessary changes, if a bonus or commission on the profits of
individual branches were given to managers and others; and the
Executive would be greatly hampered by such an arrangement,
for the changes, however desirable in the interest of the whole of
the Association, must affect the profits of individual branches to
a considerable extent.   It is improbable that branch managers
would readily and cheerfully carry out instructions as to alterations calculated to lessen the profits of the branches under their
charge, and, therefore, their own remuneration, while increasing
that of others.

26. Although giving a bonus in the form of commission on
profits is for the foregoing reasons entirely opposed to the interests
of the Association, it is necessary to introduce in some form the
system of "payment by results," and a suitable method of doing
so will have to be devised.   Men who show originality and
ingenuity in designing, or do specially good work in other directions, must be encouraged and rewarded.   A man who has taste

and talent, or ability and resourcefulness, will make money under conditions in which another, not possessed of such qualities, will fail.

III.

27. The committee recommends that there should be :—

(*a*) A Board of Directors of not less than six and not more than nine members;

(*b*) An Executive of not less than two and not more than four members;

(*c*) Advisory Committees of not less than three and not more than eight members.

The committee has ascertained that Mr. R. P. Hewit is willing to continue as Chairman of the Board of Directors, and that Mr. Neville Clegg and Mr. Frederick Schwabe have agreed to join the Board if Mr. Frank Hollins, Mr. John Stanning, and Mr. John Thomson would likewise be elected directors. These latter gentlemen have intimated their willingness to accept seats on the Board if appointed by the shareholders.

BOARD OF DIRECTORS.

ROBERT PATTERSON HEWIT, Chairman.
NEVILLE CLEGG.
FRANK HOLLINS.
FREDERICK SALIS SCHWABE.
JOHN STANNING.
JOHN THOMSON.

EXECUTIVE.

L. B. LEE, Chairman.

G. BOLDEN.   C. J. HIGGINBOTHAM.

The Chairman of the Board of Directors and the members of the Executive shall form a Finance Committee. All questions having reference to salaries and to bonuses will be dealt with by this committee.

ADVISORY COMMITTEES.

(*a*) *Works Production.*   (*b*) *Designs, Styles, etc.*
R. BORAL.   J. W. ARTHUR.
C. T. BRADBURY.   A. N. CLEGG.
O. A. BROWN.   T. NORRIS.
W. BROWNING.   F. W. STRATTON.
P. CAMPBELL.

(c) *Concentration.*
R. BORAL.
W. R. R. GEMMELL.
C. HEAPE.
R. MCKECHNIE.

(d) *Prices.*
W. BUCKLEY.
W. G. CLEGG.
R. P. EARWAKER.
J. HELM.
R. MCKECHNIE.

(e) *Trading.*
A. N. CLEGG.
W. R. R. GEMMELL.
J. H. MACMILLAN.
R. MCKECHNIE.
C. H. NEVILL.

(f) *Cloth Buying.*
J. W. ARTHUR.
W. LEES.
F. V. WILLIAMS.

(g) *Drugs, Stores, Coal, etc.*

W. BROWNING.
W. BUCKLEY.
H. COSTOBADIE.

ROSS GEMMELL.
J. KNOWLES.

N.B.:—Regarding the constitution of the foregoing, it may be advisable to state here that additional names may shortly be added on the recommendation of the Executive or of the first members of these committees.

28. In order to carry out the recommendations of the committee it is necessary for the present Board of Directors to resign. The six directors of the Association who are members of the committee have already placed their resignations in the hands of the chairman, and the other directors of the Association will doubtless follow their example, in order to avoid the delay which would otherwise occur.

29. The members of the Executive must attend the meetings of the Board of Directors, and take part in the discussions, but will have no vote.

30. The Executive shall send to the Chairman of each Advisory Committee weekly, on fixed days, a list of the subjects requiring the attention of his committee, and these agenda shall determine the frequency of the meetings of the Advisory Committees.

31. One or more members of the Executive shall be present at the meetings of the Advisory Committees. It is essential that they follow the discussions and take part in them, so as to understand and appreciate the reasons for the recommendations of these committees.

32. It is intended that the Advisory Committees shall primarily decide upon the measures necessary to increase the efficiency of the branches and upon other matters allotted to them ; and it will be the duty of the Executive to carry the recommendations of the Advisory Committees into effect. It must, however, not be inferred therefrom that the members of the Executive merely occupy

the position of managers, whose duty it is to carry out the instructions of committees competent to enforce their decisions. They will have the right to decline to adopt any recommendation of the Advisory Committees if they think that it would be hurtful to the interests of the Association to carry it into effect. Should such difference of opinion arise, it shall be submitted to the Board of Directors, whose decision must be final. If the Board of Directors is applied to with reference to a matter of this kind, it should give to the Chairman or any other member of the Advisory Committee in question an opportunity of explaining its views.

33. The Advisory Committees should elect their own Chairman, who must be confirmed by the Board. Recommendations as to additions to their number and the filling of vacancies will emanate from them or the Executive, but the appointments shall be made by the latter, subject to the approval of the Board.

34. A concise record shall be kept of the business transacted at every meeting of an Advisory Committee, and the Board of Directors shall be furnished at its monthly meetings with a written report enumerating the matters which have been referred to the Advisory Committee since the previous meeting of the Board of Directors. This report shall also state what meetings have been held and contain a table of attendance, together with a synopsis of what took place at the meeting. In addition thereto it shall be the duty of the members of the Executive to draw the attention of the Board of Directors to matters of exceptional importance which have been transacted at the meetings of the Advisory Committees or have occurred in the course of the conduct of the business generally.

35. While it is intended that the Advisory Committees shall be permanent institutions, the proposed allocation of work to different committees is tentative and may require to be modified later on, but any modification shall be made only by the Board of Directors. The number of the members constituting these committees should fluctuate, not only in accordance with changes in the volume and nature of the work they have to perform, but also with due regard to the desirableness of promoting men to a position in which their ability and knowledge will become available for the benefit of the whole Association.

36. The remuneration of the committees shall be fixed by the Board of Directors.

37. It will readily be understood that the scheme recommended by the committee aims at the avoidance of the difficulties which

have formerly beset the management and of the friction which has arisen in consequence.

38. Although these difficulties have been referred to in the first part of this report, giving the result of the investigation which the committee was asked to make, it appears desirable to point out further some aspects of the case which must be taken into consideration, in order to form a proper estimate of the probability of the scheme being successful.

39. The co-existence of three different bodies for the purpose of management is unusual, but a careful scrutiny of past and present difficulties leads to the belief that they are necessary separately to (1) Supervise (Board), (2) Administer (Executive), and (3) Advise (Advisory Committees), whilst co-operating in the general control of the business and directing its policy.

40. A division of labour and of responsibility is not only necessitated by the immense volume of the work required to make the Association as prosperous as it should and can be made, but more particularly by the great variety of the subjects which have to be dealt with.

41. The difficulties already experienced seem to prove that arrangements which may meet the requirements of other combinations would be quite inadequate to secure the success of this Association. It is not reasonable to assume that two or three managing directors or a Board of twelve or fifteen directors could give sufficient time to every important matter requiring attention, or that they would possess the requisite knowledge of all subjects to enable them to arrive at conclusions which could really be called their own.

42. In the absence of such arrangements as are proposed by the committee, they would have to rely upon the assistance of permanent officials appointed by themselves, and the casual help and advice given by others, whom they would consult if they thought it necessary, and whose advice they would adopt or disregard as they thought fit. They would in many cases have to issue instructions based upon the recommendations of others, whose identity is either not disclosed, or who, if known, might not generally be thought the most competent persons to advise, and whose functions and responsibilities are not properly defined.

43. It cannot be expected that decisions so arrived at would commend themselves to others, and it is of the greatest importance, with regard both to internal affairs and to the intercourse with customers, whose interests must be carefully studied, that all

instructions given by the Executive should be known to be the outcome of careful deliberation and of sound practical and up-to-date knowledge of the matters to which they refer. Unless this be the case, such instructions would be carried out reluctantly and without the promptness and thoroughness necessary to obtain a satisfactory result. It should be the aim to convince, not to compel; but, if compulsion has to be resorted to in extreme cases, it must be prompt and effective.

44. The directors and members of the Executive having to protect the interests of the Association as a whole, it is undesirable that they should be connected with the management of any particular branch or section, as their opinions might be influenced thereby. It must, however, be borne in mind that as soon as they assume administrative functions, and are no longer in daily contact with the practical part of the business, their expert knowledge becomes of little avail, as conditions constantly change. It is all the more necessary that they should take the fullest advantage of all the intelligence and expert knowledge available, and that they should ascertain and be guided by the opinions of the ablest men, actively engaged in the business, who are in touch with the customers as well as with the staff at the works and in the warehouses. Means must be devised for constant intercourse between these men and the Executive, and they should exercise a continuous influence upon the affairs of the Association. The committee believes that all these advantages will be secured by the constitution as recommended under paragraph 27.

45. It is also of the utmost importance to have the means of encouraging younger men by making it possible for them to obtain influential positions, and this becomes possible by the creation of the Advisory Committees. The most successful branches should become training schools for such men, from which they can be drafted to positions of responsibility, facilitating the introduction of the best methods of the leading houses into the less successful branches.

46. If the management were entrusted exclusively to a Board of twelve or fifteen directors, some of them not connected with the business of calico printing, this would entail the exclusion of a large number of men of ability, of ripe experience, and possessing an intimate knowledge of all important matters upon which the Board of Directors would have to decide. Their exclusion would be a serious loss to the Association, and in the course of time would in all probability become the cause of grave dissatisfaction and antagonism to the Board.

47. The question as to whether the grouping of businesses should be adhered to had better be left for the consideration of a new Board.

48. It shall be competent for any person employed by the Association to submit in writing to the Chairman of the Board or to the Chairman of the Executive or to the Chairman of an Advisory Committee suggestions of changes and improvements which in his opinion would materially enhance the interests of the Association. The Chairman receiving such a communication shall be pledged not to disclose the name of the sender, should the latter not desire it. If the suggestions are of practical value, a suitable pecuniary recognition should be made by the Executive.

In conclusion the committee desires to say that, after very careful consideration of the present condition of the Association and the possibilities of the future, it is of opinion that the proposed system of management, if carried out by men of the requisite knowledge and experience, will open up a successful career for this great combination.

O. E. PHILIPPI (*Chairman*).
FRANK HOLLINS.
WILLIAM MATHER.
EDWARD PARTINGTON.
JOHN STANNING.
JOHN THOMSON.

———

C. T. BRADBURY.
ASSHETON N. CLEGG.
CHAS. J. HIGGINBOTHAM.
LENNOX B. LEE.
ROBERT McKECHNIE.
J. H. MACMILLAN.

MEMORANDUM.

Referring to paragraph 21 of the Report, I desire to amplify what the committee as a whole has considered sufficient to say on the subject in the body of the report, by the following observations based on intimate knowledge of calico printing works in foreign countries as well as in Great Britain :—

Calico printing is an industry requiring a greater range of knowledge and a stricter application of science in carrying out every detail of its multifarious processes than most industrial undertakings. Chemical and mechanical science of high degree

25

are absolutely necessary to obtain the greatest excellence and economy of production; and these are the foundations upon which commercial success chiefly depends.

The Association of the Calico Printers of Great Britain affords an opportunity, unique in the history of the industry, for the application of the continuous discoveries of scientific research to practical objects in each branch works.

To make use of this opportunity I strongly urge that a central department of technical chemistry, applied to calico printing, should at once be established and equipped with necessary appliances for research and experimental work, conducted by the ablest and best trained chemists, specially qualified to pursue investigations, in which chemical processes and mechanical and electrical appliances are involved.

This department would form a "Clearing house" for difficulties experienced in any branch works in carrying out complicated processes, and in the introduction of new colours and methods of production. It would conduct research work having a direct bearing on desirable improvements and changes in processes. It would inquire into, and test if necessary, all new inventions, and obtain information from other countries of new developments in calico printing.

It would form the brain of the business, always active and alert to supply the managers of the branches with expert knowledge without interference with the responsibility of such managers in obtaining the best practical results.

A combination of many works not only renders such a department comparatively inexpensive, but these works together forming an organic whole, with varying experiences and processes according to styles produced, would afford to the Central Technical Research Department material for investigation and comparison altogether wanting in a single concern, with competition in place of co-operation on every hand.

In several large industries on the Continent (not calico printing) it has been found necessary even for independent and competing concerns to combine in forming and maintaining such a department of scientific research and experiment, to which are referred all questions any subscribing manufacturers may desire to send up, for exhaustive scientific investigation.

In countries where calico printing is carried on by individual and separate concerns it would be difficult, owing to the nature of the industry, to adopt this plan; but where practically all the calico printing works in the country are owned by one body of shareholders I regard it as indispensable, if the highest possibilities of combination are to be realised, that a Central Research Department should be established on an ample scale, conducted by a highly trained director and supported by a competent staff of assistants.

Apart from the direct practical results there would be the advantage of training a supply of scientific calico printers to act as managers of works, or assistants to managers, with experience of the Association's needs, and interest in its welfare.

In the absence of such a department I fail to see how this great Association is to be supplied continually, as time goes on, with the requisite men of trained intelligence to conduct its operations on the productive side with that degree of excellence and economy necessary to meet the competition of the highly organised and equipped calico printing works with which I am acquainted in other countries.

But with such resources as I have ventured to suggest, providing the cultured brain to direct the skilful hand of the British workman, it should not be difficult for the Association of British Calico Printers to attain a commanding position for any class of goods in foreign markets, and to supply with profit to themselves a very large portion of the world's demand.

WILLIAM MATHER.

25 *

APPENDIX V.

NOTES ON TRUST LITERATURE.

THERE is now a voluminous literature on the various aspects of the trust problem, particularly with regard to the developments in Germany and the United States. Professor von Halle gives an excellent bibliography of the earlier works in his *Trusts* (1895), and Professor C. J. Bullock contributes to *Trusts, Pools, and Corporations* (mentioned below) an article entitled "Trust Literature : a Survey and Criticism," covering the period 1897-1901. For later books and articles the current bibliography in the *Quarterly Journal of Economics* of Harvard University should be consulted. Without pretending to anything like a comprehensive survey, it may be useful for the student first approaching the subject if a few notes on some of the principal works are here appended. He must first be warned that a general knowledge of the working and development of industry is an indispensable preliminary to the special study of organisation, and, therefore, a number of books are included which will give him that particular information.

For the United Kingdom, *British Industries* (Longmans, 1903), edited by Professor W. J. Ashley, and *The Evolution of Modern Capitalism* (Walter Scott, 1906, new edition), by J. A. Hobson, form the best introduction, and may be followed up for particular trades in Professor Chapman's *Lancashire Cotton Industry* (Manchester University Press, 1904), *The Paisley Thread Industry* (Paisley, Gardner, 1907), by Matthew Blair, and the *Books on Business* series issued by Methuen & Co. *The New Trades Combination Movement* (Rivingtons, 1899) is an interesting account of the Birmingham Alliances by their inventor, Mr. E. J. Smith. Dr. A. Shadwell's *Industrial Efficiency : a Comparative Study of Industrial Life in England, Germany, and America* (Longmans, 1906, 2 vols.) covers a wide field in the discussion of many topics of importance to the student of organisation. The *Reports of the Tariff Commission* (7 Victoria Street, London,

S.W.) on the iron, textile, and agricultural industries contain abundance of statistics and a great mass of general information on the trades dealt with. Of course, they deal prominently with tariff questions, but the other side of the case is fully set forth in *British Industries under Free Trade* (Fisher Unwin, 1904), a collection of articles by business men, edited by Harold Cox.

W. R. Lawson's *American Industrial Problems* (Blackwood, 1903) forms an admirable introduction to the nineteen volumes recording the investigations of the *American Industrial Commission*, appointed in 1898, of which at least the concluding volume, or *Final Report*, must be carefully studied. Vols. i. and xiii. contain the evidence on *Trusts;* vol. ii. is a special report on *Trust and Corporation Laws*, and vol. xviii. deals with *Industrial Combinations in Europe*. The reports of the Commissioner of Corporations on *The Beef Industry* (March, 1905) and on *The Transportation of Petroleum* (May, 1906) exemplify the latest official methods of investigation with a view to control. Out of the abundant private literature, *Trusts*, by E. von Halle (Macmillan, 1895), *Monopolies and Trusts*, by Professor R. E. Ely (Macmillan, 1900), and *The Trust Problem*, by Professor J. W. Jenks (Macmillan, 1901), are still the standard works on the general problems of industrial combination, just as Professor Meade's *Trust Finance* (New York, Appleton's, 1903) is on the financial aspects. *Commercial Trusts, the Growth and Rights of Aggregated Capital*, by J. R. Passos (Putnam, 1906), sets forth the views of a great corporation lawyer, and *The Control of Trusts*, by Professor J. B. Clark (Macmillan, 1901), discusses the possibilities of regulation. Among studies of particular trusts the student will find of particular value the classic work by Miss Ida Tarbell on *The History of the Standard Oil Co.* (Heinemann, 1905, 2 vols.) and a collection of monographs, legal documents, etc., edited by Professor W. Z. Ripley, under the title *Trusts, Pools, and Corporations* (Ginn & Co., Boston, 1905).

For Germany the *Annual Reports* issued by our Consuls General at Berlin and Frankfort are of great value, and Sayous' *La Crise Allemande de 1900-2* must not be omitted. Official investigations into kartells have been proceeding for some years past. A *Bericht über Kartellwesen* was presented to the Reichstag in 1905, containing a tabular survey of kartells arranged according to industries, a collection of their rules, and a statement of their legal status. It has since been republished by Franz Siemenroth, Berlin, who also publishes *Kontradiktorische Ver-*

handlungen über Deutsche Kartelle, in twelve parts. These latter are the verbatim reports of a series of meetings in which the representatives of the great kartells in the coal, iron, steel, books, wall-paper, and spirit industries were confronted with their critics and the case for and against their organisations was discussed under the presidency of Government officials. They also contain a number of official documents. An earlier investigation is contained in vol. lx. of the *Schriften des Vereins für Sozialpolitik— Über Wirthschaftliche Kartelle in Deutschland und im Auslande* (Leipzig, Duncker und Humblot, 1904). Other books of importance are : *Die Kartelle der Gewerblichen Unternehmer,* by L. Pohle (Leipzig, 1898) ; *Die Unternehmerverbände,* by R. Liefmann (Freiburg, Volkswirthschaftliche Abhandlungen der badischen Hochschulen, 1897) ; *Ausbau des Kartellwesens,* by A. Steinmann-Bucher (Berlin, 1902) ; *Les Cartells de l'Agriculture en Allemagne* by A. Souchon (Paris, Colin, 1904) ; *Der Deutsche Stahlwerks-Verband,* by W. Kollmann ; and *Monopolistic Combinations in the German Coal Industry,* by Francis Walker (American Economic Association, 1904).

Dr. Josef Grunzel in his *Über Kartelle* (Leipzig, Duncker und Humblot, 1902) gives a valuable analysis of kartells, a full account of their development in Austria, and a sketch of their growth in other countries. De Leener's *Syndicats Industriels en Belgique* (Brussels, Misch et Thron, 1903) ; Raffalovich's *Trusts, Cartels, et Syndicats* (Paris, Guillamin, 1903) and *De l'Accaparement,* by Dr. E. Dolléans (Paris, Larose, 1902) must also be mentioned. Finally, Mr. D. H. Macgregor gives in his *Industrial Combination* (Bell, 1906), an admirable analysis of American trusts and German kartells from the standpoint of the theoretic economist.

ADDENDA.

Alkali Co., United.—The heavy expenditure on improvements at length has had its reward in the payment of an ordinary dividend of 2 per cent. for 1906, the first since 1896; £125,000 was also transferred to reserve. Net profits, 1906, £528,194.

Allsopp Combine.—This scheme has fallen through, but negotiations are proceeding for the fusion of Salt & Co. and the Burton Brewery Co.

Australian Mail Syndicate.—Mr. W. Beardmore and Messrs. Vickers, Sons, & Maxim were reported in March, 1907, to have withdrawn from the syndicate. Some difficulty was found in raising money by debentures but it is understood that the contract will be carried out.

Bell Brothers.—Net profits, 1906, £140,437 ; dividend, 10 per cent.

Borax Consolidated.—Dividend 1905-6, 20 per cent.

Bradford Dyers' Association.—In January, 1907, the Association settled a dispute with 8,000 of its workmen on terms which will be surprising to those who believe " trusts " to be inevitably hostile to working class interests. In return for recognition by the men of the masters' right to control the manning of machinery and the organisation of the branches, the Association agreed to raise wages 10 per cent. and to restrict the employment of boys and improvers. Increased output, heavier work, and greater responsibility entitle a man to higher wages. Men displaced in 1907 are to receive from the Association an amount equal and in addition to the out-of-work benefit or emigration grant paid by their trade union.

Calico Printers' Association.—The capital of the company is to be converted as to 60 per cent. into 5 per cent. preference shares and as to 40 per cent. into ordinary shares.

Cammell, Laird, & Co.—Dividend for 1906, 10 per cent.

Coal Associations.—The owners of gas-coal pits in the Midlands, suffering from the pressure of their men for higher wages, and from the skill of gas companies in beating down the prices of their coal contracts, have resolved to put an end to underselling. The

Iron and Steel Trades Journal (16th February, 1907) announced that the coal-owners of Yorkshire, Leicester, Derby, and Notts "will regulate, by a central board, the minimum selling-price of gas-coal contracts. Each district at present has, of course, its own association, but their efforts have been annulled by competition from other districts. Now delegates from each district will form the board, and a uniform price basis according to the quality of the coal will be arrived at." A rise of 2s. 6d. to 5s. per ton was expected.

Cycle Combine.—The Birmingham Small Arms Co., which was started in 1861 and began the manufacture of cycle component parts in 1893, acquired the Eadie Manufacturing Co. in February, 1907, and raised its capital from £600,000 to £1,000,000. Competition was thus eliminated, while economies are anticipated from the cessation of duplication of work.

Fairbairn, Lawson, Combe, Barbour, Ltd.—Dividend for 1906, 8½ per cent.

Rivet, Bolt, and Nut Co.—Dividend for 1906, 6 per cent.

Sponge Importers, International.—Dividend for 1906, 6 per cent.

Stewarts & Lloyds.—Dividend for 1906, 10 per cent.

Tobacco Co., Imperial.—Net profits, year to 31st October, 1906, £1,787,931; dividend on deferred ordinary shares, 10 per cent.

Vickers, Sons, & Maxim.—Net profits for 1906 were £879,904 after providing for depreciation, etc.; the sum of £250,000 was written off good-will and patents, and 15 per cent. dividend was paid. In their report the directors announce the acquisition of a quarter share in the firm of Messrs. Whitehead & Co., torpedo manufacturers. In this way they become partners with Sir W. G. Armstrong, Whitworth, & Co.

INDEX.